Whose Promised Land?

The Continuing Crisis over Israel and Palestine

Colin Chapman

Baker Books

A Division of Baker Book House Co
Grand Rapids, Michigan 49516

Published in the USA by Baker Books
a division of Baker Book House Company
P.O. Box 6287, Grand Rapids, MI 49516-6287

Second printing, December 2002

Original edition published in English under the title *Whose Promised Land?* by Lion
Publishing plc, Oxford England. Copyright © Lion Publishing plc 2002.

Printed in the United States of America

Library of Congress Cataloging-in-Publication Data

Chapman, Colin Gilbert.
    Whose promised land? : the continuing crisis over Israel and Palestine
/ Colin Chapman.
        p.   cm.
    Includes bibliographical references and index.
    ISBN 0-8010-6441-4 (pbk.)
      1. Palestine—History. 2. Israel—History. 3. Arab-Israeli conflict.
4. Palestine in the Bible. 5. Bible—Criticism, interpretation, etc. 6. Land
tenure—Religious aspects. 7. Land tenure—Biblical teaching. I. Title.
DS121 .C52 2002
956.94—dc21   2002071156

Contents

Preface   9
Acknowledgments   11
Introduction   13

PART I: UNDERSTANDING THE HISTORY   19

Chapter I: The Land in History:
Basic Facts and Their Interpretation   21

1.1 The patriarchs: Abraham, Isaac and Jacob (c. 2000–1700 BC)   21

1.2 The exodus and the conquest of the land
under Joshua (c. 1280–1050 BC)   22

1.3 The kingdom under Saul, David and Solomon (1050–931 BC)   23

1.4 The kingdoms of Israel and Judah (931–587 BC)   23

1.5 The Babylonian exile (597–539 BC)   24

1.6 Palestine under the Babylonians, Persians and Greeks (597–63 BC)   24

1.7 Palestine under the Romans (63 BC–AD 330)   25

1.8 Palestine under the Byzantine empire (AD 330–634)   25

1.9 Palestine under the Arabs and Seljuk Turks (634–1096)   26

1.10 Palestine under the Crusaders and the Mamluks (1096–1517)   26

1.11 Palestine under the Ottoman Turks (1517–1918)   27

1.12 Palestine under the Mandate (1922–48)   27

1.13 The UN Partition Plan (1947)   29

1.14 The founding of the State of Israel (1948)   30

1.15 Conflicts since 1948   31

1.16 The peace process since Madrid (1991) and Oslo (1993)   35

1.17 Jerusalem and the West Bank since 1967   37

1.18 Different interpretations of the facts   39

Chapter 2: The Seeds of Conflict: Call the Next Witness   43

2.1 Anti-Semitism   44

2.2 Zionism   49

2.3 Jewish settlement in the land   58

2.4 Arab reactions to Jewish settlement   61

2.5 The role of Britain   64

2.6 The role of the United Nations   69

2.7 Partition and war (1948–49)   73

2.8 The voice of Israel   80

2.9 Other Jewish/Israeli voices   86

2.10 The different voices of the Palestinians   92

2.11 Conclusions   106

PART 2: INTERPRETING THE BIBLE   III

Chapter 3: The Land *Before* Christ:
'A Land Flowing with Milk and Honey'   I I 3

3.1 The promise of the land   113

3.2 The boundaries of the land   117

3.3 The conquest of the land   119

3.4 The land and the temple   125

3.5 Exile from the land   127

3.6 The return to the land   130

3.7 The land and the hopes of Israel   134

3.8 Conclusions   138

Chapter 4: The Land *After* Christ:
'The Meek Shall Inherit the Earth'   I4I

4.1 The birth of Jesus the Messiah   142

4.2 Jesus and the land   145

4.3 Jesus and Jerusalem   151

4.4 The redemption of Israel   159

4.5 The land in the teaching of the apostles   161

4.6 John's vision of the final fulfilment of the covenant   168

4.7 The land and the millennium   172

4.8 Conclusions   175

Chapter 5: Other Biblical Themes:
'Is There Any Word from the Lord?' 179

5.1 A passion for truth 180

5.2 The problem of prejudice 186

5.3 The demands of the law 189

5.4 The prophetic concern for justice 194

5.5 God's judgment in history 200

5.6 Suffering injustice 206

5.7 Rethinking and repentance through disaster 210

5.8 Jew and Gentile in the Old Testament 216

5.9 Jew and Gentile after Jesus the Messiah 221

5.10 The condemnation of anti-Semitism 227

5.11 The possibility of reconciliation 231

5.12 Conclusions 236

PART 3: APPRECIATING THE ISSUES TODAY 239

Chapter 6: Realities Today: Is There
Any Hope of Resolving the Conflict? 241

6.1 A crisis for Zionism 242

6.2 The power equation in the world today 248

6.3 Christian Zionism and Dispensationalism 254

6.4 Zionism and Islam 266

6.5 Conclusions: The options for Israel and questions
for the Palestinians 274

Conclusion: Whose Land? 279

Appendix I: Principles of Christian
Interpretation of Old Testament Prophecy 287

Appendix 2: Examples of Christian
Interpretation of Old Testament Prophecy 295

Appendix 3: The Covenant of Hamas, the Islamic Resistance Movement 307

Notes 309
Index of Biblical Passages 317
General Index 321

Preface

This revised edition of *Whose Promised Land?* has been prepared during the summer and autumn of 2001, in the weeks immediately before and after the attacks on New York and Washington on September 11, 2001. These tragic events have, among other things, focused the attention of the world once again on the continuing conflict between Israel and the Palestinians. An American edition of the book, published around the first annivesary of the attacks, provides an opportunity to reflect on an issue which has been near the heart of the anger that motivated the terrorists, and to recognize the significance of recent developments in Israel/Palestine.

The first edition was written in Beirut in the early 1980s, in the period before the Israeli invasion of Lebanon in June 1982, and published in April 1983. It was revised in 1985 and 1989, and then again in 1992, following the Gulf War.

This further revision covers the relevant history up to January 2002, explaining in particular the background to the Al-Aqsa Intifada which began in October 2000.

The historical sections have made use of newer material from the recent writings of Israeli historians like Benny Morris (whose book *Righteous Victims: A History of the Zionist-Arab Conflict, 1881–1999* represents, according to one reviewer, 'the coming of age of Israeli historical self-criticism' [Stephen Sizer, *Third Way*, October 2000, p. 31]); from Martin Gilbert's *Israel: A History* (1998); and from a remarkably even-handed account by a British journalist, Anton La Guardia, *Holy Land, Unholy War: Israelis and Palestinians*, published in 2001.

The chapters on the Bible include material from recent writings of New Testament scholars like N.T. Wright (e.g. in *The New Testament and the People of God* and *Jesus and the Victory of God*) and Peter Walker (e.g. in *Land of Promise*, edited by Peter Walker and Philip Johnston).

Some chapters in Part 3 are revisions of Appendices in the last edition (6.1 A crisis for Zionism and 6.3 Christian Zionism and Dispensationalism), but others are new (6.2 The power equation in the world today, 6.4 Zionism and Islam and 6.5 Conclusions: The options for Israel and questions for the Palestinians).

The style of the original work remains unchanged. The intention is that in the historical sections there should be enough detail to explain the development of the conflict and the complexity of the issues, but not so much as to deter the general reader. The biblical sections are similarly not intended for specialists, and are deliberately as untechnical as possible. Many biblical passages are printed in full for the benefit of readers who may not have access to the Bible.

Events since the beginning of 2002 – including the Palestinian suicide bomb-ings in Israel and the incursions of the Israeli Defence Forces into the West Bank – have increased the feelings of despair, bitterness and hatred on both sides, to the point that there's little hope of reconciliation without strong intervention from outside. They have therefore drawn the United States further into the con-flict – somewhat against its will – as the only superpower that has the means and the moral authority to resolve the conflict.

These recent developments place an enormous responsibility on the shoul-ders of Americans. And since these political issues are closely tied up with the interpretation of the Bible, Jews and Christians among them have a special rea-son for facing up to this responsibility. The questions they need to address have now (in mid–2002) become much more sharply focused:

■ Are we simply dealing with 'the war against terrorism'? Or are we prepared to try to understand the anger that lies behind the terrorism – anger over the occupa-tion of the West Bank which is in defiance of UN resolutions? Do we, in other words, have the patience to investigate the nature of the conflict in general and the root causes of the recent escalation in particular?

■ If the Bible seems to say that the Jews have a divine right to the land for all time, is this the only way to interpret the Bible? Is there a direct connection between the children of Israel, the Jewish people and the State of Israel today? Is there only one way of reading the promises about the land and the predictions of a return to the land? Or is there another way of reading the text which is totally faithful to scripture, but leads to a less one-sided political stance?

■ If the USA is to play the role that it is now being called upon by the rest of the world to play, what are the demands of justice? How is the USA to balance its tra-ditional support for Israel with its government's recent commitment to work for the establishment of a viable Palestinian state? Do its people and its government have the will to work for a just and fair solution – even if it means imposing a solution on unwilling parties that are unable to make peace by themselves?

Since this new edition goes out at a time when the stakes for the Middle East and for the rest of the world seem to get higher by the day, my hope and prayer is that it expresses something of the spirit of these words written by one of the first Jewish Christians, possibly living in Jerusalem:

The wisdom from above is in the first place pure; and then peace-loving, consid-erate, and open to reason; it is straightforward and sincere, rich in mercy and in the kindly deeds that are its fruit. True justice is the harvest reaped by peace-makers from seeds sown in a spirit of peace.
JAMES 3:17–18 (NEB)

BEIRUT, 9 MAY, 2002

Acknowledgments

This new edition provides an opportunity to express my profound thanks to several people who have played significant roles at various stages in the life of this book.

I'm specially grateful to David and Pat Alexander, the founding directors of Lion Publishing, who took the risk of publishing the first edition in 1983, and persevered with reprints and revisions, assisted later by Robin Keeley. Afaf Musallam and Chris and Alison Walley made a very significant contribution in the typing and reviewing of the first drafts in Beirut during the early 1980s. Peter Riddell and Steve Motyer, both of London Bible College, checked this revised edition and made many helpful suggestions, most of which have been incorporated into the text. Finally, I have greatly appreciated working with Morag Reeve, Jenni Dutton and Rhoda Edy of Lion Publishing, who have been remarkably long-suffering in putting up with my movements between Beirut and the UK and a great deal of e-mail correspondence.

I am grateful to the Life and Peace Institute in Uppsala, Sweden, for permission to rework an article on the Intifada which appeared in March 2001 in their journal, *New Routes*.

Introduction

Two peoples – Jews and Palestinian Arabs – lay claim to the same piece of land. But who does it really belong to?

Does it belong to the Jews because Abraham and his descendants lived in it for many centuries before Christ and believed that God had promised it to them 'for ever'? Does it belong to them because, even after their expulsion from Jerusalem by the Romans in AD 135, groups of Jews lived on in several centres until steady immigration began in the 1880s? Does it belong to them because it was offered to them by the United Nations Partition Plan in 1947?

Does it belong to the Palestinian Arabs because they and their ancestors have been living continuously in the land for many centuries – since even before the Arabs came to rule in the seventh century AD? Does it belong to them because of the special place of this land in the religion of Islam?

What do we do when claims of this kind are based *both* on rights derived from previous occupation *and* on divinely given scripture? Do we ignore the scripture and concentrate on the history, or leave aside the history and focus on the scripture?

Should the land be called 'Israel' or 'Palestine'? Or 'Israel' *and* 'Palestine'? If there is already a Jewish state of 'Israel', should there also be a state of 'Palestine'? Is it possible to limit ourselves to *scripture and theology* and ignore *politics?* And if we do venture into contemporary politics, is it realistic to believe that the conflict over the land can be resolved?

If the heart of the problem we are dealing with is that two peoples are claiming the same piece of land for different reasons, how do we begin to answer the question 'Whose Promised Land?' Because we are not dealing with a single issue, but with a number of issues which are inter-related, we need to resist the temptation to reduce everything to a single dimension – 'the conflict is nothing but...' or 'the problem is nothing more than...' If we can do this, we are then free to recognize the wide variety of major ingredients like the following, which contribute to the conflict.

Jewish links with the land over centuries

An unbroken tie between our people and our land has persisted through all these centuries in full force.[1]
DAVID BEN-GURION

These words of the first Prime Minister of Israel when it was created in 1948 remind us of the feeling of many Jews that they have been bound – as if by an umbilical cord – to this piece of land for many centuries.

Biblical grounds for Jewish claims

For Jews, the creation of Israel is a modern miracle, the consummation of God's promise, long in coming, but here at last. The covenant with Abraham remains eternally valid.[2]
ANTON LA GUARDIA

Jewish claims to the land are based not only on history, but also on the Hebrew Bible, and in particular the promise of God to give the land to Abraham and his descendants 'as an everlasting possession' (Genesis 17:8). Jews can therefore point to their own scriptures as the title deeds which prove their claim of ownership.

Support for Jewish claims from many Christians

If you abandon Israel, God will never forgive you… it is God's will that Israel, the biblical home of the people of Israel, continue for ever and ever.[3]
BILL CLINTON'S PASTOR

These words addressed to Bill Clinton by his American pastor in 1980, thirteen years before he became president of the USA, sum up the conviction of many Christians, especially in Europe and the USA, who believe that the creation of the Jewish state in 1948 has real significance in God's plan for the world. While this view is not shared by all Christians and is open to question, it continues to encourage many Christians to give moral and political support to the State of Israel.

The question of Palestine and the Palestinians

The Jewish Question may have been solved by the creation of Israel. The Question of Palestine remains an open sore.[4]
ANTON LA GUARDIA

This comment by a British journalist pinpoints a basic issue at the heart of the conflict. Having missed the opportunity to establish a Palestinian state in 1948 (which they could have done at the time that Israel was created), the Palestinians have struggled ever since to find appropriate ways of establishing their own political identity and expressing their desire to be a nation.

Palestinian perceptions of Zionism and Israel

I see no way of evading the fact that in 1948 one people displaced another, thereby committing a grave injustice.[5]
EDWARD SAID

We are the aggressors, and they defend themselves… Palestine is theirs, because they inhabit it, whereas we want to come here and settle down, and in their view we want to take away from them their country.[6]
DAVID BEN-GURION

In the first statement above, **Edward Said**, a Palestinian American who is one of the most articulate advocates of the Palestinian cause in the West, does not hesitate to describe what happened in 1948 in terms of 'displacement'. **David Ben-Gurion**'s words in the second statement represent an admission that (at least at certain moments) he understood very well how the whole Zionist enterprise was perceived by the Palestinian Arabs.

Israel's policies concerning the West Bank since 1967

I do think that Israel should stay for ever and ever and ever and ever in the West Bank, because this is Judea and Samaria. This is our homeland.[7]
MOSHE DAYAN, 14 MAY 1967

Israel took control of the West Bank in 1967 and, on the grounds of security, has continued its occupation against the wishes of the Palestinian Arabs. The second Intifada, which began in October 2000, has led to a prolonged crisis and brought into sharp focus the conflicting aspirations of Israeli Jews and Palestinians. Does Israel want to make peace with the Palestinian Arabs? Will Israel ever be willing to withdraw from the West Bank and allow the Palestinians to establish their own state? Is it possible to find any political formula which would enable the two peoples to live peacefully side by side as equals?

Political realities today

There is no certainty that Israeli good-will or ill-will, flexibility or inflexibility, will decisively temper or resolve this century-old conflict. Islamic fundamentalism, Great Power rivalry or intervention, and nuclear weapons may prove far more telling.[8]
BENNY MORRIS

These final sentences of **Benny Morris**'s *Righteous Victims: A History of the Zionist-Arab Conflict, 1881–1999* draw attention to some of the other factors which enter into the equation. The escalating conflict has unleashed new forces which cannot easily be predicted or controlled.

World involvement in the conflict

Ever since Herzl lobbied the chanceries of Europe to secure a charter for the Jewish colonization of Palestine, the Jewish and Palestinian questions have been in large part in the hands of the nations of the world.[9]
ANTON LA GUARDIA

Only a miracle or a catastrophe will change the situation. If you don't believe in the first and fear the latter, you realize that the only practical hope for saving Israel and the Palestinians from mutual slaughter is heavy international pressure on both of them.[10]
DAVID GROSSMAN

The State of Israel owes its existence first to Britain and the USA, and then to the United Nations which called for its creation in 1947. Since Jews and Arabs are at present locked in a conflict they cannot resolve by themselves and which affects most of the rest of the world, intervention from the outside becomes more important than ever. The second quotation from **David Grossman**, an Israeli writer, written in June 2001, underlines the stark choices that face the world.

These different issues are explored in the book in the following way. We begin with *history* rather than with the *Bible*, since it is important to have at least a basic understanding of the history before we turn to the Bible to attempt to find meaning in historical events.

Thus *Part 1: Understanding the History* seeks to explain the historical claims of both Jews and Arabs that are based on previous occupation of the land, and to understand the events leading up to the establishment of the State of Israel and the most significant developments in its first fifty or so years of existence.

Chapter 1: The Land in History: Basic Facts and Their Interpretation is a brief historical survey of the different people who have ruled the land from the twentieth century BC to the present day, describing in particular the resurgence of the conflict in recent years.

Chapter 2: The Seeds of Conflict: Call the Next Witness attempts to explain in greater detail the nature of the conflict, using quotations from a wide variety of sources to allow individuals who have been involved in the conflict to speak in their own words.

Part 2: Interpreting the Bible explores what the Bible has to say on the theme of the land.

Chapter 3: The Land Before Christ: 'A Land Flowing with Milk and Honey' focuses on the land in the Old Testament.

Chapter 4: The Land After Christ: 'The Meek Shall Inherit the Earth' explores how Jesus understood the idea of the land, and how his disciples believed that he had redefined Jewish ideas about the land. This survey challenges the idea that the recent return of Jews to the land and the establishment of the State of Israel should be seen by Christians as the fulfilment of the promise made to Abraham and the predictions of a return.

Chapter 5: Other Biblical Themes: 'Is There Any Word from the Lord?' explores other themes in the Bible which are relevant to our understanding of the conflict today.

Part 3: Appreciating the Issues Today builds on the analysis of the history in Part 1 and the study of the Bible in Part 2, and discusses some of the major forces that seem to be determining the outcome of the conflict today.

The *Conclusion* outlines a personal answer to the question, 'Whose Promised Land?'

Appendices 1 and 2 discuss in more detail the Christian interpretation of prophecy in the Old Testament.

PART I

Understanding
the History

Who has lived in the land and who has ruled it in the past? How did the State of Israel come into being? What have been the various stages in the conflict between Israel and the Palestinian Arabs?

Chapter 1 is not a complete history of the land, but an outline of the basic facts about who has ruled the land from around the twentieth century BC to the present day, with special focus on the process leading to the establishment of the State of Israel in 1948 and the background to the resurgence of the conflict in the first Intifada of 1987 and the Al-Aqsa or second Intifada which began in 2000.

Chapter 2 is a kind of anthology of quotations. Instead of trying to argue a particular case, it presents different kinds of source material to enable readers to make up their own minds about the history of the land in recent years. Before we turn to the Bible in Part 2, we are trying to understand how the conflict has developed over the years and the particular forms that it takes at the present time.

Chapter 1

The Land in History

Basic Facts and Their Interpretation

*One can be sure that in time the world will
become conscious of what has happened.*[1]
JOHN H. DAVIS

*The plea of 'not knowing' cannot in good faith be entered
at history's bar. Those who want to know can know the truth;
at all events, enough of it to draw the just conclusions.*[2]
NORMAN FINKELSTEIN

*When we say that the Arabs are the aggressors and we
defend ourselves – that is only half the truth. As regards our
security and life we defend ourselves... But the fighting is only one aspect of the
conflict, which is in its essence a political one. And politically we are the
aggressors and they defend themselves.*[3]
DAVID BEN-GURION, 1938

*David Ben-Gurion of course was right. Zionism was a
colonizing and expansionist ideology and movement.*[4]
BENNY MORRIS

*The Intifada is a milestone – a place from which to consider the tumultuous road to
Palestinian statehood, the experiment in Palestinian autonomy, and the forces that
destroyed this attempt at 'peace'.*[5]
ANTON LA GUARDIA

1.1 The patriarchs: Abraham, Isaac and Jacob (c. 2000–1700 BC)

Some time after 2000 BC (it is difficult to know precisely when), Abraham, the head of
a small tribe, or perhaps just an extended family, migrated from Harran in Syria to the
hill country of Palestine. He did not settle permanently in any one place, but moved
between Shechem, Beersheba and Hebron. The inhabitants of the land at that time,
who were of Semitic and other stock, are named by the writer of Genesis as 'the

Kenites, Kenizzites, Kadmonites, Hittites, Perizzites, Rephaites, Amorites, Canaanites, Girgashites and Jebusites' (Genesis 15:19–21).

During a time of famine he lived in Egypt, and on a later occasion took refuge in Gerar in the northern Negev. The only piece of land he bought was the field containing the cave in which he buried his wife Sarah (see 3.1 The promise of the land).

Abraham's son Isaac may have settled more permanently in one place in the hill country. But during another severe famine Isaac's son, Jacob, moved to Egypt with his whole family at the invitation of Joseph who had by this time become, in effect, the Prime Minister of Egypt. Their descendants stayed in Egypt for over 400 years.

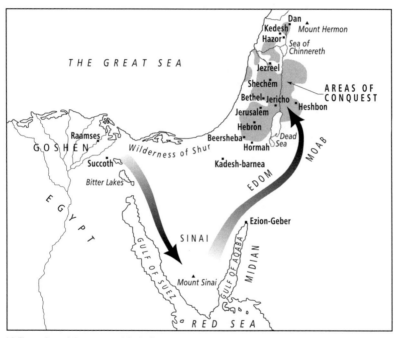

1.2 *The exodus and the conquest of the land.*

1.2 The exodus and the conquest of the land under Joshua (c. 1280–1050 BC)

After a time of severe oppression under one of the pharaohs in Egypt, the twelve tribes of Israel made their escape under the leadership of Moses. After crossing the Red Sea, they spent forty years in different parts of the Sinai Peninsula. Sometime around 1280 BC Joshua led them across the River Jordan.

The conquest of the land began with the capture of Jericho, and continued with several campaigns in the hill country to the south and north. The boundaries of the land which Joshua believed had been promised by God to the children of Israel ran from (approximately) the Mediterranean coast east to Mount Hermon, then to the southern end of the Dead Sea, and west to the Mediterranean. The east bank of the Jordan was allocated by special request to two-and-a-half tribes (see 3.2 The boundaries of the land).

It is somewhat misleading, however, to speak of 'the conquest of the land', since the Israelites did not conquer anything like the whole land. One tribe after another attempted to occupy the territory allotted to it, but not all the tribes were successful, and large areas remained under the control of the Canaanites and others who were living in the land (see 3.3 The conquest of the land).

There then followed a period of decline during which the tribes came under the control of neighbouring peoples like the Philistines, but from time to time they were able to establish their independence under their own leaders or 'judges'.

1.3 The kingdom under Saul, David and Solomon (1050–931 BC)

Saul, the first king (about 1050–1011 BC), rallied many of the tribes in an attempt to push back the Philistines who occupied most of the coastal plain and controlled most of the hill country. When he was killed in battle, he was succeeded by King David (about 1011–971 BC), who was more successful, and after breaking the power of the Philistines on the coast, turned his attention to the area east of the Jordan, where he defeated three smaller kingdoms: Edom in the south, Moab to the east of the Dead Sea, and Ammon to the north of the Dead Sea. He then defeated the states of Aram further to the north.

1.3 *Israel under the united monarchy.*

During the reign of his son, King Solomon (about 971–931 BC), the kingdom enjoyed a period of peace and prosperity, and its power extended further than at any other period in its history ('from Dan to Beersheba...').

1.4 The kingdoms of Israel and Judah (931–587 BC)

After the death of Solomon in about 931 BC, the ten northern tribes revolted against his successor, King Rehoboam, and two separate kingdoms came into being – the northern kingdom with its capital at Samaria, and the southern kingdom with its capital at Jerusalem.

The northern kingdom continued under its own kings for 200 years, until it was threatened by the growing power of Assyria in the north. It finally came to an end when Samaria was captured in 722 BC and a large proportion of the population was deported.

This deportation was very thorough, and large numbers of immigrants from other conquered territories were brought in to take their place. Those who settled in the

I.4 The divided kingdom: Israel and Judah.

province of Samaria eventually adopted the religion of the Israelites who had remained in the land. But this community, later called 'the Samaritans', was despised by the people of Judah to the south because of their mixed ancestry and because their religion was no longer considered to be pure.

The deported Israelites were settled in several different places within the Assyrian empire – in what is today NE Syria, SE Turkey and the western part of Iran. This was part of a deliberate policy aimed at making them lose their identity and assimilate more easily with the local population. Most historians seem to accept that the Assyrian policy must have achieved its aim, and that the vast majority of the exiles were fully absorbed in the communities where they settled and never returned to their land.

1.5 The Babylonian exile (597–539 BC)

When the northern kingdom of Israel was absorbed within the Assyrian empire, the southern kingdom of Judah was able to defend itself and retain some measure of independence. By the beginning of the sixth century, however, the Babylonians had taken over control of the whole area from the Assyrians, and were now threatening the small kingdom of Judah on their south-western border.

In 597 BC Nebuchadnezzar of Babylon captured Jerusalem, despoiled the temple and deported the cream of the population to Babylon.

When the people left in the land rose up in revolt against the Babylonians in 586 BC, the Babylonian army attacked and destroyed much of the city of Jerusalem and took many of the remaining people into exile.

When Cyrus, king of Persia, captured Babylon in 539 BC, his policy was to repatriate the different groups of exiles in the country. The first group of exiles therefore returned in 537 BC under Zerubbabel, while other groups returned over a period of many years – some as much as seventy or eighty years later under Ezra and Nehemiah.

1.6 Palestine under the Babylonians, Persians and Greeks (597–63 BC)

At some periods after their return from exile, the Jews enjoyed a considerable measure of independence, but they were never able to establish the kind of sovereign state which had existed from the tenth century to the sixth century BC. So from 597 BC onwards the Jewish community in Palestine lived under the control of one foreign power after another.

Palestine under the Babylonians
The Babylonian empire controlled the whole of Palestine after 597 BC until 538 BC.

Palestine under the Persians
The Persian empire dominated Palestine after Cyrus' victory in 539 BC until 330 BC.

Palestine under the Greeks
Alexander the Great conquered the coastal plain in 330 BC, although he did not interfere with the Jewish community around Jerusalem.

The Ptolemies (who were Greek) took control of Palestine after the death of Alexander the Great in 323 BC.

The Seleucids (of Syria), who were also Greek, took over control of Palestine from the Ptolemies in 200 BC. It was during this period that Antiochus Epiphanes tried to stamp out the Jewish religion – for example, by setting up an altar to Zeus in the temple. Jewish resistance was led by Judas Maccabeus, and after three years of intense guerilla warfare, the Syrians were driven out of Jerusalem and the temple was purified (165 BC).

Thus for a short period of two or three years, the Jews had a fully independent Jewish state based in Jerusalem. But the Syrians soon regained control, re-established pagan worship in the temple, and nominated their own candidate as high priest. In the years that followed, the Jews were ruled by a succession of their own priest-kings, and enjoyed a certain measure of independence.

1.7 Palestine under the Romans (63 BC–AD 330)
The Romans took over Palestine in 63 BC when Pompey invaded at the head of the Roman army. At times they ruled the country through local puppet kings such as Herod the Great (37–4 BC); at other times they ruled through Roman procurators like Pontius Pilate (AD 26–36) or through direct Roman rule (AD 135–330). Resistance to Roman rule led to the Jewish revolt of AD 66, which ended in AD 70 when Jerusalem was captured and the temple destroyed. Some Jews made a final stand at Masada near the Dead Sea, but the Romans captured the stronghold in AD 73.

Although Roman rule was not oppressive, resistance continued. A further Jewish revolt in AD 132 was led by Bar Cochba, who rallied an army of 200,000 men and proceeded to drive the Romans out of Jerusalem. When the Roman army recaptured Jerusalem in AD 135 the Jews were slaughtered. The Emperor Hadrian now turned Jerusalem into a Roman colony and called it Aelia Capitolina. He built a pagan temple in honour of Jupiter on the site of the temple, and forbade the Jews to enter Jerusalem on pain of death. Although these repressive actions killed all hopes of Jewish national independence, communities of Jews continued to live in different centres in Palestine (e.g. on the coastal plain and in Galilee).

1.8 Palestine under the Byzantine empire (AD 330–634)
In AD 330 the Roman Emperor Constantine, who had made Christianity the official religion of the Roman empire, founded a new capital city for the eastern half of his empire at Byzantium, which was thereafter known as Constantinople. In 395 the Roman empire was officially divided into two halves and the eastern half became

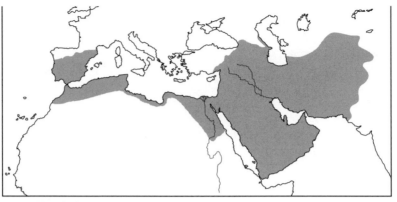

1.9 The Arab empire at the end of the Umayyad dynasty in AD 750.

known as the Byzantine empire; Palestine was thus a province of the Byzantine empire for some three-and-a-half centuries.

Treatment of the Jews (in Palestine and elsewhere) by the Byzantine emperors varied: in 438 the Empress Eudocia removed the ban on Jews praying at the temple site, but the Emperor Justinian (527–65) organized attempts to convert Jews to Christianity by force and from that time onwards Byzantine treatment of the Jews deteriorated.

In 614 the Persians invaded the Byzantine empire and occupied Syria, Palestine and Egypt. For three years Jerusalem was in the hands of the Jews, until the Byzantines defeated the Persians in 617 and reasserted their control over Palestine.

1.9 Palestine under the Arabs and Seljuk Turks (634–1096)

In 634, only two years after the death of the prophet Muhammad in 632, the Arab armies invaded Palestine and captured Jerusalem. Palestine thus became part of the Muslim empire for the next 450 years.

From 661 this empire was ruled by the Umayyads, an Arab dynasty which ruled from Damascus.

Then from 750 it was ruled by the Abbasids, a dynasty which ruled from Baghdad.

The Arab Muslims came to Palestine as conquerors; but since there was no attempt either to expel the people of the land or to convert them to Islam they remained as Christians or Jews. Gradually, however, the population began to convert to Islam, since that was the path to social advancement, and Arabic quickly became the most widely spoken language. Islam, however, did not become the religion of the majority of the population of Palestine until the thirteenth century.

1.10 Palestine under the Crusaders and the Mamluks (1096–1517)

In 1099 the Crusaders, Christian knights from Western Europe, recaptured Jerusalem from the Muslims (and massacred the entire population of the city, Jewish and Muslim). The Crusaders established a kingdom in Palestine, based in Jerusalem, but

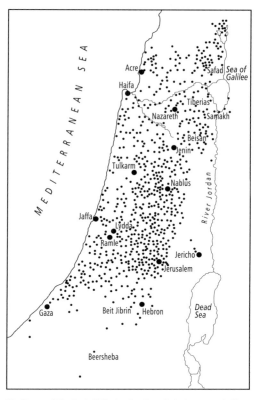

I.IIa *Ottoman Palestine in 1880, showing the main Arab towns and villages prior to Zionist colonization.*

in 1187 they were defeated and expelled from Jerusalem by Saladin. Although they retained a certain amount of territory, they were finally expelled altogether from Palestine in 1291, when their last stronghold, the port of Acre, was recaptured by the Muslims. Palestine remained under Muslim rule thereafter, ruled by various dynasties of Mamluks, slave-soldiers, mostly of Turkish descent, until its conquest by the Ottoman Turks in 1516.

1.11 Palestine under the Ottoman Turks (1517–1918)

In 1516 the Ottoman Turks conquered Palestine. At the beginning of this period there were approximately thirty Jewish communities in different parts of Palestine, with their centre in Safed. There was very heavy taxation on Jews.

In 1880 the total population of Palestine was about 480,000.

Of these the total number of Arabs was around 456,000.

The total number of Jews was around 24,000 (i.e. approximately five per cent of the population).

The first *Aliyah* (return of Jews) took place in 1881. Most of the new immigrants established new Jewish colonies.

The number of Jews gradually increased as a result of further waves of immigration, particularly during the First World War.

In 1914 there were 60,000 Jews (roughly nine per cent of the total).

1.12 Palestine under the Mandate (1922–48)

The Turks were defeated during the First World War and were driven out of Palestine in 1918 by the combined efforts of the British, the French and the Arabs. It was in November 1917 that the British government issued the famous Balfour Declaration, in which it expressed support for the idea of 'a national homeland for the Jewish people' (see 2.5 The role of Britain).

A Peace Conference of the victorious powers was held at Versailles in 1919 to decide the future of the region.

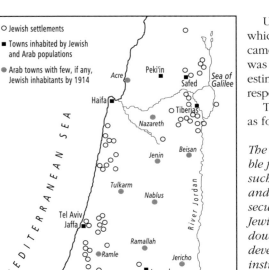

○ Jewish settlements

■ Towns inhabited by Jewish and Arab populations

● Arab towns with few, if any, Jewish inhabitants by 1914

1.IIb *Ottoman Palestine in 1914, showing the extent of Jewish settlement since 1880.*

Under the terms of the Mandate, which was granted in 1920 and came into effect in 1922, Britain was given responsibility for Palestine, while France was given responsibility for Syria.

The terms of the Mandate were as follows:

The Mandatory shall be responsible for placing the country under such political, administrative and economic conditions as will secure the establishment of the Jewish national home, as laid down in the preamble, and the development of self-governing institutions and also for safeguarding the civil and religious rights of all the inhabitants of Palestine, irrespective of race and religion.

During the twenties and thirties there were many violent clashes between the Arab communities and the more recently arrived Jewish settlers. In 1936 the Arabs rose in revolt against the British in protest at the continued Jewish immigration. The revolt was crushed. The Peel Commission sent out by the British government in 1937 concluded that the Mandate was no longer workable, and recommended that the country should be partitioned into two states, one Jewish and one Arab (see 2.4 Arab reactions to Jewish settlement).

In 1939 a British White Paper proposed a joint Arab-Jewish state and a limit on Jewish immigration of 75,000 in the next five years. This was seen by the Jews as a breach of the Balfour Declaration and the Mandate.

The period of the Second World War saw a great deal of legal and illegal Jewish immigration and further polarization of the two communities. During the Holocaust in Europe, Britain and the USA would not accept Jewish immigrants and their sole hope was Palestine. As a result, the Jews numbered thirty-one per cent of the total population in 1947.

During these years the Jews acquired more land by purchase from the Arabs:

■ In 1918 the Jews owned two per cent of the land.

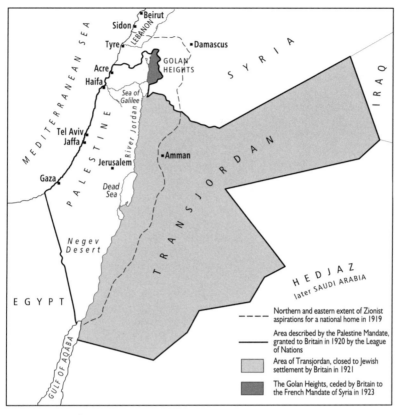

1.12 *The British Mandate for Palestine (1920–48).*

The map legend reads:

- – – – Northern and eastern extent of Zionist aspirations for a national home in 1919
- ———— Area described by the Palestine Mandate, granted to Britain in 1920 by the League of Nations
- Area of Transjordan, closed to Jewish settlement by Britain in 1921
- The Golan Heights, ceded by Britain to the French Mandate of Syria in 1923

■ In 1935 they owned about five-and-a-half per cent of the land (equivalent to twelve per cent of the cultivable land).
■ By 1947 they owned six per cent of the land.

1.13 The UN Partition Plan (1947)
In 1947 the British government announced that it intended to give up the Mandate, and to hand the whole problem of Palestine over to the United Nations (the successor to the League of Nations). At this time the Jews owned six per cent of the land and were around thirty per cent of the population.

A special commission of the UN in 1947 made detailed recommendations for the creation of two separate states:

■ A Jewish state, which would include fifty-five per cent of the land, with a population of 509,780 Arabs and 499,020 Jews (i.e. more Arabs than Jews).
■ An Arab state which would include the remaining forty-five per cent of the land, with 749,101 Arabs and 9,520 Jews.

1.13 *The UN Partition Plan (1947).*

■ Jerusalem, and the area surrounding it, would become an 'international zone'.

The General Assembly approved the Partition Plan by a 2 to 3 majority, largely through the influence of the USA.

While the Jews in Palestine accepted the plan, the Palestinian Arabs totally rejected it, partly because it was felt that the plan was imposed without consultation, and partly because it was felt that the division of the land was unfair and to the advantage of the Jews. A state of civil war developed, with both sides increasing their terrorist activities. These were the most widely publicized episodes in a series of attacks and counter-attacks, random killings and military operations that cost several thousand lives among the Palestinian Arabs and Jews:

■ On 9 April 1948, the *Irgun*, a Jewish underground group, killed between 100 and 250 Arab men, women and children in the village of Deir Yassin south-west of Jerusalem (see 2.7 Partition and war [1948–49]).

■ On 12 April 1948, as a reprisal for Deir Yassin, the Arabs attacked a convoy travelling to the Hadassah Hospital north-east of Jerusalem and killed seventy-seven Jewish doctors, nurses, university teachers and students (see 2.7 Partition and war [1948–49]).

1.14 The founding of the State of Israel (1948)

When the British Mandate ended on 14 May 1948, Dr Chaim Weizmann raised the flag of David and proclaimed the new State of Israel.

The Arabs had no plans for establishing the Arab state called for by the UN Partition Plan, and were determined to destroy the new Jewish state. Therefore, within hours of the creation of the State of Israel, Arab forces from Jordan, Syria, Egypt, Lebanon and Iraq launched an attack. In the fighting which fol-

1.14 *Israel after the war of 1948–49.*

lowed during the next seven months, the Jewish forces defeated the Arab armies and took over large areas in the north (Galilee) and in the south (the Negev), which, according to the Partition Plan, should have formed part of the Arab state. Between 700,000 and 800,000 Palestinian Arabs left or were driven from their homes (i.e. approximately sixty per cent of the pre-war Arab population of Palestine, or eighty-five per cent of the Arab population which would have been within the State of Israel). Of a total of 550 villages in the area occupied by the Jews, only 121 remained. Jerusalem was divided with the old, walled city including the holy sites falling under Arab rule, and West Jerusalem being held by the Jews.

By the time of the ceasefire in January 1949, Israel had occupied seventy-seven per cent of the land (i.e. one third more than it would have had if the Arabs had accepted the UN plan). The territory on the West Bank, including East Jerusalem, which was supposed to form part of the Arab state, was annexed by Jordan.

1.15 Conflicts since 1948

Suez (1956)
The nationalization of the Suez Canal by President Nasser of Egypt in 1956 created an international crisis which gave Israel the opportunity to attack Egypt, in order to put an end to terrorist attacks across the border.

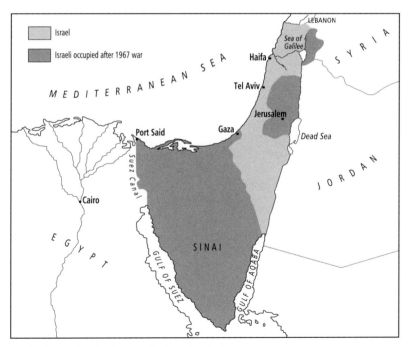

1.15a *Israel and the Occupied Territories after the Six-Day War (1967).*

1.15b *Israel today*

After concluding a secret treaty with Britain and France, Israel invaded Sinai on 29 October 1956, and in less than a week took the whole of Sinai. Britain and France then launched an airborne attack on the Suez Canal.

As a result of strong pressure from America, however, Britain and France were forced to withdraw their forces, and Israel agreed to withdraw from Sinai after receiving assurances that Egypt would not attack Israel or interfere with Israeli shipping in the Gulf of Aqaba.

The June Six-Day War (1967)

By the end of 1966 the clashes between Israel and its Arab neighbours had reached serious proportions. Condemnation of these incidents by the UN Security Council had little effect.

President Nasser closed the Gulf of Aqaba to shipping. Israel interpreted this as an act of war. Goaded on by the propaganda from other Arab countries, especially Syria, Nasser requested the UN to withdraw its emergency forces from the border between Israel and Egypt in Sinai, and moved Egyptian forces up to the border.

In order to forestall any Arab attack, Israel struck first and destroyed most of the Egyptian airforce while it was still on the ground at its airbases. In less than a week Israel had occupied the whole of Sinai, the Gaza Strip, the West Bank (including the Old City of Jerusalem) and the Golan Heights.

The Security Council Resolution of 22 November 1967 called on Israel to withdraw from territories occupied in the 1967 war. Some Israeli Jews argued that Israel should *not* hold on to the West Bank. Successive governments, however, have refused to comply with this resolution, and instead encouraged the building of settlements on the land it had occupied.

PART OF THE TEXT OF RESOLUTION 242:

The Security Council,

Expressing *its continuing concern with the grave situation in the Middle East,*

Emphasizing *the inadmissibility of the acquisition of territory by war and the need to work for a just and lasting peace in which every state in the area can live in security,*

Emphasizing *further that all member states in their acceptance of the Charter of the United Nations have undertaken a commitment to act in accordance with Article 2 of the Charter,*

1. Affirms that the fulfillment of Charter principles requires the establishment of a just and lasting peace in the Middle East which should include the application of both the following principles:

(i) Withdrawal of Israeli armed forces from territories of recent conflict;

(ii) Termination of all claims or states of belligerency and respect for and acknowledgment of the sovereignty, territorial integrity and political independence of every state in the area and their right to live in peace within secure and recognized boundaries free from threats or acts of force.

This is one of the resolutions to which Palestinians have referred repeatedly since 1967. It should be noted that it includes both a clear call for Israeli withdrawal *and* a recognition of Israel's right to exist.

The October/Yom Kippur War (1973)

The Egyptian army crossed the Suez Canal on 6 October 1973 in a surprise attack, and succeeded in penetrating some distance into Sinai. The Israeli counter-attack, however, resulted in the encirclement of a large part of the Egyptian army, and a cease-fire came into effect on 24 October.

Although Egypt did not achieve its aim of recovering Sinai, the psychological effect of the initial victory in the war enabled President Sadat in 1977 to make his historic visit to Jerusalem to propose a peace plan with Israel.

This initiative culminated in the Camp David Treaty of 1978, in which Israel, Egypt and the USA agreed that:

- Israel would withdraw from Sinai.
- Israel and Egypt would seek to normalize relations.
- These agreements would be 'linked' with negotiations between Israel and Egypt which would lead to 'full autonomy' for the Palestinians in the West Bank and the Gaza Strip.

The annexation of the Golan Heights (1981)

The Israeli government passed a bill officially annexing the Golan Heights.

The invasions of Lebanon (1978 and 1982)

In March 1978 the Israeli army invaded southern Lebanon in an attempt to crush the Palestinian forces who were using it as a base to launch attacks across the border into Israel. The Israelis withdrew in June 1978 as a result of strong pressure from the United Nations, but established a buffer zone under the control of Lebanese Christian militia instead of turning over all occupied territory to the UN forces.

On 6 June 1982 the Israeli army launched a full-scale invasion of Lebanon in order to remove Palestine Liberation Organization (PLO) forces and ensure the security of Israel's northern border. The Palestinian camps were destroyed and Beirut besieged for two months before the exodus of the PLO militia and leadership. This was followed by the Israeli army's entry into West Beirut and the massacre of Palestinian civilians by Lebanese militia in the camps of Sabra and Chatila. The

Israeli army withdrew later in the year, but maintained control over a ten-mile strip in the south of the country.

The first Intifada ('Uprising') (December 1987–September 1993)
This movement seems to have begun as a spontaneous upsurge of protest among the Palestinians in the Occupied Territories against twenty years of Israeli occupation. Children and young people took to the streets throwing stones and petrol bombs at Israeli soldiers, and a general strike was called.

At least 1,095 Palestinians were killed by Israel's security forces, and 43 by civilians, mostly settlers. 20,000 or more Palestinians were injured by bullets or truncheons. Benny Morris described the outcome as follows:

The Intifada ended in a stalemate, with the Palestinians unable to eject the Israelis from the territories and the Israelis unable to stop the violence... Ultimately, the result of the Intifada was a basic restructuring of geopolitical realities in the region, one of which was the start of the emergence of a Palestinian state.[6]

Some believe that the Intifada was an important factor in triggering the peace process which began with the Madrid Conference in 1991.

Declaration of the State of Palestine (15 November 1988)
At a meeting in Algiers the Palestinian National Council proclaimed a Declaration of Independence, thereby setting up the state of 'Palestine' in the Occupied Territories.

These declarations, together with subsequent statements made by Yasser Arafat, amounted to a recognition of the existence of the State of Israel, an acceptance of the principle of partition, a recognition of the 'two-state solution' and a renunciation of 'terrorism in all its forms'. Shortly afterwards fifty-five countries recognized the Palestinian state.

The Israeli government responded in April 1989 with its own proposal of 'free and democratic elections' among the Palestinians on the West Bank and the Gaza Strip, which would eventually lead to 'a transitional period of self-rule'.

Invasion of Kuwait and the Gulf War (August 1990–February 1991)
On 2 August 1990 the Iraqi army invaded Kuwait, partly because of long-standing border grievances, and partly because of Kuwait's recent policy on oil production. But it was widely thought that Iraq's ultimate objective was to dominate the Gulf region, unite the Arabs and harness their economic resources in the struggle against Israel. There was also fear of how Saddam Hussein might use the weapons of mass destruction that he had developed.

Arafat's support of the Iraqi invasion damaged the Palestinian cause for many years. People found it hard to understand how the leader of a movement which protests so strongly against what it sees as the illegal occupation of the West Bank by Israeli forces should approve of the occupation of Kuwait by Iraqi forces in August 1990. The explanation seems to be that Palestinians saw in Saddam Hussein the only 'strong man' in the region who had the military power to confront Israel and the courage to stand up to the USA and the rest of the world.

The UN Security Council called on Iraq to withdraw, enforcing strong economic sanctions at the same time. After some time Saddam Hussein offered to withdraw, provided the Western powers agreed to link an Iraqi withdrawal from Kuwait with a withdrawal of Israeli forces from the West Bank, and to convene an international conference to settle the Arab-Israel conflict. The five permanent members of the UN Security Council refused to accept any linkage of this kind, on the grounds that it would reward Saddam Hussein for his aggression against Kuwait.

Early in November President Bush ordered a massive increase in US forces in Saudi Arabia, and twenty-eight different countries, including Britain, France, Egypt and Syria, joined the multi-national force. Iraq refused to back down, and when the UN deadline expired on 15 January, the allies prepared to launch their attack. In operation 'Desert Storm', which involved heavy aerial bombardment of Iraqi army positions and targets all over Iraq before the ground forces moved forward, the Iraqi army was forced to withdraw and Kuwait was liberated.

A few weeks after the defeat of Iraq, President George Bush told the US Congress, 'The time has come to put an end to the Arab-Israeli conflict.' The Gulf War therefore proved to be a further factor in triggering the peace process.

1.16 The peace process since Madrid (1991) and Oslo (1993)

Madrid (1991)

An American initiative led by the President, George Bush, and his Secretary of State, James Baker, led to the convening of a three-day conference in Madrid, 30 October–1 November. Because of Israeli reluctance to recognize the PLO, the Palestinians were included as members of the Jordanian delegation, but were able to operate independently, consulting continuously with the PLO leadership in Tunis.

Discussion centred round UN Resolutions 242 and 338 and the 'land for peace' formula, and the two sides agreed to continue discussions in the following months.

Extremist Palestinian groups like *Hamas* and *Islamic Jihad* denounced the whole process as a 'sell-out of Palestine'.

Oslo Peace Accords (1993)

While the Madrid process was continuing, secret talks began in December 1992 and continued in the coming months with the mediation of the Norwegian government. Together they worked out a 'Declaration of Principles on Interim Self-Government Arrangements', and the agreement was signed by Israeli Prime Minister Yitzhak Rabin and Yasser Arafat in the presence of Bill Clinton on the lawn of the White House in Washington on 13 September.

The agreement allowed for the establishment of a 'Palestine Authority' in Gaza and Jericho, followed by gradual Israeli withdrawal and a handing over of powers to the Palestinians. One major advance was that Israel for the first time recognized the PLO as a representative of the Palestinians, while the PLO recognized Israel's right to exist, committing itself to a peaceful resolution of the conflict. Israel was to remain in overall control of most of the West Bank and much of the Gaza Strip, and discussion of the issues of Jewish settlements on the West Bank and the Gaza Strip, the status of Jerusalem and the right of return of Palestinian refugees was postponed to a future date.

Strong opposition to the Oslo agreement among Palestinians led to an upsurge of terrorism. The Israeli army withdrew from parts of the Gaza Strip and Jericho in May 1994. Arafat came to Gaza on 1 July and made it the headquarters of the Palestine Authority. Since then both sides have accused each other of failing to implement their promises according to the agreed timetable: the Palestinians accuse the Israeli government of dragging its feet over the withdrawals, while Israel accuses the Palestine Authority of continuing to allow terrorist attacks against Jewish targets.

During Benjamin Netanyahu's time as Prime Minister of Israel from 1996 to 1999, government opposition to the idea of an independent Palestinian state gave the impression to the Palestinians that it wished to halt the peace process.

The Israeli-Jordanian Peace Treaty (1994)
After secret talks between the Israeli government and King Hussein, a 'Treaty of Peace' was signed on 26 October 1994 by the Prime Minister of Jordan, the Prime Minister of Israel (Rabin), President Clinton and the Russian Foreign Minister. Both Israel and Jordan recognized each other's right 'to live in peace within secure and recognized boundaries'.

The Al-Aqsa or second Intifada (October 2000–)
In July 2000 President Clinton hosted the Israeli Prime Minister, Ehud Barak, and Arafat for talks at Camp David in order to prepare for some kind of final status agreement between the two sides, but they failed to reach an agreement. The Israeli interpretation, largely supported by Clinton, was that the Palestinians had refused very generous concessions offered by Israel. The Palestinian interpretation was that while some concessions were being offered by Israel, they were not substantial enough to meet Palestinian demands and amounted to a humiliating defeat for the Palestinians. It would seem that Barak did offer substantial concessions (including Arab East Jerusalem, in recognition of the Palestinian need for Jerusalem as its capital). Some believe that the Israeli Knesset would never have been able to ratify concessions of this kind that were unprecedented. The sticking point seems to have been the Old City of Jerusalem: Barak could not offer it, and Arafat could not renounce the Palestinian claim to it.

This was the context in which Ariel Sharon, as leader of the Likud party, visited Haram al-Sharif, the Dome of the Rock on the Temple Mount in Jerusalem on 28 September 2000. He was accompanied by 1,000 police officers, and declared his intention to make the point that Israel would never give up its claims to the Temple Mount. It is probable that Barak discouraged Sharon from making the visit, but could not afford to be seen to be preventing Sharon from doing so. The Palestinians and many others interpreted Sharon's visit as an act of extreme provocation, and this was the event which sparked off the second Intifada, the so-called Al-Aqsa Intifada, in which Palestinians took to the streets in protests which became more and more violent in the ensuing months, with a series of suicide bombings which caused the deaths of many Israeli civilians.

By the end of November 2001, 862 Palestinians had been killed and around 25,000 injured; 239 Israelis had been killed and around 800 injured. *Hamas* activists engaged in terrorist attacks on Jewish settlements. Israel kept up the pressure on the Palestinians by restricting their movement, demolishing houses, closing Israeli borders to Palestinians working in Israel, invading areas controlled by the Palestine Authority and assassinating Palestinians suspected of involvement in terrorism.

1.17 Jerusalem and the West Bank since 1967

The United Nations has on several occasions repeated its calls for Israel to withdraw from the West Bank and the Gaza Strip. In 1980, for example, the Security Council's resolution reaffirmed that 'acquisition of territory by force is inadmissable', and referred to 'the overriding necessity to end the prolonged occupation of Arab territories occupied by Israel since 1967, including Jerusalem'. The General Assembly on 20 December 1982 similarly called for unconditional withdrawal. Israel has consistently refused to implement these resolutions, arguing that occupation is the only way to ensure the security of the State of Israel.

The Geneva Convention states that the Occupying Power is not allowed to alter the status of occupied territories and 'shall not deport or transfer parts of its own civilian population into the territory it occupies'. Israel, however, has continued its policy of building settlements on the West Bank and the Gaza Strip.

In 1983, for example, the government drew up a 'Master Plan and Development Plan for Settlement in Samaria and Judea'. This Master Plan envisaged 'the eventual incorporation of the West Bank into Israel, aiming to "disperse maximally large Jewish population in areas of high settlement priority, using small national inputs and in a relatively short period by using the settlement potential of the West Bank to achieve the incorporation [of the West Bank] into the [Israeli] national system"'.

The following account illustrates the arguments used by the government to justify its building programmes:

In a court action challenging the construction of a settlement in the West Bank, the Supreme Court of Israel said that the cabinet, in approving the settlement, was 'decisively influenced by reasons stemming from the Zionist worldview of the settlement of the whole land of Israel'. Judge Moshe Landau cited an affadavit of the attorney general that quoted Prime Minister Menachem Begin as affirming 'the Jewish people's right to settle in Judea and Samaria'. Judge Landau said this 'view concerning the right of the Jewish people' was 'based on the fundamentals of Zionist doctrine'. Government officials said that settlement construction was aimed at creating a presence to prevent the Palestine Arabs from forming a state. In promoting settlement the government also sought to use the settlements as physical obstacles to separate Arab towns from one another and to decrease the possibility of united political action against the occupation.

In recent years there have been sharp differences of opinion within Israel over its policies relating to the West Bank and the Gaza Strip. Some have argued strongly that Israel should withdraw from the Occupied Territories, while others have insisted that Israel should hold onto them and continue to develop them. The latter view has prevailed at most periods since the early 1980s. Yitzhak Shamir, for example, promised in his inaugural address as Prime Minister in 1983 to continue the 'holy work' of settlement in the West Bank. In many cases Jewish settlers belonging to groups like Gush Emunim have taken the initiative to claim territory and build

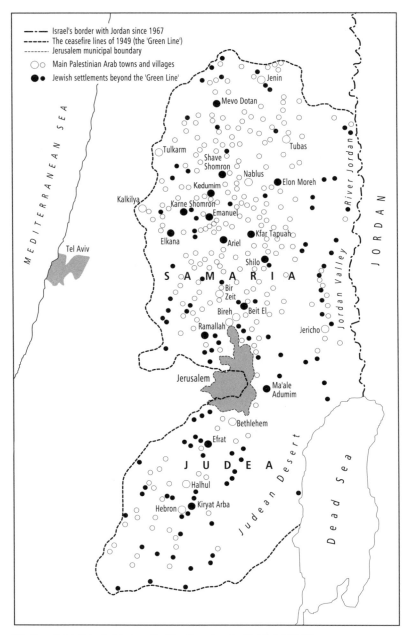

1.17a *The main Palestinian Arab towns and Jewish settlements on the West Bank (1967–97).*

settlements, and subsequently forced the hand of the government to allow them to continue their activities. Outside bodies like the International Commission of Jurists have criticized these settlements as 'a step towards eventual assertion of sovereignty over the territories or part of them'.[7]

1.18 Different interpretations of the facts

Telling the basic story is a vital part of the enquiry for those who have very sketchy or one-sided ideas about the conflict over the land. The next step is to recognize how the same history is understood by different people. Some of the main differences between Jewish and Arab interpretations of the past and more recent history can be outlined as follows:

✡ The Jews say that their ancestors first settled in Palestine some time between the twentieth and eighteenth centuries BC.

☪ *The Palestinian Arabs say they have been living in Palestine since at least the seventh century AD.*

✡ The Jews say that the kingdom which lasted from the tenth century BC (under David) to the sixth century BC was the only independent nation state which had ever existed in the land (i.e. before 1948).

☪ *The Arabs say that if we accept claims which are based on possession of the land centuries ago, then Mexico would have a right to parts of the USA, the Spaniards could claim Mexico, and the Arabs could claim Spain.*

✡ The Jews say that although many of their ancestors were driven out of Palestine by the Romans in AD 135, groups of Jews remained in several centres in the land, and have continued to live there right up to the present time. There was a regular flow of pilgrims and immigrants from Jewish communities in Europe.

☪ *The Arabs do not deny this – and they add that for 1,300 years there was hardly any friction between these small Jewish communities and their Arab neighbours.*

✡ The Jews say that since 1882 they have constituted a majority in the city of Jerusalem.

☪ *The Arabs point out that the number of Jews living in the whole of Palestine in 1882 was 24,000 – which amounted to approximately five per cent of the total population.*

✡ Jews all over the world have always thought of Palestine as their ancestral homeland, and have continually expressed the hope that they will meet 'next year in Jerusalem'.

☪ *The Arabs insist that Palestine has a special significance for all of the three monotheistic religions – Judaism, Christianity, and Islam, and that most of the world refuses to understand or to recognize the special place that Palestine has for Muslims and Islam.*

✡ The Jews argue that when they started returning to Palestine from the 1880s onwards, they came in peacefully and acquired land by legal purchase.

☪ *The Arabs bitterly regret that land was often sold to Jews out of purely selfish motives. They also point out that much of the land was sold by absentee landlords living outside the land, many of whom were not Arabs, and that much of the land now owned by Jews was not acquired by legal purchase, but by expropriation or by war.*

✡ *The Jews say that in settling in Palestine they had the approval of the Turkish government up to 1918, then the League of Nations, and finally of the British government, which was responsible for Palestine under the Mandate from 1920 to 1948.*

☾ *The Arabs can point to historical documents which prove beyond doubt that during the First World War the British government was making contradictory promises to the Jews and the Arabs. While assuring the Jews that they approved of the idea of a Jewish homeland in Palestine (the Balfour Declaration), they were at the same time secretly promising to help the Arabs to establish their own independent states after the collapse of the Turkish empire (the McMahon-Hussein Agreement). Moreover, although the Balfour Declaration and the League of Nations' Mandate included safeguards to protect the civil and political rights of the non-Jewish population, all the promises made to the Arabs were subsequently broken.*

✡ After centuries of persecution which led eventually to the killing of six million Jews under the Nazis in Germany, European Jews *had* to find a refuge – and Palestine was the obvious place to choose, because of all that the land had meant to them in the past.

☾ *The Arabs insist that at first they welcomed the Jewish immigrants, and lived peacefully alongside them for many years. They only began to be more hostile when they realized that many of the immigrants were seeking greater political power. Hostility inevitably led to violence, because the Arabs saw that the Jews would eventually become a majority and take control of the land. The Arabs point out that they were not in any way responsible for the persecution of the Jews in Europe, and wonder why they should have had to suffer for the crimes of Europe.*

✡ The Jews say they have a right to the land because of all that they have invested in it; they have drained the swamps and made the desert 'blossom like a rose'.

☾ *To which the Arabs reply: since when has an argument like this been accepted in a court of law as a valid claim to ownership?*

Against this background, this is the kind of dialogue that tends to take place between Israeli Jews and their supporters on the one hand and Palestinians and their supporters on the other:

✡ 'Israel took the opportunity provided by the 1947 UN Partition Plan to create the State of Israel. The Palestinians could have created a Palestinian state at the same time, but failed to do so and tried to destroy the Jewish state. They therefore permanently forfeited the right to have a Palestinian state.'

☾ *'There were good and understandable reasons for their refusal at the time. The 1947 Partition Plan still provides a basis for the Palestinian claim at the present time. A small state on the West Bank and Gaza Strip is less than ideal but better than nothing.'*

✡ 'Israel has won all the wars it has fought. Should we feel guilty for winning?'

☾ *'It is not just a matter of winning but of all the injustices that have been committed in the process. And if there is ever to be peace, the victors have to make significant concessions.'*

✡ 'Jews have had a strong sense of identity for centuries; but the idea of a distinct Palestinian identity is a comparatively recent invention.'

☾ *'The Arabs living in Palestine have always been aware that they were not the same as Arabs in other areas. But they admit that it was nationalism in Europe and Zionism which stimulated (but did not create) their Palestinian nationalism and their sense of a distinct identity as Palestinians.'*

✡ 'The Arabs have been responsible for starting all the conflicts since 1948 – as in 1956 and 1967.'

☾ *'In several of the conflicts it was Israel that stirred things up in order to give themselves justification for taking the initiative. Many Israelis still hold on to the goal of a Greater Israel.'*

✡ 'The fighting in 1948 was a War of Independence. Many Arabs were encouraged by their leaders to leave. The Jews were attacked by the armies of neighbouring Arab countries.'

☾ *'Many Jewish leaders planned to drive as many Arabs as possible out of the areas designated for the Jewish state by a process of ethnic cleansing.'*

✡ 'It is impossible to make peace with the Palestinians because of the many extremist Islamic groups which are not interested in making peace – like *Hamas* and *Islamic Jihad*.'

☾ *'If there are extremist fundamentalists among the Palestinians, there are extremists and fundamentalists among the Jews – like* Gush Emunim.*'*

✡ 'Israel felt compelled to build settlements and roads on the West Bank and Gaza for security reasons and to settle new immigrants from Russia. Only Israel knows what it needs to do to ensure its own security.'

☾ *'Israel continues to occupy the West Bank and Gaza in defiance of UN Resolutions. It has been creating facts on the ground in order to make it impossible for any Palestinian state to be created, or to make it as small and as weak as possible. Palestinians find it hard to understand why Israel seems to be the only country in the world that refuses to carry out UN Resolutions and yet is allowed to get away with it.'*

✡ 'Many Israeli Jews believe that force is the only language that the Arabs understand.'

☾ *'The only way for Israel to be secure is to make peace with the Palestinians and the Arabs.'*

✡ 'Arafat and the PLO say in public that they recognize the State of Israel, but if ever a Palestinian state is created, they will use it as a base from which to drive the Israelis into the sea.'

☾ *'From the very beginning Zionist leaders have said one thing in public and another thing in private.'*

✡ 'Israel can never surrender to Islamic extremism.'

☾ *'Perhaps it is Israeli intransigence and the lack of response from the rest of the world that have driven many Palestinians towards Islamic fundamentalism as the only source of hope in their despair.'*

✡ 'The Arabs have shown that they are not interested in the peace process, and that most of them would like to destroy the Jewish state.'

☾ *'When the Arabs have at different stages put out feelers and wanted to make peace, successive Israeli governments have turned a deaf ear. They wanted to maintain the hostility in the hope of eventually gaining more territory.'*

With such opposing views, is it ever going to be possible to find out the truth about what has happened in history? The following chapter (Chapter 2: The Seeds of Conflict: Call the Next Witness) attempts to explore the nature of the conflict in more detail.

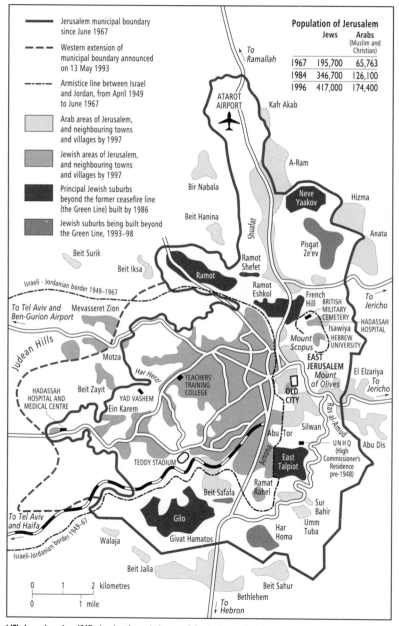

1.17b *Jerusalem since 1967, showing the encirclement of the city by new Jewish settlements.*

Chapter 2

The Seeds of Conflict
Call the Next Witness

*Two important phenomena of the same nature and yet in direct conflict,
which have so far escaped all attention, are at present developing
in the Asiatic part of Turkey. They are the awakening of the Arab nation
and the hidden attempts of Jews to re-establish the ancient kingdom of Israel
on a very large scale. These two movements are destined to be in permanent
conflict, until one gains the upper hand over the other. The fate of the whole
world will depend on the eventual outcome of the conflict between these
two peoples who represent two conflicting principles.[1]*

NAJIB AZURI, A PALESTINIAN ARAB, WRITING IN 1905

*Can it be that the dispossessed will keep silent and calmly accept
what is being done to them? Will they not ultimately arise to regain,
with physical force, that which they are deprived of through the power
of gold? Will they not seek justice from the strangers that placed
themselves over their land?[2]*

YITZHAK EPSTEIN AT THE 1905 ZIONIST CONGRESS

*It was evident twenty years ago [i.e. in 1891] that the day would
come when the Arabs would stand up against us.[3]*

AHAD HA'AM (ASHER GINSBERG), A JEW, WRITING IN 1911

*There is no example in history of a people saying we agree to renounce
our country, let another come and settle here and outnumber us.[4]*

DAVID BEN-GURION, 1944

*We are doomed to live in a constant state of war with the Arabs
and there is no escape from sacrifice and bloodshed. This is perhaps
an undesirable situation, but it is a fact. If we are to proceed with our work
against the wishes of the Arabs we shall have to expect such sacrifices.[5]*

MOSHE DAYAN, AN ISRAELI JEW, WRITING IN 1968

> *The origin of the conflict lies in the settlement of a new population*
> *on a territory already occupied by a people unwilling to accept that*
> *settlement. This is as undeniable as it is obvious. The settlement*
> *may be justified in whole or in part; but it cannot be denied.*
> *Likewise the refusal of the indigenous population to accept*
> *it may be thought justifiable, or it may not.[6]*
> MAXIME RODINSON, WRITING IN 1982

2.1 Anti-Semitism

Q What is anti-Semitism?

It is a strange irony of history that although both Jews and Arabs are Semitic peoples, the word 'anti-Semitism' has come to be used exclusively for feelings or actions against the *Jewish* people.

Theodor Herzl (1860–1904), the founder of the modern Zionist movement, explained his understanding of anti-Semitism:

I understand what anti-Semitism is about. We Jews have maintained ourselves, even if through no fault of our own, as a foreign body among the different nations. In the ghetto, we have taken on a number of anti-social characteristics... Anti-Semitism is a consequence of the emancipation of the Jews. The peoples about us who lack a historical understanding... do not see us as a historical product... When we came out of the ghetto, we were... 'ghetto Jews'. We should have been allowed time to accustom ourselves to freedom.[7]

Only anti-Semitism has made Jews out of us.[8]

Max Nordau, at the First Zionist Congress in Basle in 1897, described the effects of anti-Semitism on Jews in Europe in a speech which was later described as 'a monument of our age':

Jewish misery has two forms, the material and the moral. In Eastern Europe, North Africa and Western Asia – in those very regions where the overwhelming majority, probably nine-tenths of all Jews, live – there the misery of the Jews is to be understood literally. It is a daily distress of the body, anxiety for every day that follows, a tortured fight for bare existence. In Western Europe... the question of bread and shelter, and the question of security of life and limb concerns them less. There the misery is moral. It takes the form of perpetual injury to self-respect and honour and of a brutal suppression of the striving for spiritual satisfactions which no non-Jew is obliged to deny himself.[9]

He went on to speak of the pogroms in Eastern Europe in the early 1880s:

[After] a slumber of thirty to sixty years, anti-Semitism broke out once more from the innermost depth of the nations and his real situation was revealed to the mortified Jew... He has lost the home of the ghetto, but the land of his birth is denied to

*him as his home. He avoids his fellow Jew because anti-Semitism has made him
hateful. His countrymen repel him when he wishes to associate with them. He has
no ground under his feet and he has no community to which he belongs as a full
member. He cannot reckon on his Christian countrymen viewing either his character or his intentions with justice, let alone with kindly feelings. With his Jewish
countrymen he has lost touch. He feels that the world hates him and he sees no
place where he can find warmth when he seeks it...*

*The emancipated Jew is insecure in his relations with his fellow beings, timid
with strangers, even suspicious of the secret feelings of his friends. His best powers
are exhausted in the suppression, or at least the difficult concealment, of his own
real character. For he fears that this character might be recognized as Jewish, and
he never has the satisfaction of showing himself as he is in all his thoughts and sentiments. He becomes an inner cripple.*[10]

Q How did Christianity contribute to the growth of anti-Semitism?

Dagobert D. Runes, a Jew, expresses the feelings of many Jews who believe that
Christianity is largely responsible for anti-Semitism:

*Anti-Semitism was born with Christianity; to be sure, not with Jesus, a Jew himself,
whose followers took conviction in His descendancy from the House of David, but
rather with those who, on the basis of sermons flowing from the lips of the gentle
Nazarene, created an organized church...*

*A new era began, the era of Christianity not as the solemn teachings of a gentle
Jew, but as a powerful body of involved edicts, codes and doctrines that affected the
whole Western world. The nations of the Roman empire, without leadership and broken in spirit, submitted to the wishes of the Bishop of Rome, all except the Jews. The
Jew would not surrender, neither in Judea nor in Egypt, neither in Persia nor in
Libya. Not even in Rome. So the Bishop of Rome, who in the fourth century became
the master of the souls of Europe, put the mark of perfidy on the name and title of
every Jew in his realm and elsewhere. And this blot he willed should remain upon
the children and children's children of the House of Israel; and because of this
stigma, for more than 1500 years Christians have always found it easy to deal with
Jews as non-beings. Judai monstra sunt. [Jews are monsters.]*

*It was the Bishop of Rome who in the thirteenth century directed that the blot
which was placed upon the Jew should also be carried on his clothing, visible to all.*

*It was the Bishop of Rome who ordered in the fifteenth century that the marked
people be confined to ghettos so that they might not soil the Christians around them.*

*It was the Bishop of Rome who used the Crusades against the Muslims as an occa-
sion to heap blemish upon the Jews.*

*It was the Bishop of Rome who was the spiritual head of the auto-da-fé
[Inquisition] in which in Spain alone 9,000 Jewish patricians were burned ad
majorem Christi gloriam [for the greater glory of Christ]. And in our time, it was the
Bishop of Rome who refused to utter a single sentence of horror, nay, disapproval,
of the choking to death by German Christians of one million Jewish children and
five million Jewish women and unarmed men.*

The crucifixion of the Jew Jesus by order of the whole Jewish community has been made a cornerstone of all Christian theology, supported by the implication that in the eyes of God the Jews are for ever accursed, and that every Jewish child in your town, and every Jewish woman in your town, and every man, is a congenital sinner and criminal.[11]

Runes quotes the following passages from the writings of John Chrysostom, Augustine, Thomas Aquinas and Martin Luther to show how Christians have often been encouraged to think about the Jews:

The Jews are the most worthless of all men – they are lecherous, greedy, rapacious – they are perfidious murderers of Christians, they worship the devil, their religion is a sickness...

*   The Jews are the odious assassins of Christ and for killing God there is no expiation possible, no indulgence or pardon. Christians may never cease vengeance, and the Jews must live in servitude for ever. God always hated the Jews, and whoever has intercourse with Jews will be rejected on Judgment Day. It is incumbent upon all Christians to hate the Jews.*
JOHN CHRYSOSTOM (AD 344–407)

The true image of the Hebrew is Judas Iscariot, who sells the Lord for silver. The Jew can never spiritually understand the Scriptures and for ever will bear the guilt for the death of Jesus because their fathers killed the Saviour.
AUGUSTINE (AD 354–430).

It would be perfectly licit to hold the Jews, because of their crucifying the Lord, in perpetual servitude.
THOMAS AQUINAS (AD 1225–74)

Set their synagogues on fire, and whatever does not burn up should be covered or spread over with dirt so that no one may ever be able to see a cinder or stone of it... in order that God may see that we are Christians... Their homes should likewise be broken down and destroyed... They should be put under one roof or in a stable, like gypsies, in order that they may realize that they are not masters in our land as they boast, but miserable captives, as they complain of us incessantly before God with bitter wailing... They should be deprived of their prayer books and Talmuds, in which such idolatry, lies, cursing, and blasphemy are taught... their rabbis must be forbidden to teach under the threat of death.
MARTIN LUTHER (AD 1483–1546)

Q What forms did anti-Semitism take in nineteenth-century Europe?

James Parkes, an English historian, describes the development of modern anti-Semitism in his book *The Emergence of the Jewish Problem (1879–1939).* He begins by describing some of the basic attitudes towards Jews in the nineteenth century:

Modern anti-Semitism is a political weapon deliberately invented and artificially developed for ends which have nothing to do with the Jewish people or the Jewish religion. Its salient characteristic is that the material out of which it is forged is not only false, but known by its artificers to be false. The actual problems, prejudices, difficulties, and jealousies which arise out of the presence of actual Jewish communities are too diverse and too diffuse to have any practical value as a general weapon of the kind which anti-Semites desired. They had, however, this essential value. They provided the background of susceptibility on which the anti-Semite was able to paint his vast chimeras, and gave to the most improbable creations of his fancy the similitude of probability.

Among the peasants and the proletariat, and among the ignorant of all classes, there had survived into the nineteenth century relics of the religious intolerance of the Middle Ages, and memories of the exactions of Jewish usurers; and they were familiar with Jews as strange, ragged and 'foreign' pedlars dealing with trumpery, or as old-clothes merchants, ridiculous with their evil-smelling sacks, and the three or four old hats beloved of nineteenth-century cartoonists.

Among the middle classes and the urban artisanate the word 'Jew' stood for something quite different. It stood for the rival and competitor. The urbanization and industrialization of Europe had opened all kinds of new occupations to the more enterprising members of the Jewish population. The place which they came to occupy, if never so powerful as anti-Semites represented it, was yet a prominent one in many walks of urban life, and quite sufficient to attract jealousy among the non-Jewish urban population of similar standing, and desiring to obtain similar advantages from the expanding capitalism of the time.

To the aristocrat, the landowner, and the cleric, 'Jews' appeared in still a third light. The urbanized, capitalistic, liberal, secularist, and 'democratic' bourgeois state, which had deprived these classes of their authority and privileges, had emancipated the Jews, and given them every opportunity for influencing the public life of what had been 'Christendom'. To them the Jew was the parvenu, the sceptic, the desecrator of traditions.

Without this triple background of dislike, suspicion, or hostility arising out of actual Jewish problems the whole vast structure of anti-Semitism would have crumbled.

He goes on to describe how anti-Semitism was used as a political weapon:

The common enemy for which, in different countries, the weapon of anti-Semitism was forged, was precisely the liberal, secular, urbanized, and capitalistic state of the period; and though it proved no more than a Mrs Partington's mop in the effort to restore the aristocratic and clerical society which had perished, it was most adroitly chosen for the discomfiture of nineteenth-century politicians. In the first place Jews alone could be described by all the adjectives used above to describe the nineteenth-century state. Their politics were almost universally liberal, for it was liberalism which had secured their political emancipation, and it was in liberal circles that they were most at home. The Jewish generation which had first profited by emancipation was largely in revolt against the traditions of the Synagogue, and was by temperament secularist; for the alternative of a modernized and reformed Judaism had scarcely appeared. They had for centuries been an urban *population. And they were better equipped for the nineteenth-century* capitalist *development than any similar class of non-Jewish society. They were cosmopolitan, accustomed to handling money, and versed in all forms of commercial practice. Whatever aspect of modern society was under attack, it was therefore possible to give it the name of 'Jewish'. Anti-Semitism united 'the enemies of dissent, the enemies of wealth as well as the enemies of the alien and the enemies of the upstart – clericals, nationalists, socialists, and aristocrats'. But that was not all. A concentration on the 'Jewish' aspect of society allowed the attack to be made simultaneously on all fronts, and to bring together the most diverse elements of opposition. The traditional hostility to the Jews of the Churches, whether Roman, Protestant, or Orthodox, brought together the aristocratic prelate who disliked the diminution of his privileges, the sincere Christian who hated the secularist opportunism of the new society, and the poor rural or urban curate whose parishioners were ruthlessly exploited by the selfishness of capitalist enterprise; the old landowner and the non-Jewish industrialist united in opposing the Jewish rival of the latter; and the Christian and the freethinking intellectual found common ground in hostility to the cultural influence of Jews in the arts and professions. But even among the* petite *bourgeoisie in the towns and cities it was useful; for it brought together the jealous, the unsuccessful, and the displaced in a common movement. Only the Socialist movement resisted the temptation and refused to fall into the trap of distinguishing a Jewish from a non-Jewish capitalist. The 'Christian' Socialists, on the other hand, whether Roman or Protestant, were in the forefront of the movement.*

These are some specific examples he gives of how anti-Semitism was used:

Not only could the weapon of anti-Semitism draw together the most diverse elements in society; it could also be wielded in any one of a number of ways. The charge that opponents were 'Jewish' could be used simply as a stick with which to beat them. It was in this way that organized political anti-Semitism was first used by Bismarck in his attack on the National Liberals in 1879. The Jews could be used as a scapegoat for the failings of an unpopular regime, as they were used by the Russian bureaucracy from 1881 to 1917. Alternatively the scapegoat technique could be used to persuade people that their misery was neither the fault of their rulers, as in nineteenth-century Rumania, nor of themselves, as in the propaganda which brought the National Socialists to power in twentieth-century Germany. The Jewish bogy could be used to undermine confidence in a regime too strong for direct attack, as in the case of the French Third Republic in the period between 1880 and 1914. Finally, a concentration on supposedly anti-social or unpopular activities of Jews provided a most satisfactory smoke-screen to divert attention from the equally anti-social or unpopular activities of non-Jews engaged in similar occupations. Hence the considerable support given to fascist movements of the Mosley type by non-Jewish capitalists who have been only too glad to have attention diverted from themselves in a period in which socialism, or advanced radicalism, has been 'in the atmosphere'.

There is then nothing surprising in the emergence of anti-Semitism in the nineteenth-century picture. To present it as an unexpected return to medieval prejudice in a period of rationalism and toleration is to ignore the opportunism of modern political struggles.[12]

2.2 Zionism

Q Why have the Jews felt such a strong attachment to the land throughout their history?

Denys Baly, an Englishman who lived and worked in Palestine for many years before and after the creation of Israel in 1948, describes how for many centuries Jews have expressed their longing to return to the land:

The famous cry of hope, 'Next year in Jerusalem', which year by year is uttered at the feast of the Passover is not the only expression of this longing for return. Three times a day, at the morning, afternoon and evening services the following words are spoken, 'Sound the great horn for our freedom; lift up the ensign to gather our exiles, and gather us from the four corners of the earth. Blessed art thou, O Lord, who gatherest the banished ones of the people of Israel. Restore our judges as at the first, and our counsellors as at the beginning; remove from us sorrow and sighing; reign thou over us, O Lord, thou alone in loving-kindness, and tender mercy, and justify us in judgment. Blessed art thou, O Lord, the King who lovest righteousness and judgment. And to Jerusalem, thy city, return in mercy, and dwell therein as thou hast spoken; rebuild it soon in our days as an everlasting building, and speedily set up therein the throne of David. Blessed art thou, O Lord, who rebuildest Jerusalem'. Nor are these the only occasions. Running throughout the liturgical services, like one of the threads of which the pattern is made, is this earnest longing and hope, and this certainty that the day will come in which the hope will be fulfilled.

He goes on to explain the unbroken contact between the Jews of the Dispersion and the Jews of Palestine over many centuries:

Equally impressive is the unbroken contact which the Jews of the Dispersion maintained with the land of Palestine, and that not only as a place of pious pilgrimage but as a continuing centre of Jewish life. The Jewish community in Palestine was not always numerous, was from time to time in severe straits of poverty and privation, and on occasions was kept in existence only by the timely charity of their fellow Jews in other lands. Yet the gifts that in return went out from them to the Jews throughout the world were such that it would be true to say that had they not been given, then Judaism as we know it today would never have been. From Palestine in the grim period after the destruction of Jerusalem came the Mishnah and from Palestine also, some 500 years later, came the Massoretic text of the Hebrew Scriptures, the sole authority for the Hebrew text until the dramatic discovery of the Dead Sea Scrolls in the bloody twilight of the Mandate. The contribution of Tiberias to the development of the Talmud takes second place to the work of the Babylonian scholars of the time, but it has its place in that development. These three things, the Tanakh or Old Testament, definitively edited by the Massoretes, the Mishnah and the Talmud, are the foundation and the basis of the Jewish way of life, and if Judaism had no other debt to Palestine than that two of them had taken shape there, the Dispersion would still have had to own that Palestine was their mother.

The Jews in Palestine continued to maintain a precarious existence there throughout the succeeding centuries, surviving the massacres of the Crusades and the fitful intolerance, indifference, and magnanimity of the Muslim rulers. Left to themselves, they would probably have died out altogether or become merged in the surrounding Muslim flood, or have been preserved as a tiny fossil like the Samaritan community of Nablus. That this did not happen was due to the continual flow, irregular but never entirely ceasing, of Jews from other countries. Devout rabbis who wished to spend their final years in prayer and study in the Holy Land, desperate exiles fleeing before some new persecution, great names like that of Nahmanides, lesser men whose names today are lost for ever – they constitute a fact of history to which the Zionists may rightly call attention. After the expulsion of the Jews from Spain the life of the Jewish community in Galilee was once again vigorous and effective. At the beginning of the seventeenth century, when religious life there was already on the decline, Safad had eighteen talmudic colleges and twenty-one synagogues. Joseph Caro, the author of the authoritative code-book of Jewish conduct, the Shulhan Arukh, lived for forty years in Safad, dying there in 1575. Isaac Luria, who through his disciple Haim Vital, a native of Safad, was to have a tremendous effect on the development of Jewish mysticism, came to Safad in 1570, though he was destined to live there for only two more years. These names, though the most important, are not the only ones. During their time, in fact, the Palestinian community was among the most dynamic sections of Jewry...

The enduring continuity of Jewish contact with some part of what they believe to be their historic homeland is seen to be more impressive than it is popularly held to be... It is this enduring contact of the Jewish people with Palestine, together with the deep-seated religious and emotional ties with the country, which are the strength of the Zionist case. When in the nineteenth century the Jews began to look for somewhere to live in safety, Palestine was the only country which could stir the general interest.[13]

Q What are the origins of Zionism?

Although the prayer 'Next year in Jerusalem' had for centuries expressed the hope that the Jews would one day return to the land, few believed that it could ever become reality. The first significant development in the nineteenth century, however, was that after the emancipation of Jews in Western Europe, some wealthy Jews like the philanthropist Sir Moses Montefiore, began to work for the revival of the struggling Jewish communities in Palestine. Then in 1881 the pogroms among the Jewish communities in Western Russia led to a new upsurge of Zionist feeling.

Moshe Leib Lilienblum (1843–1910), a Russian Jew, argued that the root of the problem was that the Jew was always made to feel a 'stranger'. This is how his ideas are summed up by David Vital, professor of political science at Tel Aviv University, in his book *The Origins of Zionism*:

The 'Middle Ages' are once again upon us, with the sole difference that it is no longer religion that is the criterion for distinguishing the native from the stranger, but nationality and race. It is these that are now the household gods of Europe in both the West and the East. The Jew is not a Teuton of the German nation, or a Magyar of the Hungarian nation, or a Slav, but a son of Shem and therefore, whether he wills it or not, a 'stranger'. Thus, in the final analysis, nothing has changed... We, the Jews, may not think of ourselves as strangers, but others do. There is therefore nothing that we ourselves can do to avoid the conflict... There is only one way out of the predicament: the Jews must cease to be strangers. But how?

He totally rejected the idea that Jews should be assimilated in the countries where they lived:

The petty-minded and the small of heart propose final and absolute assimilation – a despicable and unjustifiable solution in principle, an unworkable one in practice. There was no evidence to suggest that the surrounding people wished to accept the Jews and, in any case, there was no reason to believe that it was a matter subject to deliberate decision. 'I do not speak of the flight of individuals; there have always been blackguards in mind and deed. They have never done anything to improve the condition of the Jews, on the contrary... they have reduced the ranks of the beaten and increased the ranks of the beaters.' But assimilation in toto was another matter: assimilation was national death; a nation could not commit suicide. If it occurred, it would be as a consequence of history, which is to say of processes and events over which we ourselves have no control.

Lilienblum went on to propose a return to Eretz-Israel as the only solution to the problem:

No, the solution to the troubles of the Jews and to the fears and resentments of the Gentiles was to find a place where the Jews 'would no longer be strangers but citizens and masters of the land themselves'... It might take a century for the Jews to evacuate Europe, but a beginning must be made. Where to? Not to America, where, once again, they would be strangers, but to Eretz-Israel 'to which we have a historic right which was not lost with our (lost) rule of the country, any more than the peoples of the Balkans lost their rights to their lands when they lost their rule over them'.[14]

Leon Pinsker (1821–91) was influenced by Lilienblum's writings, and in 1882 published a very significant book entitled *Auto-emancipation*, in which he argued that the problems of the Jews could only be solved if they were able to live as a nation in their own homeland. This is **David Vital**'s summary of Pinsker's ideas:

The heart of the problem, says Pinsker, is that the Jews comprise a distinctive element in every one of the nations in which they are found, an element that cannot be entirely absorbed and therefore cannot be readily and comfortably tolerated, but is, on the contrary, feared and hated and denied equality of status and treat-

ment... By the standards of others, once they had lost their country the Jewish peo-
ple should have fallen into decay long ago. But instead, uniquely, they continued
to maintain themselves as a nation and, by so doing, became in the eyes of others
an uncanny and frightening people... As such the Jews aroused superstitious fear;
fear led to hatred; hatred to a psychosis which has now, after almost twenty cen-
turies, become a malady passed down from father to son... There is, generally, little
love for strangers. But not all strangers are alike. All have a home somewhere –
except the Jew... 'The Jews are aliens who have no representatives, because they
have no country...'

It cannot be denied that the emancipation of the Jews, where instituted, is a
great achievement. But it is only legal emancipation, not social. Its basis is in rea-
son, not in natural and unencumbered feeling... Equality can be attained only by
the recreation of full Jewish nationality, by the collective return of the Jews to the
ranks of the nations as a people living in their own homeland. This will not be
achieved by the efforts of others, but by self-help. The Jews must not look to others to
emancipate them; they must strive for auto-emancipation.

Pinsker's solution is a territorial solution. He does not propose a Return. At one
point he says plainly that it is not the Holy Land that the Jews need but a land. At
another point he makes clear that he does not object to Eretz-Israel; but nor does he
believe it a suitable country for settlement... It is the fact of territory that is crucial.[15]

Whereas earlier in the nineteenth century only a few individuals and groups of
Jews had settled in Palestine, after the publication of *Auto-emancipation*, Pinsker
became the leader of a movement known as 'Hibbat Zion' (Love of Zion), which
encouraged Jews from Europe to settle in Eretz-Israel. This movement is described
by Vital as 'Proto-Zionism... a somewhat inchoate movement devoted to the reset-
tlement of the Jews in Eretz-Israel/Palestine... Institutionally it was weak. In character and ethos it was philanthropic rather than political.'

This first period of immigration lasted from 1882 to 1903. According to **Noah
Lucas** in his *Modern History of Israel*, it

resembled subsequent Zionist immigration in that it was a minuscule trickle alongside
the mass emigration to the west prompted by the outbreak of pogroms and intensified
persecution of the Jews in Russia after 1882... Most (of the early immigrants who actu-
ally reached Palestine) were of the middle class with substantial property which
enabled many of them to acquire land and develop citrus plantations and vineyards.
In the event the majority settled in the cities, especially Jerusalem where their livelihood
was at best precarious... The Zionism of these settlers was construed in terms of per-
sonal emancipation rather than a clear vision of national redemption, and their
efforts contributed little to the regeneration of Jewish national life in Palestine. By the
end of the century their settlements had degenerated into effete charitable foundations.

Lucas also describes the way in which the movement Hibbat Zion was influenced by
Ahad Ha'Am (Asher Ginsberg), one of its most outstanding leaders:

The settlement attempt in Palestine, although it was small in scale, did accustom the Jews of eastern Europe to consider immigration to Palestine as a possible concrete solution for their immediate plight. On the other hand the failures of the immigrants provoked scepticism about the efficacy of 'practical' Zionism (as the settlement effort was dubbed) and led to vigorous debate among Zionist writers and followers as to the proper strategy for the national movement. The first influential criticism of the Lovers of Zion and the early settlers came from the pen of Ahad Ha'Am (1856–1927), himself a Russian leader of the movement and possibly the most acute thinker of Zionism.

In his essay This Is Not The Way, published in 1889, Ahad Ha'Am presented the kernel of what became with subsequent elaboration a sophisticated doctrine of Zionism, advocated by a critical school of thought within the mainstream of the movement. Ahad Ha'Am suggested in his essay that the approach of the Lovers of Zion with the haphazard settlement activities it sponsored was bound to fail so long as it appealed to self interest and the desire for personal emancipation rather than to the inspiring vision of national regeneration with its cultural potentiality. The development of the national movement required the reinvigoration of Jewish education in the diaspora for the revival of Jewish spiritual unity and creativity. Settlement in Palestine was of crucial importance because it would eventually establish a centre of leadership for such creativity but not if cultural quality was subordinated to quantity.

This was the basic line of argument of 'spiritual' or 'cultural' Zionism: it selected the crisis of Judaism rather than that of the Jews as the core issue.[16]

Q How did Zionism become a political movement?

The person who drew together the many different strands of Zionism and made them into a coherent political movement was **Theodor Herzl** (1860–1904), a Hungarian Jew, who was born and brought up in Budapest. At the age of eighteen he moved with his parents to Vienna, where he studied law. After finding that because he was a Jew he could not practise law, he became a civil servant. He soon started to write, and when he moved to Paris in 1891, became a correspondent for a newspaper in Vienna. In 1894 he reported in detail the trial of Alfred Dreyfus, the French Jew who was condemned on the basis of false evidence, and this experience made him painfully aware of the problem of anti-Semitism.

In his first book, *The Jewish State: An Attempt at a Modern Solution to the Jewish Question*, written immediately after the Dreyfus affair and published in 1896, he attempted to outline a purely political solution to the problems facing Jewish communities in Europe. This was his analysis of the Jewish question:

The Jewish question exists wherever Jews live in perceptible numbers. Where it does not exist, it is carried by Jews in the course of their migrations... This is the case in every country, and will remain so, even in those highly civilized – for instance France – until the Jewish question finds a solution on a political basis. The unfortunate Jews are now carrying the seeds of anti-Semitism into England; they have already introduced it into America...

We are one people – our enemies have made us one in our respite, as repeatedly happens in history. Distress binds us together, and, thus united, we suddenly discover our strength. Yes, we are strong enough to form a State, and, indeed, a model State. We possess all human and material resources necessary for the purpose.

He proposed that Jews should create their own state as a way of solving these problems:

Let the sovereignty be granted us over a portion of the globe large enough to satisfy the rightful requirements of a nation; the rest we shall manage for ourselves.

The creation of a new State is neither ridiculous nor impossible. We have in our day witnessed the process in connection with nations which were not in the bulk middle class, but poorer, less educated, and consequently weaker than ourselves. The Governments of all countries scourged by anti-Semitism will be keenly interested in assisting us to obtain the sovereignty we want.

He described how organizations such as The Jewish Society could be set up to work towards the creation of the Jewish state:

Should the Powers declare themselves willing to admit our sovereignty over a neutral piece of land, then the Society will enter into negotiations for the possession of this land. Here two territories come under consideration, Palestine and Argentina. In both countries important experiments in colonization have been made, though on the mistaken principle of a gradual infiltration of Jews. An infiltration is bound to end badly. It continues till the inevitable moment when the native population feels itself threatened, and forces the Government to stop a further influx of Jews. Immigration is consequently futile unless based on an assured supremacy.

The Society of Jews will treat with the present masters of the land, putting itself under the protectorate of the European Powers, if they prove friendly to the plan. We could offer the present possessors of the land enormous advantages, take upon ourselves part of the public debt, build new roads for traffic, which our presence in the country would render necessary, and do many other things. The creation of our State would be beneficial to adjacent countries, because the cultivation of a strip of land increases the value of its surrounding districts in innumerable ways.

He then discussed the relative merits of Argentina and Palestine – two countries which had been suggested as possible locations for a Jewish homeland:

Shall we choose Palestine or Argentina? We shall take what is given us, and what is selected by Jewish public opinion. The Society will determine both these points.

Argentina is one of the most fertile countries in the world, extends over a vast area, has a sparse population and a mild climate. The Argentine Republic would derive considerable profit from the cession of a portion of its territory to us. The present infiltration of Jews has certainly produced some discontent, and it would be necessary to enlighten the Republic on the intrinsic difference of our new movement.

Palestine is our ever-memorable historic home. The very name of Palestine would attract our people with a force of marvellous potency. Supposing His Majesty the Sultan were to give us Palestine, we could in return undertake to regulate the whole finances of Turkey. We should there form a portion of the rampart of Europe against Asia, an outpost of civilization as opposed to barbarism. We should as a neutral State remain in contact with all Europe, which would have to guarantee our existence. The sanctuaries of Christendom would be safeguarded by assigning to them an extra-ter-ritorial status such as is well known to the law of nations. We should form a guard of honour about these sanctuaries, answering for the fulfilment of this duty with our existence. This guard of honour would be the great symbol of the solution of the Jewish Question after eighteen centuries of Jewish suffering.

Because of the enthusiastic response to his book, Herzl organized a Zionist Congress in Basle in August 1897. It is hard to overestimate the significance of this congress, which was attended by 200 Jews from all over Europe, and was the very first gathering of its kind. The Congress formally adopted the Basle Programme, which stated:

Zionism strives for the establishment of a publicly and legally secured home in Palestine for the Jewish people.
     For the attainment of this aim the Congress considers the following means:

1. The appropriate promotion of colonization with Jewish agriculturalists, artisans and tradesmen.
2. The organization and gathering of all Jews through suitable local and general institutions, according to the laws of the various countries.
3. The promotion of Jewish national feeling and consciousness.
4. Preparatory steps for the attainment of such Government consent as is necessary in order to achieve the aim of Zionism.[17]

This is how **Ahad Ha'Am** summed up the significance of the Congress:

For three days, from morning to evening, some 200 Jews from all countries and of all tendencies had debated in the open and before all the nations the matter of the foundation of a secure home for the Jewish people in the land of their fathers. Thus the national answer had burst the bounds of 'modesty' and been made public. It had been expounded to all the world aloud, in clear language, and with a straight back – something which had not occurred since Israel was exiled from the land.[18]

David Vital explains why the Congress was so crucial for the Zionist movement:

Zionism recreated the Jews as a political nation; and by so doing it revolutionized their collective and private lives. It did not do so immediately or completely or equally... It seems beyond question that this movement for revival and radical change in Jewry did attain results which may fairly be called revolutionary and, further, that its definitive form dates from 1897. For that reason alone the First

Zionist Congress must now be judged one of the pivotal events in the modern history of the Jews.

[The Congress] established a precedent – and the principle – of unity, bringing together virtually all the diverse strains of which the movement was composed: romanticists and pragmatists, orthodox and secularists, socialists and bourgeois, Easterners and Westerners, men whose minds and language were barely influenced by the non-Jewish world and those who were largely products of it, and, above all, those whose primary concern was with the condition of the Jews as opposed to those, like Ahad Ha'Am, whose eyes were on the crisis of Judaism.

The key to Herzl's influence lay in his great organizing ability and his belief that he could use the great powers to assist Jewish settlement in Palestine. He brought to the Zionist movement a drive and a confidence which the Lovers of Zion and the Eastern European Jews did not have at that time. In his own diary he summed up what he believed he had achieved at this first Zionist Congress:

Were I to sum up the Basle Congress in a word – which I shall guard against pronouncing publicly – it would be this: at Basle I founded the Jewish State… If I said this out loud today, I would be answered by universal laughter. Perhaps in five years and certainly in fifty everyone will know it.

Like most of the other leaders of the Zionist movement in his time he seemed to be more concerned about the problems of the Jews in Europe than about the possible consequences of his dreams for the people who were living in Palestine. In his diary he explained how he thought the Jewish immigrants would have to treat the Arabs:

We shall have to spirit the penniless population across the border by procuring employment for it in the transit countries, while denying it any employment in our own country… Both the process of expropriation and the removal of the poor must be carried out discreetly and circumspectly.[19]

The second great leader of the Zionist movement was **Chaim Weizmann**, a Russian Jew, who came to settle in England in 1904. After teaching chemistry at the University of Manchester for several years, he moved to London in 1916 and began working in the Admiralty under the supervision of Lord Balfour. During this time he did a great deal to explain and commend the idea of a Jewish national homeland to officials in the British government, and he was therefore one of the main architects of the Balfour Declaration (see 2.5 The role of Britain).

Some months *before* the Balfour Declaration, Weizmann wrote these words about his hopes for the gradual creation of a Jewish homeland in Palestine:

States must be built up slowly, gradually, systematically and patiently. We, therefore, say that while the creation of a Jewish Commonwealth in Palestine is our final ideal… the way to achieve it lies through a series of intermediary stages. And one of those intermediary stages, which I hope is going to come about as a result of the war, is that the fair country of Palestine will be protected by such a mighty and just Power as Great Britain. Under the wing of this Power, Jews will be able to develop, and to set up the administrative machinery which… would enable us to carry out the Zionist scheme.

In his autobiography he later explained how he thought of the Balfour Declaration merely as 'a framework' within which Jews could achieve their ultimate goals in Palestine:

The Balfour Declaration was no more than a framework, which had to be filled in by our own efforts. It would mean exactly what we would make it mean – neither more nor less. On what we could make it mean through slow, costly and laborious work would depend whether and when we should deserve to attain statehood.

In an address to a Jewish audience in London two years after the issue of the Declaration, he said:

I trust to God that a Jewish state will come about; but it will come about not through political declarations, but by the sweat and blood of the Jewish people… [The Balfour Declaration] is the golden key which unlocks the doors of Palestine and gives you the possibility to put all your efforts into the country… We were asked to formulate our wishes. We said we desired to create in Palestine such conditions, political, economic and administrative, that as the country is developed, we can pour in a considerable number of immigrants, and finally establish such a society in Palestine that Palestine shall be as Jewish as England is English, or America is American… I hope that the Jewish frontiers of Palestine will be as great as Jewish energy for getting Palestine.

On many occasions of this kind he gave assurances that the Zionists would do nothing to harm the Arabs in Palestine:

All fears expressed openly or secretly by the Arabs that they are to be ousted from their present position are due either to a fundamental misconception of Zionist aims or to the malicious activities of our common enemies.

I need hardly say that we Jews will be meticulously and scrupulously careful to respect the sentiments of any religious group or sect in Palestine.

The Zionists are not demanding in Palestine monopolies or exclusive privileges… It always was and remains a cardinal principle of Zionism as a democratic movement that all races and sects in Palestine should enjoy full justice and liberty.

Palestine must be built up without violating the legitimate rights of the Arabs – not a hair of their heads shall be touched.

It is not our objective to seize control of the higher policy of the province of Palestine. Nor has it ever been our objective to turn anyone out of his property.[20]

Sir Charles Webster, a British diplomat who knew Weizmann well during these years, has described his impressions of his brilliant diplomacy in promoting the Zionist programme:

With unerring skill he adapted his arguments to the special circumstances of each statesman. To the British and Americans he could use biblical language and awake a deep emotional undertone; to other nationalities he more often talked in terms of interest. Mr Lloyd George was told that Palestine was a little mountainous country not unlike Wales; with Lord Balfour the philosophical background of Zionism could be surveyed. For Lord Cecil the problem was placed in the setting of a new world organization; while to Lord Milner the extension of imperial power could be vividly portrayed. To me, who dealt with these matters as a junior officer of the General Staff, he brought from many sources all the evidence that could be obtained of the importance of a Jewish national home to the strategical position of the British empire, but he always indicated by a hundred shades and inflections of the voice that he believed that I could also appreciate better than my superiors other more subtle and recondite arguments.

This skillful presentation of facts would, however, have been useless unless he had convinced all with whom he came into contact of the probity of his conduct and the reality of his trust in the will and strength of Britain.[21]

2.3 Jewish settlement in the land

Q How did the Jewish settlers acquire land?

David Hirst, an English journalist who has been the Middle East correspondent of *The Guardian* for many years, describes how land was sold to Jews in the period before 1929 in his book *The Gun and the Olive Branch*:

The great bulk of the land that the Zionists acquired came from large, predominantly absentee, landowners. As resistance built up, the area relinquished by small farmers, 42.7 per cent of the total from 1891 to 1900, fell to a mere 4.3 per cent from 1900 to 1914.

The name Sursock occupies an invidious and recurrent place in this story. The Sursocks were a Levantine family of high breeding and immense wealth who spent much of their time in Western Europe. They also owned some of the richest land in Palestine. In a series of transactions from 1891 to 1920 they sold it all to the Zionists, as unmoved by high appeals to their sense of Arab history as by workaday calls on their conscience. In 1910 they sold the region of Foule, with its Crusader castle made famous by Saladin, in the fertile Vale of Esdraelon; in 1920 they disposed of the rest of their holdings, along with 8,000 peasants in twenty-two villages who made a living from them. They had acquired the whole area in 1872 from corrupt Ottoman officials for the derisory sum of £18,000 to £20,000. It brought in a revenue of £12,000 to £40,000 a year. They sold it for ten times the price they had paid for it, but subsequently complained bitterly that they had let it go so cheap – as indeed they had. The fate of the 8,000 peasants was never determined; the tenants among them – but not the labourers – received 'compensation' of £28,000 – pre-

cisely £3.5 per head for the lot. The Sursock sale was a famous and much-deplored
transaction. But there were many others.

He goes on to explain why the Arabs had only themselves to blame for the ways in
which land was sold to Jews after 1929:

Although there have been many and often fortuitous circumstances to which the
Zionists owe their astonishing success, by no means the least have been the incom-
petence and irresponsibility of the Arab leaders, the frivolity and egoism of the privi-
leged classes. The frailties which the Haifa newspaper Carmel had first denounced
a quarter of a century earlier were all the greater now. About nine-tenths of all
land acquired by the Jews up to 1929 was sold by absentee landlords. But after
that, the ever-growing 'Zionist peril' notwithstanding, the main culprits were resi-
dent landlords. It was at this time, too, that Arab usurers came most offensively into
their own; smallholders were forced to borrow at interest rates of up to fifty per
cent; they would cling desperately to their little plots of land, but in the end, under
a crushing burden of debt, were forced to abandon them to the land-hungry Jews.
There were mouth-watering profits to be made; the price of a dunum near Rishon-
le-Zion, originally eight shillings, had reached £10 to £25 by the early thirties.
Officially, of course, the willing squanderers of the Arab heritage were becoming
the pariahs of society. They were ritually condemned on every suitable occasion –
at conferences convened to consider the 'Zionist peril', in the campaign statements
of rival political parties, in the anathemas issued by religious authorities. Thus in
1932, the Independence Party issued a proclamation declaring that 'there is no
future for the nation unless the gates are closed on immigration, and the sale of
land prohibited; the delegates reaffirm their dissatisfaction at the middle-men and
the landsellers, and consider that the time has come to punish and oppose them.' In
Palestinian vocabulary simsar – 'middle-man' – has established itself ever since as
a word of abuse. In 1935, when immigration and land sales were surpassing all
limits, Haj Amin Husseini, the Mufti, assembled some 400 men of God, imams,
qadis, muftis, preachers and teachers, who issued a fatwa, or religious edict, out-
lawing the sale of land to Jewish immigrants and denouncing its perpetrators as
apostates to be denied burial in Muslim cemeteries.

These land sales revealed fatal weaknesses within the Arab community:

However – and here is the real measure of the Palestinian leadership – although the
landsellers and agents might suffer all manner of verbal abuse, they rarely suffered
much worse. Landselling, branded as 'treason', was a characteristic accusation
which one faction of notables hurled at another. It made for an immense hypocrisy.
There was no real social ostracism, let alone any condign punishment. The very
people who most vociferously condemned the practice were not infrequently the
ones who most indulged in it. In 1928, the delegates to the Seventh Palestine
Congress were described by a contemporary as a very odd assortment who included
'spies and middlemen selling land to the Jews'. In 1932, the newspaper al-Arab
found it strange indeed that the Arab Executive should wax so indignant about the

sale of Arab land when some of its own members were doing the selling. No wonder a British fact-finding team's efforts to uncover the full extent of these odious trans- actions met with resistance from the Arab as well as the Jewish leadership. If, by 1948, the landsellers had only allowed some 6.6 per cent of physical Palestine to fall into Jewish hands – though that represented a much higher proportion of its cultivable area – the damage they inflicted on the Palestinian psyche is less easy to calculate. But it was undoubtedly great. The landsellers typified the Palestinians' response to Zionism at its most self-destructive. They were the most unhealthy part of a body politic so diseased that, instead of achieving that self-renewal which, under strain, an even slightly healthier one might have achieved, it degenerated still further. It did not immunize itself against the sickness which the landsellers represented; it let the sickness spread. The disloyalty of a few, rather than fortifying the constructive patriotism of the majority, aggravated the factionalism, recrimina- tion and mistrust which poisoned the whole Palestinian struggle, and the behaviour of the politicians in particular.[22]

Q What was the official Jewish policy regarding settlement in the land and the establishment of a Jewish state?

David Ben-Gurion, who became the first Prime Minister of Israel in 1948, explained:

The Debate has not been for or against the indivisibility of the Land of Israel. The Debate concerned which of the two routes would lead quicker to the common goal.

He summed up the goals of the Zionist movement in the introduction to *The History of the Haganah*:

At the present time we speak of colonization, and only of colonization. It is our short-term objective. But it is clear that England belongs to the English, Egypt to the Egyptians and Judea to the Jews. In our country there is room only for Jews. We will say to the Arabs: 'Move over'; if they are not in agreement, if they resist, we will push them by force.[23]

Joseph Weitz, a Jewish government official responsible for Jewish colonization, wrote the following words in 1940:

After the [Second World] War the question of the land of Israel and the question of the Jews would be raised beyond the framework of 'development' among ourselves. It must be clear that there is no room for both peoples in this country. No 'development' will bring us closer to our aim, to be an independent people in this small country. If the Arabs leave the country, it will be broad and wide-open for us. And if the Arabs stay, the country will remain narrow and miserable. When the War is over and the English have won, and when the judges sit on the throne of Law, our people must bring their petitions and their claim before them; and the only solution is Eretz Israel, or at least Western Eretz Israel, without Arabs. There is no room for compro-

mise on this point! The Zionist enterprise so far, in terms of preparing the ground and paving the way for the creation of the Hebrew State in the land of Israel, has been fine and good in its own time, and could do with 'land-buying' – but this will not bring about the State of Israel; that must come all at once, in the manner of a Salvation (this is the secret of the Messianic idea); and there is no way besides transferring the Arabs from here to neighbouring countries, to transfer them all; except maybe for Bethlehem, Nazareth and Old Jerusalem, we must not leave a single village, not a single tribe. And the transfer must be directed to Iraq, to Syria, and even to Transjordan. For that purpose we'll find money, and a lot of money. And only with such a transfer will the country be able to absorb millions of our brothers, and the Jewish question shall be solved, once and for all. There is no other way out.[24]

Moshe Dayan, a hero in the wars of 1948 and 1956, who later served as Minister of Foreign Affairs in the Israeli government, described in 1967 how the state needed to be expanding continually for the sake of its own security:

People abroad ought to realize that, quite apart from their strategic importance to Israel, Sinai, the Golan Heights, the Tiran Straits and the hills west of the Jordan lie at the heart of Jewish history. Nor has the 'restoration of historical Israel' ended yet. Since the return to Zion 100 years ago a double process of colonization and expansion of frontiers has been going on. We have not yet reached the end of that road. It is the people of Israel who will determine the frontiers of their own state.[25]

2.4 Arab reactions to Jewish settlement

Q How did the Arabs react to Jewish settlement?

Najib Azuri, writing in 1905, reveals how he, as a Palestinian Arab, understood the goal of the Jewish settlers in Palestine at that time:

The Jews of our time have understood very well the mistake made by their forefathers. They are trying carefully to avoid it in the restoration of what they call their ancient fatherland. They want to get hold of a part of Palestine which their forefathers were never able to occupy, and in particular to take possession of all the natural boundaries of the country. These are two of the most important points in the Zionist plan of action.

They regard as these natural boundaries Mount Hermon in the north, the source of the Jordan, and the Leontes valley, with the territory which lies between Rasyaya and Sidon; in the south the Suez Canal and the Sinai peninsula; in the east the Arabian desert, and as a Western frontier the Mediterranean. With these frontiers, and in the hands of a people that can defend them, Palestine would be impregnable.[26]

Asher Ginsberg (known as Ahad Ha'Am, 1856–1927) was a Russian Jew who visited Palestine many times from 1891 onwards. He finally settled there in 1922 and died in 1927. After a visit to Palestine in 1891 he recorded some of the problems which the Jewish settlers in Palestine were facing and some of the problems which they were creating:

Palestine is not an uninhabited country and can offer a home only to a very small proportion of the Jews who live scattered throughout the world. Those who settle in Palestine must above all seek to win the friendship of the Palestinians, by approaching them courteously and with respect. But what do our brothers in Palestine do? Precisely the opposite. They were slaves in the land of their exile, and suddenly they find themselves with unlimited freedom, an unbridled freedom of the kind that can be found only in Turkey. This sudden change has aroused in them a tendency to despotism, which is what always happens when slaves come to power. They treat the Arabs with hostility and cruelty, rob them of their rights in a dishonest way, hurt them without reason and then pride themselves on such actions; and no one attacks this despicable and dangerous tendency...

We abroad have a way of thinking that Palestine today is almost desert, an uncultivated wilderness, and that anyone who wishes to buy land there can do so to his heart's content. But this is not in fact the case. It is difficult to find any uncultivated land anywhere in the country... We abroad have a way of thinking that the Arabs are all savages, on a level with the animals, and blind to what goes on around them. But that is quite mistaken. The Arabs, especially the townsmen, see through our activities in their country, and our aims, but they keep silent and make no sign, because for the present they anticipate no danger to their own future from what we are about. But if the time should ever come when our people have so far developed their life in Palestine that the indigenous population should feel more or less cramped, then they will not readily make way for us.

In 1911 he wrote to a friend in Jaffa:

As to the war against the Jews in Palestine, I was a spectator from afar with an aching heart, particularly because of the want of insight and understanding shown on our part to an extreme degree. As a matter of fact, it was evident twenty years ago, that the day would come when the Arabs would stand up against us.[27]

The **Emir Faisal**, son of Sherif Hussein of Mecca, and **Chaim Weizmann** met in January 1919, and signed an agreement in which they pledged their good faith in 'carrying into effect the British Government's Declaration of 2 November 1917' (i.e. the Balfour Declaration). This document shows the willingness of a prominent Arab leader at the time to allow Jews to settle in Palestine:

All necessary measures shall be taken to encourage and stimulate immigration of Jews into Palestine on a large scale, and as quickly as possible to settle Jewish immigrants upon the land through close settlement and intensive cultivation of the soil. In taking such measures the Arab peasant and tenant farmers shall be protected in their rights, and shall be assisted in forwarding their economic development.

After signing the agreement, however, Faisal added a proviso in his own handwriting in Arabic to qualify his position:

Provided the Arabs obtain their independence as demanded in my Memorandum dated 4 February 1919, to the Foreign Office of the Government of Great Britain, I shall concur in the above articles. But if the slightest modification of departure were to be made I shall not be bound by a single word of the present Agreement which shall be deemed void and of no account or validity.

Three months later he expressed his fear of what would happen if the Jews wanted to establish a state:

Let the unhappy Jews find refuge there... under a Muslim or a Christian government... But if the Jews desire to establish a state and obtain sovereign rights in the country, I foresee serious dangers and conflicts between them and other races.[28]

Some Zionist leaders expressed their understanding of the Arab reaction to what the Jews were doing in Palestine.

Moshe Sharett, in speeches to the Mapai Political Committee in 1936:

There is no Arab in Palestine who is not harmed by Jewish immigration; there is no Arab who does not feel himself part of the Great Arab Nation which includes Iraq, the Hedjaz, and Yemen. For him Palestine is an independent unit that had an Arab face. That face is now changing. In his eyes Haifa was an Arab town, and now it is Jewish. His reaction cannot but be resistance.

I am convinced that the Arabs genuinely fear Jewish growth and domination. If this is not true, then all the years I studied Arabic and have met with Arabs were in vain. And if I am wrong on this fundamental question I am not fit to be here.[29]

David Ben-Gurion, commenting on Arab terrorism in a speech to the same committee in 1938:

I want to destroy first of all the illusion among our comrades that the [Arab] terror is a matter of a few gangs, financed from abroad... We are facing not terror but a war. It is a national war declared upon us by the Arabs. Terror is one of the means of war... This is an active resistance by the Palestinians to what they regard as a usurpation of their homeland by the Jews – that's why they fight. Behind the terrorists is a movement, which though primitive is not devoid of idealism and self-sacrifice...

In our political argument abroad, we minimize Arab opposition to us. But let us not ignore the truth among ourselves. I insist on the truth, not out of respect for scientific but political realities. The acknowledgment of this truth leads to inevitable and serious conclusions regarding our work in Palestine... let us not build on the hope the terrorist gangs will get tired. If some get tired, others will replace them. A people which fights against the usurpation of its land will not tire so easily... it is easier for them to continue the war and not get tired than it is for us... The Palestinian Arabs are not alone...

But the fighting is only one aspect of the conflict which is in essence a political one. And politically we are the aggressors and they defend themselves. Militarily, it is we who are on the defensive, who have the upper hand... but in the political sphere they are superior. The land, the villages, the mountains, the roads are in their hands. The country is theirs, because they inhabit it, whereas we want to come here and settle down, and in their view we want to take away from them their country, while we are still outside.[30]

British officials in Palestine explained how they understood the Arab reaction:

Commander Hogarth sent the following report to the Foreign Office in 1918:

Weizmann's disclaimers of political aims are not credited, partly because associates of his at home and in Palestine have not always endorsed them... Anti-Jew feeling is as strong as – perhaps stronger than ever among all classes of Arabs...[31]

Herbert Samuel, a British Jew, who was appointed in 1920 by the British government as High Commissioner for Palestine, wrote the following in a personal letter to Weizmann in 1921:

After a year in Palestine I have come to the conclusion that the importance of the Arab factor had been underestimated by the Zionist movement: unless there is very careful steering it is upon the Arab rock that the Zionist ship may be wrecked.[32]

Gilbert Clayton, one of Weizmann's chief advisers among the British military, wrote the following in 1924:

In general, a year in Palestine has made me regard the whole adventure with apprehension. We have become an alien and detested element into the very core of Islam, and the day may well come when we shall be faced with the alternative of holding it there by the sword or abandoning it to its fate; the Arabs are under-dogs for the moment but they will bide their time and wait.[33]

Eric Mills:

The real trouble was that the Jews were not willing to gain the good will of the Arabs, and to allay their fears by agreeing to limit the extent of their infiltration and to reassure them that the Jews were not going to crowd them out.[34]

2.5 The role of Britain

Q What promises did Britain make to the Jews?

Britain's promises to the Jews were contained in the Balfour Declaration which was a letter written on 2 November 1917 by **Arthur Balfour**, the British Foreign Secretary, to Lord Rothschild, a prominent English Jew. Since Palestine at that time was still part of the Ottoman empire, the British government had no authority to decide the future of the country, but hoped to be able to do so after the defeat of Turkey in the First World War.

Foreign Office
2 November 1917

Dear Lord Rothschild,
I have much pleasure in conveying to you, on behalf of His Majesty's Government, the following declaration of sympathy with Jewish Zionist aspirations which has been submitted to, and approved by the Cabinet:

'His Majesty's Government view with favour the establishment in Palestine of a national home for the Jewish people, and will use their best endeavours to facilitate the achievement of this object, it being clearly understood that nothing shall be done which may prejudice the civil and religious rights of the existing non-Jewish communities in Palestine, or the rights and political status enjoyed by Jews in any other country.'

I should be grateful if you would bring this declaration to the knowledge of the Zionist Federation.

Yours sincerely,

Arthur Balfour

In making this declaration the British government hoped to encourage Jews both in America and in Russia to support the cause of the Allies in the war against Germany. There was also the hope that a Jewish homeland established in Palestine with the support of Britain would protect the Suez Canal and thus safeguard British interests in India and the East.

Another motive which prompted this letter was the desire to avoid a large influx of Jewish refugees into Britain. Balfour had expressed this desire several years earlier when he supported the introduction of an Aliens Act, which was intended to restrict Jewish immigration into Britain:

A state of things could easily be imagined in which it would not be to the advantage of the civilization of the country that there should be an immense body of persons who, however patriotic, able and industrious, however much they threw themselves into the national life, still, by their own action, remained a people apart, and not merely held a religion differing from the vast majority of their fellow-countrymen, but only intermarried among themselves.[35]

Arthur Koestler once described the Balfour Declaration as:

a document in which one nation solemnly promises to a second nation the country of a third nation.[36]

Q What promises were made to the Arabs?

During the First World War the British government made several promises to Arab leaders in order to enlist their support in the war against the Turks. Some of these promises were contained in letters written by **Sir Henry McMahon**, the British High Commissioner in Egypt, to Sherif Hussein of Mecca. The following are extracts from two of these letters:

We hereby confirm to you the declaration of Lord Kitchener... in which was manifested our desire for the independence of the Arab countries and their inhabitants, and our readiness to approve an Arab Caliphate upon its proclamation.
DATED 30 AUGUST 1915

I am authorized to give you the following pledges on behalf of the Government of Great Britain, and to reply as follows to your note:

1. That, subject to the modifications stated above, Great Britain is prepared to recognize and uphold the independence of the Arabs in all the regions lying within the frontiers proposed by the Sharif of Mecca [i.e. the area now corresponding to the Arabian Peninsular, Iraq, Syria, Lebanon, Jordan and Palestine];
2. That Great Britain will guarantee the Holy Places against all external aggression, and will recognize the obligation of preserving them from aggression;
3. That, when circumstances permit, Great Britain will help the Arabs with her advice and assist them in the establishment of governments to suit those diverse regions...

I am confident that this declaration will convince you, beyond all doubt, of Great Britain's sympathy with the aspirations of her friends the Arabs; and that it will result in a lasting and solid alliance with them, of which one of the immediate consequences will be the expulsion of the Turks from the Arab countries and the liberation of the Arab peoples from the Turkish yoke which has weighed on them all these long years.
DATED 24 OCTOBER 1915

The following Anglo-French Declaration, dated 7 November 1918, was publicized widely all over Palestine:

The goal envisaged by France and Great Britain in prosecuting in the East the War set in train by German ambition is the complete and final liberation of the peoples who have for so long been oppressed by the Turks, and the setting up of national gov-

*ernments and administrations that shall derive their authority from the free exercise
of the initiative and choice of the indigenous populations.*

*In pursuit of those intentions, France and Great Britain agree to further and
assist in the setting up of indigenous governments and administrations in Syria [i.e.
Syria and Palestine] and Mesopotamia which have already been liberated by the
Allies, as well as in those territories which they are endeavouring to liberate, and to
recognize them as soon as they are actually set up.*

*Far from wishing to impose this or that system upon the populations of those
regions, their [i.e. France's and Great Britain's] only concern is to offer such support and efficacious help as will ensure the smooth working of the governments and
administrations which those populations will have elected of their own free will to
have; to secure impartial and equal justice for all; to facilitate the economic development of the country by promoting and encouraging local initiative; to foster the
spread of education; and to put an end to the dissensions which Turkish policy has
for so long exploited. Such is the task which the two Allied Powers wish to undertake
in the liberated territories.*[37]

Q How could the promises made to the Jews and the Arabs be reconciled?

Sir Edward Grey, who had been the British Foreign Secretary from 1905 to 1916,
admitted the inconsistency between the promises made to the Jews and the Arabs in
a speech to the House of Lords in March 1923:

*A considerable number of these engagements, or some of them, which have not
been officially made public by the Government, have become public through other
sources. Whether all have become public I do not know, but I seriously suggest to
the Government that the best way of clearing our honour in this matter is officially
to publish the whole of the engagements relating to the matter, which we entered
into during the war. If they are found to be not inconsistent with one another our
honour is cleared. If they turn out to be inconsistent, I think it will be very much
better that the amount, character and extent of the inconsistencies should be
known, and that we should state frankly that, in the urgency of the war, engagements were entered into which were not entirely consistent with each other.*

*I am sure that we cannot redeem our honour by covering up our engagements
and pretending that there is no inconsistency, if there really is inconsistency. I am
sure that the most honourable course will be to let it be known what the engagements are, and, if there is inconsistency, then to admit it frankly, and, admitting
that fact, and having enabled people to judge exactly what is the amount of the
inconsistency, to consider what is the most fair and honourable way out of the
impasse into which the engagements may have led us. Without comparing one
engagement with another, I think that we are placed in considerable difficulty by
the Balfour Declaration itself. I have not the actual words here, but I think the
noble Duke opposite will not find fault with my summary of it. It promised a Zionist
home without prejudice to the civil and religious rights of the population of
Palestine. A Zionist home, my Lords, undoubtedly means or implies a Zionist
Government over the district in which the home is placed, and if ninety-three per*

cent of the population of Palestine are Arabs, I do not see how you can establish other than an Arab Government, without prejudice to their civil rights. That one sentence alone of the Balfour Declaration seems to me to involve, without overstating the case, very great difficulty of fulfilment.[38]

Q How did Britain attempt to carry out these promises?

In a secret memorandum submitted to the British cabinet in 1919, **Lord Balfour** made it very clear that the British government had no intention of applying the principle of self-determination and allowing the Arabs in Palestine to decide their own future:

Do we mean, in the case of Syria, to consult principally the wishes of the inhabitants? We mean nothing of the kind... The contradiction between the letter of the Covenant and the policy of the Allies is even more flagrant in the case of the 'independent nation' of Palestine than in that of the 'independent nation' of Syria. For in Palestine we do not propose even to go through the form of consulting the wishes of the present inhabitants of the country... The four great powers are committed to Zionism. And Zionism, be it right or wrong, good or bad, is rooted in age-long traditions, in present needs, in future hopes, of far profounder import than the desires and prejudices of the 700,000 Arabs who now inhabit that ancient land... In short, so far as Palestine is concerned, the Powers have made no statement of fact which is not admittedly wrong, and no declaration of policy which, at least in the letter, they have not always intended to violate.

He made the same admission in a letter to Lloyd George:

The weak point of our position is of course that in the case of Palestine we deliberately and rightly decline to accept the principle of self-determination.[39]

Erskine Childers, an English journalist and writer, has described the frame of mind in which **Lloyd George**, then the British Prime Minister, approached the question of Palestine at the Peace Conference in Versailles in 1919 following the defeat of Germany and its ally, Turkey, in the First World War. His main concern was to do all he could to implement the Balfour Declaration:

Lloyd George, without whose personal support the Balfour Declaration certainly could never have been obtained, was almost lyrical in his Welsh scriptural romanticism about Zionism. We know from documents that he had it fixed in his mind that he was being given the chance to recreate the Holy Land of the scriptures, as he constantly put it, 'from Dan to Beersheba'. And if I may digress into greater detail for a moment, it is only because I think that what this led to provides both a fascinating and perhaps tormenting glimpse of the way in which our Western notions and emotions, played out in the hands of men wielding total military supremacy, have so gravely injured Arabs.

In the first place, Foreign Office experts in London tried to explain very tactfully to the Prime Minister that there simply was no such place as Dan on any twentieth-century map of Palestine. It did not matter. It is a fact of documentary record that Lloyd George went to the Peace Conference at Versailles determined to draw upon the Palestine of 1919, political boundaries for a new Hebrew State 'from Dan to Beersheba'. It is a fact of documentary record that the Zionists themselves were placed in an extremely delicate situation over this; because they in fact wanted very much more territory than from Dan to Beersheba – they also wanted most of the Sinai Peninsula, all of Transjordan, the whole southern portion of what is today Lebanon, and all south-western Syria almost to the edge of Damascus. Yet the Prime Minister on whose enthusiasm they so counted kept on saying 'Dan to Beersheba', like a kind of ritual incantation...

I believe that I can state with a degree of absolute, mathematical certainty, that no other indigenous people in this century has been disposed of by European Powers and a European settler movement on the basis of a map reputedly showing the area of a tribal kingdom that had briefly existed there 3,000 years earlier. To come upon these facts in the sober archives of twentieth-century government is to have one's brain reel and – in my case at least – to be filled with a sense of shame.[40]

In the end, therefore, British and French promises to the Arabs were totally disregarded, and the Versailles Peace Conference gave Britain the Mandate for Palestine, and France the Mandate for Syria.

2.6 The role of the United Nations

Q How did the UN come to accept the plan that was put forward in 1947? What was the background? (See 1.13 The UN Partition Plan [1947])

David Hirst describes some of the diplomacy which prepared the way for the acceptance of the Partition Plan:

The United Nations, to which a despairing Britain had handed over the whole problem, ruled in favour of partition. That vote was a story of violence in itself – albeit diplomatic violence – in which the United States went to the most extraordinary lengths of backstage manipulation on behalf of its Zionist protégés. Partition went against the better judgment of many of those nations which cast their vote in favour of it. America too – at least its State Department officials who knew something about the Middle East – had grave misgivings. But the White House, which knew a good deal less, overruled them. It sanctioned what a deeply distressed James Forrestal, the Secretary of Defense, described as 'coercion and duress on other nations' which 'bordered on scandal'. President Truman warned one of his secretaries that he would demand a full explanation if nations which normally lined up with the United States failed to do so on Palestine. Governments which opposed partition, governments which could not make up their minds, were swayed by the most unorthodox arguments. The Firestone Tyre and Rubber Company, with plantations in Liberia, brought pressure to bear on the Liberian Government. It was hinted to

Latin American delegates that their vote for partition would greatly increase the chances of a pan-American road project. The Philippines, at first passionately opposed to partition, ended up ignominiously in favour of it: they had too much at stake in seven bills awaiting the approval of Congress. Important Americans were persuaded to 'talk' to various governments which could not afford the loss of American good will.[41]

President Truman had earlier admitted that he was under strong pressure from Jewish voters in the USA. In an address to American ambassadors to Arab countries in 1945 he said:

I am sorry, gentlemen, but I have to answer to hundreds of thousands who are anxious for the success of Zionism; I do not have hundreds of thousands of Arabs among my constituents.

In his memoirs he speaks of the intense pressure put on him in 1947 by Zionists who wanted the USA to support the resolution recommending the establishment of the State of Israel:

The facts were that not only were there pressure movements around the United Nations unlike anything that had been seen there before but that the White House, too, was subject to a constant barrage. I do not think that I ever had so much pressure and propaganda aimed at the White House as I had in this instance. The persistence of a few of the extreme Zionist leaders – actuated by political motives and engaging in political threats – disturbed and annoyed me. Some were even suggesting that we pressure sovereign nations into favourable votes in the General Assembly.[42]

Q What did the Jews and the Arabs think of the plan?

David Hirst sums up Jewish and Arab reactions:

For the Zionists the Partition Plan ranked, as a charter of legitimacy, with the Balfour Declaration which, in their view, it superseded and fulfilled. Certainly, it was a no less partisan document. Palestine comprises some 10,000 square miles. Of this, the Arabs were to retain 4,300 square miles while the Jews, who represented one-third of the population and owned some six per cent of the land, were allotted 5,700 square miles. The Jews also got the better land; they were to have the fertile coastal belt while the Arabs were to make do, for the most part, with the hills. Yet it was not the size of the area allotted to the Jews which pleased them – indeed, they regarded it as the 'irreducible minimum' which they could accept – it was rather the fact of statehood itself. Conversely it was not merely the size of the area they were to lose, it was the loss of land, sovereignty and an antique heritage that angered the Arabs. The Partition Plan legitimized what had been, on any but the most partisan interpretation of the Balfour Declaration and the Mandate, illegitimately acquired. The past was, as it were, wiped out. Overnight, the comity of nations solemnly laid the foundations of a new moral order by which the Jews, the great majority of whom had been in Palestine less than thirty years, were deemed to have claims equal, indeed superior, to those of the Arabs who had lived there from time immemorial.[43]

Maxime Rodinson, a French Jew, formerly Professor of Old Ethiopic and Old South Arabian languages at the Sorbonne in Paris, explains how the UN Partition Plan was received by the Arab states:

For the Arab masses, the acceptance of the UN resolutions meant an unconditional surrender to a European Diktat, of the same kind as the capitulation of black or yellow kings in the nineteenth century to the gunboats which had fired shots on their palaces.

European countries had supported colonists with the intention of gaining control of part of the national territory. During the period when the native population could have forced out these colonists easily enough, they had been prevented from reacting by the British police and the British army, who had received their mandate from the nations of Europe and America. Their reaction was also morally hamstrung by the fallacious assurance that what was going on was no more than the peaceful settlement of a number of unfortunate people with no evil intentions, who in any case would remain in the minority.

When the real concerns of the colonists became known publicly and when it became evident how they had gradually developed collective strength under the protection of the mandate, the European and American world wanted to force the Arabs to accept the fait accompli (for all their internal differences, all following the same line, from the socialist Soviet Union to the ultra-capitalist USA).

For the Arabs, the aftermath of the Second World War was a bitter repetition of the deception of the First. Once again, people had made all kinds of promises to them in order to secure their collaboration or at least their neutrality. But after the war was won, the promises were broken by a malevolent confederacy of Europeans, agreed in their rich nations' complicity against the people that had had confidence in them.

Did not the 1922 Mandate stipulate that 'there should be no infringement of the rights and the position of other parts of the population' (euphemistically called non-Jews)? Had not the American Presidents Roosevelt and Truman promised Ibn Saud, in their letters of 5 April 1945 and 28 October 1946, that they would not make any decision about Palestine without full consultation with the Arabs and the Jews, and that nothing would be resolved which went against Arab interests?

All these promises were now broken. There was not an Arab who could openly contradict the statement made by the Arab High Committee: 'Any attempt by the Jews or any other group of powers to set up a Jewish state on Arab territory is an act of oppression which will be met with force on grounds of justified self-defence.'[44]

Q How are we to explain the role played by the great powers in the passing of the Partition Plan?

The British Council of Churches Report entitled *Towards Understanding the Arab-Israeli Conflict* explains how the Holocaust influenced world opinion:

*The most significant and terrible action by an outside power which contributed to
the establishing of the State of Israel (and consequently the Arab-Israeli conflict) was
the Holocaust in Europe. It was the experience of persecution in Europe, culminating
in the Nazi attack on the Jews, which gave the longings for a state practical form.
Persecution amounting to threatened genocide motivated the Jews to make a life or
death attempt to create a state of their own. The European Holocaust precipitated an
irresistible surge of world opinion and support and put what the major powers of the
day (though not the Arabs) regarded as an undeniable authority behind the claim
to the land.*

*The Yad Vashem museum, memorial to the victims of the Holocaust, reminds all
who visit it of the dreadful details. 'Yad Vashem' is a quotation from Isaiah 56,
verse 5; it means a 'place – or a memorial – and a name' and it commemorates
those millions of victims who in death by gas, or bullet or hanging had neither
memorial nor name. Its grim stone, monochrome photographs and shelves full of
the books which record the names of the dead, still being added to as more details
become known, leave one aware of how once Europe treated its Jews, and of their
determination never to leave their fate to others again.[45]*

Edward W. Said, a Palestinian who is Professor of Comparative Literature at
Columbia University in the USA, sums up the role of the great powers in the fulfilment of the vision of Zionism in the following words:

*For indeed it was the world that made the success of Zionism possible, and it was
Zionism's sense of the world as supporter and audience that played a considerable
practical role in the struggle for Palestine.[46]*

The Quaker Report of 1970, *The Search for Peace in the Middle East*, points out how
the Palestinian Arabs feel that *they* have had to suffer for the sins of the great powers of the 'Christian West':

*How many of the Jews who went to Palestine in the 1930s and 1940s would have
migrated to some other country if they had been given encouragement cannot be
known. In any case, the Christian West was able to escape in large measure from its
accumulated centuries of anti-Semitic guilt, by co-operating with the dedicated
Zionist leadership in helping displaced Jews find refuge in a predominantly Arab
land.*

*At the time the UN Partition Plan was adopted, the Jewish third of the population
of Palestine owned about six per cent of the land. The Arab two-thirds of the population owned about a third of the land, and felt they had good claim on that major
portion of public lands listed as Government domain. At partition the Palestinian
Arabs saw themselves being forced to give up much of their lands, private and com-
munal, to Jewish settlers as part of a grand-scale international effort at restitution
and compensation to the Jews. The Palestinian Arabs, a Semitic and largely Muslim
people, concluded that they were being required to pay for the anti-Semitic sins of
the Christian West.*

This is obviously a simplified and only partial explanation of how the Zionist movement and the present State of Israel came to gain broad Western support, but it will be impossible to understand current Arab attitudes apart from this unflattering interpretation of why the United States and Western Europe gave support to the creation of Israel and have continued to support it. In fact, some Arabs came to feel that in Western nations pro-Zionism for Jews abroad was the natural corollary of continued anti-Semitism at home.[47]

Erskine Childers makes the same point in commenting on the way Jews have been treated by Christians over the centuries:

The ironies here are scarcely to be contemplated. Who in fact pleaded with the Arabs to cross the Pillars of Hercules – the straits of Gibraltar – into Spain? The Jews of Spain who were being persecuted by their Visigothic rulers. Some decades earlier, when the Arabs had first arrived outside the gates of Jerusalem, they had signed a treaty with its inhabitants guaranteeing Christians and Jews alike complete autonomy and freedom of worship. When our Crusader ancestors arrived outside Jerusalem some centuries later, they entered by a trick, and as they made the streets run red – to quote an eyewitness – they assembled all Jews in the synagogue and burned them alive. The first great wave of anti-Semitism in Europe followed the Crusades, which had carried out perhaps the first mass incineration of Jews, nearly 1,000 years before Hitler, in Palestine. And 1,000 years later we, the descendants of those Crusaders, decided that Arab-inhabited Palestine should be taken from its Arabs and given to a Jewish settler movement to pay for our latest crimes in Europe.[48]

2.7 Partition and war (1948–49)

Q How did the Jews and Arabs prepare for partition?

Denys Baly describes how both the Jews and the Arabs prepared for the implementation of the UN Partition Plan in May 1948:

There seems little point in spending much time upon the question of whether the Arabs were the aggressors in 1948, except that it is an accusation which the Arabs themselves resent bitterly. Anyone who lived in Palestine during the last five years of the Mandate and had the good fortune to be intimate with both Arabs and Jews could not but be aware that both sides had every intention of fighting, if necessary. The Jewish preparations, as one might expect of them, were better organized, more thorough and more efficient, and had been going on for a longer time than those of the Arabs, who do not normally exhibit efficiency as one of their virtues.[49]

Benny Morris describes the aim of the *Haganah*'s 'Plan D', which was originally intended to be carried out in May 1948 when the British were withdrawing, but was brought forward to April:

*Its aim was to take over strategic areas vacated by the British, gain control of the
main towns and the internal lines of communication, and secure the emergent
state's border areas in preparation for the expected invasion by the Arab armies.
Implementation in effect meant crushing the Palestinian Arabs' military power
and subduing their urban neighbourhoods and rural settlements in the areas
earmarked for Jewish statehood. The various areas held by the* Haganah *were to
be soldered together by conquest of those lying in between into a single geo-
graphic-political-military continuum. Blocs of settlements outside the statehood
areas – such as the Etzion Bloc and Nahariya – were also to be secured and
linked up. Brigade and battalion commanders were given permission to raze or
empty and mine hostile or potentially hostile Arab villages.*[50]

David Ben-Gurion frequently stated his expectation that the Arabs would be
expelled from their land:

*We must expel Arabs and take their places... and if we have to use force – not to
dispossess the Arabs of the Negev and Transjordan, but to guarantee our own right
to settle in those places – then we have force at our disposal.*
      The Arabs of the Land of Israel, they have but one function left, to run away.[51]

*We should adopt a system of aggressive defence. With every Arab attack we should be
ready to reply with a decisive blow, destroy the site, or expel the inhabitants and take
their place.*[52]

He later summed up what the Jewish underground group known as the *Haganah*
had achieved before partition:

*Until the British left, no Jewish settlement, however remote, was entered or seized by
the Arabs, while the Haganah... captured many Arab positions and liberated
Tiberias and Haifa, Jaffa and Safad... So, on the day of destiny, that part of
Palestine where the* Haganah *could operate was almost clear of Arabs.*[53]

Joseph Weitz:

'*Among ourselves it must be clear that there is no place in the country for both peoples together... With the Arabs we shall not achieve our aim of being an independent people in this little country.*' Weitz wanted '*at least the western part [west of the
Jordan River] of Eretz Israel without Arabs.*' He saw '*no other way but to transfer
the Arabs from here to the neighbouring countries; transfer all of them, not one village or tribe should remain*'.[54]

Menachem Begin, a former leader of the *Irgun*, the other main group of the Jewish
underground, has described in detail the objectives which they set for themselves
in the months between January and March 1948:

In the months preceding the Arab invasion… we continued to make sallies into the Arab area. In the early days of 1948, we were explaining to our officers and men, however, that this was not enough… It was clear to us that even the most daring sallies carried out by partisan troops would never be able to decide the issue. Our hope lay in gaining control of territory. At the end of January 1948, at a meeting of the Command of the Irgun in which the planning section participated, we outlined four strategic objectives: (1) Jerusalem, (2) Jaffa, (3) the Lydda-Ramleh plain, (4) the Triangle [the towns of Nablus, Jenin and Tulkarm], comprising the bulk of the non-desert area west of Jordan.[55]

Edward Said gives the perspective of the Palestinians on Jewish intentions in their preparations for declaring the state, speaking about

how deeply, how thoroughly, and how determinedly Israeli politicians, military men, and intellectuals continued well after 1948 to prosecute the same policy of trying to get rid of the Palestinians, either by actual transfer, by massacre (as in Kafr Qasim), or by forcing submission on them as a whole. The entire idea has always therefore been to reduce the Palestinians' actuality to nil, to efface Palestinians as a people with legitimate rights, to render them alien in their own land. And indeed Israel has so far succeeded in its own mind.[56]

Q What kind of atrocities were committed?

Benny Morris describes the blowing up of the King David Hotel in Jerusalem on 22 July 1946, by the *IZL* (*Irgun Z'vai Leumi*):

Without coordinating with the Haganah, sappers placed a number of bomb-laden milk containers in the basement of the King David Hotel in Jerusalem, which served as a British military and administrative headquarters. The resulting explosion, which demolished an entire wing of the building and killed ninety-one people – Britons, Arabs and Jews – was the biggest terrorist action in the organization's history. The IZL subsequently claimed it had given the occupants ample warning, but they had failed to evacuate the building; the British maintained that no such warning had been issued.[57]

This is Morris' account of the massacre of the Palestinian village of Deir Yassin:

The attack, on the morning of 9 April, was carried out with the prior approval of, and in cooperation with, the Jerusalem command of the Haganah. Some 130 IZL and LHI [the Lohamei Herut Israel, Lehi or the Stern Gang] fighters took part. During the battle, Haganah machine-gunners stationed nearby supplied covering fire, and two Palmah squads in armoured cars joined in the actual battle. Palmah squads also helped evacuate the wounded, and the Haganah helped the combatants with amunition.
   The advance through the village proved far more difficult than anticipated. By its end the IZL and LHI had suffered five dead and more than thirty wounded – or

more than one quarter of the attacking force. The units, pinned down by sniper fire, advanced slowly, throwing grenades through windows and dynamiting house after house. Much of the population, including most of the able-bodied males, fled. Soon after the start of the battle an IZL armoured truck with a loudspeaker began calling on the villagers to lay down their arms and flee. But the truck got stuck in a ditch some thirty metres from the village and apparently went unheard.

Deir Yassin is remembered not just as a military operation, but rather for the atrocities committed by the IZL and LHI troops during and immediately after the drawn-out battle: whole families were riddled with bullets and grenade fragments and buried when houses were blown up on top of them; men, women and children were mowed down as they emerged from houses; individuals were taken aside and shot. At the end of the battle, groups of old men, women and children were trucked through West Jerusalem's streets in a kind of 'victory parade' and then dumped in (Arab) East Jerusalem.

According to Jerusalem Shai commander Levy (reporting on 12 April), 'the conquest of the village was carried out with great cruelty. Whole families – women, old people, children – were killed, and there were piles of dead [in various places].'

The Jewish agency and the Haganah *leadership immediately condemned the massacre. Deir Yassin became the one Jewish atrocity that it was permissible to write about – and to condemn. The* Haganah *made great efforts to hide its part in the operation, and during the following decades, Menachem Begin's Herut Party and its successor, the Likud, were continually berated for Deir Yassin in internal Israeli political squabbling. And over the years, the incident came to be used in Arab propaganda to blacken the name of the Yishuv as a whole.*

During the next three days a variety of outsiders – Israeli doctors, Haganah *officers, a Red Cross representative named Jacques de Reynier – visited the village to investigate. All saw bullet-riddled, sometimes charred bodies of men, women and children. In 1948 participants, observers and journalists wrote that as many as 254 villagers were killed that day. Everyone had an interest in publicizing a high Arab casualty figure: the* Haganah, *to tarnish the IZL and LHI; the Arabs and British, to blacken the Jews; the IZL and LHI, to provoke terror and frighten Arabs into fleeing the country. Recent Arab and Jewish investigations, and supporting interviews, however, suggest that these numbers were an exaggeration and that the real number of Arab dead was 100–110.*

Deir Yassin had a profound political and demographic effect. Despite a formal Jewish Agency Executive letter of apology and explanation to King Abdullah, the incident seemed to push Jordan into the arms of those pressing for direct intervention by the Arab states, and to undermine the secret Yishuv-Abdullah agreement. It may also have contributed to the decision of leaders of other nations – principally Egypt – to join the fray. Certainly the news enraged Arab fighting men, and 'Deir Yassin!' became a rallying cry for combatants bent on revenge.

At the same time, however, the news of what had happened – extensively covered and exaggerated in the Arab media for weeks – had a profoundly demoralizing effect on the Palestinian Arabs and was a major factor in their massive flight during the following weeks and months. The IDF [Israeli Defence Forces] Intelligence Service called Deir Yassin 'a decisive accelerating factor' in the general Arab exodus.[58]

The Arabs sought to revenge what happened in the village of Deir Yassin by attacking a Jewish convoy on its way to Mount Scopus in Jerusalem:

The affair had an immediate and brutal aftermath. On 13 April, Arab militiamen from Jerusalem and surrounding villages attacked a ten-vehicle convoy of mostly unarmed lecturers, nurses and doctors on their way to the Hadassah Hospital-Hebrew University campus on Mount Scopus. (The convoy was also carrying two IZL fighters who had been wounded at Deir Yassin.) Four vehicles, including two packed buses, were trapped. For hours the British refrained from intervening and warned the Haganah not to do so. Three Palmah armoured cars arrived on the scene but were overwhelmed by the ambushers. The shooting continued for more than six hours, the Arabs eventually dousing the armoured buses with gasoline and setting them alight. When the British finally intervened, more than seventy Jews had died. Deir Yassin and the death of 'Abd al-Qadir had been avenged.[59]

Q Why did so many Arabs leave their homes?

Edgar O'Ballance, writing in a semi-official history of the 1948 war entitled *The Arab-Israeli War of 1948*:

It was Jewish policy to encourage the Arabs to quit their homes and they used psychological warfare in urging them to do so. Later, as the war wore on, they ejected those Arabs who clung to their villages. This policy, which had such amazing success, had two distinct advantages. First, it gave the Arab countries a vast refugee programme to cope with, which their elementary economy and administrative machinery were in no way capable of attacking, and secondly ensured that the Jews had no Fifth Column in their midst.[60]

I.F. Stone, an American Jewish journalist who was decorated by the *Irgun* in 1948:

The argument that the refugees ran away 'voluntarily' or because their leaders urged them to do so until after the fighting was over, not only rests on a myth but is irrelevant. Have refugees no right to return? Have German Jews no right to recover their properties because they had to flee?

Jewish terrorism, not only by the Irgun in such savage massacres as Deir Yassin, but in milder forms by the Haganah itself, 'encouraged' Arabs to leave areas the Jews wished to take over for strategic or demographic reasons. They tried to make as much of Israel as free of Arabs as possible.[61]

Benny Morris plays down the idea of deliberate intent on the part of the Jews to expel Arabs from their homes:

The Palestinian refugee problem was born of war, not by design, Jewish or Arab. It was largely a by-product of Arab and Jewish fears and of the protracted, bitter fighting that characterized the first Israeli-Arab war; in smaller part, it was the deliberate creation of Jewish and Arab military commanders and politicians.[62]

Norman Finkelstein summarizes Morris's explanation of the Arab exodus as follows:

War, without a Jewish masterplan or indeed, without any preplanning whatsoever, brought a Palestinian exodus of itself... with a little nudging in the right direction, the low-key exodus... turned into a mass flood and a fait accompli.

He is critical of Morris's conclusion, however, suggesting that the evidence presented by Morris himself actually supports a different conclusion:

I suggest that Morris's own evidence points to the conclusion that Palestine's Arabs were expelled systematically and with premeditation.[63]

Finkelstein's conclusions are supported by what several involved in the operations wrote after the event. When **Yitzhak Rabin**, for example, was asked by Yigal Allon what to do with the Arab inhabitants of Lydda, the reply was 'Expel them'. Later Rabin wrote:

'Driving out' is a term with a harsh ring. Psychologically, this was one of the most difficult actions we undertook. The population of Lod did not leave willingly. There was no way of avoiding the use of force and warning shots in order to make the inhabitants march the ten or fifteen miles to the point where they met up with the Legion. The inhabitants of Ramleh watched and learned the lesson. Their leaders agreed to be evacuated voluntarily.[64]

Joseph Weitz, Director of the Lands Department of the Jewish National Fund, writing in his diary on 11 January concerning Arab tenant farmers in two villages in a predominantly Jewish area in the north of Palestine:

Is it not now the time to be rid of them? Why continue to keep in our midst these thorns at the time when they pose a danger to us?[65]

Writing his diary on 21 April:

Our army is steadily conquering Arab villages and their inhabitants are afraid and flee like mice. You have no idea what happened in the Arab villages. It is enough that during the night several shells will whistle over them and they flee for their lives. Villages are steadily emptying and if we continue on this course – and we shall certainly do so as our strength increases – then villages will empty of their inhabitants.[66]

Yigal Allon, one of the main heroes of the war of 1948, later recorded in the *Book of Palmach* some of the tactics which he and other Jews used in the months before the UN Partition Plan was due to come into effect:

There were left before us only five days, before the threatening date, 15 May. We saw a need to clean the inner Galilee and to create a Jewish territorial succession in the entire area of the upper Galilee. The long battles had weakened our forces, and before us stood great duties of blocking the routes of the Arab invasion. We therefore looked for means which did not force us into employing force, in order to cause the tens of thousands of sulky Arabs who remained in Galilee to flee, for in case of an Arab invasion these were likely to strike us from the rear. We tried to use a tactic which took advantage of the impression created by the fall of Safed and the [Arab] defeat in the area which was cleaned by Operation Metateh – a tactic which worked miraculously well.

I gathered all of the Jewish mukhtars, who have contact with Arabs in different villages, and asked them to whisper in the ears of some Arabs, that a great Jewish reinforcement has arrived in Galilee and that it is going to burn all of the villages of the Huleh. They should suggest to these Arabs, as their friends, to escape while there is still time. And the rumours spread in all the areas of the Huleh that it is time to flee. The flight numbered myriads. The tactic reached its goal completely. The building of the police station at Halsa fell into our hands without a shot. The wide areas were cleaned, the danger was taken away from the transportation routes and we could organize ourselves for the invaders along the borders, without worrying about the rear.

Allon admitted that if the Arab armies had not invaded, the Jews would have seized even more territory than they in fact did before the final cease-fire in early 1949:

There would have been no stop to the expansion of the forces of Haganah who could have, with the same drive, reached the natural borders of western Israel, because in this stage most of the local enemy forces were paralysed.[67]

Chaim Weizmann, speaking later about the fighting which took place between 1948 and 1949 described its results in the following terms:

It was a miraculous clearing of the land: the miraculous simplification of Israel's task.[68]

John H. Davis, an American who was Commissioner-General of the United Nations Relief and Works Agency for Palestine Refugees (UNRWA) for five years, explains his understanding of why so many Arabs fled from their homes:

The cause of the panic flight of nearly three-quarters of a million men, women and children from their homes has been obscured by veils of propaganda. It is only recently that careful sifting of the evidence has helped to clarify the picture. For long, a widely publicized view was that the refugees left voluntarily or because the Arab authorities themselves ordered them to leave, to clear the way for the advancing armies of the Arab States. As General Glubb has pointed out, voluntary emigrants do not leave their homes with only the clothes they stand up in, or in such a hurry and confusion that husbands lose sight of wives and parents of their children. Nor does there appear to be one shred of evidence to substantiate the claim that the fleeing refugees were obeying Arab orders. An exhaustive examination of

the minutes, resolutions and press releases of the Arab League, of the files of leading
Arabic newspapers, of day-by-day monitorings of broadcasts from Arab capitals
and secret Arab radio stations, failed to reveal a single reference, direct or indirect,
to an order given to the Arabs of Palestine to leave. All the evidence is to the con-
trary; that the Arab authorities continuously exhorted the Palestinian Arabs not to
leave the country...

What now seems clear... is that the Arab Governments, by inept and exaggerated
publicizing of Jewish atrocities in press and radio in an effort to justify to the world
the impending arrival of their troops in Palestine to 'restore order', in fact unwit-
tingly added to the panic and confusion in a population that had for years wit-
nessed the spectacle of Jewish terrorists holding the armed might of the Mandatory
Power to ransom and therefore had cause to fear the ruthless efficiency of their tac-
tics. Panic and bewilderment thus played decisive parts in the flight. But the extent
to which the refugees were savagely driven out by the Israelis as part of a deliberate
master-plan has been insufficiently recognized.[69]

2.8 The voice of Israel

Q How do Jews in Israel express the philosophy of the state?

David Ben-Gurion, speaking about the Law of Return in 1951:

It [Israel] is not a state for its citizens alone, but for the whole Jewish people, for
every Jew whoever he be, who chooses to live in his homeland, who chooses Israeli
independence in preference to life in the Diaspora. The peculiar sign that singles
out the State of Israel and fixes its central mission, the Zionist-Jewish mission, is the
'Law of Return', the foundation scroll of the rights of the Jewish people in Israel.
This law has its origins in the Declaration of Independence of 14 May 1948, which
says 'The State of Israel shall be open to immigration and to the Ingathering of the
Exiles'. It may be said that for that purpose the State was founded. The Law of
Return establishes that it is not the State that confers upon the Jew abroad the right
to settle in Israel, this right being inherent in his being a Jew, if he only has the
desire to join the population of the State.[70]

Abba Eban, a former Israeli Foreign Minister and ambassador in Washington, writing
in *An Autobiography* (1978):

Zionism and Israel made great promises to the Jewish people. They may even have
promised too much. There has always been a Utopian element in our national
movement. The higher the expectation, the greater the possibility of disappointment.
We have restored our nation's pride. We have given the Jewish people a renewed
sense of its collective creativity. We have created a sanctuary in which our special
legacy can be preserved and enlarged. We have taken Jewish history out of provin-
cialism and caused it to flow into the mainstream of human culture. We have
given mankind a special communication of social originality and intellectual vital-
ity. We have revealed an immense power of Jewish recuperation. Above all, we have

*fulfilled our human vocation by redeeming hundreds of thousands of our kinsmen
from sterility, humiliation and death. So Israel has no cause for comprehensive
apology. It is a society inspired by a positive vision, a nation in which tomorrow is
more vivid than yesterday, and in which it seems more important to build than to
destroy... it is in Israel alone that the Jew can face the world in his own authentic
image, and not as a footnote in the story of other societies. It is only as a nation in
its own soil, its own tongue and its own faith that the Jewish people can hear what
it has to hear, say what it has to say – do what it has to do.*[71]

Moshe Davis, Executive Director of the Office of Britain's Chief Rabbi, in the book
I am a Jew (1978):

*Israel is the only country in the world which is a Jewish country, and where the
majority of the citizens are Jewish. The mere fact of its existence causes many Jews
to sleep more peacefully in their beds. It represents an ultimate asylum, should it be
needed. And few Jews would ever categorically guarantee that Jews – in any country – will always live where they are safely. They would not rule out as absurd the
possibility that, one day, they or their children might indeed buy that air ticket, for
whatever reasons. The uncertainty of the Jew in the world – even in the closing
decades of the twentieth century – is still a very real factor in determining Jewish
attitudes towards Israel.*

*I know that when I went to visit the State of Israel for the first time twenty-seven
years ago [i.e. 1951] (I was the first of my family for many generations to do so), I
felt that I was returning home for myself and also for countless others before me
whose great dream it was to see the Land but who were never so privileged. I have
been back many times since, and each time I find there is something special about
it. I always find it an emotional and spiritual experience, a return to roots, drink-
ing from the ancient wells of my tradition and my history.*

*The religious aspect of the contemporary Jewish State – notwithstanding its
many real problems – seems to have Biblical undertones. A measure of prophetic
fulfilment is apparent in its achievements. The Hebrew language has been revived.
A unique system of social justice embraces the total living system of that quarter of
a million of its inhabitants who live in the Kibbutzim and co-operative settlements.
Israel has become the home of one-fifth of the Jewish people. The country has resisted the combined and repeated attacks of all its neighbours to destroy it. Half a million of its Jewish population derive from the backward countries of the Middle East,
whose civilizations are several hundred years behind the West. They have been
absorbed into the modern, twentieth-century culture and technology of Israel.*[72]

One of those present during the independence ceremony (14 May 1948) was **Golda
Meir**, who later recalled how, when Ben-Gurion spoke the words 'the State of
Israel',

*my eyes filled with tears and my hands shook. We have done it. We had brought the
Jewish state into existence – and I, Golda Mabovitch Meyerson, had lived to see the*

day. Whatever price any of us would have to pay for it, we had re-created the Jewish national home.

The long exile was over. From this day on, we would no longer live on sufferance in the land of our forefathers. Now we were a nation like other nations, masters – for the first time in twenty centuries – of our own destiny. The dream had come true – too late to save those who had perished in the Holocaust, but not too late for the generations to come.[73]

Moshe Dayan, describing his feelings on hearing of the 1947 UN Resolution partitioning the country:

The UN decision recognizing Israel's right to statehood was an historic event. The successful passage of the resolution represented an enormous political achievement, in which Ben-Gurion had played the major role. However, underlying our expression of joy was a far deeper emotion, one that I felt as a Jew – indeed, more as a Jew than I had ever known before. I felt in my bones the victory of Judaism, which for 2,000 years of exile from the Land of Israel had withstood persecutions, the Spanish Inquisition, pogroms, anti-Jewish decrees, restrictions, and the mass slaughter by the Nazis in our own generation, and had reached the fulfilment of its age-old yearning – the return to a free and independent Zion.[74]

Q How do non-Jews who are sympathetic towards Israel explain and defend its ideals?

W. Laqueur, writing in one of the standard histories of Zionism:

The Arab-Jewish conflict was inevitable, given the fact that Zionism wanted to build more than a cultural centre in Palestine. Nor is it certain that a cultural centre would not have encountered Arab resistance. Zionism, the transplantation of hundreds of thousands of Jews, was bound to effect a radical change in Palestine, as a result of which the Palestinian Arabs were bound to suffer. It was not the Arabs' fault that the Jews were persecuted in Europe, that they had awakened to the fact that they wanted again to be a nation and therefore needed a state in the country in which they had lived 2,000 years before.

The effects of Zionism on the Arabs should not be belittled. The fact that they derived economic and other benefits from Jewish immigration is immaterial in this context. This is not to say that Zionism was bound to result in the evacuation or expulsion of many Palestinian Arabs from Palestine. Had the Arabs accepted the Peel Plan in 1937, the Jewish state would have been restricted to the coastal plain between Tel Aviv and Haifa. Had they not rejected the UN partition of 1947, most of Palestine would still have remained in their hands. The Arab thesis of inevitable Zionist expansion is a case of self-fulfilling prophecy: the Arabs did everything in their power to make their prophecy come true, by choosing the road of armed resistance – and losing. The Zionist movement and the yishuv matured in the struggle against the Arab national movement. Eventually it reached the conclusion that it was pointless to seek Arab agreement and that it could achieve its aims only against the Arabs.

Arab intransigence was the natural reaction of a people unwilling to share its country with another. For European Jewry the issue was not an abstract one of preserving a historical connection, religious and national ties. With the rise of Hitler it became a question of life or death, and they felt no pangs of conscience: the danger facing the Jews was physical extinction. The worst fate that could befall the Arabs was the partition of Palestine and minority status for some Arabs in the Jewish state. Zionism is guilty no doubt of many sins of commission and omission in its policy on the Arab question. But whichever way one looks at it, the conflict on immigration and settlement could not have been evaded since the basis for a compromise did not exist. Zionism could and should have paid more attention to Arab grievances and aspirations. But despite all concessions in the cultural or economic field, the Arabs would still have opposed immigration with an eye to the inevitable consequences of mass immigration.

Seen from the Arab point of view, Zionism was an aggressive movement, Jewish immigration an invasion. Zionists are guilty of having behaved like other peoples – only with some delay due to historical circumstances. Throughout history nation-states have not come into existence as the result of peaceful development and legal contracts. They developed from invasions, colonization, violence and armed struggle. It was the historical tragedy of Zionism that it appeared on the international scene when there were no longer empty spaces on the world map. Wherever the Jews would have chosen to settle, they would have sooner or later come into conflict with the native population. The creation of nation-states meant the perpetration of acts of injustice. The native population was either absorbed and assimilated or it was decimated or expelled. The expulsion of ten million Germans from Eastern Europe was almost immediately accepted as an established fact by the outside world and those unwilling to put up with it were denounced as revanchists and war-mongers. Given the realities of Soviet power, it was clear that the new order in eastern Europe could not be challenged except through a new world war. But Zionism was not in a position of such strength, nor was there a danger of world war. Hence the fact that the territorial changes in eastern Europe have been accepted as irreversible, while those in the Middle East continue to be challenged by many.[75]

A resolution of the General Assembly of the United Nations on 10 November 1975 condemned Zionism as 'a form of racism and racial discrimination'. The **Ecumenical Theological Research Fraternity in Israel** responded immediately by issuing an appeal to churches around the world, in which it attempted to explain and defend Zionism against this criticism:

Christians should be aware that Zionism, far from being itself a racist movement, was for most Jews the only viable answer to anti-Jewish racism culminating in the destruction of European Jewry during the Nazi Holocaust. Christians have to acknowledge that the Church's age-long teaching of contempt for the Jewish people, and the long history of Christian anti-Jewish practices, have in a large measure contributed to the perpetration of terrible crimes against Jews. Recognizing this fact, the least that Christians can do is to attempt a fair and proper assessment of what Zionism is and what it means to the Jewish people.

For this reason, it is impossible to present Judaism and Zionism as two entirely different things. There is only a very thin line between anti-Zionism and anti-Semitism or anti-Judaism. Zionism has to be seen as an important and valid expression of a fundamental dimension of Judaism. The basic aspiration of Zionism is to free and unite the Jewish people; free it from alienation, oppression and persecution, and unite it in the Land from which it has been exiled but which it has never abandoned... Zionism is an attempt of the Jewish people to give contemporary expression to its identity, and to take its place in freedom, dignity and co-operation among the community of nations, and make its contribution to the one world of which the prophets have spoken.

When we come to the political implications of Zionism and the Jewish-Arab conflict, it should be borne in mind that the main-stream of the Zionist movement never had the intention to deprive the Arab population living in the land of their rights, but desired to live in peace with them. If there was an underestimation of the Arab position towards Zionist settlement in the country, and even insensitivity to their fears and their feelings, this did not originate from ill-will or bad intentions, but from human limitations and weaknesses.

The fundamental Zionist principles enshrined in Israel's Declaration of Independence of 1948 include the following: 'The State of Israel will be open for Jewish immigration and for the Ingathering of the Exiles; it will foster the development of the country for the benefit of all its inhabitants; it will be based on freedom, justice and peace according to the vision of the prophets of Israel; it will ensure complete equality of social and political rights for all its citizens, irrespective of religion, conscience, language, education and culture; it will safeguard the Holy Places of all religions; and it will be faithful to the principles of the Charter of the United Nations'.[76]

Q How have Israeli Jews understood their conflict with Palestinians over the land?

Moshe Dayan, speaking in April 1956 in a eulogy over an Israeli killed by Arabs, showed that he understood the feelings of Arabs towards the Jews:

Let us not condemn the murderers today. What do we know of their fierce hatred for us? For eight years they have been living in refugee camps in Gaza while right before their eyes we have been turning the land and the villages in which they and their forefathers lived into our own land. We should demand Roi'i's blood not from the Arabs in Gaza but from ourselves, for closing our eyes to our cruel fate and the role of our generation... We are a generation of settlers, and without the combat helmet and the barrel of a gun, we will not be able to plant a tree or build a house. This is the fate of our generation, and the choice before us it to be ready and armed, strong and hard, or to have the sword snatched from our hands and be cut down.[77]

Yitzhak Rabin, in his speech on the White House lawn at the signing of the Oslo Accords on 13 September 1993, held out a hand of friendship and reconciliation to the Arabs:

We are destined to live together, on the same soil in the same land. We, the soldiers who have returned from battle stained with blood, we who have seen our relatives and friends killed before our eyes, we who have attended their funerals and cannot look into the eyes of parents and orphans, we who have fought against you, the Palestinians – We say to you today in a loud and clear voice: Enough of blood and tears. Enough. We harbour no hatred towards you. We have no desire for revenge. We, like you, are people who want to build a home, plant a tree, love, live side by side with you – in dignity, in empathy, as human beings, as free men. We are today giving peace a chance and saying to you: Enough. Let's pray that a day will come when we all will say, 'Farewell to arms.'[78]

Anton La Guardia describes the views of many of the more moderate Israelis in the year 2001:

In an atmosphere of what political scientists call 'post-Zionism' – a climate in which Israeli patriotism is less blinding – Israelis have slowly and painfully re-examined their national myths, their selective history and even the impact of the Holocaust. They are beginning to understand the cost which the creation of their state has exacted from the Palestinian people. No longer can Israelis argue that there is no such thing as a Palestinian people. The mainstream argument in Israel is now what kind of Palestinian state should exist, and how to balance Israel's need for security with the cost of military occupation of the West Bank and Gaza Strip.[79]

Alongside these moderate voices, however, a strident kind of fundamentalism has developed since 1967. Some religious Jews have taken the opportunity of the occupation of the West Bank to press home their claims to Jewish ownership and permanent settlement in these occupied areas. This is how **Anton La Guardia** explains the development of these views and the parting of the ways between moderates and fundamentalists:

Where a substantial portion of secular Jews were drifting towards 'post-Zionism', the other half of Israel was becoming increasingly nationalist and religious, zealously attached to the notion of settling the biblical heartland of 'Judaea and Samaria'.[80]

Martin Gilbert explains the significance of the development of 'religious Zionism' and its claims to the West Bank during this period:

As well as the rapid growth of the Land of Israel Movement after the Israeli occupation of the West Bank in 1967, religious Zionism substantially transformed itself into a movement of settlement in the West Bank, impelled by a messianic vision that the Jewish occupation of the whole of the Land of Israel was a decisive step on the road to Redemption. The Jewish historian Ehud Luz, in his book on religion and nationalism in the early Zionist movement (1882–1904) wrote, twenty years after the Six-Day War, of how since 1967 'religious Zionism has begun to demonstrate self-confidence and feelings of superiority, whereas secular Zionism has retreated to apologetics'.[81]

The following are examples of the views of two of these fundamentalist groups:

Rabbi Shlomo Avner, spiritual leader of *Ateret Cohanim*:

We must settle the whole land of Israel, and over all of it, establish our rule. The Arabs are squatters. I don't know who gave them authorization to live on Jewish land. All mankind knows that this is our land. Arabs came here recently. And even if some Arabs had been here for 2,000 years, is there a statute of limitations, that gives a thief a right to its plunder?[82]

Gush Emunim, meaning 'Block of the Faithful', a group founded in 1974 to work for Jewish settlement in the Occupied Territories and national spiritual renewal:

The main purpose of the Jewish people is to attain both physical and spiritual redemption by living in and building up an integral Eretz Yisrael. The territory of Eretz Yisrael is assigned a sanctity which obligates its retention once liberated from foreign rule, as well as its settlement, even in defiance of government authority.[83]

Benny Morris recognizes how these policies on the West Bank have influenced the situation and ultimately led to the recent crisis:

In 1967, with the conquest of the West Bank and Gaza Strip (and Sinai and the Golan Heights), the original, full dream of Zionism – of Jewish statehood in the whole of Palestine – once again burst forth, to inflame and complicate the conflict. Again the concept of transfer came to the fore, with 200,000 to 300,000 Palestinians fleeing the newly conquered territories, some of them under duress, and with Israeli policy in the following years geared, at least in part, to squeezing out of East Jerusalem, the West Bank and Gaza Strip as many additional Arabs as possible.[84]

2.9 Other Jewish/Israeli voices

Q Are all Jews Zionists? Why have some Jews rejected the idea of a Jewish state?

In May 1917 (six months before the Balfour Declaration) the **Board of Deputies of British Jews and the Anglo-Jewish Association** published a joint manifesto in *The Times*, in which they expressed strong reservations about the concept of a Jewish state in Palestine:

Zionist theory regards all the Jewish communities of the world as constituting one homeless nationality incapable of complete social and political identification with the nations among whom they dwell and it is argued that for this homeless nation-ality a political centre and an always available homeland in Palestine are neces-

sary. Against this theory, the conjoint committee strongly and earnestly protest. Emancipated Jews in this country regard themselves primarily as a religious community, and they have always based their claims to political equality with their fellow citizens of other creeds on this assumption – that they have no separate aspirations in a political sense.

The second point in the Zionist programme which has aroused the misgivings of the conjoint committee is the proposal to invest the Jewish settlers in Palestine with certain special rights in excess of those enjoyed by the rest of the population... Any such action would prove a veritable calamity for the whole Jewish people. In all the countries in which they live the principle of equal rights for all religious denominations is vital for them.[85]

Asher Ginsberg (Ahad Ha'Am) became the leader of the movement known as 'Moral Zionism', which was critical of the 'Political Zionism' of Weizmann and others. In 1922 he wrote the following letter to the Tel Aviv newspaper *Haaretz*, after hearing that a group of Zionists had killed an Arab as a reprisal for anti-Jewish riots:

Is this the goal for which our fathers have striven and for whose sake all generations have suffered? Is this the dream of a 'Return to Zion', to stain its soil with innocent blood? Many years ago I wrote an essay in which I stated that our people will willingly give their money to build up their state, but they will never sacrifice their prophets for it. This was to me an axiomatic truth. And now God has afflicted me to have to live and to see with my own eyes that I apparently erred. The people do not part with their money to rebuild their national home, but instead, their inclination grows to sacrifice their prophets on the altar of their 'renaissance': the great ethical principles for the sake of which they have suffered, and for the sake of which alone it is worthwhile to return and become a people in the land of our fathers. For without these principles, my God, what are we and what can our future life in this country be, that we should bring all the endless sacrifices without which this land cannot be rebuilt? Are we really doing it only to add in an Oriental corner a small people of new Levantines who vie with other Levantines in shedding blood, in desire for vengeance, and in angry violence? If this be the 'Messiah', then I do not wish to see his coming.[86]

Albert Einstein:

I should much rather see reasonable agreement with the Arabs on the basis of living together in peace than the creation of a Jewish State. Apart from practical considerations, my awareness of the essential nature of Judaism resists the idea of a Jewish State, with borders, an army, and a measure of temporal power, no matter how modest. I am afraid of the inner damage Judaism will sustain – especially from the development of a narrow nationalism within our own ranks, against which we have already had to fight strongly, even without a Jewish State. We are no longer the Jews of the Maccabean period. A return to a nation in the political sense of the word would be equivalent to turning away from the spiritualization of our community which we owe to the genius of our prophets.[87]

Q Why have some orthodox Jews opposed the idea of a Jewish state and criticized its policies and actions?

Rabbi Benjamin, former editor of the magazine *Ner.*

In the end we must come out publicly with the truth; that we have no moral right whatever to oppose the return of the Arab refugees to their land… that until we have begun to redeem our sin against the Arab refugees, we have no right to continue the Ingathering of Exiles. We have no right to demand that American Jews leave their country to which they have become attached, and settle in a land that has been stolen from others, while the owners of it are homeless and miserable. We had no right to occupy the house of an Arab if we had not paid for it at its value. The same goes for fields, gardens, stores, workshops. We had no right to build a settlement and then to realize the ideal of Zionism with other people's property. To do this is robbery. I am surprised that Rabbi Herzog and all those who speak in the name of Jewish ethics and who always quote the Ten Commandments should consent to such a state of affairs. Political conquest cannot abolish private property…

In the end we must speak the truth. We are faced with this choice: to listen to the voice of truth for the sake of our own good and genuine peace, or, not to listen to it, and to bring evil and misfortune upon us and the future generations.[88]

In an article entitled 'A Place for Palestinians in Passover Prayers', in April 2001, **Rabbi Marc Ellis**, Professor of American and Jewish Studies and Director of the Center for American and Jewish Studies at Baylor University in Waco, Texas, described how he as a Jew related his understanding of the Passover to his relationship with Palestinians:

This week, Jews all over the world celebrate Passover, the ancient festival commemorating the exodus of Israelites from Egypt. The narrative of liberation is read within the context of food and fellowship. As Jews we are commanded to place ourselves in the original struggle to be free, to experience the suffering and hope of the ancient Israelites as they did, to see this ancient liberation as our own. Despite the plagues and death, the wanderings in the desert and the admonishments of God, Passover is a festive holiday. Food and wine are plentiful. Family and friends come together.

How we celebrate our freedom in the past with the complexities of the present is always a challenge. Over time, as Jews became free, struggles of other peoples were mentioned in the Seder meal. As a child being raised in the 1950s and 1960s, at Passover we incorporated the civil rights struggle into our narrative. In the 1980s and 1990s, there were specific Passover narratives featuring the struggle of women, and freedom movements in Central America and elsewhere. And, in some Jewish homes and synagogues, Palestinians were featured as a people struggling for liberation.

There is hope in remembrance applied to the present. If we are there in Egypt demanding our freedom, the Passover story accompanies us as we demand freedom now. Freedom is interdependent, across time and community boundaries. No one is truly free if others are not also free.

Today, with Israeli gunships daily firing rockets into defenceless Palestinian towns, cities and refugee camps, it is difficult to accept the Passover narrative in its deepest implications. We as Jews are free, are 'in Jerusalem', but is that freedom at the expense of others? If Palestinians are being taught the 'lesson' of opposing Israeli power and standing up for their rights and dignity, if the message from the Israeli government to the Palestinian people is surrender or die – a message not unfamiliar to Jews – do we repeat this story at the Passover table?

The call for Jewish unity is a caution against Jewish dissent and the dissent of others who see the Passover story as embodying their own struggle today. Should we as Jews celebrate our own liberation while being silent about or even denigrating the Palestinian struggle? Are helicopter gunships guarding Jews in Israel and Jews around the world on these Passover nights? Or are these gunships a symbol of our own need to reconsider the road we as Jews are travelling?...

My heart is not in the celebration this year. And it can never be again until freedom for Jews is also freedom for Palestinians.

What do I answer my children when they ask the simple and difficult questions they are commanded to ask as we gather to tell the story of our origins thousands of years ago? That helicopter gunships are like the parting of the sea? That Israeli Prime Minister Ariel Sharon is like Moses leading us through the difficult times of desert and rebellion?

I no longer have the answers to their questions. But I will respond as a Jew in the only way possible today. That the Palestinians are part of our story of liberation and until they are free, we are not.[89]

Q Why are some Jews critical of the continuing occupation of the West Bank?

Abba Eban, at one time Foreign Minister of Israel and one of the most urbane and convincing advocates on behalf of Israel, speaking in June 1983:

Not a single country in the world community, including those most in favour of Israel, was prepared to support the idea that Israel's security required the imposition of permanent Israeli jurisdiction over a foreign nation. At least half the Israeli nation opposed the idea of the incorporation of the West Bank and Gaza into Israel.

There does not exist on the surface of the inhabited globe a single State that resembles what Israel would look like if it were to incorporate the West Bank and Gaza coercively into Israel. A democratic country ruling a foreign nation against its will and against the will of the world would be a unique reality.[90]

Arie Lova Eliav, writing in 1988:

Following the Six-Day War, Israel 'became a conqueror and an occupying power', with subsequent evil consequences that had… lasted for two decades.

The results of the brilliant military victory achieved in the 1967 war included a horrifying exposure of all the evil impulses hidden within Israel as individual human beings and as a people: arrogance, vanity, indifference to the fate of the defeated, a strong desire to control the conquered territories and to enslave their population to the economy of the victors, and a mystic ritual of 'sanctification' of the conquered lands. And one more thing: the insouciance of those who led the victory.

Drunk and dizzy with glory and fame, gorged on the fruits of victory, the leaders imagined themselves all-powerful and believed that time was bound to work on their behalf. They began to think, speak, and act in terms of the supremacy of force, of 'might is right', to which they added a sort of 'The sword shall devour for ever' fatalism on the one hand, and a belief in divine miracles, which would hasten the coming of the Messiah, on the other.

These patterns of thought, speech, and action have led ever-increasing sections of Israeli society, and primarily Israeli youth, to hate the 'stranger' in their midst, and to increase their hostility toward the Arabs. This, in turn, has engendered the settlements on the West Bank – some of them built upon the tricks of land speculators.

The 'Greater Israel' movement, whose main goal is to incorporate the West Bank and Gaza into the nation's borders, had led Zionism and Israel astray, diverting them from their proper path and deflecting them from the achievement of their fundamental goals.

We must now ask ourselves some painful questions: Is Israel still a Jewish state? Is Israel still a democratic state? Are Israel's economy and society still productive? Is Israel a state – or a society – of tolerance? And Is Israel approaching peace?[91]

Many Israelis have been critical of the brutality of their own forces in suppressing the Palestinians. These are some of the voices that have been raised in public:

We are gradually losing our humanity. The local population are gradually becoming objects in our eyes – at best mere objects, at worst something to be degraded and humiliated.[92]
BENNY BARABASH, SPEAKING AT A PRESS CONFERENCE ON ISRAELI POLICIES ON THE WEST BANK, 10 MAY 1982

How many wars will our boys fight before they will become animals?[93]

The war in Lebanon, which began in 1982, similarly was fiercely criticized by many Israeli Jews:

Ze'ev Schiff:

Israel must now bear the cost of its venture in Lebanon: hundreds of dead, thousands of wounded, and the shattering of a long-standing consensus on security that has produced an alarming rift within Israeli society.

From the sobering consequences of Operation Peace for Galilee one may be forced to conclude that a country can be victorious on the battlefield but lose a war strategically; that a small nation whose leaders fail to appreciate the limits of military power is doomed to pay dearly for their arrogance; and that a democracy like

Israel, whose defence is based on a militia army, cannot possibly win a war that lacks not only broad public support but even the slimmest national consensus regarding its very necessity.[94]

Anton La Guardia describes the significance of the Israeli protest against the Lebanon war and the suppression of the Intifada:

The Yom Kippur War made Israelis question the competence of their army and government, the Lebanon War made them doubt its morality and the Intifada made them accept the futility of trying to deny the existence of Palestinians as a separate people.

The daily scenes of soldiers shooting stone-throwers was a deeply disquieting, if not revolting, spectacle for many Israelis. When Yizhak Rabin, defence minister in the unity government, called on soldiers to 'break their bones', many did just that in front of television cameras. The most powerful armed forced in the Middle East, the embodiment of everything that was considered noble in Zionism – an army of 'humanists and fighters', as Ben-Gurion had put it – was reduced to chasing, beating and shooting poverty-stricken Arab children through the slums of Gaza. The callousness of military occupation, the legalized torture carried out by the Shin Bet (the domestic intelligence service) and the squalor of the Palestinian refugee camps prompted many Israelis to re-examine their justification for holding on to the Occupied Territories. The stone-throwers did not present a mortal threat to Israel, and the occupation seemed only to corrupt Israeli society. A significant number of soldiers, usually reservists, refused to serve in Lebanon or the Occupied Territories. Dozens were given jail terms for their insubordination; many others were simply allowed to stay at home discreetly.[95]

He also explains the consequences of Israel's continuing occupation of the West Bank:

Imperceptibly at first, the great victory of the Jews in 1967 was transformed into prolonged and debilitating military occupation. In contrast with 1948, the Palestinians for the most part stayed in their towns and villages. Israel inherited a large and resentful Palestinian population. The Arab states' defeat of 1967 crystallized the revolutionary Palestinian guerrilla groups. In Israel, victory energized a Jewish national-religious movement that would become increasingly militant.[96]

The conquered territory was a poisoned chalice. Israel had become a mini-empire, occupying a sullen and resentful Palestinian population in the West Bank. On the first day of the war, Dayan had told the nation on radio: 'Soldiers of Israel, we have no aims of conquest.' In the aftermath of victory, however, the Israeli government was ambivalent about the return of captured territory... The victorious doctrine of striking the first blow and fighting the war on the enemy's territory gave way to a defensive posture – and hubris.[97]

2.10 The different voices of the Palestinians

Q Who are the Palestinians?

There are approximately 8.4 million Palestinians today (of whom around 3.5 million are registered with UNRWA as refugees), located in the following regions:

■ The State of Israel, within which approximately one million Palestinians live, where they form twenty per cent of the population of Israel.
■ The West Bank and Gaza, in which approximately three million Palestinians live, some of them still under Israeli military rule, and some in areas controlled by the Palestine Authority.
■ Other countries, in which approximately 4.4 million Palestinians live. In Jordan there are 2.3 million; in Lebanon there are 0.4 million; and in North and South America there are 0.2 million.

Everett Mendelsohn, in a report entitled *A Compassionate Peace* (October 1982), a follow-up of the Quaker Report of 1970, describes the great variety of situations in which these Palestinian communities find themselves:

No single description would fit the experiences of Palestinian communities in different parts of the Arab world. They form different proportions of the populations in their host lands, ranging from sixty per cent in Jordan to below one per cent in Iraq, so that the importance of their political and social roles varies. Although the Palestinians share Arabic as a common language and Islam as a common religion (except in Lebanon, where there is a large Christian minority), in the various societies in which they reside they have established very different forms of social and political organization and have set up different means of receiving or integrating the Palestinian inhabitants. In Jordan many have been able to achieve full citizenship and participate in the affairs of the state (including even cabinet membership), a result of the inclusion of the West Bank in the kingdom of Jordan after the 1949 armistice agreement. In other countries, however, they remain refugees or, even in the second generation, outsiders. Many live in camps or in city districts or neighborhoods which are effectively separate, and they are often discriminated against. Like other foreign nationals they may engage in business in the Gulf or Arabian states, but a national must be either the senior partner or the business registrant. Palestinians, aware of European history, often compare their present status to that of the Jews in the ghettos of Europe. They have come to fill the role of expatriate professionals, teachers, technicians, and skilled artisans in many societies.[98]

Edward Said speaks of the Palestinians' attachment to the land they have cultivated for centuries, and describes how they have been conscious of their identity throughout the conflicts of the last 100 years:

For any Palestinian there was no doubt that his country had its own character and identity. True, Palestine had been part of the Ottoman empire until the end of the

First World War, and true also that in any accepted sense it had not been inde-
pendent. Its inhabitants referred to themselves as Palestinians, however, and made
important distinctions between themselves, the Syrians, the Lebanese, and the
Transjordans. Much of what we can call Palestinian self-assertion was articulated
in response to the flow of Jewish immigrants into Palestine since the 1880s, as well
as to ideological pronouncements made about Palestine by Zionist organizations.
Under the constantly felt sense of foreign invasion, Palestinian Arabs grew together
as a community during the interwar years. The things that had been taken for
granted – the structure of the society, village and family identity, customs, cuisine,
folklore, dialect, distinctive habits and history – were adduced as evidence, to
Palestinians by Palestinians, that even as a colony the territory had always been
their homeland, and that they formed a people. Sixty per cent of the population was
in agriculture; the balance was divided between townspeople and a relatively small
nomadic group. All these people believed themselves to belong in a land called
Palestine, despite their feelings that they were also members of a large Arab nation;
and for all of the twentieth century, they referred to their country as Filastinuna
(our Palestine).

He speaks of how the world is being forced to acknowledge their existence as a people:

There is a Palestinian people, there is an Israeli occupation of Palestinian lands, there
are Palestinians under Israeli military occupation, there are Palestinians – 650,000
of them – who are Israeli citizens and who constitute fifteen per cent of the population
of Israel, there is a large Palestinian population in exile: these are actualities which
the United States and most of the world have directly or indirectly acknowledged,
which Israel too has acknowledged, if only in the forms of denial, rejection, threats of
war, and punishment. The history of the past forty years has shown that Palestinians
have grown politically, not shrunk, under the influence of every kind of repression
and hardship; the history of the Jews has shown too that time only increases attach-
ment to the historically saturated land of Palestine. Short of complete obliteration, the
Palestinians will continue to exist and they will continue to have their own ideas
about who represents them, where they want to settle, what they want to do with their
national and political future.[99]

Anton La Guardia explains the origins of the awareness of Palestinian identity:

The point at which Arab resentment of Zionist encroachment developed into a
separate Palestinian national consciousness is the subject of heated debate
among academics. In Palestinian Identity, the Palestinian academic, Rashid
Khalidi, finds the first glints of nationalist identity among the literate notables in
Ottoman days. The sense of nationhood then gradually spread wider with the
shock of the First World War, the losing struggles against the British and the
Zionists, and finally crystallized with the trauma of dispossession and dispersion
in 1948.[100]

John H. Davis answers the charge that the Arab governments used the Palestinian refugees as a pawn for political purposes:

The fact is that the Palestinian refugee problem has never been well understood in the Western world. One common belief, even among responsible persons, is that the refugees have remained unsettled and unemployed largely because the Arab Governments have inhibited their settlement or have even held them as hostages by not allowing them to settle or go to work. Supposedly, their motivation has been the desire to keep alive the Palestine issue in the eyes of the world. The evidence is quite to the contrary. Following the upheaval of 1948, virtually all able-bodied male refugees who possessed skills needed in Arab countries, or for that matter, elsewhere, found jobs almost immediately and became self-supporting and have never been dependent on international charity. This group comprised some twenty per cent of the total working force which left their homes in Palestine in 1948–1949; for the most part they were persons from the urban sector of Palestine, their good fortune being that the world needed the skills which they possessed.

In contrast, the farming sector of the refugee population, which comprised about seventy per cent of the total refugee numbers in 1948, did not fare so well. Their problem has been, and is, that as refugees they became surplus farm workers in an era when the world at large, and Arab countries in particular, already had a surplus of people in their rural sectors. In fact, in the Arab countries as a group rural youth is still reaching maturity at a rate per generation more than three times that required to replace the farm parents – a situation that is further aggravated by the fact that the typical rural holding is already too small adequately to support a family of eight to ten persons, or use modern equipment efficiently. Hence, it was the rural refugees from Palestine who, for the most part, became dependent on international charity. The reason they became dependent was not that they were held as hostages, but that they were unemployable under the competitive employment conditions that then prevailed, and for that matter prevail to this day.[101]

Abdel-Shai, one of the Palestinian delegates at the Madrid Peace Conference, 1991, tried to explain Palestinian self-understanding:

We, the people of Palestine, stand before you in the fullness of our pain, our pride and our anticipation, for we have long harboured a yearning for peace and a dream of justice and freedom. For too long, the Palestinian people have gone unheeded, silenced and denied – our identity negated by political expedience, our rightful struggle against injustice maligned, and our present existence subsumed by the past tragedy of another people. It is time for us to narrate our own story.[102]

Q Why do many if not most Palestinians feel so bitter towards Israel?

Fawaz Turki, a young Palestinian living in France, expresses the feelings of many young Palestinians in exile in a book called *The Disinherited*, published in 1974:

*The deportations, the blowing up of homes, the expropriation of property, the arro-
gance on the faces of Israeli soldiers walking into Arab coffee shops in Jerusalem to
slap the patrons on the face and demand identity cards, and the primitive torture
of members of the resistance – all these go on, and to the outside world 'the Arabs'
have never had it so good. Look at how our standard of living is better than ever.
We earn excellent wages under occupation. We drive cars. We watch television.
Our health standards have improved. And they show pictures of our West Bank
'notables', our Uncle Toms and Beni oui oui, as if to attest to this, shaking hands
with Israeli military governors. And nobody seems to realize that, during all this,
Palestinians called and fought for a secular state and not for a struggle to inflict on
Israeli society the same devastation they inflicted on us.*

*I begin to lose my patience and my sense of rationality. I begin to feel that our
lives are not worth living anywhere in this world, anywhere. It is impossible for me
to be oblivious of my situation; to be, as it were, happy. Moments of gloom and fury
overwhelm my being as I spend restless days in Paris and I see pictures of robust
Israelis tilling our land, growing our oranges, inhabiting our cities and towns, co-
opting our culture, and talking in their grim stubborn way about how we do not
'exist' and how our country was a 'desert' before they went there. And I gag with
anger and mortification.*[103]

Edward Said expresses the longings of Palestinians in exile to return to their country, and of those within Israel to have self-government:

*Those Palestinians in manifest exile want to return; those in internal exile (inside
Israel or under military occupation) want independence and freedom and self-government where they are. A refugee from Galilee or Jaffa who now lives either in
Lebanon or in Kuwait thinks primarily in terms of what he lost when he left in
1948 or later; he wants to be put back, or to fight his way back, into Palestine. He
wants to return. Conversely, the present Palestinian resident of Gaza, Nazareth or
Nablus faces or in some way daily rubs up against an occupying power, its symbols
of authority, its basically unchecked domination over him; he wants to see that
power removed or, in the case of the Arab Israeli citizen, he no longer wishes to be
known and treated negatively as a 'non-Jew'. He wants novelty. One Palestinian
wants to move, the other to stay; both want a pretty radical change.*[104]

Anton La Guardia sums up the basic feeling among Arabs of what Israel represents:

*Israel formed – and still forms – a Jewish dagger in the heart of the Arab world, sever-
ing Egypt and North Africa from the Fertile Crescent and the Arabian peninsula. For
Arabs, its very existence is a humiliation, a new Crusader state.*[105]

Palestinians have frequently expressed their nationalistic feelings in poetry. **Tawfiq
Zayyad**, a Palestinian living in Israel, expressed the conviction that Israel cannot get
rid of the Arabs. In a poem called *Baqun* ('We Shall Remain'), he says that in spite of
all the indignities they have to suffer, the Arabs will remain:

Here – we have a past
  a present
  and a future.
Our roots are entrenched
Deep in the earth.
Like twenty impossibles
We shall remain.[106]

Kamal Nasr, a Christian Palestinian poet, was fully committed to the aims and
ideals of the Palestine Liberation Organization, and was one of a number of
Palestinians murdered in their homes in Beirut by a group of Israeli commandos one
night in 1973. This is how he expressed the feelings of the Palestinian refugees:

The refugees are ever kindling
  In their camps, in that world of darkness,
The embers of revolt,
  Gathering force, for the return,
They have lost their faith in the doctrine of love,
  Even here in this land of love and peace
Their stolen rights cry in their hearts,
  Inflamed by misery and hunger.
Dismayed by the persistent throng.
  The enemy spreads poison and hatred abroad;
'They are Communists,' he says. 'Their hopes are false,
  Let us kill their hopes to return!'[107]

Mahmoud Darwish:

We travel like other people, but we return to nowhere.[108]

Q What is the Palestine Liberation Organization (PLO)?

Everett Mendelsohn describes the position of *Fatah*, one of the most important
groups within the PLO, in the context of the whole Palestinian movement:

One recent study lists more than twenty Palestinian resistance groups. Among
these, Fatah (Palestine National Liberation Movement) is the oldest, largest and
most influential. While it is only one of many units of the PLO, it now accounts for
seventy per cent of the umbrella group and its leadership has assumed effective con-
trol. Fatah's membership runs the spectrum of belief and social orientation in the
Palestinian community. It is more conservative than other guerrilla groups and
reflects a generally Arab orientation, broadly construed Islamic religious beliefs,
and a politically neutralist stance. It contains segments that are Christian and also
a strong secular, socialist wing.
  Eight guerrilla groups now make up the PLO along with Fatah, and Yasser
Arafat, the Fatah leader, is Chairman of the PLO executive committee. In the wake

of the 1967 war, the PLO filled a vacuum. From the point of view of outsiders, the PLO took on the qualities of a 'government in exile', although in fact it has rejected that political choice. Although known in the media primarily for guerrilla military activities, and terrorism, the PLO has assumed responsibility for many aspects of Palestinian life, especially in refugee communities. It has established a social service system and formed a Palestinian branch of the Red Crescent (headed by a physician, younger brother of Yasser Arafat); it conducts schools and operates an industrial co-operative (SAMED) in Lebanon. The PLO offered a political defence for their resort to terrorism, arguing it 'gives our cause resounding coverage – positive or negative it mattered little'.[109]

Yehoshafat Harkabi, formerly director of Israeli Military Intelligence, and later a professor at the Hebrew University in Jerusalem, explained in an article in the *Washington Post* in 1988 how he, as an Israeli Jew, saw the PLO:

I do not endorse the PLO position. I find ugliness in the position it takes. But I cannot delude myself into thinking that it does not represent the Palestinians. Had there been a referendum most Palestinians would say the PLO represents them, not because they love its leaders or endorse every article in its doctrine but because it symbolizes the idea that the Palestinians deserve to have a state. The Palestinians are fed up with others thrusting themselves forward as their representatives. The PLO is the only authentic Palestinian representation; it has no competition. Criminalizing the PLO as a terrorist organization amounts to criminalizing the Palestinian people which is both politically and morally wrong. If one accepts that the Palestinians should be included in any negotiations for settlement, they must be able to choose who will represent them, just as the Americans and Soviets appoint their own delegations in arms control talks.[110]

Q What are the aims of the PLO? How have they changed over the years?

We need to distinguish at least four crucial stages in the development of the PLO, and recognize the significant changes in its stated goals at each of these stages.

'The Liberation of Palestine' (1964–67)

In January 1964 the PLO was set up by Arab leaders at a summit conference of the Arab League, with the aim of 'Organizing the Palestinian people to enable them to carry out their role of liberating their homeland and determining their destiny'. During this early period the movement was largely under the control of President Nasser and other Arab governments, and groups of *fedayeen* (freedom fighters) began to make raids into Israel from the surrounding Arab countries.

The following are articles from the *Palestine National Charter*, which was written in 1964 and amended in 1968:

1. Palestine is the homeland of the Arab Palestinian people; it is an indivisible part of the Arab homeland, and the Palestinian people are an integral part of the Arab nation...

3. The Palestinian Arab people possess the legal right to their homeland and have the right to determine their destiny after achieving the liberation of their country in accordance with their wishes and entirely of their own accord and will...

8. The phase in their history, through which the Palestinian people are now living, is that of national struggle for the liberation of Palestine...

9. Armed struggle is the only way to liberate Palestine. Thus it is the overall strategy, not merely a tactical phase. The Palestinian Arab people assert their absolute determination and firm resolution to continue their armed struggle and to work for an armed popular revolution for the liberation of their country and their return to it. They also assert their right to normal life in Palestine and to exercise their right to self-determination and sovereignty over it.

10. Commando action constitutes the nucleus of the Palestinian popular liberation war...

15. The liberation of Palestine, from an Arab viewpoint, is a national duty and it attempts to repel the Zionist and imperialist aggression against the Arab homeland, and aims at the elimination of Zionism in Palestine. Absolute responsibility for this falls upon the Arab nation – peoples and governments – with the Arab people of Palestine in the vanguard...

19. The partition of Palestine in 1947 and the establishment of the State of Israel are entirely illegal, regardless of the passage of time, because they were contrary to the will of the Palestinian people and to their natural right in their homeland, and inconsistent with the principles embodied in the Charter of the United Nations, particularly the right to self-determination.[111]

'The Democratic State of Palestine' (1967–74)

Before 1967 the Palestinians were very reliant on the Arab states. But because of the failure of the 1967 war and the disastrous defeat of the Arab armies, a more grass-roots Palestinian leadership emerged in the PLO with a determination that Palestinians should be masters of their own destiny. Thus in 1968 Yasser Arafat, who had worked as an engineer in the Gulf before joining the *fedayeen* in southern Lebanon, was elected Chairman of the PLO. The leadership of the movement was from now on in the hands of those who had been actively involved in fighting for the cause, and were prepared to take the fight into Israel itself.

After a significant battle in which a large number of Palestinians resisted an Israeli raid on the town of Karakeh inside Jordan, many young Palestinians joined the movement and committed themselves to fight with the *fedayeen*.

During this period the PLO stated its goals as the dismantling of the Zionist State of Israel and the establishment in its place of a 'Democratic State of Palestine', covering the whole of Israel and the West Bank. This was to be a 'democratic secular state', in which Jews and Arabs would have equal rights.

David Hirst explains the significance of this new concept:

The Jew-as-Zionist was still the enemy, of course, and against him and all he stood for Fatah would pursue its 'Revolution Till Victory'. Complete liberation was still the aim. And complete liberation still meant 'liquidating the Zionist aggressor-state – politically, militarily, socially and ideologically'. There was no question of accepting some kind of mini-state to be set up in such territories as Israel, under a general settlement, might be induced to evacuate; together, the West Bank and Gaza represented no more than twenty-three per cent of original Palestine; it would, the Fatah theorist said, be a mere puppet – Israel's Bantustan. Only through complete liberation could the Palestinians fulfil their inalienable right to return; only thus could they assure themselves, as a people, of a free and decent life. But it was no longer a call for a literal and absolute justice, a restoration, pure and simple, of the status quo ante. If it did not acknowledge the Zionist fait accompli itself, it acknowledged the fundamental consequence of it, a physical Jewish presence in Palestine. It was a great leap forward in their thinking.[112]

Salah Ta'mari, formerly a PLO military commander, speaking in 1998:

I have not abandoned my dream of a democratic state in all of Palestine where Palestinians – Jews and non-Jews – will live together.[113]

'National authority over every part of liberated Palestinian territory' (1974–88)
The twelfth meeting of the Palestine National Council in June 1974 marked the next decisive turning point. Yasser Arafat, chairman of the PLO, began to move away from concepts of 'armed struggle' and 'total liberation' in favour of a diplomatic settlement. A resolution at this conference, therefore, called for an 'independent combatant national authority over every part of Palestinian territory that is liberated'.

There were three other significant developments during this period:

■ In 1974 the PLO was recognized at the Summit Conference of the Arab League at Rabat in Morocco as 'the sole legitimate representative' of the Palestinian people.
■ In November 1974 the UN General Assembly recognized the PLO as the representative of the Palestinians, and gave it observer status. It was then that **Yasser Arafat**, as Chairman of the PLO, made his famous speech in which he said, 'I have come bearing an olive branch and a freedom fighter's gun. Do not let the olive branch fall from my hand.'
■ In 1975 the USA adopted the Israeli policy of refusing to recognize the PLO and excluding it from any role in negotiations.

A Palestinian professor from Bir Zeit College on the West Bank expressed the significance of this change in Palestinian attitudes and aspirations in these words:

It is very difficult for us to say goodbye to what is ours – Haifa, Jaffa and most of Jerusalem – but we are in effect telling the Israelis that we are ready to do so. We are saying that we no longer want to drive them out of the land from which they drove us. Some of us still want to do so, but they are not the dominant voice. But in return the Israelis must withdraw from at least all the territories occupied in 1967. Nothing less is feasible. They must grasp this.[114]

'The Two-State Solution' (1988–)

At a meeting in Algiers in November 1988 the Palestine National Congress took the step of declaring a Palestinian State on the West Bank and the Gaza Strip. Yasser Arafat was thus, in effect, playing his last card, in an attempt to persuade the Israeli government and the USA to make concessions. The PLO was therefore changing its position in three significant ways:

- It was recognizing Israel's legal right to exist.
- It was renouncing terrorism as a means of achieving its goals.
- It was accepting the UN Security Council Resolution 242 (which recognized Palestinian rights to self-determination and called for an exchange of territories for peace) and Resolution 338 (which called for negotiations) as part of the basis for an international peace conference.

The following are extracts from the Palestinian Declaration of Independence:

Palestine, the land of the three monotheistic faiths, is where the Palestinian Arab people was born, on which it grew, developed and excelled. The Palestinian people was never separated from or diminished in its integral bonds with Palestine. Thus the Palestinian Arab people ensured for itself an everlasting union between itself, its land and its history...

Nourished by an unfolding series of civilizations and cultures, the Palestinian Arab people adds to its stature by consolidating a union between itself and its patrimonial land.

Injustice: when in the course of modern times a new order of values was declared with norms and values fair to all, it was the Palestinian Arab people that had been excluded from the destiny of all other peoples by a hostile array of local and foreign powers...

And it was the Palestinian people, already wounded in its body, that was submitted to yet another type of occupation over which floated the falsehood that 'Palestine was a land without people'. This notion was foisted upon some in the world, whereas in Article 22 of the Covenant of the League of Nations (1919) and in the Treaty of Lausanne (1923), the community of nations had recognized that all the Arab territories, including Palestine, of the formerly Ottoman provinces were to have granted to them their freedom as provisionally independent nations.

Partition: despite the historical injustice inflicted on the Palestinian Arab people resulting in their dispersion and depriving them of their right to self-determination following upon UN General Assembly Resolution 181 (1947), which partitioned Palestine into two states, one Arab, one Jewish, yet it is this resolution that provides those conditions of international legitimacy that ensure the right of the Palestinian Arab people to sovereignty and national independence.

By stages, the occupation of Palestine and parts of other Arab territories by Israeli forces, the willed dispossession and expulsion from their ancestral homes of the majority of Palestine's civilian inhabitants was achieved by organized terror.

Identity: in Palestine and on its perimeters, in exile distant and near, the Palestinian Arab people never faltered and never abandoned its conviction in its rights of return and independence. And the collective Palestinian national will forged for itself a political embodiment, the Palestine Liberation Organization, its sole legitimate representative, recognized by the world community as a whole, as well as by related regional and international institutions.

Whereas the Palestinian people reaffirms most definitely its inalienable rights in the land of its patrimony:

Now by virtue of natural, historical and legal rights and the sacrifices of successive generations who gave of themselves in defence of the freedom and independence of their homeland;

in pursuance of resolutions adopted by Arab summit conferences and relying on the authority bestowed by international legitimacy as embodied in the resolutions of the United Nations Organization since 1947;

and in exercise by the Palestinian Arab people of its rights to self-determination, political independence, and sovereignty over its territory;

The Palestinian National Council, in the name of God, and in the name of the Palestinian Arab people, hereby proclaims the establishment of the State of Palestine on our Palestinian territory with its capital Jerusalem (Al-Quds Ash-Sharif).

Freedoms: the State of Palestine is the state of Palestinians wherever they may be. The state is for them to enjoy in it their collective national and cultural identity, theirs to pursue in it a complete equality of rights. In it will be safeguarded their political and religious convictions and their human dignity by means of a parliamentary democratic system of governance, itself based on freedom of expression and the freedom to form parties.

The State of Palestine herewith declares that it believes in the settlement of regional and international disputes by peaceful means, in accordance with the UN Charter and resolutions. Without prejudice to its natural right to defend its territorial integrity and independence, it therefore rejects the threat or use of force, violence, and terrorism against territorial integrity, or political independence, as it also rejects their use against the territorial integrity of other states.[115]

Q What are some of the other voices of the Palestinians?

Hamas is a more radical Palestinian resistance group that is critical of the PLO. It developed out of the Muslim Brotherhood as a response to the Intifada which began in 1987. It called itself 'the Islamic Resistance Movement' or *Hamas* (meaning 'zeal' in Arabic). Being an unashamedly Islamic movement, *Hamas* takes the Qur'an as its constitution, and bases its ideology firmly on the Qur'an. The significance of this Qur'anic basis is explained by **Peter Riddell** as follows:

The starting point, the very foundation, for Hamas *as an organization, as well as for individual members, is founded upon:*

■ *Endemic hostility to governments which do not base themselves upon Islamic values, whether these governments consist of Muslims or non-Muslims.*
■ *A perception that God is 'incensed' with the Jews.*
■ *A belief that the Jews are destined to be the first sent to Hell on the Day of Judgment.*
■ *Deriving from the above, a firm belief that Muslim lands should not be under the sovereignty of non-Muslims.*[116]

Riddell's summary of the contents of each of the 36 articles of the Covenant of *Hamas* is shown in the table in Appendix 3.

Edward Said, a prominent Arab-American, and professor of English Literature at Columbia University, New York, has been one of the most articulate spokespeople for the Palestinians for many years. The following are extracts from his writings on different subjects related to the conflict.

The world needs to recognize the dispossession that took place in 1948:
Israel's constant demands for security conceal, I think, a deep insecurity about Israel's 'original sin', the fact that there was always another people in Palestine, and that every village, kibbutz, settlement, city, and town had an Arab history also. Dayan used to admit it publicly. This generation of leaders hasn't the honesty... there is tragedy beneath every road, every act of military prowess, every settlement. What sort of hypocrisy is it to rail against Islamic fundamentalism and to say nothing of Jewish fundamentalism that dehumanizes every non-Jew and relies on biblical promises that go back two millennia?[117]

There is a fundamental blindness in the Israeli conscience which the PLO encouraged, instead of forcing responsibility on Zionism for its crimes against an entire people. There can never be peace between Palestinian Arabs and Israeli Jews (and their many diaspora supporters) until public acknowledgment of Israel's dispossession, and continuing oppression of the Palestinian people is recognized as a matter of state policy.[118]

He describes the significance of the first Intifada, which began in 1987:

At no point in modern Middle Eastern history has a mass uprising been so vast and protracted in scale, so radical in its results, so profoundly meaningful as the current one in the Israeli-occupied territories.

For one thing, this uprising has totally discredited the notion that the Palestinian issue – the Palestinian people themselves – can be finessed or ignored, or that, given the proper mixture of benign neglect and intimidation, the Palestinians will simply go away as a 'problem'. For another, the Palestinians as a whole have now gone into direct mass confrontation with the Israeli military in the Occupied Territories, and politically they have successfully defied and stalemated what is in effect one of the most redoubtable armies in the world. More important, in showing no fear but acting with great resourcefulness, the Palestinians have reduced the Israeli presence and its schemes on the West Bank and Gaza to reactive measures – cruel, stupid, politically bankrupt.

The entire Palestinian nation is now unified; the distinctions between classes, communities and interests have been scrubbed; all are together. Internationally, there is little sympathy for Israel now as, unconditionally armed and supported politically by the United States, it lurches from refusal and negation to killing and bombing, pretending that the issue is simply one of law and order. Whose law and order?

The uprising is an eruption of history compressed into the daily energies of a long-suffering, often forgotten and routinely abused people. Slowly the great disparity diminishes between Western praise and admiration for Israel as a democracy and pioneering state, on the one hand, and, on the other, the ignorant opprobrium Palestinians have had heaped on them since their world was shattered in 1948. Yet if there can be no return to the past for us, the same is at least as true for Israel and the United States. Here a new set of problems has emerged.

It is surprisingly difficult to shift from having hardly any status to a position of relative and acknowledged centrality, but this is what has happened to the Palestinian people. By sheer force of will, this has been our achievement, symbolized by the uprising. No one, I think, doubts that our march to self-determination is now irreversible. But the course is still for us to map; our leaders and representatives remain ours to choose. Even the United States tacitly accepts these realities…

It is not enough for well-intentioned people to talk about the need for peace. Peace has to be made with us, not with a 'demographic problem' – and the occupation must end. Respond to what Palestinians, as the aggrieved party, propose; argue with it, modify it, suggest alternatives. But do not throw it out, any more than you would advocate throwing Palestinians off their land.[119]

He has consistently been very critical of the Oslo Accords:

It has taken almost exactly four years (writing in 1997) for the Oslo peace process inexorably to peel off its cosmetic wrappings in order to reveal the stark truth hidden at its core: there was no real peace agreement, only an agreement to keep Israeli hegemony over the Palestinian territories safeguarded by hypocritical rhetoric and military power. In this… there was a lamentable Palestinian failure to judge Israeli motives – especially under Labor – and to preserve a degree of skepticism. Instead we entered an appalling spiral of loss and humiliation, gulled by the United States and the media into thinking that we had at last achieved some measure of respectability and acceptance, all of which has impoverished our people whose per capita income had been slashed by half; we have lost our ability to move around freely, confined to the dreadful little Bantustans (about three per cent of the West Bank) that we insist on calling liberated zones, obliged to watch more settlements being built and more land taken, more houses destroyed, more people evicted, and sadistic collective punishment meted out without proportion or reason. Western liberals must remember that Oslo was not a fresh start: it was built on twenty-six years of Israeli military occupation and, before that, nineteen years of Palestinian dispossession, exile, and oppression. If Israel has all along insisted that it is not responsible for what has been visited on the Palestinian people since 1948, then it should explain to us why we, alone of all people, should forget the past, remain uncompensated, our travails unacknowledged, even as all other victims of injustice have the right to reparations, apologies, and the like. There is no logic to that, only the cold, hard, narcissistic indifference of amoral power.[120]

I have no doubt that the only acceptable form of peace between Israel and Palestine must really be a mutual one, in which Israel cannot enjoy benefits like sovereignty, security, territorial continuity, real political independence, and national self-determination, and Palestine not. Peace must be between equals, which is exactly what is wrong with the Oslo peace process.[121]

Everything we now know about what happened in Oslo suggests that the Palestinian leadership believed that it was getting a state, whereas the Israelis in fact were planning exactly the opposite.[122]

He explains his perception of the real underlying intentions of Israel concerning the West Bank:

The Israelis were not just passing laws here and there but were operating with a plan and a vision for bringing these territories – which they clearly never planned to give up – under the rule of law for their purposes… carefully prepared plans to consolidate their hold on the territories and by no means to concede sovereignty or self-determination to the Palestinians.[123]

He has been extremely critical of Arafat and the leadership of the Palestinian Authority:

All I can come up with is a series of unflattering rationales for going on as before, with equally bad results and equally tragic consequences for the whole people. One rationale is that so long as the peace process guarantees the centrality of the PLO and its leader, then more or less anything goes. A second is that being so outmanoeuvered, outgunned, outsmarted by Israel, you feel you have no choice but to go on trying to brazen it out vis-à-vis your own people, with a lot of hopeful but ultimately misleading speeches and promises; meanwhile you surround yourself with supporters who tell you what you want to hear and are anxious to help you set up more feel-good things like a bagpipe band, a few luxurious cars and houses, postage stamps with your face on them, and so on. The best thing of all is to go on

*as many state visits (few of them necessary) as possible: one day Stockholm, anoth-
er Paris, another Beijing, another Cairo. Third is the tactic of making more concessions, accepting all the humiliating Israeli conditions in the wishful fantasy that
some day you'll either stop having to make concessions or the Israelis will give you a
few things back. Fourth is the rationale that this is politics, a dirty business, so we
proceed with the Israelis like partners in crime; never mind that they get all the
advantages, a lot of commercial deals have come out this way.[124]*

He pleads with Palestinians to recognize the challenge that has been posed by
Israel:

*The fundamental challenge that Israel poses is to ourselves – our inability to organ-
ize, our inability to dedicate ourselves to a basic set of principles from which we do
not deviate, our inability to marshal our resources singlemindedly, our inability to
devote all our efforts to education and competence, finally, our inability to choose a
leadership that is capable of the task.[125]*

He outlines what he sees as the basic conditions of peace and changes of thinking
that are required on the part of all the parties concerned:

*The only peace worth its name is an exchange of land for peace on the basis of
rough parity between the two sides. There can be no peace without some genuine
attempt on the part of Israel and its powerful supporters to take a step toward the
people they have wronged, a step they must take in humility and reconciliation, not
in clever talk and cruel behaviour.[126]*

*What is needed now (writing in 1997) – and certainly the United States can take
the step – is a restatement of the basic premise that there is peace only when land
is given back, and that, for the short time that it may still be possible, the goal is
independence and statehood for two peoples in Palestine. Start from that, and it
might be possible to move toward the goal in as many steps as are necessary. But
one cannot expect peace and security while Palestinians continue to suffer and
not one word is said about the causes of that suffering.[127]*

*What we ask for is acknowledgment, not destruction; equality, not subordination. I
think also that we must always be very clear in our understanding of Jewish suffering and in making it apparent that what binds us together is a common history of
persecution, which must be shown not to be the exclusive possession of the Jewish
people.[128]*

This was his perception of the prospects for peace in the late 1990s:

*It is... evident that on both sides the inclination toward a real peace with justice
and equality is lacking. Israelis feel that after thirty years of military supremacy
they can do what they want in either peace or war; Palestinians refuse to reconcile
themselves to a state of permanent subjugation despite their leaders' weakness. So*

long as the fundamental reality is denied or avoided – that Israel exists as a Jewish state by virtue of its having supplanted the rights of all Palestinians with a 'superior' Jewish right – there can neither be reconciliation nor true coexistence. If the past thirty years have taught one lesson, it is that a yearning for peace and self-fulfilment among Palestinians cannot be abrogated or totally suppressed, no matter how militarily and politically powerful Israel is. What is now needed is a change of consciousness: Israelis must realize that their future depends on how they face up to and deal courageously with their collective history of responsibility for the Palestinian tragedy. And Palestinians, as well as other Arabs, must discover that the struggle for Palestinian rights is indivisible from the need to create a real civil and democratic society, to invest massively in innovative education, and to explore modes of secular community now unavailable in the 'returns' either to Judaism, Christianity, or Islam which are characteristic of contemporary religious fundamentalism.[129]

In rejecting the two-state solution, he has for many years argued for one democratic state in which Jews and Arabs are equal as the only ultimate solution:

The present crisis is, I think, a glimmering of the end of the two-state solution, whose unworkability Oslo, perhaps unconsciously, embodies. Israelis and Palestinians are too intertwined with each other in history, experience, and actuality to separate, even though each proclaims the need for separate statehood and will in fact have it. The challenge is to find a peaceful way in which to coexist not as warring Jews, Muslims, and Christians, but as equal citizens in the same land.[130]

I see no other way than to begin now to speak about sharing the land that has thrust us together, sharing it in a truly democratic way, with equal rights for all citizens. There can be no reconciliation unless both peoples, two communities of suffering, resolve that their existence is a secular fact, and that it has to be dealt with as such. This does not mean a diminishing of Jewish life as Jewish life or surrendering Palestinian Arab aspirations and political existence; on the contrary, it means self-determination for both peoples. But it does mean being willing to soften, lessen, and finally give up special status for one people at the expense of the other. The Law of Return for Jews and the right of return for Palestinian refugees have to be considered and trimmed together. But the notions of Greater Israel as the land of the Jewish people given to them by God and of Palestine as an Arab land that cannot be alienated from the Arab homeland need to be reduced in scale and exclusivity.[131]

2.11 Conclusions

Anti-Semitism

Prejudices against Jews which had developed over many centuries in Christian Europe combined with various political, social and economic factors in Europe (and especially Eastern Europe) in the nineteenth century to create strong feelings against Jews, and these led to violent attacks on a number of Jewish communities and individuals. Herzl understood the basic source of anti-Semitism to be the fact that 'we Jews have maintained ourselves, even if through no fault of our own, as a foreign body among the different nations'. 'The guilty conscience of Christendom translated into support of Zionism, most importantly in the United States' (Benny Morris)[132] (2.1 Anti-Semitism).

Zionism
The early leaders of the Zionist movement, many of whom were secular Jews, like Theodor Herzl and Chaim Weizmann, worked for the creation of a Jewish homeland in Palestine as a solution to the problem of anti-Semitism in Europe. In spite of all they said to the contrary in public, their ultimate goal was the setting up of some kind of Jewish state in Palestine. Some of the new Israeli historians now recognize that from the beginning 'Zionism was a colonizing and expansionist ideology and movement' (Benny Morris)[133] (2.2 Zionism).

Jewish settlement in the land
When the modern period of Jewish immigration began in the 1880s, the Jews numbered only about five per cent of the total population, and were living in a limited number of centres. Most of the land they acquired was bought from absentee Palestinian landowners, and these sales, which were later bitterly regretted, exposed fatal weaknesses in Arab society. The intention of many of the settlers was to say to the Arabs 'Move over'. Throughout the conflict there has been a 'mutual lack of empathy' between Jewish settlers and the Arabs (Benny Morris)[134] (2.3 Jewish settlement in the land).

Arab reactions to Jewish settlement
When the Arabs realized that the Jews might eventually outnumber them and gain control of the country, they naturally did all they could to prevent this happening. It was inevitable that the steady influx of Jewish immigrants would sooner or later lead to friction and to conflict. Since the aims of the Jewish leadership were so totally incompatible with the Arabs' desire for self-determination, the struggle between the two communities was bound to lead to violence. When the Arabs resorted to violence, it was in order to protect their interests and avoid being submerged by the immigrant community. When Jews resorted to violence it was to establish themselves as an independent community in a hostile environment. 'Paradoxically it was in large part the thrust and threat of Zionism that generated... consciousness of collective self, that is a distinct Palestinian and Arab identity and nationalism' (Benny Morris)[135] (2.4 Arab reactions to Jewish settlement).

The role of Britain
The promises made by the British government during the First World War to the Jews (in the Balfour Declaration) and to the Arabs (e.g. in the Hussein-McMahon correspondence), appear to us now to have been contrary and incompatible. The British government was at best totally unrealistic, and at worst simply dishonest in thinking that a Jewish homeland could be established in Palestine without in any way harming the interests of the Arabs in Palestine. The Arabs had special reason

to feel bitter and resentful at the way the British and the other Western powers represented at the Peace Conference at Versailles in 1919 broke all the promises they
had made, and instead of granting the Arabs independence, established their own
authority throughout the Middle East largely to further their own interests. In the
period between the two world wars, the Jewish enterprise in the land 'unfolded
under the protective carapace of British rifles and under a beneficent and efficient
administration that made the task of the settlers and the Jewish Agency infinitely
easier' (Benny Morris)[136] (2.5 The role of Britain).

The role of the United Nations

When the British government felt that it could not resolve the growing conflict
between the two sides, it declared its intention to end the Mandate and to hand the
problem over to the United Nations. The delegation who visited the country recommended partition: a Jewish state including fifty-five per cent of the land and a
population of 509,780 Arabs and 490,020 Jews; an Arab state including the remaining forty-five per cent of the land and a population of 749,101 Arabs and 9,520 Jews;
and Jerusalem becoming an 'international zone'. In voting for the plan, many of the
member states of the UN were influenced by self-interest and by pressure both from
Jews and from the American government (2.6 The role of the United Nations).

Partition and war (1948–49)

The Jews prepared much more carefully than the Arabs, and many of their leaders
talked about the idea of 'transfer'. Atrocities were committed by both sides. Arab
armies from Egypt, Jordan, Iraq, Syria and Lebanon invaded. As the conflict spread,
between 700,000 and 800,000 Arabs left their homes (i.e. approximately sixty per
cent of the pre-war Arab population of Palestine, or eighty-five per cent of the Arab
population which would have been within the State of Israel). The Palestinians
could have established their own state at the time, but rejected the idea because
they felt that the division of the land was unfair and favoured the Jews, and because
they felt that the plan went against the principle of self-determination and was
imposed on them without adequate consultation (2.7 Partition and war).

The voice of Israel

Israel sees itself as a state for the whole Jewish people, and its 'Law of Return' gives
any Jew anywhere in the world the right to settle in Israel. Jews feel that the establishment of the state has restored their pride, and enabled them to be masters in
their own land and a nation among the nations. After the destruction of the
Holocaust they have created a haven, 'the ultimate asylum' in which Jewish life, culture and values can be preserved. Thousands of Jews have been saved from death
or discrimination in other countries. Amounting to around one-fifth of the total number of Jews in the world, they can feel that they are a nation on their own soil, with
their own language and faith, and believe that they have much to give to the world.
They recognize that the creation of the Jewish state has caused suffering and injustice to others, but point out that territorial changes have been a fact of life for many
centuries. 'Zionism is an attempt of the Jewish people to give contemporary expression to their identity.' The crisis in relationships with the Palestinians during 2000

and 2001 exposed deep divisions within Israel which had existed for many years, with some wanting to withdraw from the West Bank and Gaza, and others insisting on holding on to it whatever the cost (2.8 The voice of Israel).

Other Jewish/Israeli voices

Not all Jews, whether in Israel or outside, are Zionists. Some have been opposed to the very idea of a Jewish state, while others have been very critical of the way the state has acted. Israel functions as a democracy, and strongly critical voices have been raised within Israel against the suppression of the Palestinians on the West Bank and Gaza Strip since 1967, and against the war in Lebanon in 1982 and the occupation of the south of Lebanon which continued until 2000. Many believe that the conquest of the West Bank has turned out to be a 'poisoned chalice' (2.9 Other Jewish/Israeli voices).

The different voices of the Palestinians

Of the eight million Palestinians in the world today, one million live in Israel, where they form twenty per cent of the total population, three million live on the West Bank and Gaza (either under the Palestinian Authority or under Israeli military rule), while four million live outside Israel/Palestine, with 3.5 million of them officially registered as refugees (making the largest number of refugees of any nationality in the world). All Palestinians have a strong sense of their Palestinian identity and believe that it needs to be expressed in the form of some kind of Palestinian state. They feel that few people in the world have recognized the injustices they have suffered or been prepared to do anything to redress them. The Palestine Liberation Organization (PLO) has since 1964 been the strongest voice of the Palestinians in the outside world, representing a secular, non-religious response to the conflict, and has changed its position at several stages. *Hamas*, the Islamic Resistance Movement, and *Islamic Jihad* represent a strongly Islamic response to the Jewish state and are critical of both Israel and the PLO, totally rejecting the so-called 'Peace Process' since 1991 and 1993. Others of a more liberal and moderate persuasion have also been critical of the Peace Process, believing that it has involved a virtual surrender to Israel. In the crisis of 2000 and 2001 the Palestinian position was weakened by the divisions between these three different approaches (2.10 The different voices of the Palestinians).

PART 2

Interpreting
the Bible

How is the Bible used to explain the significance of what has been happening in
the land?

Chapter 3 is a study of the theme of the land through the Old Testament. If, as
Brueggeman says, the land is 'a central, if not *the central theme* of Biblical faith' (his
italics), how is this idea developed in the different stages of the Old Testament history? How in particular do the writers of the Old Testament understand the promise
of the land to Abraham and his descendants? And how do the prophets understand
the predictions about a return of Jewish exiles to the land?

Chapter 4 is a study of the theme of the land in the New Testament. How did
Jesus as a Jew living in the first century AD understand hopes about the land which
had developed among his people over many centuries? And how did the disciples
of Jesus and the writers of the New Testament think about the land? What difference,
if any, did the coming of Jesus make to their Jewish ideas about the land and the
purposes of God?

Chapter 5 explores other themes from the Old and New Testaments which may
shed light on some of the issues at the heart of the conflict over the land today. If
the Bible, taken as a whole, does not give any encouragement to believe that one
people has a divine right to a piece of land or that God is working out a pre-
arranged plan in the land, regardless of how people behave, does it have anything
else that can guide our thinking about resolving the conflict between Jews and
Arabs over the land?

Chapter 3

The Land *Before* Christ
'A Land Flowing with Milk and Honey'

The Lord said... 'I have come down to rescue them from the hand of the Egyptians and to bring them up out of that land into a good and spacious land, a land flowing with milk and honey.'
EXODUS 3:8

[The land]... a central, if not the central theme *of biblical faith.[1]*
WALTER BRUEGGEMANN

Land... is more than acreage or territory. It is a theological symbol, through which a series of messages are conveyed... But if land is more than acreage or territory and symbolic of promise, gift, blessing and lifestyle, it is nevertheless still soil and territory. It has theological aspects, but it is not thereby an ethereal thing, nor should it be spiritualized.[2]
E.A. MARTENS

The land, like the Torah, *was a temporary stage in the long purpose of the God of Abraham. It is as though... the land were a great advance metaphor for the design of God that his people should eventually bring the whole world into submission to his healing reign.[3]*
PETER WALKER

3.1 The promise of the land

Why was it that Abraham left his ancestral home in Ur of the Chaldees (near the town of Basra in southern Iraq) to settle in a foreign country? The book of Genesis gives us the answer:

The Lord had said to Abram, 'Leave your country, your people and your father's household and go to the land I will show you.

'I will make you into a great nation
  and I will bless you;
I will make your name great,
  and you will be a blessing.
I will bless those who bless you,
  and whoever curses you I will curse;
and all peoples on earth
  will be blessed through you.'
GENESIS 12:1–3

Soon after he entered the land, the promise concerning the land was made even more specific in these words that God addressed to Abraham:

To your descendants I give this land, from the river of Egypt to the great river, the Euphrates...
GENESIS 15:18

I am God Almighty; walk before me and be blameless. I will confirm my covenant between me and you... The whole land of Canaan, where you are now an alien, I will give as an everlasting possession to you and your descendants after you; and I will be their God.
GENESIS 17:1, 8

Abraham was then commanded to practise circumcision as the sign that he accepted the terms of this 'everlasting covenant':

As for you, you must keep my covenant, you and your descendants after you for the generations to come. This is my covenant with you and your descendants after you, the covenant you are to keep: Every male among you shall be circum-cised. You are to undergo circumcision, and it will be the sign of the covenant between me and you... My covenant in your flesh is to be an everlasting covenant.
GENESIS 17:9–11, 13

The covenant was therefore a kind of 'package deal', which included four basic promises – with no conditions attached:

- 'I will give you *the land* as an everlasting possession.'
- 'I will greatly increase your numbers... and I will make you into *a great nation*.'
- 'I will make an *everlasting covenant to be your God* and the God of your descendants.'
- 'I will bless those who bless you, and *all people on earth will be blessed through you*.'

These were incredible promises to make to an old man without children, who had just entered the land as a foreigner. The rest of the book of Genesis describes how

God began to fulfil his side of the covenant – and in particular the promises about the land and the nation.

The land

Abraham continued his semi-nomadic way of life in the hill-country of Palestine, moving his tents between Shechem, Bethel and Hebron. On one occasion he left the land because of famine, and went down to Egypt, no doubt assuming that God could no longer fulfil his promise to give him a permanent foothold in the land. But he soon found himself telling half-truths to protect his wife, and caused Pharaoh such embarrassment that he was sent back to where he had come from (Genesis 12:6–20).

Abraham did not actually own any piece of land until his wife Sarah died many years later. And it is strange that one whole chapter of Genesis is devoted to Abraham's negotiations for the purchase of the cave in Hebron where he buried his wife (Genesis 23). But these details begin to make sense when we see that this marked the very first stage of the fulfilment of God's promises. Abraham did not assume that God's promise about the land gave him the right to steal it from its current owners. And he was not interested in accepting the cave as a gift. He insisted on buying the land, paying its full value and making a legal contract in the presence of witnesses. Parts of the chapter even sound as if they are taken straight from a written contract:

So Ephron's field in Machpelah near Mamre – both the field and the cave in it, and all the trees within the borders of the field – was deeded to Abraham as his property in the presence of all the Hittites who had come to the gate of the city.
GENESIS 23:17–18

When Abraham's son, Isaac, was tempted to go to Egypt – once again because of famine – he was told by God to stay in the land, and given an assurance that the covenant promise extended also to him:

Do not go down to Egypt; live in the land where I tell you to live. Stay in this land for a while, and I will be with you and will bless you. For to you and your descendants I will give all these lands and will confirm the oath I swore to your father Abraham. I will make your descendants as numerous as the stars in the sky and will give them all these lands, and through your offspring all nations on earth will be blessed.
GENESIS 26:2–4

Similarly, when Isaac's son, Jacob, was leaving the country to find a wife among his relatives in Padan Aram, he received a vivid confirmation of the promises in his dream at Bethel:

I am the LORD, the God of your father Abraham and the God of Isaac. I will give you and your descendants the land on which you are lying. Your descendants will be like the dust of the earth, and you will spread out to the west and to the east, to the north and to the south. All peoples on earth will be blessed through you and your offspring. I

am with you and will watch over you wherever you go, and I will bring you back to this
land. I will not leave you until I have done what I have promised you.
GENESIS 28:13–15

God therefore assured Abraham's son and grandson that he fully intended to fulfil
his promise about the land.

The nation

For many years Abraham and Sarah must have wondered how this part of the promise could possibly be fulfilled, since they were getting on in years and still had no
children. Abraham soon came to the conclusion that, according to custom, his servant Eliezer would have to become his legal heir. But God had other plans:

Then the word of the LORD came to him: 'This man will not be your heir, but a son
coming from your own body will be your heir.' He took him outside and said,
'Look up at the heavens and count the stars – if indeed you can count them.' Then
he said to him, 'So shall your offspring be.'
   Abram believed the LORD, and he credited it to him as righteousness.
GENESIS 15:4–6

It was one thing, however, for Abraham to believe God's promise; it was very much
harder for him to wait patiently while Sarah grew older and older. Eventually they
felt they must take matters into their own hands. So following an accepted custom,
they planned for Abraham to have a child by Hagar, Sarah's Egyptian maid, in order
to continue the family line. But the arrival of Ishmael only created friction within
the family (Genesis 16:1–16).

   In the end, after receiving a further confirmation of the divine promise from three
mysterious visitors, Abraham and Sarah finally had a son of their own, whom they
called Isaac (Genesis 18:1–15; 21:1–7).

   If Abraham now felt more confident of God's ability to fulfil his promise, he must
have been thrown into utter confusion some years later when he was called by God
to offer his son Isaac as a sacrifice. It must have seemed as if God was mocking
Abraham. But this harrowing experience was intended as a test of Abraham's faith.
When he proved that he was willing to obey the divine call, he received a further
confirmation that the covenant would be fulfilled:

'I swear by myself, declares the LORD, that because you have done this and have not
withheld your son, your only son, I will surely bless you and make your descendants
as numerous as the stars in the sky and as the sand on the seashore. Your descen-
dants will take possession of the cities of their enemies, and through your offspring
all nations on earth will be blessed, because you have obeyed me.'
GENESIS 22:16–18

The 'title deeds' of the land

The terms of the original covenant promise given to Abraham seem to leave no
room for doubt about the divine right of the Jews to possess the land for all time: 'I

will give you the land as an everlasting possession.' But when we see the promise about the land in the context of the whole covenant, it becomes difficult, if not impossible, to separate it from the other three promises:

- 'I will make you into a great nation.'
- 'I will... be your God.'
- 'All people on earth will be blessed through you.'

We cannot have the promise about the land without everything else that goes with it – including the privilege and responsibility of belonging to a group of people who have a special relationship with God, and being part of his plan that will eventually bring blessing to all the peoples of the world.

3.2 The boundaries of the land

If Abraham and his descendants believed that God had promised this particular land to them, what area of land were they thinking about? How did the writers of the Old Testament describe the boundaries of this promised land?

Different writers describe it in different ways, and there does not appear to be any attempt to give one fixed description of the boundaries of the land. Sometimes it is simply described in terms of its earlier inhabitants, as 'the land of Canaan' (Genesis 12:5), or 'the land of the Kenites, Kenizzites, Kadmonites, Hittites, Perizzites, Rephaites, Amorites, Canaanites, Girgashites and Jebusites' (Genesis 15:19–21). In the first promise of the land to Abraham the boundaries of the land are given as 'from the river of Egypt to the great river, the Euphrates' (Genesis 15:18).

One statement of the land promise is particularly significant:

The LORD appeared to Isaac and said, 'Do not go down to Egypt; live in the land where I tell you to live. Stay in this land for a while, and I will be with you and will bless you. For to you and your descendants I will give all these lands and will confirm the oath I swore to your father Abraham. I will make your descendants as numerous as the stars in the sky and will give them all these lands, and through your offspring all nations on earth will be blessed.'
GENESIS 26:2–4

This restatement of the promise to Isaac, which speaks not just of 'the land' but of 'all these lands', leaves the promise very open. It also shows clearly that the writer believed the fulfilment of the promise concerning the land to be intimately bound up with the promise that Abraham would have many descendants and that through these many descendants God's blessing would eventually include 'all nations on earth'. The land is clearly part of a bigger plan in the mind of God.

In the books of Exodus, Deuteronomy and Joshua the land is described in several different ways:

... from the Red Sea to the Sea of the Philistines [the Mediterranean Sea], and from the desert to the River [the River Euphrates].
EXODUS 23:31

... from the desert to Lebanon, and from the Euphrates River to the western sea [the Mediterranean Sea].
DEUTERONOMY 11:24

... from Gilead to Dan, all of Naphtali, the territory of Ephraim and Manasseh, all the land of Judah as far as the western sea, the Negev and the whole region from the Valley of Jericho, the City of Palms, as far as Zoar.
DEUTERONOMY 34:1–3

... from the desert to Lebanon, and from the great river, the Euphrates – all the Hittite country – to the Great Sea on the west.
JOSHUA 1:4

The reign of King Solomon in the tenth century BC was a period of unparalleled peace. During this time the area of land occupied by the Israelites was probably more extensive than at any other period of their occupation of the land:

He (Solomon) ruled over all the kingdoms west of the River, from Tiphsah to Gaza, and had peace on all sides. During Solomon's lifetime Judah and Israel, from Dan to Beersheba, lived in safety, each man under his own vine and fig tree.
1 KINGS 4:24–25

He ruled over all the kings from the River to the land of the Philistines, as far as the border of Egypt.
2 CHRONICLES 9:26

One way of explaining the variety in these descriptions of the land is to say that they reflect the hand of different writers at different stages in the history of Israel. Another possible explanation is that the Israelites never controlled the whole area of Palestine, that they never had any idea of clearly defined borders. There always was considerable flexibility and fluidity in their understanding of the boundaries of the land. In the words of **Paul Williamson**:

Clearly, none of these descriptions ties down the geographical parameters suffi-ciently to reconstruct a map of the promised land... While it is reasonable to conclude that the promised land, strictly speaking, was the territory formerly occupied by the Canaanites, Amorites, Hittites, Perizzites, Hivites and Jebusites, the inclusion of additional groups in such lists, to give what are probably sym-bolic totals of seven and ten, may suggest that the ideal envisaged is less suscep-tible to rigid delineation than many have imagined. This would also account for the rather vague description of the promised land in terms of present occupation or ancestral promise. The territorial promise, in its most comprehensive sense, was not limited by geographical borders, therefore such borders were not mapped out with the rigidity and consistency which otherwise we might expect.[4]

The considerable variety in the descriptions of the boundaries of the land makes it hard to believe that anyone – whether Jew or Gentile – could use the Old Testament to define the area of land in which Jews returning to the land since the nineteenth century should have a right to live. When we see further how promises about the land are so closely related not just to the descendants of Abraham but also to 'all nations on earth', we are forced to see the land promises in the wider context of God's concern for the whole human race.

3.3 The conquest of the land

At the end of the book of Genesis we are left wondering how God is going to ful-fil the promise about the land. All the twelve sons of Jacob (i.e. Israel) have gone to settle in Egypt, partly because of yet another famine, and partly because one of the sons, Joseph, is virtually Prime Minister of Egypt. It looks as if they have left the land and gone to settle in Egypt for good (Genesis 50:22–26).

Earlier in the book, however, we are given a hint of how God will eventually bring the children of Israel back to the land. When God is reassuring Abraham about the covenant promise, he says:

Know for certain that your descendants will be strangers in a country not their own, and they will be enslaved and mistreated four hundred years. But I will pun-ish the nation they serve as slaves, and afterward they will come out with great pos-sessions… In the fourth generation your descendants will come back here, for the sin of the Amorites has not yet reached its full measure.
GENESIS 15:13–14, 16

The return to the land began with the dramatic exodus from slavery in Egypt under the leadership of Moses (described in the book of Exodus), and was completed through the conquest of the land under his successor, Joshua. This conquest, as described in the book of Joshua, began with the capture of Jericho in the Jordan Valley (Joshua 5:13 – 6:27). The first areas to be occupied were in the central and southern parts of the hill country (Joshua 8:1 – 10:45), and later campaigns in the north brought parts of Galilee under Israelite control (Joshua 11). A number of towns were completely destroyed, including Jericho, Ai and Hazor. There are many indications in the text, however, that the conquest of the land was never complete (e.g. Joshua 13:1–32; Judges 1:1–36), and that many of the original inhabitants con-tinued to live alongside the Israelites (e.g. Joshua 9:1–27).

Many Israeli Jews today probably have little difficulty in appreciating the biblical account of the conquest of the land. They can hardly fail to notice the similarities and the differences between the conquest of the land under Joshua and the settle-ment of Jews in the land since the 1880s. It is not surprising that Israeli politicians should describe the West Bank as 'Judea and Samaria' in order to make the con-nection with the Old Testament, or that the Israeli government has sometimes made the book of Joshua compulsory reading in schools.

But what if you happen to be an Arab Christian, and find that you are identified in the minds of Israeli Jews with the ancient Canaanites and all the other tribes which Joshua defeated in the thirteenth century BC? How are you likely to think about the book which seems to give the Jews a divine right to take away your land in the twentieth century AD?

And what can any reader in the twenty-first century make of the biblical account which says that God not only condoned the conquest and all that went with it, but actually *commanded* it? Is it conceivable that a God of love could actually have *ordered* the Israelites to engage in what we today would call 'ethnic cleansing'? For many today, including Christians, these are some of the hardest questions in the whole Bible.

One way of resolving the problem is to see these stories simply as a Jewish interpretation of their history. Since they believed that they were 'the chosen people' who enjoyed a special relationship with God, they wrote their history in such a way as to justify their ideas about their special status and their superiority over other people. The Old Testament should therefore be seen as a very ethnocentric interpretation of Israelite history.

Another approach is to admit the seriousness of the problem, and to wrestle with the text of the Bible to see if it contains any perspectives which might make it easier to accept all that is involved in the conquest of the land. Christians in particular who believe that the Bible is to be seen as *both* the words of human beings *and* the Word of God at the same time, will want to read this part of the Old Testament in the light of the New Testament.

This approach is likely to focus on four particular issues:

The reality of what happened

Only a few cities were completely destroyed. We therefore need to be careful not to exaggerate the extent of the destruction. An archaeologist, **Alan Millard**, makes the point in the following way:

The Bible's accounts of Israel's entry into Canaan record the actual destruction of only a few cities. Throughout, they emphasize that Israel drove out the former inhabitants and took over (inherited) their property. A desolate land with its towns in ruins would be of little benefit to the Israelites, just emerging from 40 years of semi-nomad life. What had to be destroyed were the pagan shrines of the Canaanites with their cultic paraphernalia.

Jericho was a special case. The city was an offering to God, a 'firstfruit' of the conquest. Ai and Hazor were also sacked. But again they were exceptional cases, perhaps as focal points of opposition.[5]

The problem of judging past actions by the moral standards of today

It is always easy to apply the moral standards of today to the past – but sometimes dangerous and often unhelpful. The concept of human rights, for example, that has developed in the last fifty years may seem to us today to be very obvious and almost self-evident. We naturally feel that it represents a huge step forward for the human race. But this progress is very recent, and has not taken place without a struggle. It was largely because of the religious wars in Europe during the eighteenth century and the excesses of Nazism, Fascism and Communism in the twentieth century that the idea of the rights of individuals over the rights of the state came to be widely accepted.

From the vantage point of our present century, it is inevitable that we are shocked, if not disgusted, at so much in history, and may feel some moral superiority in passing judgments of this kind. But instead of judging everything in the past by the standards of today, we need to try to appreciate the ethical values by which individuals and societies have functioned in the past – however unenlightened they may seem by our standards.

The Romans, the Goths, the Vandals, the Crusaders, the Mongols and slave traders, to name but a few, have caused unspeakable suffering and misery to millions. Now, after many centuries in which ethnic cleansing was accepted as a fact of life, we have reached the stage where international law does not allow one people to take over the territory of another by force. But if we today have been sensitized to the horrors of ethnic cleansing, it is partly because the painful developments of the twentieth century enabled us – if not forced us – to reach this stage, and partly because we can read about what happens in places like Bosnia in our newspapers and watch it on television only hours after it has happened, and later see those responsible for these atrocities being tried and declared guilty by an international court.

No doubt we would all want to say that by the standards of today many of the actions of Joshua and the Children of Israel in the conquest of the land were evil and should never be held up as an example for people to follow today. But if moral development in the human race has taken place gradually, it does not help us to be standing in judgment over people in the past. If generations to come are sensitized to other moral issues to which we today are comparatively blind, they may be as horrified with certain things that happen today as we are with many actions in the past.

Although this argument does not begin to address the problem of how a God of holiness and justice could ever be thought of as condoning, if not commanding, something that we consider to be evil, it should at least encourage a certain humility in the way we think about the past.

Other Old Testament perspectives

Even if the Old Testament writers do not seem to have been quite as sensitive to the problem as we are (or think we are) today, they do offer some substantial reasons to explain why the land had to be taken by the children of Israel in this way. These reasons are contained in five important themes which are repeated in many different forms:

THE LAND IS A GIFT FROM GOD

The land is described with almost monotonous regularity as 'the land which the Lord your God is giving you' or 'the land the Lord your God is giving you as an inheritance' or 'the land which the Lord your God has given you'.

These expressions are repeated so often that it is easy to miss the point. The land did not belong to the Israelites and their ancestors since the beginning of time. They could not claim that they had owned it from time immemorial. It came to them at this particular time as a gift from God. They had done nothing to deserve it, and they had not acquired it through their own cleverness or skill in war. God had said very clearly and simply:

The land is mine and you are but aliens and my tenants.
LEVITICUS 25:23

Since this is how the land came to them, it must always be seen as something given by God – an undeserved, unsolicited gift. It is a sign of the incredible generosity of God.

GOD HAS GIVEN THE LAND TO FULFIL HIS PROMISE TO ABRAHAM
In giving the land to the children of Israel under Joshua, God is simply fulfilling the promise he made centuries before to Abraham. He therefore encourages the people to enter the land in the following words:

See, I have given you this land. Go in and take possession of the land that the LORD *swore he would give to your fathers – to Abraham, Isaac and Jacob – and to their descendants after them.*
DEUTERONOMY 1:8

This means that the conquest of the land should not be seen as an end in itself. It is merely one stage in the unfolding of God's plan for history, which is to lead to blessing for *all* the nations of the earth.

THE CONQUEST OF THE LAND WAS GOD'S WAY OF JUDGING ITS
INHABITANTS
The earlier promise given to Abraham indicates that the other tribes occupying the land at that time had already come under the judgment of God, but that the judgment was being postponed until a future date. Speaking to Abraham, God says:

In the fourth generation your descendants will come back here, for the sin of the Amorites has not yet reached its full measure.
GENESIS 15:16

Many passages in the Old Testament law describe the social customs and religious practices of the inhabitants of the land as 'abominations' or 'detestable things'; and archaeologists have confirmed this picture of a corrupt society and a degraded religion. The people are urged not to follow these detestable practices, since it was because of them that the previous inhabitants had been turned out of the land:

Do not defile yourselves in any of these ways, because this is how the nations that I am going to drive out before you became defiled. Even the land was defiled; so I punished it for its sin, and the land vomited out its inhabitants... The native-born and the aliens living among you must not do any of these detestable things, for all these things were done by the people who lived in the land before you, and the land became defiled.
LEVITICUS 18:24–27

GOD WILL BE JUST AS SEVERE IN HIS JUDGMENT ON THE ISRAELITES AS HE HAS BEEN ON THE CANAANITES

If we are inclined to think that God showed special favouritism in his dealings with the children of Israel, we should notice that God warned his people that if they were disobedient, he would judge them just as severely and in exactly the same way as he judged those other nations before them:

And if you defile the land, it will vomit you out as it vomited out the nations that were before you.
LEVITICUS 18:28 (COMPARE LEVITICUS 26:1–45; DEUTERONOMY 13:1–18; 18:9–22; 27:15–26; 28:1–68)

If God used the children of Israel as his instrument of judgment on the inhabitants of the land, the time would come when they would experience the same kind of judgment if they disobeyed the covenant.

AN APPEAL TO OBEY GOD'S LAW

The gift of the land and God's judgment on its previous inhabitants are closely linked with an appeal to obey God's law. While God commands the people to destroy all vestiges of Canaanite religion, he is at the same time urging them to obey the new law revealed through Moses. If they are to follow this new way, they must make a clean break with the religious practices of their neighbours:

Keep my requirements and do not follow any of the detestable customs that were practised before you came and do not defile yourselves with them. I am the LORD your God... Be holy because I, the LORD your God, am holy.
LEVITICUS 18:30; 19:2

When you enter the land the LORD your God is giving you, do not learn to imitate the detestable ways of the nations there. Let no one be found among you who sacrifices his son or daughter in the fire, who practices divination or sorcery, interprets omens, engages in witchcraft, or casts spells, or who is a medium or spiritist or who consults the dead. Anyone who does these things is detestable to the LORD, and because of these detestable practices the LORD your God will drive out those nations before you. You must be blameless before the LORD your God.
   The nations you will dispossess listen to those who practise sorcery or divination. But as for you, the LORD your God has not permitted you to do so. The LORD your God will raise up for you a prophet like me from among your own brothers. You must listen to him.
DEUTERONOMY 18:9–15 (COMPARE 20:18)

All these five themes – the land as a gift, the land and the covenant, judgment (both on the Canaanites and on Israel) and obedience – are brought together in Moses' exhortations to the people before they enter the Promised Land:

If you ever forget the LORD your God and follow other gods and worship and bow down to them, I testify against you today that you will surely be destroyed. Like the nations the LORD destroyed before you, so you will be destroyed for not obeying the LORD your God. Hear, O Israel...

After the LORD your God has driven them out before you, do not say to yourself, 'The LORD has brought me here to take possession of this land because of my righteousness.' No, it is on account of the wickedness of these nations that the LORD is going to drive them out before you. It is not because of your righteousness or your integrity that you are going in to take possession of their land; but on account of the wickedness of these nations, the LORD your God will drive them out before you, to accomplish what he swore to your fathers, to Abraham, Isaac and Jacob. Understand, then, that it is not because of your righteousness that the LORD your God is giving you this good land to possess, for you are a stiff-necked people.
DEUTERONOMY 8:19; 9:1, 4–6

The New Testament perspective of progressive revelation

The writers of the New Testament clearly believed that God has been revealing himself gradually to the Israelites over a period of many centuries, and that the climax of God's revelation had come in the person of Jesus. This is how the writer to the Hebrews understood this process of gradual and progressive revelation:

In the past God spoke to our forefathers through the prophets at many times and in various ways, but in these last days he has spoken to us by his Son...
HEBREWS 1:1–2

According to this understanding of revelation, we would have to say that God was obliged, as it were, to limit himself in the process of revelation. The truth that he wanted to reveal had to be adapted and accommodated to what people could understand at any given time in history. The idea of God as trinity, for example, could only be understood by people who had come to believe that there is only *one* God. It could never have been developed in a polytheistic context in which people believed in many different gods and goddesses, because it would have been totally misunderstood. The full Christian understanding of the love of God as it has been expressed in the life, death and resurrection of Jesus would never have been understood at the time of Abraham, Moses, Joshua or David. It took many centuries to prepare the Children of Israel for the fuller revelation that was to come in the person of Jesus.

Anyone, therefore, who sees Christ as the fullest possible revelation of what God is like and of the kind of moral standards that God sets for human beings, will see many of the actions of Joshua as very wrong and abhorrent. But if, as the biblical account suggests, God was involved in the conquest of the land under Joshua, it was because he had to work within a particular cultural and religious context, revealing gradually as much new truth as people were able to grasp. Given the level of culture and religion at the time, God's revelation of a new way had to be gradual. He had to work *within* a culture that practised ethnic cleansing as something that was acceptable, in order ultimately to change the culture from within by exposing this evil in its true light and showing the human race a better way.

Since the name 'Jesus' in Hebrew is basically the same name as 'Joshua', the New Testament writers clearly thought of Jesus as a new Joshua – but a Joshua who achieved something very different and infinitely greater than the earlier Joshua had achieved. This Joshua did not lead the Children of Israel out of the wilderness and into the Promised Land, but led everyone who follows him – from whatever race – into the kingdom of God. As we shall see later (see 4.5 The land in the teaching of the apostles), there are good reasons for believing that the book of Acts was intended to correspond in certain ways to the book of Joshua, showing this time not the conquest of the land of Palestine, but the spread of the message about Christ all over the Mediterranean world (see especially Acts 1:8).

So those who see Jesus as the climax of God's revelation to the human race can never imagine him acting in the way that Joshua did. It is inconceivable that Jesus would have taken up weapons to attack the Romans in the way that Joshua attacked the Canaanites. Christians who live *after* Jesus can never, as it were, put the clock back and regress to a way of thinking that prevailed *before* the time of Jesus. The life of Jesus becomes a kind of filter through which they interpret everything in the Old Testament. Or, to change the metaphor, Jesus becomes the lens through which everything in the Old Testament is seen and interpreted. Christians should never, therefore, get used to the cruelty in the story of the conquest and read it without any difficulty, and should probably be far more careful about how they tell the story to children. If at any stage they wonder whether God could have done things differently and whether this really was the only way for God to get the message through to humankind, they may realize that it is a dangerous business for us to 'play God' and start imagining how he could (and should) have done things differently.

In coming to terms with the biblical account of the conquest, therefore, we may at the end of the day be left with a choice: *either* we solve the problem in the story of the conquest by reading it as a purely human and distorted interpretation of history and not in any sense as inspired scripture; *or* we try to take seriously *everything* that the Bible (both Old and New Testaments) says about the conquest. Seen in this light, the conquest of the land becomes one stage in the unfolding of God's plan for history – a shameful but vital stage, one that was not to be repeated, and need never be repeated.

3.4 The land and the temple

Since the land was seen as the place where God was revealing himself more fully through his dealings with the Israelites, Jerusalem came to be seen as a central place in the whole land which had special significance in the relationship between God and his people. And within the city of Jerusalem, the temple that was built by Solomon in the tenth century was seen as the place in which God's purpose was brought into sharper focus. This building expressed the idea that God wanted in some way to live among his people. In the words of **N.T. Wright**,

The symbolism of the temple was designed to express the belief that it formed the centre not only of the physical world but also of the entire cosmos, so that, in being YHWH's dwelling place, it was the spot where heaven and earth met.[6]

In the period of the wandering in the wilderness, the tabernacle or tent in which the Israelites worshipped was called 'the house of Yahweh', 'the dwelling place of Yahweh'. Thus in the instructions about the building of the tabernacle, Moses was told by God:

Have them make a sanctuary for me, and I will dwell among them.
EXODUS 25:8

So I will consecrate the Tent of Meeting and the altar and will consecrate Aaron and his sons to serve me as priests. Then I will dwell among the Israelites and be their God. They will know that I am the LORD their God, who brought them out of Egypt so that I might dwell among them. I am the LORD their God.
EXODUS 29:44–46

Later we are told that when the tabernacle had been built,

The cloud covered the Tent of Meeting, and the glory of the LORD filled the tabernacle. Moses could not enter the Tent of Meeting because the cloud had settled upon it, and the glory of the LORD filled the tabernacle.
EXODUS 40:34–35

These same ideas about God's presence among his people were taken up by Solomon in his prayer at the dedication of the temple:

The LORD has said that he would dwell in a dark cloud; I have indeed built a magnificent temple for you, a place for you to dwell forever... But will God really dwell on earth? The heavens, even the highest heaven, cannot contain you. How much less this temple I have built! Yet give attention to your servant's prayer and his plea for mercy, O LORD my God. Hear the cry and the prayer that your servant is praying in your presence this day. May your eyes be open toward this temple night and day, this place of which you said, 'My Name shall be there,' so that you will hear the prayer your servant prays toward this place.
1 KINGS 8:12–13, 27–30

Solomon ended his prayer with the hope that what happens in the temple would somehow have implications for every human being:

... so that all the peoples of the earth may know that the LORD is God and that there is no other.
1 KINGS 8:60

In the pages of the Old Testament, therefore, clear connections develop between the *land*, the *city* of Jerusalem and the *temple*. The significance of the land as a whole comes to be focussed in a special way on the city of Jerusalem; and at the heart of the city is the temple. Peter Walker describes the relationship as being 'like concentric circles',[7] and quotes R. Kreider: 'already in the Hebrew Bible as well as in Judaism, Jerusalem had come to symbolize all that the Land stood for', and 'just as Jerusalem became the symbol of the Land, so the temple became the symbol of the City'.[8] And in the words of W.D. Davies, 'Just as Jerusalem became the quintessence of the land, so the temple became the quintessence of Jerusalem.'[9]

3.5 Exile from the land

If the land was a gift which carried with it an obligation to obey the law of God, it followed naturally that when this obligation was not honoured, the gift could be taken away. The children of Israel were not to assume that they could live in the land for ever regardless of the way they lived. It was perfectly possible for them to forfeit the right to live in the land.

This sanction was made very clear by Moses in his explanation of the Law before the children of Israel entered the land:

After you have had children and grandchildren and have lived in the land a long time – if you then become corrupt and make any kind of idol, doing evil in the eyes of the LORD your God and provoking him to anger, I call heaven and earth as witnesses against you this day that you will quickly perish from the land that you are crossing the Jordan to possess… The LORD will scatter you among the peoples, and only a few of you will survive among the nations to which the LORD will drive you.
DEUTERONOMY 4:25–27

Similarly, if the temple was a sign of God living among his people, this sign could be removed if the people failed to honour the covenant. This was the warning that was given at the dedication of Solomon's temple.

If you or your sons turn away from me and do not observe the commands and decrees I have given you and go off to serve other gods and worship them, then I will cut off Israel from the land I have given them and will reject this temple I have consecrated for my Name.
1 KINGS 9:6–7

The exile of Israel

The subsequent history of the nation proved that these warnings were no idle threats. This was the fate of the northern kingdom of Israel when its capital Samaria was captured in 721 BC:

The king of Assyria invaded the entire land, marched against Samaria and laid siege to it for three years. In the ninth year of Hoshea, the king of Assyria captured Samaria and deported the Israelites to Assyria. He settled them in Halah, in Gozan on the Habor River and in the towns of the Medes. All this took place because the Israelites had sinned

against the LORD their God, who had brought them up out of Egypt from under the
power of Pharaoh king of Egypt. They worshiped other gods and followed the practices
of the nations the Lord had driven out before them, as well as the practices that the
kings of Israel had introduced... So the LORD was very angry with Israel and removed
them from his presence.
2 KINGS 17:5–8, 18

The exile of Judah

One hundred years later, when the Babylonian army was threatening the southern
kingdom of Judah, the prophet Jeremiah tried to warn the people of the disaster
which was approaching:

The LORD said, 'It is because they have forsaken my law, which I set before them;
they have not obeyed me or followed my law. Instead, they have followed the stub-
bornness of their hearts; they have followed the Baals, as their fathers taught them.'
Therefore, this is what the LORD Almighty, the God of Israel, says: 'See, I will make
this people eat bitter food and drink poisoned water. I will scatter them among
nations that neither they nor their fathers have known, and I will pursue them with
the sword until I have destroyed them.'
JEREMIAH 9:13–16

The same prophet, speaking on behalf of God, warns that the coming judgment on
the *people* (here described as 'my house', and 'my inheritance') will also involve
judgment on the *land*:

I will forsake my house,
  abandon my inheritance;
I will give the one I love
  into the hands of her enemies.
My inheritance has become to me
  like a lion in the forest.
She roars at me;
  therefore I hate her.
Has not my inheritance become to me
  like a speckled bird of prey
  that other birds of prey surround and attack?
Go and gather all the wild beasts;
  bring them to devour.
Many shepherds will ruin my vineyard
  and trample down my field;
they will turn my pleasant field
  into a desolate wasteland.
It will be made a wasteland,
  parched and desolate before me;
the whole land will be laid waste
  because there is no one who cares.
JEREMIAH 12:7–11

This message of doom began to be fulfilled in 597 BC, when Nebuchadnezzar of Babylon captured Jerusalem, despoiled the temple and deported the cream of the population:

Nebuchadnezzar removed all the treasures from the temple of the LORD and from the royal palace, and took away all the gold articles that Solomon king of Israel had made for the temple of the LORD. He carried into exile all Jerusalem: all the officers and fighting men, and all the craftsmen and artisans – a total of ten thousand. Only the poorest people of the land were left… It was because of the LORD's anger that all this happened to Jerusalem and Judah, and in the end he thrust them from his presence.
2 KINGS 24:13–14; 20

The king's uncle, Zedekiah, was installed by the Babylonians as a puppet king; but when he tried to lead an insurrection some years later (586 BC), Jerusalem was largely destroyed, and the land was depopulated even further:

On the seventh day of the fifth month, in the nineteenth year of Nebuchadnezzar king of Babylon, Nebuzaradan commander of the imperial guard, an official of the king of Babylon, came to Jerusalem. He set fire to the temple of the Lord, the royal palace and all the houses of Jerusalem. Every important building he burned down. The whole Babylonian army, under the commander of the imperial guard, broke down the walls around Jerusalem. Nebuzaradan the commander of the guard carried into exile the people who remained in the city, along with the rest of the populace and those who had gone over to the king of Babylon. But the commander left behind some of the poorest people of the land to work the vineyards and fields… So Judah went into captivity, away from her land.
2 KINGS 25:8–12, 21

Israel had already gone into captivity away from her land 135 years before – and never returned. Now it was Judah's turn to go into exile.

The exile and the covenant
It may be hard for us today to appreciate what a catastrophe the exile was to the people of Judah. All their leaders were banished from the land. The king was deported and stripped of all his powers. The temple was in ruins and the priests were no longer able to offer the sacrifices. It must have seemed as if God had broken every promise he had ever made to Abraham and to David.

We can feel something of the despair and bitterness of the people in exile in a foreign land in this well-known psalm:

By the rivers of Babylon we sat and wept
 when we remembered Zion.
There on the poplars
 we hung our harps,
for there our captors asked us for songs,

our tormentors demanded songs of joy;
they said, 'Sing us one of the songs of Zion!'
How can we sing the songs of the Lord
   while in a foreign land?
PSALM 137:1–4

During the exile the people had plenty of time to look again at their scriptures to
find out why they had gotten themselves into this situation. Those who understood
the Law and the prophets must have realized that God had not broken his covenant
with his people. He was simply applying the sanctions which had been written into
the covenant long ago. While the promise and gift of the land were *unconditional,*
their continued possession of the land was *conditional* and depended on their loyalty and obedience to the God who had given it to them.

3.6 The return to the land
One reason why the Jews survived the exile was that their Babylonian captors kept
them together as a community instead of scattering them in different places as the
Assyrians had done with the Israelites. Another reason was that their prophets were
able to interpret all that had happened and give them hope for the future.

   This hope would have been based partly on promises in the Mosaic law that if
the people returned to God in genuine repentance, he would restore them to their
land:

When all these blessings and curses I have set before you come upon you and you
take them to heart wherever the Lord *your God disperses you among the nations,*
and when you and your children return to the Lord *your God and obey him with*
all your heart and with all your soul… then the Lord *your God will restore your*
fortunes and have compassion on you and gather you again from all the nations
where he scattered you. Even if you have been banished to the most distant land
under the heavens, from there the Lord *your God will gather you and bring you*
back. He will bring you to the land that belonged to your fathers, and you will take
possession of it.
DEUTERONOMY 30:1–5

How then did the prophets build on this promise? What kind of hopes did they hold
out to the Jewish exiles? These are examples of the hopes held out by different
prophets of a return to the land and a restoration of the people.

Isaiah
The prophecies in the first part of Isaiah (chapters 1–39) were delivered more than
100 years before the exile and spoke of the great judgment to come and the restoration which would follow. Whether the rest of the book (chapters 40–66) was written
by the same writer or by a later writer during the exile, it speaks even more clearly
of the deliverance of the people after submitting to God's judgment:

Comfort, comfort my people, says your God.
Speak tenderly to Jerusalem,

*and proclaim to her
that her hard service has been completed,
   that her sin has been paid for,
that she has received from the LORD's hand
   double for all her sins.*

*A voice of one calling:
   'In the desert prepare
   the way for the LORD;
make straight in the wilderness
   a highway for our God.
Every valley shall be raised up,
   every mountain and hill made low;
the rough ground shall become level,
   the rugged places a plain.
And the glory of the LORD will be revealed,
   and all mankind together will see it.
      For the mouth of the LORD has spoken.*

*You who bring good tidings to Zion,
   go up on a high mountain.
You who bring good tidings to Jerusalem,
   lift up your voice with a shout,
lift it up, do not be afraid;
   say to the towns of Judah,
   'Here is your God!'
See, the Sovereign LORD comes with power,
   and his arm rules for him.*
ISAIAH 40:1–5, 9–10

Jeremiah

Unlike Isaiah, who had spoken about events which to him were in the distant future, Jeremiah lived through the Babylonian invasion in 597 BC and the destruction of Jerusalem in 586 BC, and remained with those who were left behind in Jerusalem. He prophesied that the exile would last for a limited period:

*This is what the LORD says: 'When seventy years are completed for Babylon, I will come to you and fulfill my gracious promise to bring you back to this place...
Then you will call upon me and come and pray to me, and I will listen to you. You will seek me and find me when you seek me with all your heart. I will be found by you,' declares the LORD 'and will bring you back from captivity. I will gather you from all the nations and places where I have banished you,' declares the LORD, 'and will bring you back to the place from which I carried you into exile.'*
JEREMIAH 29:10–14 (COMPARE 16:14–15)

Ezekiel

Ezekiel must have been in his mid-twenties when he witnessed the surrender of Jerusalem to the Babylonian army and was taken into exile in Babylon. His first prophecies were about the glory of God and the inevitability of judgment on the sinful people of Judah. Then sometime after hearing of the final destruction of Jerusalem in 586 BC, he began to look forward to the restoration of the nation to the land.

The word of the LORD came to me...

Therefore say: 'This is what the Sovereign LORD says: Although I sent them far away among the nations and scattered them among the countries, yet for a little while I have been a sanctuary for them in the countries where they have gone.'

Therefore say: 'This is what the Sovereign LORD says: I will gather you from the nations and bring you back from the countries where you have been scattered and I will give you back the land of Israel again.' They will return to it and remove all its vile images and detestable idols.
EZEKIEL 11:14, 16–18

The fulfilment of these prophecies

When King Cyrus of Persia captured Babylon in 539 BC, his policy was to repatriate the different groups of exiles in the country. The edict allowing the Jews to return to Jerusalem is recorded in 2 Chronicles and Ezra, and it is significant that they speak of this return as a fulfilment of the prophecies of Jeremiah:

In the first year of Cyrus king of Persia, in order to fulfill the word of the LORD spoken by Jeremiah, the LORD moved the heart of Cyrus king of Persia to make a proclamation throughout his realm and to put it in writing: 'This is what Cyrus king of Persia says: "The LORD, the God of heaven, has given me all the kingdoms of the earth and he has appointed me to build a temple for him at Jerusalem in Judah. Anyone of his people among you – may the LORD his God be with him, and let him go up."'
2 CHRONICLES 36:22–23; EZRA 1:1–3

The exiles who returned to Judah and Jerusalem settled in the places which their parents and grandparents had left when they were taken into exile. Ezra gives a list of all those who returned at this time 'each to his own town':

Now these are the people of the province who came up from the captivity of the exiles, whom Nebuchadnezzar king of Babylon had taken captive to Babylon (they returned to Jerusalem and Judah, each to his own town...)
EZRA 2:1 (COMPARE 1 CHRONICLES 9:2)

At every stage this was a peaceful return. There is no suggestion either in the prophecies or in the historical accounts that there was any fighting involved in the resettling of the exiles in their own land. This is the idyllic picture of the return painted by Isaiah:

Only the redeemed will walk there,
  and the ransomed of the LORD will return.
They will enter Zion with singing;
  everlasting joy will crown their heads.
Gladness and joy will overtake them,
  and sorrow and sighing will flee away.
ISAIAH 35:9–10

Anything less like the conquest under Joshua is hard to imagine!

Popular ideas about the land

As Judaism developed in the centuries after the exile, the Jews came to believe that there was an inseparable connection between the people of Israel and the land. Since the land had been given to them by God as an everlasting possession, it was *here* that he wanted them to live, and it was *here* that they had the ideal opportunity to live in total obedience to the law of God. It was as if there were a kind of 'umbilical cord' between Israel and the land.

This is why they always expressed a strong desire to possess soil in the land, and, if they lived away from the land, to make pilgrimage to it, and if possible to die in the land. It also explains why they always considered it vital that the land should be under their own control. The greatest threat to their existence as a nation living under the law of God came from having to live under an alien, occupying power. W.D. Davies has summed up their attitude: 'They could only dwell securely in the promised land when it was not occupied territory.'[10]

Another development during this period was that the Jews began to see even more clearly the special significance of the city of Jerusalem and the temple. This was because they summed up for them the meaning of the land.

When they became discouraged and depressed about their situation as a nation in the land, some started to dream dreams and to hope that God would one day intervene in an obviously supernatural way to vindicate his people. This led to the development of a new kind of writing called 'Apocalyptic', which generally described visions and dreams using many strange symbols. These writers tried to explain why the powers of evil were frustrating the fulfilment of God's promises, and looked forward to the time when God would establish his kingdom in the land for all the world to see. This kind of writing was particularly popular between 200 BC and AD 100, when the Jews were under the power of the Seleucids and the Romans.

The scholars' interpretation of the land

Some Jewish writers continued to interpret everything the Old Testament said about the land in a very *literal* way; but at the same time they developed a *spiritual* interpretation of the land.

For example, **Philo**, the Jewish philosopher-theologian who died in Alexandria in AD 50, held firmly to traditional Jewish hopes for the land, but also gave a symbolic interpretation to passages in the Old Testament about the land. Thus in a discussion of Genesis 15:7–8, he begins with the literal meaning of the promised land, and then goes on to interpret the land as a symbol of 'fruitful wisdom':

What is the meaning of the words, 'I am the Lord God who led thee out of the land of the Chaldeans to give thee this land to inherit?' The literal meaning is clear. That which must be rendered as the deeper meaning is as follows. The 'land of the Chaldeans' is symbolically mathematical theory, of which astronomy is a part. And in this (field) the Chaldeans labour not unsuccessfully or slothfully. Thus He honours the wise man with two gifts. For one thing He takes away from Chaldean doctrine, which in addition to being difficult to seize and grasp, is the cause of great evils and impiety in attributing to that which is created the powers of the Creator, and persuades men to honour and worship the works of the world instead of the Creator of the world. And again, He grants him fruitful wisdom which he symbolically calls 'land'... [11]

Their own yet not their own

The Jews after the exile were therefore no more than a small remnant of the southern kingdom of Judah, and an even smaller remnant of the twelve tribes which had occupied the land under Joshua. They had a limited amount of territory around Jerusalem which was only a fraction of the land ruled by David and Solomon. They had no king; and although at times they had some degree of independence, they lived constantly under the shadow of foreign powers. They could take comfort from the fact that they were in the land; but they could hardly ever feel that they were masters in their own land.

3.7 The land and the hopes of Israel

Was this the glorious future that the prophets had spoken of? Was this all that God had in store for his people – that they should live in a small section of their own land and under the control of foreigners? God had fulfilled his promise about the return to the land. But what about all the other things that went with it – like the spiritual renewal of the nation?

Could it be that the promise of a return was to be fulfilled *again* – but this time not in another return of exiles to the land, but rather as part of the fulfilment of *all* the promises contained within the Abrahamic covenant and *all* the hopes of Israel? Our task now is to go back to the prophets and see how the theme of the land is woven into everything else that they said about the future. These are examples of how four of the prophets understood the glorious future that was to unfold.

Isaiah

Isaiah's description of the restoration of the people speaks of much more than a mere return to the land:

The desert and the parched land will be glad;
  the wilderness will rejoice and blossom...
Strengthen the feeble hands,
  steady the knees that give way;

say to those with fearful hearts,
  'Be strong, do not fear;
your God will come,
  he will come with vengeance;
with divine retribution
  he will come to save you.'
Then will the eyes of the blind be opened
  and the ears of the deaf unstopped.
Then will the lame leap like a deer,
  and the mute tongue shout for joy.
Water will gush forth in the wilderness
  and streams in the desert...
And a highway will be there;
  it will be called the Way of Holiness.
The unclean will not journey on it;
  it will be for those who walk in that Way;
  wicked fools will not go about on it.
ISAIAH 35:1, 3–6, 8

Jeremiah

Jeremiah links the return to the land with several other important prophetic themes – a promise of national security, the knowledge of God, repentance, and the covenant relationship between God and his people:

This is what the LORD, the God of Israel, says: 'Like these good figs, I regard as good the exiles from Judah, whom I sent away from this place to the land of the Babylonians. My eyes will watch over them for their good, and I will bring them back to this land. I will build them up and not tear them down; I will plant them and not uproot them. I will give them a heart to know me, that I am the LORD. They will be my people, and I will be their God, for they will return to me with all their heart.'
JEREMIAH 24:5–7

Ezekiel

Chapters 36 and 37 are a favourite hunting ground for students of prophecy. Here we find that the prophecy of a return to the land is just one of many different themes concerning what God is going to do for his people:

■ 'I will gather you from all the countries and bring you back into your own land' (36:24; 37:12, 14, 21).
■ 'I will sprinkle clean water on you, and... I will cleanse you from all your impurities' (36:25, 29, 33; 37:23).
■ 'I will give you a new heart and put a new spirit in you; I will . . . give you a heart of flesh' (36:26).
■ 'I will put my Spirit in you and move you to follow my decrees and be careful to keep my laws' (36:27; 37:14, 24).

- 'You will live in the land I gave your forefathers' (36:28; 37:25).
- 'You will be my people, and I will be your God' (36:28; 37:23, 27).
- 'I will call for the grain and make it plentiful… the desolate land will be cultivated' (36:29, 34).
- 'Then the nations… will know that I the LORD have rebuilt what was destroyed' (36:36; 37:28).
- 'I will make their people [the house of Israel] as numerous as sheep' (36:37; 37:26).
- 'Then you, my people, will know that I am the LORD' (37:13–14; 36:38).
- 'I will make them one nation in the land' (37:22).
- 'There will be one king over all of them… My servant David will be king over them… forever' (37:22, 24, 25).
- 'They will all have one shepherd' (37:24).
- 'I will make a covenant of peace with them… an everlasting covenant' (37:26).
- 'I will put my sanctuary among them forever. My dwelling place will be with them' (37:26, 27).

The remaining chapters of the book (38–48) are also important because they have much to say about Jerusalem and the land, and because many of these themes are taken up and developed in the New Testament.

Chapters 38 and 39 consist of prophecies against Gog, a nation in the far north, which we are told will one day join with many other nations to attack the land of Israel. Chapters 40 to 48 consist of a series of visions, which are introduced in the following words:

In the twenty-fifth year of our exile, at the beginning of the year, on the tenth of the month, in the fourteenth year after the fall of the city – on that very day the hand of the LORD was upon me and he took me there. In visions of God he took me to the land of Israel and set me on a very high mountain, on whose south side were some buildings that looked like a city.
EZEKIEL 40:1–2

In his vision Ezekiel sees a plan of the whole temple area and describes the temple ritual. At one stage he sees the glory of God filling the temple (43:1–9), and later sees a river flowing from the temple down to the Dead Sea (47:1–12). We are then given the boundaries of the land (47:13–23):

These are the boundaries by which you are to divide the land for an inheritance among the twelve tribes of Israel, with two portions for Joseph. You are to divide it equally among them. Because I swore with uplifted hand to give it to your forefathers, this land will become your inheritance.
EZEKIEL 47:13–14

The final chapter explains how the land is to be divided between the tribes. These boundaries should be understood as 'stylized rather than geographically feasible':[12]

*'This is the land you are to allot as an inheritance to the tribes of Israel, and these
will be their portions,' declares the Sovereign LORD.*
EZEKIEL 48:29

After some details about the exits of the city of Jerusalem (48:30–35) the book ends
with the words:

And the name of the city from that time on will be: THE LORD IS THERE.
EZEKIEL 48:35

Zechariah
Zechariah lived in the period immediately following the return from exile, and his
prophecies date from around 520 to 518 BC. He looks forward to yet another return
of exiles 'from the countries of the east and the west':

*Again the word of the LORD Almighty came to me. This is what the LORD Almighty
says: 'I am very jealous for Zion; I am burning with jealousy for her.'*
   *This is what the LORD says: 'I will return to Zion and dwell in Jerusalem. Then
Jerusalem will be called the City of Truth, and the mountain of the LORD Almighty
will be called The Holy Mountain.'*
   *This is what the LORD Almighty says: 'Once again men and women of ripe old
age will sit in the streets of Jerusalem, each with cane in hand because of his age.
The city streets will be filled with boys and girls playing there.'*
   *This is what the LORD Almighty says: 'It may seem marvelous to the remnant of
this people at that time, but will it seem marvelous to me?' declares the LORD
Almighty.*
   *This is what the LORD Almighty says: 'I will save my people from the countries of
the east and the west. I will bring them back to live in Jerusalem; they will be my
people, and I will be faithful and righteous to them as their God.'*
ZECHARIAH 8:1–8

Another passage speaks of the return of exiles of the northern kingdom of Israel
(referred to here as 'the house of Joseph' and 'the Ephraimites') and exiles of the
southern kingdom of Judah:

*I will strengthen the house of Judah
  and save the house of Joseph.
I will restore them
  because I have compassion on them.
They will be as though
  I had not rejected them,
for I am the LORD their God
  and I will answer them.
The Ephraimites will become like mighty men,
  and their hearts will be glad as with wine...
I will signal for them*

and gather them in.
Surely I will redeem them;
    they will be as numerous as before.
Though I scatter them among the peoples,
    yet in distant lands they will remember me.
They and their children will survive,
    and they will return.
I will bring them back from Egypt
    and gather them from Assyria.
I will bring them to Gilead and Lebanon,
    and there will not be room enough for them.
ZECHARIAH 10:6–10

Hope for the nation

Here indeed was a glorious future to look forward to! The prophets were speaking of the time when God would fulfil the promises he had made to Abraham. Their message was simply that:

- The people would live in *the land* for ever.
- They would become a *great nation*.
- God would be *their God*.
- Through them *all people on earth* would be blessed.

Would these promises ever be fulfilled? If so, when and how?

3.8 Conclusions

The promise of the land

The original promise about the land belonging to Abraham and his descendants 'as an everlasting possession' was part of the whole covenant with Abraham, which also included a promise about the nation, about the covenant relationship between God and his people, and about the blessing which would come to all people on earth (3.1 The promise of the land).

The boundaries of the land

The different ways in which the boundaries of the land are described in different parts of the Old Testament make it impossible to reconstruct an accurate map of the Promised Land (3.2 The boundaries of the land).

The conquest of the land

The promise about the land began to be fulfilled through Abraham's legal purchase of land, and found further fulfilment in the conquest of the land under Joshua. This conquest was partial and never complete (3.3 The conquest of the land).

The land and the temple

In the thinking of the Old Testament the significance of the *land* is closely related to the significance of *the city of Jerusalem* and of the *temple*. What happens to the temple and the city, therefore, is intimately bound up with what happens to the land (3.4 The land and the temple).

Exile from the land

Continued possession of the land was conditional on obedience. Since the land was a gift from God, he could easily withdraw the people's right to live in the land for a time if they did not fulfil the terms of the covenant. The northern kingdom of Israel was taken into exile in Assyria in 721 BC, and as far as we know, never returned to the land. The cream of the southern kingdom of Judah was taken into exile in Babylon in 597 and 586 BC (3.5 Exile from the land).

The return to the land

Prophecies about a return to the land were primarily concerned with the Jews who were exiles in Babylon. 2 Chronicles and Ezra described the return of exiles from Babylon to Jerusalem from 539 BC onwards as the fulfilment of the prophecies of Jeremiah (3.6 The return to the land).

The land and the hopes of Israel

Promises about the land and the predictions about a return to the land should not be separated from other promises and predictions in the Old Testament and must be interpreted according to the same principles. The prophets looked forward to the complete political and spiritual restoration of the nation in the land, a restoration through which God's purposes for the nation and for the world would be fulfilled (3.7 The land and the hopes of Israel).

If this is how the theme of the land is developed in the Old Testament, how is it taken up in the New Testament? The next chapter (Chapter 4: The Land *After* Christ) explores how Jesus and his disciples understood these ideas which they took from the Old Testament.

Chapter 4

The Land *After* Christ:
'The Meek Shall Inherit the Earth'

Jesus said, 'Blessed are the meek, for they will inherit the earth.'
MATTHEW 5:5

In the last resort this study drives us to one point: the person of a Jew, Jesus of Nazareth, who proclaimed the acceptable year of the Lord only to die accursed on a cross and so to pollute the land, and by that act and its consequences to shatter the geographic dimension of the religion of his fathers. Like everything else, the land also in the New Testament drives us to ponder the mystery of Jesus, the Christ, who by his cross and resurrection broke not only the bonds of death for early Christians but also the bonds of the land.[1]
W.D. DAVIES

The Land which once was the specific locale of God's redemptive working served well within the old covenant as a picture of Paradise lost and promised. Now, however, in the era of new-covenant fulfilment, the land has expanded to encompass the cosmos.[2]
O. PALMER ROBERTSON

In the christological logic of Paul, the land (like the law, particular and provisional) had become irrelevant... The people of Israel living in the land had been replaced as the people of God by a universal community which had no special territorial attachment... The land has for him been 'christified'. It is not the promised land (much as he loved it) that became his 'inheritance', but the Living Lord, in whom was a 'new creation'... To be 'in Christ'... has replaced being 'in the land' as the ideal life.[3]
W.D. DAVIES

The horizons of the land have been shaped by the revelation of Jesus Christ. [Paul's] previous Jewish focus on a particularistic fulfillment has been transformed into a Christian universalism focussed on the new creation. Just as in Christ the temple had become a universal dwelling-place and the seed of

*Abraham had been transformed into a universal people, so the promise of the
land already embraces the world.[4]*

D.E. HOLWERDA

*The Land no longer functioned as the key symbol of the geographical identity
of the people of god, and that for an obvious reason: if the new community
consisted of Jew, Greek, barbarian alike, there was no sense in which one
piece of territory could possess more significance than another. At no
point in this early period do we find Christians eager to define or
defend a 'holy land'... Jesus and the church together are the new temple;
the world, I suggest, is the new Land.[5]*

N.T. WRIGHT

4.1 The birth of Jesus the Messiah

We need to begin our study of the land in the New Testament by noting once again
the hopes of the Jewish people as they developed during the period of the Old
Testament and until the first century AD. These hopes are summed up by **N.T.
Wright** as follows:

*The 'salvation' spoken of in the Jewish sources of this period has to do with the res-
cue from the national enemies, restoration of the national symbols, and a state of
shalom in which every man will sit under his vine or fig-tree. 'Salvation' encapsu-
lates the entire future hope... For first-century Jews it could only mean the inauguration of the age to come, liberation from Rome, the restoration of the temple, and
the free enjoyment of their own Land.[6]*

*We may state categorically that what Jews in general were expecting and longing
for was the release of Israel from exile and the return of YHWH in Zion.[7]*

This, therefore, is the context in which we need to read the accounts of the life of
Jesus in the four gospels.

Luke's account of his birth, for example, contains many important clues about
whom he thought Jesus was and what he was going to do for his people – all of them
related to promises and hopes in the Old Testament.

The annunciation to Mary

The words of the angel announcing the birth of Jesus contain a very clear echo of
the original promise concerning the line of David described in 2 Samuel 7:

*You will be with child and give birth to a son, and you are to give him the name
Jesus. He will be great and will be called the Son of the Most High. The Lord God will
give him the throne of his father David, and he will reign over the house of Jacob
forever; his kingdom will never end.*

LUKE 1:31–33

The promise to David

The LORD declares to you that the LORD himself will establish a house for you: When your days are over and you rest with your fathers, I will raise up your offspring to succeed you, who will come from your own body, and I will establish his kingdom. He is the one who will build a house for my Name, and I will establish the throne of his kingdom forever. *I will be his father, and he will be my son... Your house and* your kingdom will endure forever *before me;* your throne shall be established forever.

2 SAMUEL 7:11–14, 16

Whereas David was told that his kingdom would last for ever through an unbroken line of *his descendants,* Mary is told that *Jesus himself* will reign for ever. He is to reign over 'the house of Jacob' – which means the whole house of Israel. His kingdom will not be limited to 'the house of Judah', as was the kingdom of all David's descendants who ruled in Jerusalem after Solomon; he will reign over the whole nation, united into one.

The Song of Mary

In her song of praise to God (the Magnificat), Mary speaks of the 'great things' that God has done for her personally and relates them to the fulfilment of what God had promised to Abraham:

My soul glorifies the Lord
 and my spirit rejoices in God my Savior,
for he has been mindful
 of the humble state of his servant.
From now on all generations will call me blessed,
 for the Mighty One has done great things for me – holy is his name.
He has helped his servant Israel,
 remembering to be merciful
to Abraham and his descendants forever,
 even as he said to our fathers.

LUKE 1:46–49, 54–55

The Song of Zechariah

Soon after the birth of John the Baptist, his father Zechariah connects all that is happening with the promises given to the prophets and the covenant with Abraham:

Praise be to the Lord, the God of Israel,
 because he has come and has redeemed his people.
He has raised up a horn of salvation for us
 in the house of his servant David
(as he said through his holy prophets of long ago),
salvation from our enemies
 and from the hand of all who hate us –
to show mercy to our fathers

and to remember his holy covenant,
the oath he swore to our father Abraham:
to rescue us from the hand of our enemies,
    and to enable us to serve him without fear
in holiness and righteousness before him all our days.
LUKE 1:68–75

The first part of the song defines salvation as *'salvation from our enemies'*; the second part defines salvation in terms of *'the forgiveness of their sins'*:

And you, my child, will be called a prophet of the Most High;
    for you will go on before the Lord to prepare the way for him,
to give his people the knowledge of salvation
    through the forgiveness of their sins,
because of the tender mercy of our God,
    by which the rising sun will come to us from heaven
to shine on those living in darkness
    and in the shadow of death,
    to guide our feet into the path of peace.
LUKE 1:76–79

The Song of Simeon

One person who recognized the significance of the birth of Jesus was the aged Simeon, who was present when Joseph and Mary brought Jesus to be presented in the temple on the fortieth day after his birth:

Now there was a man in Jerusalem called Simeon, who was righteous and devout. He was waiting for the consolation of Israel, and the Holy Spirit was upon him. It had been revealed to him by the Holy Spirit that he would not die before he had seen the Lord's Christ.
LUKE 2:25–26

When he took Jesus in his arms he praised God with the words:

Sovereign Lord, as you have promised,
    you now dismiss your servant in peace.
For my eyes have seen your salvation,
    which you have prepared in the sight of all people,
a light for revelation to the Gentiles
    and for glory to your people Israel.
LUKE 2:29–32

Simeon clearly understood that Jesus was to be 'the Lord's Christ', the one who would bring about 'the consolation of Israel' (or 'the restoration of Israel'). He also believed that the consolation or restoration of Israel was about to take place in the person of Jesus.

Anna the prophetess

Another person who recognized the identity of Jesus was Anna:

There was also a prophetess, Anna... She never left the temple but worshiped night and day, fasting and praying. Coming up to them at that very moment, she gave thanks to God and spoke about the child to all who were looking forward to the redemption of Jerusalem.
LUKE 2:36–38

There must have been a circle of people known to Anna who were looking forward to 'the redemption of Jerusalem', or 'the liberation of Jerusalem'. Anna's message to them after seeing Jesus was that *he* was the one who would have a vital role to play in the fulfilment of their hopes.

If Mary, Zechariah, Simeon and Anna, like the vast majority of their fellow-Jews in the first century, thought of 'the consolation of Israel' and 'the redemption of Jerusalem' as historical events which would one day take place in the city of Jerusalem and the land of Palestine, they now believed that the restoration of Israel and the liberation of Jerusalem *had already begun to take place* through the birth of Jesus the Messiah.

4.2 Jesus and the land

Jesus had very little to say specifically about the land – in fact we shall see that there is only one clear and obvious reference to the land in his teaching. This is all the more surprising when we see his message against the background of typical Jewish hopes and expectations of the first century AD, in which the land played a vital role. As an indication of the centrality of the land in the teaching of the rabbis, **W.D. Davies** quotes the following saying of a rabbi, which suggests that a thanksgiving over a meal cannot be counted as a proper grace unless it includes a specific reference to the land:

Our rabbis have said that anyone who does not mention in the Grace before Meals the blessing, 'For the land and for the food', 'a desirable land', the covenant of circumcision, the Torah *and life, has not fulfilled his duty. The Holy One, blessed be He, said, 'The Land of Israel is more precious to Me than everything. Why? Because I sought it out.'*[8]

Some have argued that if Jesus was so silent about the land, it was because he accepted typical Jewish teaching about the land at the time and took it for granted. He did not need to say anything about the land because he affirmed what his fellow Jews believed about it and the hopes that they had for its future. According to this view, the silence of Jesus concerning the land simply means that Jesus had no desire to challenge accepted ideas about the land in the minds of his contemporaries or to modify them in any way.

It is far more likely, however, that Jesus had so little to say specifically about the land because the main focus of his teaching was on the coming of the kingdom of God. According to Mark the main thrust of Jesus' message was, 'The kingdom of

God is near. Repent and believe the good news!' (Mark 1:15). Jesus' understanding of the land, therefore, has to be seen in the light of his overall message about the way God was about to establish his kingly rule in the world. These crucial ideas about the kingdom are summed up by **N.T. Wright** as follows:

'The kingdom of god'… is a slogan whose basic meaning is the hope that Israel's god is going to rule Israel (and the whole world), and that Caesar, or Herod, or anyone else of their ilk, is not. It means that Torah *will be fulfilled at last, that the temple will be rebuilt and the Land cleansed.*[9]

First-century Jews looked forward to a public event, a great act of liberation for Israel, in and through which their god would reveal to all the world that he was not just a local, tribal deity, but the creator and sovereign of all. YHWH would reveal his salvation for Israel in the eyes of all the nations; the ends of the earth would see that he has vindicated his people.[10]

In order, therefore, to understand Jesus' thinking about the land, we need to look for any clues which show how he thought about the fulfilment of the covenant made with Abraham. And since predictions of a return to the land were interwoven with everything else that the prophets said about the future, we have to take note of anything which indicates how Jesus understood the fulfilment of the hopes and longings of the people of Israel.

'The meek… will inherit the earth'
The Sermon on the Mount begins with these eight well-known sayings describing the characteristics and the blessings of those who belong to the kingdom of God:

Blessed are the poor in spirit,
  for theirs is the kingdom of heaven.
Blessed are those who mourn,
  for they will be comforted.
Blessed are the meek,
  for they will inherit the earth.
Blessed are those who hunger and thirst for righteousness,
  for they will be filled.
Blessed are the merciful,
  for they will be shown mercy.
Blessed are the pure in heart,
  for they will see God.
Blessed are the peacemakers,
  for they will be called sons of God.
Blessed are those who are persecuted because of righteousness,
  for theirs is the kingdom of heaven.
MATTHEW 5:3–10

It is not too difficult to understand what it means to be comforted, to be filled, to be shown mercy, to see God and to be called sons of God. But what does it mean to 'inherit the earth'? The Greek word translated 'earth' (*gen*) can also mean 'land'; and the Hebrew word which lies behind this Greek word is *eretz*, the word that is used throughout the Old Testament for 'the land'. Hermann Sasse in the *Kittel Theological Dictionary of the New Testament* suggests that the word 'land' is used here in the eschatological sense to mean 'the land of promise', and comments:

The kingdom which Psalm 37:11 promises to the anawin, *'the poor', is Palestine perfected in the Messianic glory.*[11]

Jesus is therefore saying that 'the meek will inherit *the land*', and the expression is taken straight from Psalm 37, which contains no fewer than seven references to 'the land' or 'the inheritance':

dwell in the land *and enjoy safe pasture...*
   those who hope in the LORD *will* inherit the land...
But the meek will inherit the land...
the blameless...
   their inheritance *will endure forever...*
those the LORD *blesses will* inherit the land...
the righteous will inherit the land...
He will exalt you to inherit the land.
PSALM 37:3, 9, 11, 18, 22, 29, 34

The Psalmist was obviously thinking of the land of Palestine, 'the land which the Lord has given you as an inheritance'. On the lips of Jesus, however, the land now begins to take on a new meaning: those who will inherit and possess the land and dwell securely in it for ever are the poor in spirit – presumably of any nation – who mourn and are meek.

These words, therefore, contain clear echoes of the promise made to Abraham:

■ Abraham had been promised that the land would belong to his descendants for ever; but now Jesus gives his description of who those descendants are.
■ Abraham had been promised that he would be the ancestor of a great nation; now Jesus spells out his understanding of who are the true people of God.
■ Abraham had been promised that there would be a special relationship between God and his descendants; Jesus now describes the kind of people who will be called sons of God, and will see God.
■ Abraham had been promised that through his descendants all peoples on earth would be blessed; now Jesus extends God's blessing to anyone who is poor in spirit and hungers and thirsts for righteousness.

'Freedom for the prisoners'
At the very beginning of his public ministry, Jesus read some words from Isaiah in a

service in the synagogue at Nazareth, and claimed that they had been fulfilled in himself:

The scroll of the prophet Isaiah was handed to him. Unrolling it, he found the place where it is written:

'The Spirit of the Lord is on me,
* because he has anointed me*
* to preach good news to the poor.*
He has sent me to proclaim freedom for the prisoners
* and recovery of sight for the blind,*
to release the oppressed,
* to proclaim the year of the Lord's favor.'*

Then he rolled up the scroll, gave it back to the attendant and sat down. The eyes of everyone in the synagogue were fastened on him, and he began by saying to them, 'Today this scripture is fulfilled in your hearing.'
LUKE 4:17–21

In their original context in Isaiah 61:1–2 the words he quoted were referring to 'the prisoners' and 'the oppressed' among the people of Judah in exile in a foreign country. He knew as well as his audience that Isaiah's prophecy of a return to the land had been fulfilled in the return of the exiles from Babylon. But here he stands up before a Jewish congregation and makes the astonishing claim, 'Today this scripture is fulfilled in your hearing.'

In the mind of Jesus, therefore, the prisoners, the blind and the oppressed were the people sitting in the same synagogue and walking the streets of Nazareth. Using Old Testament language about leading exiles back to the land from a foreign country he claimed that he had been appointed and commissioned by God to meet their deepest needs. The Israel of Jesus' day is about to have an opportunity to return from its exile.

'Good news is preached to the poor'

When John the Baptist was in prison, he sent some of his disciples to ask Jesus the question, 'Are you the one who was to come, or should we expect someone else?' In his reply Jesus used expressions from Isaiah chapters 35 and 61 to describe what he believed he had been called to do, and thus to explain who he was:

At that very time Jesus cured many who had diseases, sicknesses and evil spirits, and gave sight to many who were blind. So he replied to the messengers, 'Go back and report to John what you have seen and heard: The blind receive sight, the lame walk, *those who have leprosy are cured,* the deaf hear, *the dead are raised, and* the good news is preached to the poor.'
LUKE 7:21–22

Then will the eyes of the blind be opened
   and the ears of the deaf unstopped.
Then will the lame leap like deer,
   and the mute tongue shout for joy.
ISAIAH 35:5–6

The Spirit of the Sovereign LORD *is on me,*
   because the Lord has anointed me
to preach good news to the poor.
ISAIAH 61:1

We have already seen (in 3.7 The land and the hopes of Israel) that Isaiah 35 is a poetic description of the return of exiles to the land. It speaks of 'the redeemed' who will return and 'enter Zion with singing'. Jesus is therefore once again taking poetic imagery from an Old Testament passage about the return of Jewish exiles from Babylon, and using it to describe what he is doing in his public ministry.

A New Testament scholar, **R.T. France**, makes this comment on the significance of Jesus using the Old Testament in this way:

The inevitable conclusion seems to be that Jesus presented his ministry as the fulfilment of the whole future hope of the Old Testament, the day of the Lord and the coming of the Messiah. Even where the original reference seems to be focused on a political restoration of God's people (especially true in Isaiah 35) Jesus can find the fulfilment in his own ministry.[12]

'Many will come from the East and the West'

Jesus was astonished at the faith of the Roman centurion who believed that Jesus could heal his servant who was sick at home simply by saying the word, and without having to go to him. This is what he said to those who were following him at the time. His words contain a clear echo of Isaiah 43 and Psalm 107:

I tell you the truth, I have not found anyone in Israel with such great faith. I say to you that many will come from the east and the west, and will take their places at the feast with Abraham, Isaac and Jacob in the kingdom of heaven. But the subjects of the kingdom will be thrown outside, into the darkness, where there will be weeping and gnashing of teeth.
MATTHEW 8:10–12

I will bring your children from the east
   and gather you from the west.
I will say to the north, 'Give them up!'
   and to the south, 'Do not hold them back.'
Bring my sons from afar
   and my daughters from the ends of the earth –
everyone who is called by my name.
ISAIAH 43:5–7

Let the redeemed of the LORD say this...
those he gathered from the lands,
  from east and west, from north and south
PSALM 107:2–3

Here again, therefore, Jesus takes expressions which, in their original context, speak of the ingathering of Jewish exiles *to the land*, and uses them to speak of the future ingathering of people from all over the world *into the kingdom of God*. He even goes further and no doubt shocks many of his Jewish hearers when he warns that many Jews will be excluded from the kingdom. **R.T. France** concludes:

It seems, therefore, that, far from looking for some future regathering of the Jewish people to Palestine, Jesus actually took Old Testament passages which originally had that connotation, and applied them instead to the ingathering of the Christian community from all nations, even in one case, to the exclusion of some Jews![13]

These ideas are reflected in another saying of Jesus recorded by John:

I have other sheep that are not of this sheep pen. I must bring them also. They too will listen to my voice, and there shall be one flock and one shepherd.
JOHN 10:16

They are also expressed even more explicitly by John in his comment on what the high priest said about the death of Jesus:

He did not say this on his own, but as high priest that year he prophesied that Jesus would die for the Jewish nation, and not only for that nation but also for the scattered children of God, to bring them together and make them one.
JOHN 11:51–52

It was not that Jesus was simply 'spiritualizing' Old Testament prophecies, and thereby leaving open the possibility that they might one day be interpreted literally. Rather, according to him, the gathering of believers into the kingdom of God was the true fulfilment of these prophecies.

Some Christian writers have pointed out that the prophets predicted the return of the exiles from *all* countries – from north, south, east and west. Moreover, they say, some of the prophets (notably Zechariah) specifically predicted that exiles of the northern kingdom of Israel would return to the land as well as exiles from the southern kingdom of Judah. They go on to ask: has anything happened in history which fits this description – *except* the recent return of Jews to the land?

The question at first sight seems unanswerable; it sounds a convincing 'knock-down' argument. But if the Christian is to interpret Old Testament prophecy in the light of the teaching of Jesus, the question simply does not arise. Why? Because in the perspective of Jesus, the ingathering of the exiles – from the north, south, east and west – takes place when people of all races are gathered into the kingdom of God. This is the true, the real, the intended fulfilment of the prophecy.

This new understanding of the land in the context of the kingdom of God is summed up by **N.T. Wright** in this way:

He [Jesus] had not come to rehabilitate the symbol of holy land, but to subsume it within a different fulfilment of the kingdom, which would embrace the whole creation...[14]

Jesus spent his whole ministry redefining what the kingdom meant. He refused to give up the symbolic language of the kingdom, but filled it with such new content that... he powerfully subverted Jewish expectations.[15]

4.3 Jesus and Jerusalem

Jerusalem had figured prominently in the prophetic hopes concerning the future of Israel. In the teaching of Jesus, however, the main significance of Jerusalem was that it was the place where he would die and rise again, and that it would soon be destroyed as a judgment from God.

Predictions of the passion

When Jesus predicted his suffering, death and resurrection in Jerusalem, he spoke of them as the fulfilment of prophecy:

We are going up to Jerusalem, and everything that is written by the prophets about the Son of Man will be fulfilled. He will be handed over to the Gentiles. They will mock him, insult him, spit on him, flog him and kill him. On the third day he will rise again.
LUKE 18:31–33 (COMPARE MARK 8:31)

It is widely accepted that when Jesus spoke of his resurrection as being 'on the third day', he was using the words of Hosea 6:1–2. In their original context, these verses express the hope of a national restoration – in other words, the resurrection of the people of Israel:

Come, let us return to the LORD.
He has torn us to pieces
  but he will heal us;
he has injured us
  but he will bind up our wounds.
After two days he will revive us;
  on the third day he will restore us,
  that we may live in his presence.
HOSEA 6:1–2

These hopes and aspirations for the nation were hardly fulfilled in the centuries following the prophet's lifetime. So what did Jesus mean when he made such a deliberate reference to these hopes and said that he would be raised from the dead 'on the third day'? The answer suggested by **R.T. France** is that 'Jesus could only apply Hosea's words to himself if he saw himself as in some way the heir to Israel's hopes.' He goes on to quote this significant sentence from C.H. Dodd's book *According to the Scriptures*: 'The resurrection of Christ *is* the resurrection of Israel of which the prophets spoke.'[16]

N.T. Wright makes the same point in this way:

Jesus was claiming in some sense to represent Israel in himself... he regarded himself as the one who summed up Israel's vocation and destiny in himself. He was the one in and through whom the real 'return from exile' would come about, indeed, was already coming about. He was the Messiah.[17]

Jesus is therefore claiming that in some way *he himself* is a representative of the whole people of Israel, and that the promised restoration of the nation is going to take place *in and through him*.

Predictions of the fall of Jerusalem
Mark, Luke and Matthew all record sayings of Jesus about the end of the age, which were spoken in Jerusalem during the last week of his life. Here we study only the accounts in Mark and Luke.

MARK'S ACCOUNT
The thirteenth chapter in Mark begins with a prediction of the destruction of the temple:

As he was leaving the temple, one of his disciples said to him, 'Look, Teacher! What massive stones! What magnificent buildings!'

'Do you see all these great buildings?' replied Jesus. 'Not one stone here will be left on another; every one will be thrown down.'

As Jesus was sitting on the Mount of Olives opposite the temple, Peter, James, John and Andrew asked him privately, 'Tell us, when will these things happen? And what will be the sign that they are all about to be fulfilled?'
MARK 13:1–4

In his answer to these questions Jesus speaks of false prophets, wars, earthquakes and famines which are to be 'the beginning of birth pains'; and warns his disciples to expect persecution from civil and religious authorities, and even from their own families. He then speaks about the time when the temple will be desecrated, using expressions borrowed from the book of Daniel (9:27; 11:31; 12:11):

When you see 'the abomination that causes desolation' standing where it does not belong – let the reader understand – then let those who are in Judea flee to the mountains. Let no one on the roof of his house go down or enter the house to take anything out. Let no one in the field go back to get his cloak. How dreadful it will be in those days for pregnant women and nursing mothers! Pray that this will not take place in winter, because those will be days of distress unequalled from the beginning, when God created the world, until now – and never to be equalled again. If the Lord had not cut short those days, no one would survive. But for the

sake of the elect, whom he has chosen, he has shortened them. At that time if any-
one says to you, 'Look, here is the Christ!' or, 'Look, there he is!' do not believe it. For
false Christs and false prophets will appear and perform signs and miracles to
deceive the elect – if that were possible. So be on your guard; I have told you every-
thing ahead of time.
MARK 13:14–23

The next two verses speak about cosmic disturbances:

But in those days, following that distress,
'the sun will be darkened,
*   and the moon will not give its light;*
the stars will fall from the sky,
*   and the heavenly bodies will be shaken.'*
MARK 13:24–25

These words have generally been interpreted as referring to disturbances in the universe which will occur at the end of the world. It is more likely, however, as R.T.
France and others have argued, that they should be taken very closely with the previous verses to refer to the fall of Jerusalem.[18] The main reason for this interpretation
is that the quotation is taken straight from a prophecy of Isaiah about the fall of
Babylon, Isaiah 13:10. If Isaiah could speak of cosmic disturbances accompanying
the fall of *Babylon* (which took place in 539 BC), it is perfectly understandable that
Jesus could use the same kind of poetic language to describe the fall of *Jerusalem*.
We do not have to think in terms of literal disturbances in the cosmos at the end of
the world.

   If this is the most likely interpretation, it means that Jesus wanted his Jewish hearers to understand that God was going to punish the holy city of Jerusalem in the
same way as he had punished the pagan city of Babylon. Since they probably
understood the point of the quotation, they would no doubt have been shocked
and deeply offended at the comparison.

   The following verse speaks about the coming of the Son of man:

At that time men will see the Son of Man coming in clouds with great power and
glory.
MARK 13:26

Here again we have a saying which has generally been interpreted as referring to
the second coming of Jesus Christ at the end of the world, but which could *also and*
primarily be speaking about events in the near future. The picture of the coming of
the Son of man on the clouds is almost certainly taken from one of Daniel's visions
in the Old Testament:

In my vision at night I looked, and there before me was one like a son of man, com-
ing with the clouds of heaven. He approached the Ancient of Days and was led into
his presence. He was given authority, glory and sovereign power; all peoples,

nations and men of every language worshiped him. His dominion is an everlasting dominion that will not pass away, and his kingdom is one that will never be destroyed.
DANIEL 7:13–14

Since this passage (like many others in Daniel) is about the kingdom of God, it is natural to connect it with another important saying in Mark's Gospel about the coming of the kingdom of God:

I tell you the truth, some who are standing here will not taste death before they see the kingdom of God come with power.
MARK 9:1

If there was a connection in Jesus' mind between the coming of the kingdom of God 'with power' (Mark 9:1) and the coming of the Son of man 'with great power' (Mark 13:26), when were they to happen? The answer must be that since Jesus said the kingdom would come while many of his hearers were still alive, the coming of the Son of man would also take place during this period. We can hardly avoid making a connection between the words 'the present generation will live to *see* it all' (Mark 13:30) and the words 'then they will *see* the coming of the Son of man' (Mark 13:26).

What then could the coming of the kingdom of God and the coming of the Son of man mean at this particular time? The 'coming' described in Daniel's vision is a coming to God; the Son of man is presented before God and receives authority, glory and sovereign power. This 'coming' might, therefore, relate to the resurrection and ascension, since it was supremely through these events that Jesus was vindicated by God, raised to glory and established in his kingdom. And if the fall of Jerusalem and the destruction of Jerusalem are linked with this sequence of events, it is because it was one more event by which Jesus was vindicated before people. **N.T. Wright** relates the 'coming' closely to the events of AD 70:

He was the true king, who had authority over the temple. As such, he would be vindicated when his prediction came true, and the temple was finally destroyed.[19]

Jesus is saying, therefore, that in the years to come it will become clear through all that happens that God has vindicated him openly. Men will 'see' with the eyes of faith that the Son of man has entered into his eternal kingdom and that the kingdom of God has come in the world.

This interpretation of the coming of the Son of man does not rule out the traditional interpretation of these words, which relates them to the second coming. It simply means that the *primary* reference in the words about the coming of the Son of man is to his public vindication in the near future.

The next verse speaks about something closely related to the coming of the Son of man:

And he will send his angels and gather his elect from the four winds, from the ends
of the earth to the ends of the heavens.
MARK 13:27

The Greek word translated as 'angels' is *aggelous*, which is the common word for
'messengers'. It would therefore be perfectly legitimate to translate the sentence, 'he
will send *his messengers* and gather his elect'. This saying echoes several Old
Testament passages which speak of the gathering of exiles; and in Matthew's version of the same saying, the 'trumpet call' comes from a verse in Isaiah which
describes the return of exiles from Assyria and Egypt:

Even if you have been banished to the most distant land under the heavens, from
there the LORD your God will gather you and bring you back.
DEUTERONOMY 30:4

*'Come! Come! Flee from the land of the north,' declares the LORD. . . 'Come, O Zion!
Escape, you who live in the Daughter of Babylon!'*
ZECHARIAH 2:6–7

And he will send his angels with a loud trumpet call, *and they will gather his elect
from the four winds, from one end of the heavens to the other.*
MATTHEW 24:31

And in that day a great trumpet *will sound. Those who were perishing in Assyria
and those who were exiled in Egypt will come and worship the LORD on the holy
mountain in Jerusalem.*
ISAIAH 27:13

Thus when we compare the words of Jesus with the Old Testament sources from
which some of their ideas and expressions are taken, it appears that once again the
primary reference in Jesus' words is not to the end of the world, but to an event in
history. He has already said that 'the gospel must first be preached to all nations'
(Mark 13:10). Now he is saying the same thing, but this time using a poetic image
from the Old Testament: God will soon send out his messengers to all nations to
gather all his chosen people into the kingdom.

The remaining verses of this part of Mark 13 underline the point that everything
Jesus has predicted up till now will happen in the near future:

*Now learn this lesson from the fig tree: As soon as its twigs get tender and its leaves
come out, you know that summer is near. Even so, when you see these things happening, you know that it is near, right at the door. I tell you the truth, this generation will certainly not pass away until all these things have happened. Heaven and
earth will pass away, but my words will never pass away.*
MARK 13:28–31

When we reach Mark 13:32, however, there can be no doubt that Jesus is speaking
about events in the more distant future. The time is described as 'that day or hour',

and it is generally agreed that the reference is to the second coming of Jesus Christ and the end of the world:

No one knows about that day or hour, not even the angels in heaven, nor the Son, but only the Father. Be on guard! Be alert! You do not know when that time will come.
MARK 13:32–33

What then does Mark's version of the discourse about the end of the age contribute to our understanding of how Jesus thought about Jerusalem and its future? At the very least, we can draw three conclusions:

■ Apart from predicting the fall of Jerusalem and the destruction of the temple, Jesus was silent about the future of the land.
■ Jesus spoke of the fall of Jerusalem and the destruction of the temple as an act of divine judgment.
■ Jesus spoke of the events in the coming years (including the resurrection, the ascension and the fall of Jerusalem) as a sequence of events by which God would vindicate the Son of man and bring in the kingdom of God.

LUKE'S ACCOUNT
Luke's version of the part of the discourse dealing with the future of Jerusalem is as follows, with some of the unique features printed in roman type:

When you see Jerusalem being surrounded by armies, you will know that its desolation *is near. Then let those who are in Judea flee to the mountains, let those in the city get out, and let those in the country not enter the city. For this is the time of* punishment *in fulfillment of all that has been written. How dreadful it will be in those days for pregnant women and nursing mothers! There will be* great distress in the land *and* wrath against this people. *They will* fall by the sword *and will be taken as prisoners to all the nations. Jerusalem will be trampled on by the Gentiles until the times of the Gentiles are fulfilled. There will be* signs in the sun, moon and stars. *On the earth, nations will be in anguish and perplexity at the roaring and tossing of the sea. Men will faint from terror, apprehensive of what is coming on the world, for the heavenly bodies will be shaken. At that time they will see the Son of Man coming in a cloud with power and great glory. When these things begin to take place, stand up and lift up your heads, because your redemption is drawing near.*
LUKE 21:20–28

At least four sayings in this version are not found either in Mark or in Matthew:

1. There are several very clear (and presumably deliberate) echoes of Isaiah's prophecy concerning the fall of Babylon (Isaiah 13):

Luke 21
… *its* desolation *is near (20)*
… *the time of* punishment… *(22)*

... wrath *against this people (23)*
They will fall by the sword *(24)*

Isaiah 13
... *to make the land* desolate *(9)*
... *I will* punish *the world... (11)*
... wrath *and fierce* anger *(9)*
... *the* wrath *of the Lord... his burning* anger *(13)*
... *all who are caught will* fall by the sword... *(15)*

2. *'This is the time of punishment in fulfillment of all that has been written'* (Luke 21:22). Jesus here emphasizes what is implied in his use of the quotation from Isaiah: the fall of Jerusalem is to be seen as an act of divine judgment on the city and the people. Moreover, these events are to be seen as the fulfilment of '*all* that has been written' – in other words, presumably *all* that has been written about Jerusalem.

3. *'When these things begin to take place, stand up and lift up your heads, because your redemption is drawing near'* (Luke 21:28). We have already seen the word 'redemption' in the birth narratives, and noticed that Anna the prophetess spoke about Jesus to all who were looking forward to 'the redemption of Jerusalem' (Luke 2:38). The word occurs again in Luke 24:21 where the two disciples express their hopes that Jesus was 'the one who was going to redeem Israel'.

If the quotation about cosmic disturbances is a poetic way of speaking about the fall of Jerusalem (Luke 21:25–26), and if the words about the coming of the Son of man with power and great glory speak of his vindication through his death, resurrection and ascension and through the coming judgment of Jerusalem, then the redemption which Jesus speaks about here is not primarily something which will be achieved at the end of the world. It must be no different from the 'redemption of Jerusalem' (Luke 2:38), 'the consolation of Israel' (Luke 2:25) and the 'redemption of Israel' (Luke 24:21). In Luke's thinking, this process of redemption was set in motion the moment Jesus was born. And this saying of Jesus speaks of the redemption being completed in the near future.

4. *'Jerusalem will be trampled on by the Gentiles until the times of the Gentiles are fulfilled'* (Luke 21:24). Other translations of this verse read: *'Jerusalem will be trampled down by foreigners until their day has run its course'* (NEB). *'The heathen will trample over Jerusalem until their time is up'* (TEV).

This verse is often interpreted as a prediction that Jerusalem would be under the domination of non-Jews *until* the times of the Gentiles were fulfilled, but *after* that time, it would again come under Jewish rule. Many popular books on prophecy not only insist that Jesus was clearly predicting the eventual return of Jerusalem to Jewish rule; they also conclude that the return of Jerusalem to Jewish rule must be regarded as an important sign pointing forward to 'the last days'. They therefore attach great importance to the recapture of the Old City of Jerusalem by the Israelis in the war of June 1967.

The main problem with this interpretation is that it reads ideas into the text which can hardly be found in the text itself. Some sentences using the word 'until' *do* imply something about the more distant future. If I say 'I will go on discussing this question with you *until* I have convinced you', the obvious implication is that when I have convinced you, I will stop talking! But there are just as many sentences in which it makes no sense to try to draw implications about what will happen after the time referred to. For example, when God promised Jacob, 'I will not leave you *until* I have done what I have promised you' (Genesis 28:15), he could hardly mean that he would be with Jacob until he had fulfilled his promise, but that *after* that time he would leave him!

The real key to the interpretation of this verse, however, is probably to be found in the Old Testament, where several prophets speak of the way God will use foreign nations as instruments of judgment on the people of Israel, and will then in turn judge these foreign nations. The 'times of the nations (Gentiles)' that Jesus is referring to, therefore, in the words of **John Nolland**, are:

> *the period for a judgment upon the gentile nations that corresponds to the judgment on Jerusalem: after the kairos, 'time' of Jerusalem... come the kairoi, 'times' of the nations... The underlying pattern here of judgment upon Jerusalem/Judah/Israel followed by judgment upon the instruments of their judgment may be found in Isaiah 10:12–14; 33; 47; Jeremiah 50–51; Daniel 9:26–27 and compare Ezekiel 38; Habakuk 1:11 – 2:3.*[20]

In other words Jesus sees the coming destruction of Jerusalem as a judgment from God, but at the same time indicates that his judgment will in due course also fall on the Romans who will trample on the holy city of Jerusalem. The emphasis in Jesus' words, therefore, is on the significance of the coming destruction of Jerusalem (which will take place in the lifetime of many of his hearers) rather than on the status of Jerusalem in the more distant future. And if there is any hint about this future, it has more to do with *Rome* and the judgment that will eventually fall on the *Romans* than with *Jerusalem* ceasing to be trampled on by the Gentiles and once again coming under Jewish rule.

Luke's version of the discourse therefore points to the same conclusions as the discourse in Mark: that Jesus was silent about the future of the land; that the fall of Jerusalem was to be an act of divine judgment; and that through all the events of the coming years God was going to bring in his kingdom.

How then did Jesus understand the significance of Jerusalem for his ministry as the Messiah? It was in Jerusalem that his death and resurrection would fulfil 'all that is written by the prophets about the Son of Man'. And before long the holy city of Jerusalem would be attacked and destroyed, simply because its people had failed to recognize 'the time of God's coming' in the person of the Messiah.

Like Isaiah, Jeremiah and Ezekiel centuries before, Jesus spoke of God's judgment on the people, the temple and the land. But unlike them, he did *not* tell them that if they repented in their exile, God would restore them to their land and the temple. Was this because he assumed that the same pattern of exile and return would be repeated all over again, and that a return in the twentieth century would play just as vital a part in God's plan for the world as the return in the sixth century BC? This explanation seems far from convincing.

The alternative is to understand that when the majority of the Jewish people refused to accept Jesus as their Messiah, God could no longer deal with them on exactly the same basis as he had done before. God's plan for the Jewish people was entering a completely new phase, which included people of all races, lands and cultures within the loving purposes of God for the world.

4.4 The redemption of Israel

Once again we are indebted to Luke – this time for his vivid account of two significant meetings between the risen Jesus and his disciples. When Jesus appears to the two disciples on the road to Emmaus they do not recognize him at first, and start describing the events of the past week in Jerusalem leading up to his death. They express the extreme disappointment, even disillusionment, that they have experienced:

He was a prophet, powerful in word and deed before God and all the people. The chief priests and our rulers handed him over to be sentenced to death, and they crucified him; but we had hoped that he was the one who was going to redeem Israel. And what is more, it is the third day since all this took place. In addition, some of our women amazed us. They went to the tomb early this morning but didn't find his body. They came and told us that they had seen a vision of angels, who said he was alive. Then some of our companions went to the tomb and found it just as the women had said, but him they did not see.
LUKE 24:19–24

Jesus, however, does not seem at first sight to show a great deal of sympathy for their hopes for the nation of Israel. Instead he rebukes them for their dullness and slowness to understand the prophets:

'How foolish you are, and how slow of heart to believe all that the prophets have spoken! Did not the Christ have to suffer these things and then enter his glory?' And beginning with Moses and all the Prophets, he explained to them what was said in all the Scriptures concerning himself.
LUKE 24:25–27

One of the surprising things about this reply is that Jesus appears to ignore the subject that they are really interested in – namely, the redemption of Israel. He simply speaks of himself as 'the Christ' (i.e. the Messiah, God's anointed agent), and goes on to say why it was necessary for him to suffer and die. He then explains everything in the Scriptures concerning *himself* – not Israel.

Was Jesus thinking only of himself? Was he deaf to what the two men were saying? Was he talking at cross-purposes with them? No! He wanted them to understand that *all* that the prophets had said about *Israel* and its redemption had been fulfilled in *himself*. It was not that he was disinterested in their hopes for the nation. Rather he was trying to tell them that he *had* accomplished the redemption of Israel – although not in the way they had expected. The redemption of Israel *had already* been carried out through the suffering, death and resurrection of the Christ.

The kingdom of Israel and the kingdom of God

In his summary of the appearances of Jesus during the forty days between the resurrection and the ascension, Luke says that he was teaching the disciples 'about the kingdom of God' (Acts 1:3). When he spoke about the coming of the Holy Spirit, they still found it difficult to see the connection between Jesus' concept of the kingdom of God and their own ideas of the kingdom of God:

On one occasion, while he was eating with them, he gave them this command: 'Do not leave Jerusalem, but wait for the gift my Father promised, which you have heard me speak about. For John baptized with water, but in a few days you will be baptized with the Holy Spirit.'

So when they met together, they asked him, 'Lord, are you at this time going to restore the kingdom to Israel?'
ACTS 1:4–6

The disciples seem to have had a kind of mental block. Even if they accepted and believed all Jesus' teaching about the kingdom of God, they still held onto their Jewish hopes for the future of the nation of Israel. They were looking forward to the establishment of an independent Jewish state, no longer under Roman control. And they assumed that since this was a vital part of the establishment of the kingdom of God on earth, the resurrection of Jesus provided the unique opportunity for this next stage in the unfolding of God's plan.

This, however, was Jesus' reply:

It is not for you to know the times or dates the Father has set by his own authority [verse 7]. But you will receive power when the Holy Spirit comes on you; and you will be my witnesses in Jerusalem, and in all Judea and Samaria, and to the ends of the earth [verse 8].
ACTS 1:7–8

There are two possible interpretations of this answer, and the crucial question we need to decide is: what is the connection of thought between verse 7 and verse 8?

According to the first interpretation, we need to separate verses 7 and 8, because there is no vital connection between them. Jesus was not challenging the disciples' *idea* of a restored Jewish state, but only correcting their ideas about the *time* when it would come into being. Jesus was saying in effect: 'A restored, independent Jewish state is certainly part of God's plan for the coming of the kingdom; but it will not come into being now and it is not for you to know when it will be established.' Those who accept this interpretation often go on to claim that we in our day *do know* something about 'dates and times', since we have witnessed the establishment of an independent Jewish state in Palestine.

According to the second interpretation, verses 7 and 8 need to be taken very closely together, because both of them are answering the disciples' question. Jesus was not only trying to correct the disciples' idea about the *timing* of these events (verse 7), he was also trying to correct the *idea* that was implied in the question (verse 8). In his commentary on this passage, **John Calvin** makes the point in this way: 'There are as many mistakes in this question as there are words.'[21] If this is true, Jesus must have wanted his disciples to put to one side the idea of the kingdom which they had inherited from their Jewish background, and to accept a completely new idea of the kingdom of God. It was to be a kingdom which would include anyone from Jerusalem, Judea, Samaria and from the ends of the earth who would believe the testimony of the apostles.

It was therefore as if he was saying, 'I want you to put out of your minds once and for all the idea that the establishment of a sovereign Jewish state has any special significance in the establishment of the kingdom of God. I want you to see the kingdom of God in a different light – as a kingdom which is spiritual and therefore has nothing to do with any piece of land; a kingdom which is international and has no connection with any nation or state.'

In the words of **Peter Walker**:

When he [Luke] records Jesus' answer to the disciples' agitated question in Acts 1, he almost certainly intends us to hear this as meaning, 'Your understanding of restoration is wrong; Israel has been restored in my resurrection, and you will be witnesses of this fact from Jerusalem to the ends of the earth. The restored kingdom of Israel is the world coming under the rule of Israel's true king.' The throne of David is no longer empty, but in accordance with God's promise it has now been occupied by the risen Jesus (Acts 2:30–31). Israel's kingdom has therefore been restored through the resurrection of her king – the one whom God has made both Lord and Messiah (2:36).[22]

In the conclusion of his book, *The New Testament and the People of God*, **N.T. Wright** sums up the hopes of first-century Jews in terms of 'a public event, a great act of liberation for Israel', and ends with these words:

The early Christians, not least in the writings that came to be called the New Testament, looked back to an event in and through which, they claimed, Israel's god had done exactly that. On this basis, the New Testament, emerging from within this strange would-be 'people of god', told the story of that people as a story rooted in Israel's past, and designed to continue into the world's future. It repeated the Jewish claim: this story concerns not just a god but God. It revised the Jewish evidence: the claim is made good, not in national liberation, but in the events concerning Jesus.[23]

4.5 The land in the teaching of the apostles

Is there anything to suggest that after the ascension of Jesus his disciples continued to look forward to a restored Jewish state in the land? Given the political situation in first-century Palestine, the writers of the New Testament had every reason to hope for a national restoration for the Jewish people. But did they in fact do so? There is nothing whatsoever to suggest that they held onto these hopes. On the contrary, we find a great deal of evidence which indicates that they grasped the new concept of the kingdom of God which Jesus had tried to teach them. This means that our ideas of how they understood the meaning of the land need not be based simply on an argument about their silence concerning the land.

Peter

The testimony of Peter is of special value, because he was the first of the disciples to realize that there was a significant difference between his own typically Jewish idea of the 'Messiah' and Jesus' understanding of what the Messiah must be and do.

In the following passage from his first epistle, written about thirty years after the death of Jesus, he uses the familiar Old Testament word 'inheritance' and gives it a new meaning:

Praise be to the God and Father of our Lord Jesus Christ! In his great mercy he has given us new birth into a living hope through the resurrection of Jesus Christ from the dead, and into an inheritance that can never perish, spoil or fade – kept in heaven for you, who through faith are shielded by God's power until the coming of the salvation that is ready to be revealed in the last time.
1 PETER 1:3–5

A first-century Jew would inevitably have associated the word 'inheritance' with the land, because this is one of the main ways in which the word is used all through the Old Testament. For example:

He brought his people out like a flock...
brought them to the border of his holy land,
*   to the hill country his right hand had taken.*
He drove out nations before them
*   and allotted their lands to them as an inheritance;*
*   he settled the tribes of Israel in their homes.*
PSALM 78:52, 54–55

We can be sure that this is the background of the word 'inheritance' in Peter's mind, because he goes on to make an implied contrast between the inheritance of the land and the inheritance of the Christian believer: the land *could* perish, or be spoiled, whereas the spiritual inheritance of the believer *cannot* perish or be spoiled in any way, because it is kept in heaven for all who believe.

In the following chapter we find a similar example of the bold way in which Peter reinterprets Old Testament themes: he takes titles which were reserved exclusively for the Jews and applies them to *all* who believe in Christ – whether Jew or Gentile:

You are a chosen people, a royal priesthood, a holy nation, a people belonging to God, that you may declare the praises of him who called you out of darkness into

his wonderful light. Once you were not a people, but now you are the people of God; once you had not received mercy, but now you have received mercy.
1 PETER 2:9–10

In these words there is a clear and deliberate echo of the words in Exodus 19:6, which define the identity of the children of Israel: 'you will be for me a kingdom of priests and a holy nation'.

The Acts of the Apostles

It is possible to make out a good case for saying that the book of Acts was intended by Luke to be (among other things) a counterpart to the book of Joshua in the Old Testament. Whereas Joshua describes the gradual conquest of the land beginning from Jericho, Acts describes the gradual spread of the Christian church beginning from Jerusalem.

The book of Joshua begins with God's command to enter and conquer the land: 'go in and take possession of the land the LORD your God is giving you for your own' (Joshua 1:11). The book of Acts begins with the command of the risen Jesus to his disciples to start a different kind of conquest: 'you will be my witnesses in Jerusalem, and in all Judea and Samaria, and to the ends of the earth' (Acts 1:8).

Joshua and the tribes were to possess their allotted inheritance by killing its inhabitants 'with the edge of the sword'. In Acts, however, Paul speaks of the word of God as the weapon by which Christians are to occupy their inheritance: 'Now I commit you to God and to the word of his grace, which can build you up and give you an inheritance among all those who are sanctified' (Acts 20:32).

The book of Joshua describes the different stages by which the land was conquered – beginning with the capture of Jericho and Ai, then going on with the campaigns in the south and the north. The book of Acts describes how the gospel was first preached in Jerusalem, in Samaria, and then in Caesarea to the first Gentile; from Antioch the message was taken by Paul into Asia Minor, then to Greece, and finally to Rome.

Both Joshua and Acts describe the many difficulties which had to be faced and overcome. Thus the story in Acts of Ananias and Sapphira and their deception over the sale of their land (Acts 5:1–11) is an exact parallel to the story in Joshua of Achan, whose theft and lying held up the advance of the whole army (Joshua 7). In Joshua we find repeated several times in different forms a formula which describes times of peace and consolidation after times of fighting: 'then the land had rest from war' (Joshua 11:23; see also 14:15; 21:44; 23:1). We find something similar in Acts with sentences like 'then the church... enjoyed a time of peace. It was strengthened; and... grew in numbers' (Acts 9:31). 'So the word of God spread' (Acts 6:7; see also 2:47; 12:24; 13:49; 19:20).

If Luke and the early Christian church thought in terms of conquest, they were thinking of the conquest not of the land but of the whole world. The only sword that would be used for this conquest was the sword of the word of God which would enable those who believed it to possess the inheritance that God had promised them. The gospel of Jesus was not only for the people in the land, but for all nations of the world. 'Mission to the whole world', in the words of **N.T. Wright**, 'seems to have taken the place held, within the Jewish symbolic universe, by the land.'[24]

Paul

The subject of the land is conspicuous by its absence in the letters of Paul. He seems to show no interest in the land in the purposes of God. Even in a passage in Romans where he lists several of the privileges of the Jewish people he makes no mention of the land:

I speak the truth in Christ – I am not lying, my conscience confirms it in the Holy Spirit – I have great sorrow and unceasing anguish in my heart. For I could wish that I myself were cursed and cut off from Christ for the sake of my brothers, those of my own race, the people of Israel. Theirs is the adoption as sons; theirs the divine glory, the covenants, the receiving of the law, the temple worship and the promises. Theirs are the patriarchs, and from them is traced the human ancestry of Christ, who is God over all, forever praised! Amen.
ROMANS 9:15

The promise of the land was included in the 'covenants', and the prophecies about the land must have been included in 'the promises' which he refers to here. But it can hardly be an accident that, whereas the land figured prominently in the thinking of orthodox Jews at the time, Paul does not include the land in his list. Although he writes in Romans 11 of the glorious future that they can look forward to as a people, there is no suggestion that it is associated with the land.

A highly significant clue about the thinking of Paul is found earlier in the same letter where he writes:

It was not through law that Abraham and his offspring received the promise that he would be heir of the world, but through the righteousness that comes by faith.
ROMANS 4:13

Kenneth Bailey has pointed out that Paul is referring here to the promise in Genesis that Abraham and his descendants would inherit the land, but that in referring to this promise he substitutes 'the world' (Greek *kosmos*) for 'the land'. He explains Paul's thinking as follows:

For Paul, the 'children of Abraham' are those Jews and Gentiles who through faith in Christ have been made righteous. The 'land' becomes the 'world' (kosmos), which is the inheritance of the righteous.[25]

In Paul's thinking, therefore, *all* the divine promises in one way or another find their fulfilment in Christ. Thus, in writing to the Corinthians, he says, 'no matter how many promises God has made, they are "Yes" in Christ' (2 Corinthians 1:20).

Similarly, in one of his earliest letters, he describes *all* Christians, both Jews and Gentiles, as 'Abraham's seed' and therefore inheritors of the promise given to Abraham:

You are all sons of God through faith in Christ Jesus, for all of you who were baptized
into Christ have clothed yourselves with Christ. There is neither Jew nor Greek, slave
nor free, male nor female, for you are all one in Christ Jesus. If you belong to Christ,
then you are Abraham's seed, and heirs according to the promise.
GALATIANS 3:26–29

Christians have no difficulty in believing that the promises concerning Abraham's
descendants, about the covenant relationship between God and his people, and
about the blessing for all people on earth have been fulfilled in and through Christ.
But what about the promise concerning the land? Does it have to be put in a category of its own? Can we say that the other three aspects of the covenant have been
fulfilled in a *spiritual* way in Christ, while the promise about the land must be interpreted *literally* – and that the land therefore belongs by a God-given right to
Abraham's physical descendants for all time?

If Paul thought in these terms, it is very strange that he does not add any kind of
qualification concerning the land. If this is what he really meant, one might have
expected him to say: 'You are the heirs of the promise given to Abraham – *except*
that part of the promise which refers to the land, which applies only to the Jews
who are the physical descendants of Abraham.' It is difficult to see how he could
say that *all* believers are the seed of Abraham and therefore inheritors of the promise, but at the same time believe that one aspect of the promise does *not* apply to all
believers.

Later in the same letter he gives an allegorical interpretation to the story of Sarah
and Hagar, and draws a distinction between the actual city of Jerusalem and 'the
heavenly Jerusalem':

These things may be taken figuratively, for the women represent two covenants.
One covenant is from Mount Sinai and bears children who are to be slaves: This is
Hagar. Now Hagar stands for Mount Sinai in Arabia and corresponds to the pres-
ent city of Jerusalem, because she is in slavery with her children. But the Jerusalem
that is above is free, and she is our mother.
GALATIANS 4:24–26

This kind of 'spiritualizing' of the Old Testament was not strange or new for orthodox Jews. What *is* significant, however, is that Paul should describe 'the present city
of Jerusalem' as being 'in slavery with her children'. Presumably it was not just
because Jerusalem was under Roman occupation that he could speak of the city in
these terms; it must have been because the vast majority of the Jewish people had
rejected their promised Messiah:

The Jews… killed the Lord Jesus and the prophets and also drove us out. They dis-
please God and are hostile to all men in their effort to keep us from speaking to the
Gentiles so that they may be saved. In this way they always heap up their sins to the
limit. The wrath of God has come upon them at last.
1 THESSALONIANS 2:14–16

If Paul had lived to see Jerusalem regaining its freedom and coming under Jewish rule in 135 or 1967, he would no doubt have *continued* to think of Jerusalem as being in slavery with all her children. Political freedom for the Jewish people had little or nothing to do with the kingdom of God in the thinking of Paul.

At the end of Galatians Paul gives another striking example of how the coming of Christ has transformed his Jewish attitudes. He takes the name 'Israel' and applies it to those of all races who have come to recognize Jesus as God's Messiah:

May I never boast except in the cross of our Lord Jesus Christ, through which the world has been crucified to me and I to the world. Neither circumcision nor uncircumcision means anything; what counts is a new creation. Peace and mercy to all who follow this rule, even to the Israel of God.
GALATIANS 6:14–16

If the translation '*even* to the Israel of God' is correct, it would seem that for Paul the name 'Israel' is no longer the exclusive possession of the physical descendants of Abraham, Isaac and Jacob: 'The Israel of God' embraces all who have taken up their cross to follow in the footsteps of the crucified Messiah.

It is possible, however, that the sentence can be translated '*and* to the Israel of God' (NEB). In this case 'the Israel of God' must be those among the Jewish people who believe in Christ and therefore 'follow this rule' that Paul had laid down. In view of all that he has already said in the same letter, he could hardly still be thinking of the whole Jewish people as 'the Israel of God'.

The letter to the Hebrews
This letter was written by an unknown author to Christians from a Jewish background. The writer takes up one theme after another from the Old Testament and shows how its full meaning has been revealed in and through Jesus – in his birth, life, death, resurrection and ascension.

In chapter 4 he takes the theme of the land, which he describes as 'that rest' or 'God's rest'. It is believers in Christ who inherit this kind of rest:

Therefore, since the promise of entering his rest still stands, let us be careful that none of you be found to have fallen short of it. For we also have had the gospel preached to us, just as they did; but the message they heard was of no value to them, because those who heard did not combine it with faith. Now we who have believed enter that rest...
HEBREWS 4:1–3

In chapter 10 he speaks of Jesus as the fulfilment of the sacrificial system in the temple:

Day after day every priest stands and performs his religious duties; again and again he offers the same sacrifices, which can never take away sins. But when this priest [Jesus] had offered for all time one sacrifice for sins, he sat down at the right hand of God.
HEBREWS 10:11–12

In chapter 11 he speaks of Abraham living in the promised land, but looking forward to 'a better country – a heavenly one':

By faith he [Abraham] made his home in the promised land like a stranger in a foreign country; he lived in tents, as did Isaac and Jacob, who were heirs with him of the same promise. For he was looking forward to the city with foundations, whose architect and builder is God... People who say such things show that they are looking for a country of their own... They were longing for a better country – a heavenly one. Therefore God is not ashamed to be called their God, for he has prepared a city for them.
HEBREWS 11:9–10, 14, 16

At the climax of the letter in chapter 12 the writer draws a contrast between the literal Mount Sinai where Moses received the Law, and 'Mount Zion... the heavenly Jerusalem':

You have not come to a mountain that can be touched and that is burning with fire; to darkness, gloom and storm; to a trumpet blast or to such a voice speaking words... But you have come to Mount Zion, to the heavenly Jerusalem, the city of the living God. You have come to thousands upon thousands of angels in joyful assembly, to the church of the firstborn, whose names are written in heaven. You have come to God, the judge of all men, to the spirits of righteous men made perfect, to Jesus the mediator of a new covenant, and to the sprinkled blood that speaks a better word than the blood of Abel...

Therefore, since we are receiving a kingdom that cannot be shaken, let us be thankful, and so worship God acceptably with reverence and awe, for our God is a consuming fire.
HEBREWS 12:18–19, 22–24, 28–29

The significance of this passage and of the understanding of Hebrews concerning the land and Jerusalem is summed up by **C.J.H. Wright** as follows:

Hebrews' affirmations of what 'we have' are surprisingly comprehensive. We have the land, described as the 'rest' into which we have entered through Christ, in a way which even Joshua did not achieve for Israel (3:12 – 4:11); we have a High Priest (4:14; 8:1; 10:21) and an Altar (13:10); we have a hope, which in the context refers to the reality of the covenant made with Abraham (6:13–20). We enter into the Holy Place, so we have the reality of the tabernacle and temple (10:19). We have come to Mount Zion (12:22) and we are receiving a kingdom, in line with Haggai 2:6 (12:28). Indeed, according to Hebrews (13:14), the only thing which we do not have is an earthly, territorial city![26]

Most if not all Christians would believe that the temple and its sacrifices have been fulfilled once and for all in Jesus. When we have seen their deeper meaning fulfilled in the person of Jesus, we no longer expect or want to see a purely literal fulfilment. A literal fulfilment of such promises would seem rather like lighting a candle when the sun is shining; it is no longer necessary! But if this is true for the temple and its sacrifices, why can it not also be true for the land? Why make it an exception, and insist that unlike other themes, everything associated with the land must be interpreted literally?

It is perfectly understandable that Jews should believe that the establishment of Israel holds out a hope of survival for the Jewish people in a hostile world in the twentieth century. And Christians may or may not accept the ideals of Zionism. But if we understand how the writer of the letter to the Hebrews thought about the land, how can we believe that the establishment of a Jewish state in the land is the fulfilment of Old Testament hopes and aspirations for the land? Now that the Messiah has come, we cannot possibly go back!

4.6 John's vision of the final fulfilment of the covenant

There is one book in the New Testament more than any other which describes the hopes of a Jewish Christian about the final fulfilment of the covenant God made with Abraham and of all the hopes of Israel – the book of Revelation. It does this by describing a series of visions of past, present and future realities.

If we can assume that John the disciple was the author of both the Gospel according to John and the book of Revelation, we have the opportunity to see how one writer develops Old Testament themes about the land and Jerusalem in two books which are very different in character from each other. Moreover, the book of Revelation is specially important because so much Christian teaching about prophecy (for example, about the millennium) is based on this book (see 4.7 The land and the millennium).

The following are two examples of how John takes up themes concerning the land, Jerusalem and the temple and gives them a Christian interpretation:

The glory of the Lord filling the temple

Ezekiel's visions of the temple in the new Jerusalem form part of 'the visions of God' which he describes to the exiles in Babylon (see 3.5 Exile from the land). In one of these visions he sees the glory of God returning to the new temple:

Then the man brought me to the gate facing east, and I saw the glory of the God of Israel coming from the east. His voice was like the roar of rushing waters, and the land was radiant with his glory... The glory of the LORD *entered the temple through the gate facing east. Then the Spirit lifted me up and brought me into the inner court, and the glory of the* LORD *filled the temple.*
EZEKIEL 43:1–5

John in his Gospel records a saying of Jesus in which he claimed indirectly to be the fulfilment of all that the temple stood for:

Then the Jews demanded of him, 'What miraculous sign can you show us to prove your authority to do all this?'
    Jesus answered them, 'Destroy this temple, and I will raise it again in three days.'

*The Jews replied, 'It has taken forty-six years to build this temple, and you are
going to raise it in three days?' But the temple he had spoken of was his body.*
JOHN 2:18–21

In the words of **N.T. Wright**:

*For Jesus, part of the point of the kingdom he was claiming to inaugurate would be
that it would bring with it all that the temple offered, thereby replacing, and making redundant, Israel's greatest symbol... He has in effect replaced the temple with
himself.*[27]

Once John had seen Jesus in this light, it was only natural that he should speak of
seeing the glory of God – not in a restored temple in Jerusalem, but in the face of
Jesus:

*The Word became flesh and made his dwelling among us. We have seen his glory,
the glory of the one and Only who came from the Father, full of grace and truth.*
JOHN 1:14

When we come to the book of Revelation, we find that John has developed
Ezekiel's vision of the new Jerusalem and the new temple into a picture of the final
consummation of God's plans for the universe:

*Then I saw a new heaven and a new earth, for the first heaven and the first earth
had passed away, and there was no longer any sea. I saw the Holy City, the new
Jerusalem, coming down out of heaven from God, prepared as a bride beautifully
dressed for her husband. And I heard a loud voice from the throne saying, 'Now the
dwelling of God is with men, and he will live with them. They will be his people,
and God himself will be with them and be their God.'*
*I did not see a temple in the city, because the Lord God Almighty and the Lamb
are its temple.*
REVELATION 21:1–3, 22

In his Gospel, therefore, John relates Ezekiel's vision of the new temple to the *first*
coming of Jesus Christ: Jesus himself is the new temple and the glory of God is
revealed through him. In Revelation, he relates it to the *second* coming of Christ: he
sees 'a new heaven and a new earth', when this world as we know it ('the first
earth') has passed away. The words from the throne indicate that what he is seeing
in the vision is the final and complete fulfilment of the covenant promise made to
Abraham: 'Now the dwelling of God is with men, and he will live with them. *They
will be his people, and God himself will be with them and be their God.'*

The river of living water
This picture is found in three different prophets: Ezekiel, Zechariah and Joel. It
occurs first of all in Ezekiel, where it is part of his vision of the new temple (see 3.5
Exile from the land):

The man brought me back to the entrance to the temple, and I saw water coming out from under the threshold of the temple toward the east (for the temple faced east). The water was coming down from under the south side of the temple, south of the altar. He then brought me out through the north gate and led me around the outside to the outer gate facing east, and the water was flowing from the south side.

As the man went eastward with a measuring line in his hand, he measured off a thousand cubits and then led me through water that was ankle-deep... He measured off another thousand, but now it was a river that I could not cross, because the water had risen and was deep enough to swim in – a river that no one could cross...

Then he led me back to the bank of the river. When I arrived there, I saw a great number of trees on each side of the river. He said to me, 'This water flows toward the eastern region and goes down into the Arabah, where it enters the Sea. When it empties into the Sea, the water there becomes fresh. Swarms of living creatures will live wherever the river flows... Fruit trees of all kinds will grow on both banks of the river. Their leaves will not wither, nor will their fruit fail. Every month they will bear, because the water from the sanctuary flows to them. Their fruit will serve for food and their leaves for healing.'
EZEKIEL 47:1–3, 5–9, 12

It seems that the prophets felt free to borrow pictures and images from each other – and even sometimes to adapt them. Thus when Zechariah takes up the same picture, he speaks of water flowing *both* to the east *and* to the west:

On that day living water will flow out from Jerusalem, half to the eastern sea and half to the western sea, in summer and in winter. The LORD will be king over the whole earth.
ZECHARIAH 14:8–9

Joel at a later date uses the image as part of his picture of the prosperity of the new age when God will establish his people in the land:

In that day the mountains will drip new wine,
*   and the hills will flow with milk;*
all the ravines of Judah will run with water.
*   A fountain will flow out of the LORD's house*
and will water the valley of acacias.
*   Judah will be inhabited forever*
and Jerusalem through all generations.
JOEL 3:18, 20

When this same picture is used by Jesus, the streams of living water flow not from the temple, but from every individual who believes in him *or* (according to another possible interpretation) from Jesus himself. The words 'streams of living water will flow from within him' in John 7:38 must be taken from these visions in the prophets, since there is no other saying resembling it anywhere else in the Old Testament.

On the last and greatest day of the Feast, Jesus stood and said in a loud voice, 'If anyone is thirsty, let him come to me and drink. Whoever believes in me, as the Scripture has said, streams of living water will flow from within him.' By this he meant the Spirit, whom those who believed in him were later to receive. Up to that time the Spirit had not been given, since Jesus had not yet been glorified.
JOHN 7:37–39

The same theme appears once again in John's vision of 'a new heaven and a new earth'. Here the city from which the water is flowing is 'the Holy City, the new Jerusalem coming down out of heaven from God':

Then the angel showed me the river of the water of life, as clear as crystal, flowing from the throne of God and of the Lamb down the middle of the great street of the city. On each side of the river stood the tree of life, bearing twelve crops of fruit, yielding its fruit every month. And the leaves of the tree are for the healing of the nations.
REVELATION 22:1–2

The apostle John therefore sees the prophetic vision of the river of living water as being fulfilled in two ways: firstly, in Jesus' giving of the Spirit to the believer or in the experience of the believer who is filled with the Spirit and is therefore able to bring life to others, and secondly in the new heaven and new earth. If these were the thoughts that were going through John's mind when he read the visions in Ezekiel, Zechariah and Joel, could he *also and at the same time* be looking forward to the time when a brilliant irrigation scheme would be devised to bring water from Jerusalem across the desert of Judea and down to the Dead Sea? If in John's mind the earthly city and the earthly temple are merely reflections of the reality of heaven, where God dwells with his people and is worshipped by them, the heavenly city and the heavenly temple realistically replace their earthly counterparts.

These ideas are summed up by **N.T. Wright** as follows:

No new temple would replace Herod's, since the real and final replacement was Jesus and his people. No intensified Torah would define this community, since its sole definition was its Jesus-belief. No Land claimed its allegiance, and no Holy City could function for it as Jerusalem did for mainline Jews; Land had now been transposed into World, and the Holy City was the new Jerusalem, which, as some Jewish apocalyptic writers had envisaged, would appear, like the horses and chariots of fire around Elisha, becoming true on earth as it was in heaven.[28]

Christians generally believe that the New Testament writers give them an authoritative interpretation of the Old Testament – or rather, the normative interpretation of the Old Testament. This means, for example, that if they want to know what the sacrificial system in the temple was all about, they look to the writings of the apostles. Since the risen Jesus 'opened their minds so they could understand the Scriptures' (Luke 24:45), Christians can look to their writings to find out how Jesus interpreted the Old Testament.

Christians today do not have the liberty to interpret the Old Testament in any way that appeals to them. Everything in the Old Testament has to be read through the eyes of the apostles. It is they who, so to speak, give us the right spectacles for a genuinely Christian reading of the Old Testament.

Therefore if Christians today find that certain details in books like Ezekiel appear to fit certain situations in the Middle East today, they should resist the temptation to draw direct connections with these contemporary events. The reason is that since the apostle John has given *his* interpretation of Ezekiel's visions, this should be seen as *the normative Christian interpretation* of these visions, and not only *one possible interpretation*. Christians do not have the liberty to work out from Ezekiel 38 the scenario for a Russian invasion of Palestine in contemporary history; *or* to draw a plan of Ezekiel's temple from chapters 40–47 and expect that it will one day be built in Jerusalem; *or* to draw a map of Palestine according to Ezekiel's division of the land in chapter 48 and expect that this will one day be the territory occupied by the State of Israel. Christians do not have this liberty simply because this is not how the apostle John interpreted these visions.

Our study of the land in the Bible has now brought us full circle – back to the point at which we began. What John has described in his visions is simply the final and complete fulfilment of the covenant which God made with Abraham:

■ The promise of *the land* has now given way to the promise of 'a new heaven and a new earth' (Revelation 21:1).
■ *The nation* which God promised would become great and numerous has now become 'the 144,000 from all the tribes of Israel' (Revelation 7:4).
■ The promise of *a special relationship between God and his people* is fulfilled because now 'the dwelling of God is with men, and he will live with them. They will be his people, and God himself will be with them and be their God' (Revelation 21:3).
■ The promise of *blessing for all peoples on earth* will finally be fulfilled in the 'great multitude that no one could count, from every nation, tribe, people and language, standing before the throne and in front of the Lamb' (Revelation 7:9).

With this hope before him, it is no wonder that John should end the book with a prayer, which expresses a longing for this complete fulfilment, and a blessing:

Come, Lord Jesus. The grace of the Lord Jesus be with God's people. Amen.
REVELATION 22:20–21

4.7 The land and the millennium
Some Christian readers may well be asking at this point: why has there been no discussion of 'the millennium'? How is it possible to study biblical teaching about the future (and the book of Revelation in particular) without discussing this idea which has been so central for generations in the thinking of many Christians? How can we explore the theme of the land without reference to the debate about the millennium?

The word 'millennium' is used to refer to the period of 1,000 years described in one of John's visions in the book of Revelation (20:1–6). The passage comes towards the end of the book and speaks of how the reign of Christ has severely limited Satan's power, with the result that Christian martyrs are able to share Christ's victory and his reign. The text is as follows, with the references to 'the millennium' printed in roman type:

And I saw an angel coming down out of heaven, having the key to the Abyss and hold-ing in his hand a great chain. He seized the dragon, that ancient serpent, who is the devil, or Satan, and bound him for a thousand years. *He threw him into the Abyss, and locked and sealed it over him, to keep him from deceiving the nations anymore until* the thousand years *were ended. After that, he must be set free for a short time.*

I saw thrones on which were seated those who had been given authority to judge. And I saw the souls of those who had been beheaded because of their testimony for Jesus and because of the word of God. They had not worshiped the beast or his image and had not received his mark on their foreheads or their hands. They came to life and reigned with Christ a thousand years. *(The rest of the dead did not come to life until* the thousand years *were ended.) This is the first resurrection. Blessed and holy are those who have part in the first resurrection. The second death has no power over them, but they will be priests of God and of Christ and will reign with him for* a thou-sand years.
REVELATION 20:1–6

The debate about the millennium has centred round the following questions:

■ Is the millennium as described in Revelation 20 to be understood as a literal period of 1,000 years which has still to come in the future? Or is it to be understood symbol-ically in the context of John's highly symbolic descriptions in his visions as a way of describing some other reality?
■ Does the millennium come *before* or *after* the second coming of Christ? Does the millennium prepare the way for the return of Christ, or does the coming of Christ inaugurate the millennium?
■ How many other passages in the Bible (e.g. in the Old Testament prophets) should be related to the millennial rule of Christ? Is it possible to work out any kind of chronology to enable us to know in advance about the sequence of events leading to the end of the world?

Out of the different answers given to these questions, three main schools of inter-pretation have been developed concerning the millennium:

■ The *premillennial* position holds that the second coming of Christ will take place *before* the millennium. The return of Christ to this world will usher in a liter-al period of 1,000 years in which Christ will reign over the world.
■ The *postmillennial* position is that the second coming of Christ will take place *after* the millennium. The 1,000 years represents a period in which Christianity spreads throughout the world. At the end of this period of gradual conversion and transformation for the better, Christ will come once again to the world.

■ The *amillennial* interpretation is that the 1,000 years in the book of Revelation is not to be understood as a literal period of 1,000 years, but rather as a symbol describing the period of time in which we now live, following the victory that Christ has won through his death and resurrection. This was John's way of describing what is a present reality – namely the victory of Christ in which all Christian believers (and especially Christian martyrs) can share.

It should be evident by now that it is this third position that underlies the whole of this book. The issue of the millennium is discussed further in a later chapter because it plays such an important part in the thinking of Christian Zionists (6.3 Christian Zionism and Dispensationalism). At this stage, however, it should be sufficient to explain briefly why the study of the land in the last two chapters has not been discussed in terms of the debate about the millennium:

■ While the premillennial and postmillennial positions are widely held in certain churches (especially evangelical Protestant denominations), they are not always well known or understood outside these traditions. There are many Christians of other traditions who want to relate the Bible to what is happening in the Middle East, but are blissfully ignorant about the different prophetic schemes that have been developed within these Protestant traditions in the West.
■ Prophetic schemes based on interpretations of the millennium in evangelical Protestant churches have forced the discussion about biblical prophecy – and the Bible as a whole – into a strait-jacket. What has happened is that an idea which is based initially on only *one* passage in the Bible has been made the basis for prophetic schemes which are then used to interpret the *whole* Bible. An interpretation that has been created (at least initially) out of interpretations of one difficult passage in Revelation has been made into a grid through which the whole of the Bible has to be interpreted.

These interpretations appear to many to be thoroughly artificial constructions which have to be imposed on the text and do not arise naturally out of it. Since the theme of the land, on the other hand, as we have seen, is such a fundamental category for understanding the Bible, it seems more appropriate to understand the *millennium* within the framework of a biblical understanding of the *land* than to force its teaching about the *land* into the framework of the *millennium*.
■ In a later chapter (see 6.3 Christian Zionism and Dispensationalism) we shall see that the premillennial position leads in practice to a strangely one-sided interpretation of what has been happening in the Middle East. The insistence on a literal interpretation of everything in the Bible means that there can never be any questioning of the assumption that the Jewish people have a divine right to the land for all time. It is also taken for granted that predictions in the prophets about a return of Jews to the land have been fulfilled not only in the return from Babylon in the sixth century BC, but also in the return to Palestine since 1880. Many Christians who have been brought up with this kind of teaching have found it particularly difficult to appreciate or to have any sympathy for the Palestinians, although some of them have been forced to think again when they have seen how their theology expresses itself in human and political terms.

In case this section, however, should end on a purely controversial note, the following paragraphs, written by **Anthony A. Hoekema**, an American theologian, present the interpretation of John's millennium which is most consistent with the approach developed in this book. According to this understanding the millennium has nothing whatever to do with Jewish sovereignty over the land of Palestine. Rather it describes 'what takes place during the entire history of the church, beginning with the first coming of Christ':

The book of Revelation is full of symbolic numbers. Obviously the number 'thousand' which is used here must not be interpreted in a literal sense. Since the number ten signifies completeness, and since a thousand is ten to the third power, we may think of the expression 'a thousand years' as standing for a complete period, a very long period of indeterminate length…. We may conclude that this thousand-year period extends from Christ's first coming to just before his second coming… That period… spans the entire New Testament dispensation, from the time of the first coming of Christ to just before the time of Christ's second coming…

We can appreciate the significance of this vision when we remember that in John's time the church was sorely oppressed and frequently persecuted. It would be of great comfort to those believers to know that though many of their fellow Christians had died, some even having been cruelly executed as martyrs, these deceased fellow believers were now actually alive in heaven as far as their souls were concerned – living and reigning with Christ. This living and reigning with Christ, John goes on to say, shall continue throughout the thousand years – that is, throughout the entire gospel era, until Christ shall come again to raise the bodies of these believers from the grave.

There is no indication in these verses that John is describing an earthly millennial reign. The scene… is set in heaven. Nothing is said in verses 4–6 about the earth, about Palestine as the center of this reign or about the Jews. The thousand-year reign of Revelation 20:4 is a reign with Christ in heaven of the souls of believers who have died. This reign is not something to be looked for in the future; it is going on now, and will be until Christ returns. Hence the term realized millennialism *is an apt description of the view here defended…*[29]

4.8 Conclusions

The birth of Jesus the Messiah

The birth of Jesus is described in the gospels as the fulfilment of the promise made to Abraham and of the hopes expressed by the prophets (4.1 The birth of Jesus the Messiah).

Jesus and the land

Jesus seems to be silent about the subject of the land because for him the theme of the kingdom of God took the place of the theme of the land and everything else associated with it in the Old Testament. He used language from the Old Testament about the land, the ingathering of the exiles to the land and the redemption or restoration of the nation of Israel to describe his own ministry (4.2 Jesus and the land).

Jesus and Jerusalem
Jesus predicted the destruction of Jerusalem (which took place in AD 70), and interpreted it as a judgment from God for the refusal of the majority to recognize him as Messiah. Apart from these predictions, Jesus had nothing to say about the future status of the land or of Jerusalem (4.3 Jesus and Jerusalem).

The redemption of Israel
Jesus claimed that through his life, death and resurrection he had fulfilled the hopes of the Jewish people and accomplished 'the redemption of Israel' (4.4 The redemption of Israel).

The land in the teaching of the apostles
In contrast to Jewish writers who developed both literal and spiritual interpretations of the land side by side, the New Testament writers showed no interest in a literal interpretation. Since they were silent about the future of the land and at the same time interpreted the concept of the land in the light of Jesus and his kingdom, they must have believed that this was the only possible interpretation of the significance of the land for Christians, whether Jews or Gentiles (4.5 The land in the teaching of the apostles).

John's vision of the final fulfilment of the covenant
When New Testament writers like John had seen the significance of the land and the nation in the context of the kingdom of God which had come into being in Jesus of Nazareth, they ceased to look forward to a literal fulfilment of Old Testament prophecies of a return to the land and a restored Jewish state. The one and only fulfilment of all the promises and prophecies was already there before their eyes in the person of Jesus. The way they interpreted the Old Testament should be the norm for the Christian interpretation of the Old Testament today (4.6 John's vision of the final fulfilment of the covenant).

The land and the millennium
Instead of forcing biblical teaching about the land into the categories suggested by particular interpretations of 'the millennium', it is more helpful to study the theme of the land in the Old and New Testaments as far as possible in its own terms. The nature of the book of Revelation and the style of John's writing make it impossible to interpret the period of 1,000 years literally or to suggest that it bears any relationship to historical events of the past, present or future in Palestine. The millennial debate can easily turn out to be a blind alley because it does not help anyone to understand the realities of what has actually been happening in the land (4.7 The land and the millennium).

If it is not appropriate for Christians to interpret the recent history of Israel/Palestine in terms of the fulfilment of the promise of the land to Abraham and his descendants and the prophecies of a return of Jewish exiles to the land, does this mean that the Bible has nothing to say about the conflict?

The next chapter (Chapter 5: Other Biblical Themes) suggests that there are many other ways in which the Bible can shed light on the conflict. A number of different themes are developed to suggest the relevance of various biblical themes to a number of issues in the conflict.

The question of Christian interpretation of Old Testament prophecy is explored in greater detail in Appendix 1: Principles of Christian Interpretation of Old Testament Prophecy, and Appendix 2: Examples of Christian Interpretation of Old Testament Prophecy.

Chapter 5

Other Biblical Themes
'Is There Any Word from the Lord?'

*Jeremiah was put into a vaulted cell in a dungeon,
where he remained a long time. Then King Zedekiah sent
for him and had him brought to the palace, where he
asked him privately, 'Is there any word from the LORD?'*
JEREMIAH 37:16–17

*Let justice roll on like a river,
righteousness like a never-failing stream!*
AMOS 5:24

*Blessed are those who hunger and thirst for
righteousness...Blessed are the peacemakers.*
MATTHEW 5:6, 9

*The religious commitment can best help mankind avoid
another Holocaust and more tragic memories, not by
deifying the present state of Israel, but rather by insisting that
the majestic vision of God in Zion must stand in the same
rigorous, stern, moral judgment of this Zionist state as you
demand this same God stand in judgment of this nation of yours.*[1]
RABBI ELMER BERGER

*Repentance is not merely an act; it is an attitude of mind.
It is a passion for the truth, an urgent desire to know the worst
as well as the best, a readiness to begin again in a new way, a constantly
proceeding examination of one's way of life, and
with it all an ever remade decision to put right what is wrong.*[2]
DENYS BALY

> *Theologically speaking, what is at stake today in the*
> *political conflict over the land of the West Bank and Gaza is*
> *nothing less than the way we understand the nature of God.*[3]
> NAIM STEFAN ATEEK

5.1 A passion for truth

Will it ever be possible to find out the truth about what has actually happened in the conflict between Jews and Palestinians in the land? Each side has its own understanding of the events leading to the establishment of the State of Israel, and frequently accuses the other of deliberately concealing or distorting the truth.

For example, the book *Palestine Comes First* by Lucas Grollenberg, a Dutch Dominican priest, received a very critical review from **Walter Barker**, at the time General Secretary of a Christian mission agency working among Jews:

The writer claims to give an account of what really happened as opposed to the Zionist propaganda view supposedly accepted uncritically by the Christians and the West. One of the intriguing facets of this bitter controversy is how convinced both sides are that the other's propaganda is the most successful! The historical survey, while having every sympathy with Arab hopes, aspirations and needs, lacks any sensitivity to the Jewish point of view...

It is essential that if Christians from the West write or speak about this tragic controversy they should do so with balance. This is obviously lacking here, so as a Christian contribution it is a poor one.[4]

Margaret Brearley, in a paper published by the Anglo-Israel Association in 1998:

There has been a highly sophisticated Palestinian propaganda campaign, funded by oil wealth and devised by American PR experts, which has skillfully suggested a mythical identity for the Palestinians based on the historical identity of the Jews: hence the themes of the 'Holocaust' and 'genocide' of the Palestinians, who are presented as the new Jews under [Jewish] fascist oppression. But the facts of life in the occupied teritories give the lie to this fiction.[5]

Allegations of distortion of the truth by Arabs and those sympathetic with their position have been matched by equally strong accusations about distortions that have been circulated by Jews.

Edward Said, writing in August 2001 concerning the reporting of the second Intifada in the Western media:

Never have the media been so influential in determining the course of war as during the Al-Aqsa Intifada, which, as far as the Western media are concerned, has essentially become a battle over images and ideas. Israel has already poured hundreds of millions of dollars into what in Hebrew is called hasbara, *or information for the outside world (hence, propaganda). This has included an entire range of efforts: lunches and free trips for influential journalists; seminars for Jewish university students who over a week in a secluded country estate can be primed to 'defend' Israel on the campus; bombarding congressmen and –women with invitations and visits; pamphlets and, most important, money for election campaigns; directing (or, as the case requires, harassing) photographers and writers of the current Intifada into producing certain images and not others; lectures and concert tours by prominent Israelis; training commentators to make frequent references to the Holocaust and Israel's predicament today; many advertisements in the newspapers attacking Arabs and praising Israel; and so on. Because so many powerful people in the media and publishing business are strong supporters of Israel, the task is made vastly easier. Although these are only a few of the devices used to pursue the aims of every modern government, whether democratic or not, since the 1930s and 1940s to produce consent and approval on the part of the consumer of news – no country and no lobby more than Israel's has used them in the US so effectively and for so long.*[6]

William Zuckermann, a Jew, writing in the *Jewish Newsletter* in 1958:

The terrifyingly gruesome power of modern propaganda to take over men's minds and lives, to manipulate their emotions and turn them into animals, is to my mind nowhere expressed more clearly than in the Zionist propaganda about Arab refugees put out over the last ten years. This propaganda has literally succeeded in changing black into white, lies into truth and serious social injustice into an act of justice, praised by thousands. This propaganda has turned capable men with more than average understanding into dupes and fools who believe everything that they are told; it has made friendly and gentle men and women with a strong sense of compassion into harsh fanatics, without any feeling for anyone other than their own people.[7]

General Carl von Horn, the Swedish Commander of the United Nations Truce Supervisory Organization (UNTSO) in Palestine from 1951 to 1963, was very critical about Israeli reporting of events during this period:

The highly skilled Israeli Information Service and the entire press combined to manufacture a warped, distorted version which was disseminated with professional expertise through every available channel to their own people and their sympathizers and supporters in America and the rest of the world. Never in all my life had I believed the truth could be so cynically, expertly bent.[8]

What would the Old Testament prophets have had to say about a situation of this kind? At the very least they would have pleaded for people to face up to the truth about themselves and their situation. The following are examples of different prophets who challenged their people to face the truth, pointing out the terrible consequences for any society that refuses to acknowledge the truth about itself.

In speaking to God on behalf of the people, **Isaiah** realizes that truth and justice go together, so that when there is no truth, there can be no justice:

For our offences are many in your sight,
  and our sins testify against us.
Our offences are ever with us,
  and we acknowledge our iniquities:
rebellion and treachery against the LORD,
  turning our backs on our God,
fomenting oppression and revolt,
  uttering lies our hearts have conceived.
So justice is driven back,
  and righteousness stands at a distance;
truth has stumbled in the streets,
  honesty cannot enter.
Truth is nowhere to be found,
  and whoever shuns evil becomes a prey.
ISAIAH 59:12–15

Amos describes the reaction of the majority to anyone who dares to speak the truth and expose what was wrong:

You hate the one who reproves in court
  and despise him who tells the truth.
AMOS 5:10

Jeremiah speaks of God in his wrath having to reject a whole generation of the people because 'truth has perished':

This is the nation that has not obeyed the Lord its God or responded to correction. Truth has perished; it has vanished from their lips. Cut off your hair and throw it away; take up a lament on the barren heights, for the Lord has rejected and abandoned this generation that is under his wrath.
JEREMIAH 7:28–29

'Friend deceives friend,
  and no one speaks the truth.
They have taught their tongues to lie;
  they weary themselves with sinning.
You live in the midst of deception;
  in their deceit they refuse to acknowledge me,' declares the LORD.
JEREMIAH 9:5–6

Zechariah, however, looks forward to a better future for his people, and in his vision of the restored Jerusalem, the city is called 'The City of Truth':

This is what the LORD says: 'I will return to Zion and dwell in Jerusalem. Then Jerusalem will be called The City of Truth, and the mountain of the LORD Almighty will be called The Holy Mountain.'
ZECHARIAH 8:3

This is what the LORD Almighty says: 'Just as I had determined to bring disaster upon you and showed no pity when your fathers angered me,' says the LORD Almighty, 'so now I have determined to do good again to Jerusalem and Judah. Do not be afraid. These are the things you are to do: Speak the truth to each other, and render true and sound judgment in your courts; do not plot evil against your neighbor, and do not love to swear falsely. I hate all this,' declares the LORD.
ZECHARIAH 8:14–17

What would it mean in practical terms for all who are concerned about this conflict – whether as participants or as spectators – to demonstrate this kind of prophetic passion for truth in all their thinking about the land?

The writers of the 1970 *Quaker Report* entitled *The Search for Peace in the Middle East* explained how their report arose out of a concern to find 'the most complete truth we could understand':

> *Out of our own concern, and with the urging of both Jews and Arabs, a group of Quakers began in 1968 the exploration of possible approaches to peace in the Middle East. As we listened to people in many walks of life, and to high officials in Jordan, Israel, Lebanon, the United Arab Republic, at the UN, and in various world capitals, we were drawn into an effort to record the viewpoints we encountered and to make some attempt at assessing the possibilities of finding a solution…*
>
> *Having listened long and carefully to the many viewpoints of the interested parties, we believe we have a reasonably clear understanding of those viewpoints and how they developed. We have tried to hear all of the assorted and contradictory voices as the cries of real people overcome by real fears and frustrations – and explainable hatreds. We are convinced that no solution to the conflict can be found until it is possible for the outer world and the antagonists themselves, to hear – really hear – what the divergent voices are trying to say. No one truly interested in eventual peace in the Middle East can dismiss any of these voices as manifestations of depersonalized evil or demonic unreason…*
>
> *We have had this manuscript reviewed in detail by many Jews and Arabs, including high Israeli, Lebanese, Jordanian and United Arab Republic officials and by scholarly experts of varied nationalities. Acting on their advice, we have made many changes, while writing more than a dozen drafts, to correct mistakes of fact and to eliminate phrases and nuances deemed unfair or unsound by either side. We must assume that defects will still be found in the document. But, more important, we must accept the fact that on some issues we have had to declare ourselves in ways that put us clearly, with respect to a given point, on one side or the other.*
>
> *We have tried simply to follow the best light we could find toward the most complete truth we could understand.*[9]

Writing about the period immediately after the establishment of the State of Israel, **General Carl von Horn** described the difficult task faced by the United Nations Truce Supervisory Organization (UNTSO) in trying to remain neutral and objective in the conflict. His comments underline the need for knowing the truth – the whole truth about what has happened and is still happening:

Our raison d'être *as peacekeepers was objectivity and impartiality. Yet these very qualities were exactly those which led to hostility. It was understandable; time and time again in the course of frank discussions with Israeli officers and officials, I had heard them openly repudiate the idea of objectivity. Their flat statement 'You are either for or against us', explained why – having dared to be entirely objective – I had now been branded as irrevocably 'against'. I had seen it happen many times before from my predecessors down to the ordinary observer on the frontiers who, in the course of his duty, had incurred Arab or Israeli hostility simply because his* impartial *version had been very different from theirs. Even nastier was an Israeli tendency immediately to brand objectivity as anti-Semitic; a convenient label which could be smeared on to any UN soldier whose impartial report did not weigh down in favour of the Israelis.*

We had from time to time incurred a certain degree of animosity in our dealings with the Arabs, but never in the same implacable and frenetic way. The Arabs could be difficult, intolerant, indeed often impossible; but their code of behaviour was on an infinitely higher and more civilized level. I think that we all came to this conclusion in the UNTSO, which was strange, because there was hardly a man among us who had not originally arrived in the Holy Land without the most positive and sympathetic attitude towards the Israelis and their ambitions for their country.

Never in my life have I encountered a nation with such an infinite talent for turning goodwill into disillusion and so often disgust. It seemed as though the state were possessed of some demon with a capacity to turn potential friends into enemies. I am certain that I shall be bitterly attacked for setting down my impressions so frankly, but unfortunately they are the truth. All of us who went to Israel knew very little about Arabs, but a great deal about the Jews and their appalling sufferings in the Second World War. I have never been – and I am not – anti-Semitic; I have always numbered Jews among some of my closest friends since boyhood. I have good friends in Israel, wonderful families who stood by me and welcomed me into their homes during the height of the boycott. Many of our personnel, too, had close friends in the new state long before they came out to Jerusalem, and I would think that seldom before have the members of any organization – and this was a truly international one – started off with such a fund of goodwill towards a state which had emerged at the cost of such dreadful suffering.

What went wrong? I always had a talk with staff members who were leaving the Mission. Invariably it was the same story. Nearly all of them had arrived with the honest intention to help both parties to the Armistice Agreement, but with a conscious sympathy for the people of 'poor little Israel'. Yet after two or three years in daily contact with officials, soldiers and private individuals on both sides, there had been a remarkable change in their attitude. I found it sad but very significant that when I asked them what their most negative experiences had been during their service with UNTSO the reply was almost invariably: 'The consistent cheating and deception of the Israelis'.[10]

One positive development in recent years has been the new approaches to the history of the conflict among the so-called 'new historians' or 'revisionist historians' in Israel. Using newly available source material and with a more even-handed interpretation of the evidence, they have in recent years produced histories of the conflict which come very much closer to Arab interpretations of the same events.

Stephen Sizer, an Anglican priest who has written extensively about Christian responses to the conflict, sums up the significance of Benny Morris's *Righteous Victims: A History of the Zionist-Arab Conflict, 1881–1999*:

Righteous Victims… represents the coming of age of Israeli historical self-criticism. In a review for the New York Times, Ethan Bronner concludes, 'Benny Morris writes with clinical dispassion. While that makes for a less lively narrative, it also makes for a more responsible and credible one. This is a first-class work of history, bringing together the latest scholarship. It is likely to stand for some time as the most sophisticated and nuanced account of the Zionist-Arab conflict from its beginnings in the 1880s. In short, this is new history as one would like it – not as part of a political or scholarly campaign but in the genuine pursuit of complete truth.'

Righteous Victims is quite simply mandatory reading; a monumental work of narration and explication for all who want to make sense of the history of the Arab-Israeli conflict and the prospects for peace.[11]

Facing the truth, however, involves more than admitting all the facts of what has happened. It involves also a willingness to recognize the truth about ourselves and our communities. **Denys Baly** sees this as a special problem for Arabs, who have often found it hard to hear or to admit the truth about themselves:

The blindness of the Arab leaders and of the people is a fact – an ugly undeniable fact. There have been those who have grown rich by the sufferings of their countrymen and those who have been content to flee to lands where they could live in greater security and then pour scorn on the foreign nations for not giving that help which they themselves were not prepared to give. It cannot be denied, even by the most fervent admirer of the Arabs, that they have done nothing like as much to help their own people as the Jews have done to help theirs, nor can it be denied that their politicians have often callously used the misery of the refugees as a means to an end; that the very existence of the refugees is partly the result of Arab misunderstanding of the situation; that the Arabs have from time to time encouraged violence and hatred and have again and again refused to face self-evident facts; and that they have been far too ready to blame their unhappiness on anyone but themselves. One meets many of the Arab people who in private conversation are ready to admit these things and are deeply troubled about them. It is true, as we found with the Jews, that reasons can be found to explain these weaknesses, but reasons do not make black white, nor do they convert weakness into strength.

He also suggests what a prophetic passion for truth might do to the whole Christian church:

Repentance is not merely an act; it is an attitude of mind. It is a passion for the truth, an urgent desire to know the worst as well as the best, a readiness to begin again in a new way, a constantly proceeding examination of one's way of life, and with it all an ever remade decision to put right what is wrong...

What is needed there [in the Middle East] almost more than anything else is a ruthless intellectual honesty which will break every barrier of emotionalism, sentiment, tradition and nationality, so that at the last people will be found able to question their own motives and behaviour. Hardly anywhere does it exist, and neither Islam nor the type of Judaism which is found in Israel encourage it... Only if the Christian Church can regain this passion for truth, whatever it may cost, will they begin to see it as a way of life.[12]

Edward Said recognizes the need for intellectual honesty:

We need a discourse that is intellectually honest and complex enough to deal both with the Palestinian as well as the Jewish experience, recognizing where the claims of one stop and where the other begin.[13]

If, therefore, the Bible does not provide an easy way of understanding the conflict, at least it underlines the need for all concerned to know the truth about what has actually happened. One basic precondition in attempting to put right the wrongs that have been done in the past is that all the parties in the conflict should be willing to face the truth about the present and the past for all the parties in the conflict – however uncomfortable or damning it may be.

5.2 The problem of prejudice

When **Mark Twain** visited Palestine in 1876 he was critical of the books he read that were written by Christians, because they reflected the very Protestant sympathies of their authors:

Honest as these men's intentions may have been, they were full of partialities and prejudices, they entered the country with their verdicts already prepared, and they could no more write dispassionately and impartially about it than they could about their own wives and children.[14]

Is it ever possible, therefore, to own up to our natural bias and allow it to be challenged? Even if it cannot be fully corrected, is it ever possible that an awareness of our bias and prejudice can make us open to reach out to the person on the other side with new understanding and sympathy?

There are at least two passages in the Bible which are relevant to the question of prejudice.

'Who made me a judge or divider over you?'

Luke records a revealing incident in which Jesus was invited to intervene in a family dispute:

Someone in the crowd said to him, 'Teacher, tell my brother to divide the inheritance with me.'

Jesus replied, 'Man, who appointed me a judge or an arbiter between you?' Then he said to them, 'Watch out! Be on your guard against all kinds of greed; a man's life does not consist in the abundance of his possessions.'

And he told them this parable...

LUKE 12:13–16

If this was a simple case of injustice, with the older brother refusing to give his younger brother his legitimate share of the family property, we might expect Jesus to support the younger brother in his demand for justice. This is precisely what Jesus did *not* do. Luke's account is remarkably brief, and we are left wondering if this is all that Jesus said. Did he, for example, begin by asking more questions and investigating the case in greater detail? Or did he refuse to get involved in any way? We do not know because Luke does not tell us.

What is clear, however, from this account is that Jesus did not immediately take sides. One reason that has been suggested for this is that the words of Jesus are an echo of the words addressed to Moses by the Egyptians in Exodus 2:14: 'Who made you ruler and judge over us?' This would mean, as **N.T. Wright** suggests, that 'Jesus is refusing to be, in that sense, a new Moses, one who will parcel out the promised land. He has come to bring Israel to her real "return from exile"; but, just as this will not underwrite Israel's ethnic aspirations, so it will not reaffirm her symbolic, and zealously defended, territorial inheritance and possession'.[15]

Another possible explanation for Jesus' reply is that he wanted to tackle the deeper issue of covetousness which lay beneath the surface. But who was doing the coveting? Was it the older brother who was holding on to the whole property? Or was it the younger brother who, even though he had a legitimate right to the property, was motivated primarily by selfishness and greed? Again, we do not know. It could have been either, or it could have been both.

A modern version of the same incident might read like this: 'An Israeli in the crowd said to him, "Master, tell my Arab neighbours to let me live in peace in the land of my fathers..."' Or it might begin: 'An Arab in the crowd said to him, "Master, tell the Israelis to give us back the land which they have taken from us..."' It is hard to imagine that Jesus is not concerned about the rights and wrongs of every human situation – not least in the land today. But if he were approached in this way, he would probably see more clearly than we do the rights and wrongs on *both* sides (or rather on *all* sides); and before taking sides in any way with one group against the other, he would no doubt want to deal with some of the underlying issues and attitudes and have something to say to *every* party involved in the conflict.

'If any one of you is without sin, let him be the first to throw a stone'

The story of Jesus' dealings with the woman taken in adultery underlines the need to be careful in passing judgment on others. Jesus does not in any way condone the woman's adultery, since it is still described as 'sin'. There is, therefore, no blurring of the moral issue. But he refuses to approve of stoning the woman or to condemn her in the same tones that his audience expected. He simply says to her, 'Neither do I condemn you... Go now and leave your life of sin' (John 8:11).

There is one reason why the Christian church needs to be particularly careful about pointing the finger at the Jewish people over this issue of the land. Christians today ought to blush with shame when they read what some of the greatest names in church history have said about the Jews (see 2.1 Anti-Semitism). They may protest that they themselves have no anti-Semitic feelings whatsoever, and that they cannot be held responsible for what Christians said and did in the past. As far as the Jew is concerned, however, Christians today are inevitably identified with them, just as members of the same family are identified with each other in the eyes of the world. If Christians do not want to forget all the good that has been done in the name of Christ, Jews can hardly forget all the suffering that Christians have brought to Jews in the name of Christ.

Does this mean that Christians, like those who tried to get Jesus to condemn the woman taken in adultery, must 'go away one at a time' (John 8:9)? Or are there ways of challenging wrong and helping the wrong-doer that are more Christ-like than taking up stones in order to carry out the final sentence ourselves?

If we try to embark on this task, we have to be willing to admit with the psalmist, 'We have sinned, even as our fathers did' (Psalm 106:6), and confess with the prophet Isaiah, 'I am a man of unclean lips, and I live among a people of unclean lips' (Isaiah 6:5). For the message of Jesus to all would-be prophets is: 'First take the plank out of your own eye, and then you will see clearly to remove the speck from your brother's eye' (Matthew 7:5).

How can this awareness of the danger of prejudice contribute to our thinking about the conflict over the land?

The writers of the *Quaker Report* explain what it meant for them to write about justice in the Middle East:

Despite our best efforts to treat this issue with objectivity and candour and to win the widest possible agreement for a peaceful solution, we face these realities:

1. It is impossible to come to a fair and responsible judgment on the Arab-Israeli conflict on the basis of endorsing the Israeli government position or the positions of the Arab governments or of the Palestinian Arab organizations. No side has a case so right and just that all its past or present actions can be defended.
2. Many on each side will denounce any comment which does not support their position on the grounds that 'if you are not for us, you are against us'.
3. It is impossible to reach an even-handed judgment on the basis of some neat compromise. On some issues, we believe, the Arabs have been clearly wrong and on other issues, the Israelis have been clearly wrong.

They state their conviction that it is possible to be 'both pro-Jewish and pro-Arab':

We wish to make clear to all, particularly to our countrymen of Jewish and Arab backgrounds, that our position is one of concern for both peoples and is based on

*the conviction that the rights and interests of both must be recognized and recon-
ciled on some just and peaceful basis. We believe that to ignore or to deny the essential rights of one group will lead to the ultimate destruction of the rights of the other.
Peace and decent living conditions, if not available to both, will be unavailable to
either. We firmly believe that it is possible to be both pro-Jewish and pro-Arab. And
for both the essential need is peace.*[16]

Denys Baly points out why people who are prejudiced cannot do anything to bring
about reconciliation:

*The New Testament presents the reconciliation of God and man as possible only
when there is someone who can properly be identified with both God and man...
Political reconciliation can come about only when there are those who struggle
earnestly to belong to both sides... It is fatally easy in the circumstances of increasing polarization to become so vividly aware of the sufferings and the injustice
done to one side that we become wholly identified with them, and see no virtue at
all in the other side... Certainly it may be right to go to the defence of those who
seem to be the underdogs (though we should beware always of a merely emotional
and superficial assessment), but our concern for the underdog should not prevent
us from entering fully into the hopes and fears even of those who seem to be the
oppressors, of struggling to comprehend why they are doing what they are doing...
and think in their terms. To neglect this task is utterly to fail to speak the word of
reconciliation and to betray the cause of Christ. I use the strongest words that I
know, partly because every effort will be made by those who are embroiled in the
battle to obtain your 100 per cent allegiance and to deny it to the other side, and
partly also because this is a polarized world... A necessary part of the defence
against the betrayal of Christ is the rejection of absolute moral standards as a
basis for positive political action.*[17]

5.3 The demands of the law

One of the biggest dangers in using the Bible to interpret the conflict between Israeli
Jews and the Palestinians is the selective use of passages which support one particular argument. It is easy to appeal to the divine promise to Abraham concerning the
land and the predictions of a return, and to ignore quietly other aspects of its teaching about the land. The books of the *Torah* which contain the divine promises concerning the land, however, also contain the divine law revealed to Moses. This law
constantly emphasizes that since God is a God of righteousness and justice, he
demands and expects that his people will be concerned about justice in society.

Two aspects of this law are particularly relevant to the issue of the land in recent
history. One concerns the seriousness of theft and murder, while the other has to do
with the treatment of foreigners or aliens in the land.

'Thou shalt... thou shalt not...'

There are three commandments in particular which may need to be spelt out, since
we are concerned with rights to ownership of the land and all the violence committed by those who in recent years have claimed it as their own:

You shall not murder...
You shall not steal...
You shall not covet your neighbor's house. You shall not covet your neighbor's wife,
or his manservant or maidservant, his ox or donkey, or anything that belongs to
your neighbor.
EXODUS 20:13, 15, 17

In the Mosaic Law murder is clearly distinguished from manslaughter, and the penalty for murder leaves no doubt about the seriousness of this crime:

Anyone who strikes a man and kills him shall surely be put to death. However, if he
does not do it intentionally, but God lets it happen, he is to flee to a place I will des-
ignate. But if a man schemes and kills another man deliberately, take him away
from my altar and put him to death.
EXODUS 21:12–14

One particular form of stealing – stealing land – is strongly condemned:

Do not move your neighbor's boundary stone set up by your predecessors in the
inheritance you receive in the land the LORD your God is giving you to possess.
DEUTERONOMY 19:14

Cursed is the man who moves his neighbor's boundary stone.
DEUTERONOMY 27:17

Some Jews in the last century *have* been willing to recognize the relevance of the
Mosaic law and to be judged by it. **Chaim Weizmann** for example, speaking at
the twenty-second Zionist Congress in Basle in 1946, spoke of terrorism as 'a can-
cer in the body politic of Palestinian Jewry' and called for 'the courage of
endurance and the heroism of super-human restraint'. When accused of being a
demagogue he replied:

If you think of bringing the redemption nearer by un-Jewish methods, if you lose
faith in hard work and better days, then you commit idolatry and endanger what
we have built.[18]

He made this admission when speaking to a UN Commission of enquiry in 1947:

In all humbleness, thou shalt not kill *has been ingrained in us since Mount*
Sinai. It was inconceivable ten years ago that Jews should break this command-
ment. Unfortunately, they are breaking it today, and nobody deplores it more
than the vast majority of the Jews. I hang my head in shame when I have to
speak of this fact before you.[19]

'Do not oppress an alien'
Since the Israelites had so recently come out of slavery in Egypt, they were expected

to remember what it was like to be aliens who are vulnerable and powerless in a foreign land. When they entered the promised land and established themselves as a nation, they were therefore told not to oppress any aliens living in their midst:

Do not mistreat an alien or oppress him, for you were aliens in Egypt.
EXODUS 22:21

Do not oppress an alien; you yourselves know how it feels to be aliens, because you were aliens in Egypt. (Thou shalt not oppress a stranger: for ye know the heart of a stranger, seeing ye were strangers in the land of Egypt [Authorized Version].)
EXODUS 23:9

If, as Chaim Weizmann said, 'the Jewish problem revolves fundamentally round the homelessness of the Jewish people', one might have expected that the Jews of all people in the twentieth century would 'know the heart of a stranger'.

How has it happened, therefore, that the Jews in Israel, after returning to their land and creating a Jewish state in order to escape from oppression elsewhere, have found themselves in a position of having to take harsh measures to deal with the aliens in their midst? In spite of what the constitution says about equal rights for all communities and all religions, the Arabs, who have been living in their own land, have often had good reason to complain that they have not been not treated as native-born Israeli Jews.

One recurring theme in *both* Jewish *and* Arab writing about the conflict is the apparent inability of many Jews coming into the land to recognize or respect the rights of Palestinians Arabs. The following are examples of Jews who at different stages in the conflict have recognized this problem among themselves.

W. Brunn, a Jew, writing in 1919, points out the irony of the situation in which many Jews in Palestine have given the Arabs the same kind of treatment from which they themselves suffered in Europe:

We who are suffering persecutions throughout the world and who claim all human rights for ourselves are going to Palestine reversing the roles.[20]

Simha Flapan, an Israeli historian, writing in *Zionism and the Palestinians*, one of the most extensive studies on the attitudes of Zionists to the Palestinians (1979), describes Weizmann's attitude towards the Palestinians all through his life:

Weizmann's attitude towards the Palestinians was the gravest error of his political leadership, more serious than any other because Weizmann did not deviate from his attitude for even a brief period. His disdain for the Palestinians originated not only in the fact that lacking previous contact with them, he was influenced by his British advisers. From the very beginning, he approached the Palestinians with a prejudice that blinded him to the most obvious facts.

He must have known of the existence of the Palestinian people and their opposition to Zionist colonization, because as early as 1891, his major spiritual mentor and close associate, Ahad Ha'Am, had warned of major Arab resistance to Jewish immigration and settlement. Ahad Ha'Am had no solution to the problem, but urged that at least it be taken seriously. To lessen the conflict, he suggested prudent behaviour, just treatment and respect for Arab customs and culture. Weizmann followed Ahad Ha'Am's guidance in his relations with all Arabs except the Palestinians; with regard to them he listened to Aaron Aaronsohn, who viewed the Palestinians as backward, treacherous and corrupt.

He sums up the effects of Weizmann's 'non-recognition of the Palestinians':

Weizmann was sincere in his desire for a just solution to the conflict with the Palestinians. But his non-recognition of the Palestinians as a national entity could not but lead to a policy of injustice...

Unfortunately, Weizmann's legacy in this most vital aspect of Jewish-Arab relations has had a more lasting impact than any other. The Palestinians were never regarded as an integral *part of the country for whom long-term plans had to be made, either in the Mandatory period or since the establishment of the state. This explains why the Palestinian problem has remained at the heart of the Israeli-Arab conflict until the present day...*

Non-recognition of the Palestinians remains until the present the basic tenet of Israel's policy-makers who, like the Zionist leadership before 1948, nurture the illusion that the Palestinian national problem disappeared with the creation of the state of Jordan, leaving only the residual humanitarian problem of the refugees to be solved.

The war of 1948 was deemed to have vindicated the policy of non-recognition of the Palestinians; on the surface, the Palestinian people, dispersed as refugees all over the Middle East, had ceased to exist, and only the conflict between Israel and the Arab states remained unresolved.

Nearly 30 years had to pass before it became clear that the 1948 war did not liquidate the national problem of the Palestinians, but only aggravated and complicated it, changing some of its aspects and adding new ones, coming to resemble the problem of the Jews dispersed throughout the world, which the Zionist movement proposed to solve by 'ingathering of the exiles'.[21]

David Ben-Gurion spelt out very clearly how he understood the status of the Arabs in a Jewish state:

Israel is the country of the Jews and only of the Jews. Every Arab who lives there has the same rights as any minority citizen in any country of that world, but we must admit the fact that he lives in a Jewish country.[22]

Golda Meir went to the extent of denying the existence of the Palestinian people:

It was not as though there was a Palestinian people in Palestine considering itself as a Palestinian people and we came and threw them out and took their country away from them. They did not exist.[23]

Samuel Katz dismissed claims about the existence of the Palestinian Arabs as a people:

There was never a 'Palestinian Arab' nation. To the Arab people as a whole, no such entity as Palestine existed. To those of them who lived in its neighbourhood, its lands were a suitable object for plunder and destruction. Those few who lived within its bounds may have had an affinity for their village (and made war on the next village), for their clan (which fought for the right of local tax-gathering) or even for their own town. They were not conscious of any relationship to a land, and even the townsmen would have heard of its existence as a land, if they heard of it at all, only from such Jews as they might meet...

The feeling of so many nineteenth century visitors that the country had been waiting for the return of its lawful inhabitants was made the more significant by the shallowness of the Arab imprint on the country...[24]

Menachem Begin, former leader of the *Irgun* and Prime Minister from 1977 to 1983:

In our country there is only room for Jews.[25]

Dr Nahum Goldmann, a leader in the Zionist movement from the 1940s, recognized the vital importance of the Arab problem for the Jewish state; this is what he wrote in his autobiography in 1970:

One of the great oversights in the history of Zionism is that when the Jewish homeland in Palestine was founded, sufficient attention was not paid to relations with the Arabs. Of course, there were always a few Zionist speakers and thinkers who stressed them... And the ideological and political leaders of the Zionist movement always emphasized – sincerely and earnestly, it seems to me – that the Jewish national home must be established in peace and harmony with the Arabs. Unfortunately these convictions remained in the realm of theory and were not carried over, to any great extent, into actual Zionist practice. Even Theodor Herzl's brilliantly simple formulation of the Jewish question as basically a transportation problem of 'moving people without a home into a land without a people' is tinged with disquieting blindness to the Arab claim to Palestine. Palestine was not a land without people even in Herzl's time; it was inhabited by hundreds of thousands of Arabs, who in the course of events, could sooner or later have achieved independent statehood, either alone or as a unit with a larger Arab context.[26]

Anton La Guardia sums up the problem that the Palestinians have presented to Israel:

The hostility to Palestinians can best be explained as a hatred bred by fear. It is not just what the Palestinians do that troubles Israel, but who they are – Palestinians – people, a people who lay claim to the same piece of land as the Jews. A weak people who refused to disappear, just as the Jews were not wiped out by history. Israel fears the challenge which Palestinians pose to its moral legitimacy, fears losing the exclusive claim to suffering and fears that Israel will, in turn, be forced to recognize the tragedy it inflicted on the Palestinians. It is a fear of the ghosts of the past. It is a fear that the dead body of Palestine will reappear decades after the murder, or manslaughter, depending on one's view of history.[27]

Jews coming to the land since 1880 have been confronted with 'aliens' in the form of Palestinian Arabs. Among those who were aware of the words of the Mosaic law 'do not oppress an alien' some may have sincerely tried to obey them, while others have no doubt dismissed them as hopelessly idealistic in the hard world of modern Palestine.

Since Palestinians have been living in the land for centuries, they find it particularly hard to be put by Jews in Israel into the same category as the 'aliens' of the Old Testament. But perhaps they would not mind so much if they felt that the Jews had treated them in the way that the law required them to be treated.

If Jews and others make *no* connection between the State of Israel today and Old Testament scripture, they can certainly protest if the world seems to judge Israel by different standards. But the stronger the appeal that Jews make to the *Torah*, the stronger must be the insistence that they can, and should, be judged by the moral teaching of this same *Torah*. The more both Jews and Christians appeal to the Old Testament to demonstrate Jewish connections with the land, the more they are asking to be judged by the moral law contained in these same scriptures.

The words of **Chaim Weizmann**, therefore, written in his autobiography *Trial and Error* in 1949, begin to sound frighteningly prophetic in the light of the recent escalation of the conflict:

I am certain the world will judge the Jewish state by how it will treat the Arabs.[28]

5.4 The prophetic concern for justice

Is the God of the Bible concerned about justice? How does he respond to injustice? Is he working according to a predetermined plan which he will implement in detail, however people behave?

Many of the popular Christian books about the interpretation of Old Testament prophecy assume that since the land belongs to the Jews, and since the return of Jews to the land and the establishment of the State of Israel are so obviously the fulfilment of what is predicted in the Bible, there is no need to enter into the rights and wrongs of all that has been done. The land belongs to them by right, and God predicted a return long ago, and now it has happened – so it must be the will of God! Since this is what God planned and wanted to happen, there is no need to ask questions about *how* it happened.

Derek Prince, for example, is clearly aware of questions about injustice, but puts these on one side in his discussion of the Bible's teaching. He says that nothing can compare with the suffering of the Jews in the Holocaust, and refers to his own personal experience of suffering:

Many claims have been made that injustice has resulted from Israel being restored to their own land. Even some sincere Christians hold this point of view. The Bible is emphatic, however, that God is incapable of injustice... From our earthly point of view, it is hard to discern the pattern which God is weaving. Often it all seems jumbled and meaningless. But when we are able to see it from heaven's perspective, we agree with Moses: 'His work is perfect, and all his ways are just.'

This is not to deny that, on the human level, there have been acts of injustice perpetrated by the various parties involved in the return of Israel to their land. There has also been great suffering on the parts of many people. Of all the parties involved, however, none have suffered as much as the Jews. After six million had perished in the Holocaust, a tiny remnant have had to face more than 40 years of life-and-death struggle for survival in their own land. I myself have experienced at first hand at least some small measure of both the injustice and the suffering that accompanied the rebirth of the State of Israel.[29]

One of the problems in interpreting Old Testament prophecy in this way is that it seems to ignore a major aspect of the teaching of the prophets. In concentrating on the predictive element in prophecy, it passes over all the moral judgments that the prophets made about the attitudes and actions of their people. The prophets were not simply speaking about the future, describing how God was going to act in their affairs, but addressing their people about the present and the past.

The following are many examples of prophets who spoke out about things that were wrong in the society around them, condemning what they knew to be inconsistent with the law of God.

'You are the man!'

The Law of Moses very easily became a dead letter if there was no one around who could interpret and apply it both to individuals and to the community. When David arranged for Uriah the Hittite to be killed in battle and then took his wife Bathsheba for himself, it cannot have been because he did not know the commandments 'you shall not murder' and 'you shall not commit adultery'. He simply did not see his actions in terms of murder and adultery – until the prophet Nathan told the parable about the rich man stealing the poor man's lamb, and then pointed his finger at him with the words 'You are the man!' (2 Samuel 12:1–7).

'Have you murdered a man and seized his property?'

The prophet Elijah made several predictions about the future (for example, concerning the drought, 1 Kings 17:1); but there was more to his ministry than mere prediction.

King Ahab no doubt had many good reasons for trying to obtain possession of the vineyard belonging to Naboth which adjoined his own property. His first attempt to acquire the vineyard was perfectly fair and above-board:

Let me have your vineyard to use for a vegetable garden, since it is close to my palace. In exchange I will give you a better vineyard or, if you prefer, I will pay you whatever it is worth.

1 KINGS 21:2

The vineyard, however, was worth more to Naboth than its cash value, and he refused to sell it:

The LORD forbid that I should give you the inheritance of my fathers.
1 KINGS 21:3

Urged on by Jezebel, his wife, Ahab then resorted to deceit and finally to violence:

So the elders and nobles who lived in Naboth's city did as Jezebel directed in the letters she had written to them. They proclaimed a fast and seated Naboth in a prominent place among the people. Then two scoundrels came and sat opposite him and brought charges against Naboth before the people, saying, 'Naboth has cursed both God and the king.' So they took him outside the city and stoned him to death. Then they sent word to Jezebel: 'Naboth has been stoned and is dead' ... When Ahab heard that Naboth was dead, he got up and went down to take possession of Naboth's vineyard.
1 KINGS 21:11–14, 16

The sequel to the story indicates the seriousness of Ahab's crimes in the eyes of God:

Then the word of the LORD came to Elijah the Tishbite: 'Go down to meet Ahab king of Israel, who rules in Samaria. He is now in Naboth's vineyard, where he has gone to take possession of it. Say to him, "This is what the LORD says: Have you not murdered a man and seized his property?" Then say to him, "This is what the LORD says: In the place where dogs licked up Naboth's blood, dogs will lick up your blood – yes, yours!"'
1 KINGS 21:17–19

This story is specially relevant to this conflict since, in the words of **Naim Ateek**, 'the death and dispossession of Naboth and his family has been re-enacted thousands of times since the creation of the State of Israel'. His words have particular authority, since his book, *Justice and Only Justice*, begins with a detailed account of how he and his family were dispossessed of their family home in Beisan (Beth Shean) twenty miles south of the Lake of Galilee in May 1948.[30]

It is not just Palestinian Arabs, however, who speak in these terms. The writings of many Jews amount to an admission that there have been many 'Naboth's vineyards' in Palestine since 1880.

Max Nordau, a prominent Zionist leader, on hearing for the first time that there was an Arab population in Palestine, ran to Herzl crying:

I did not know that; but then we are committing an injustice.[31]

Moshe Dayan:

Jewish villages were built in the place of Arab villages. You don't even know the names of these Arab villages, and I don't blame you, because these geography books no longer exist. Not only do the books not exist, the Arab villages are not there either. Nahalal (Dayan's own village) arose in the place of Mahlul, Gvat (a kibbutz) in the place of Jibta, Sarid (another kibbutz) in the place of Haneifa, and Kfar-Yehoshua in the place of Tel-Shaman. There is not one single place built in this country that did not have a former Arab population.[32]

Nathan Chofshi, a Russian Jew, and contemporary of David Ben-Gurion:

If Rabbi Kaplan (an American Zionist rabbi) really wanted to know what happened, we old Jewish settlers in Palestine who witnessed the flight could tell him how and in what manner we, Jews, forced the Arabs to leave cities and villages. In the last analysis, these are the bare facts which strike our eyes: here was a people who lived on its own land for 1,300 years. We came and turned the native Arabs into tragic refugees. And still we dare to slander and malign them, to besmirch their name. Instead of being deeply ashamed of what we did and of trying to undo some of the evil we committed by helping these unfortunate refugees, we justify our terrible acts and even attempt to glorify them.[33]

Martin Buber, writing to the Speaker of the Knesset, 7 March 1953:

We know well... that in numerous cases land is expropriated not on grounds of security, but for other reasons, such as expansion of existing settlements, etc. These grounds do not justify a Jewish legislative body in placing the seizure of land under the protection of the law. In some densely populated villages, two thirds and even more of the land have been seized.[34]

'Filled... with the Spirit of the Lord... to declare to Jacob his transgression'
When the prophet **Amos** started denouncing the crimes of one foreign nation after another, the people of Judah and Israel must have felt confident, if not complacent, since they were innocent of the catalogue of crimes for which their neighbours were going to be punished (Amos 1:1 – 2:3). But before long they discovered that the severest judgment was reserved for themselves, because of their special relationship with God. Religious observance is meaningless in an unjust society:

You only have I chosen
  of all the families of the earth;
therefore I will punish you
  for all your sins.
AMOS 3:2

Making moral judgments about the life of the nation was therefore just as much a part of the prophetic ministry as making predictions about the future.

I hate, I despise your religious feasts;
  I cannot stand your assemblies...

But let justice roll on like a river,
  righteousness like a never-failing stream!
AMOS 5:21, 24

Micah had something to say about the distant future:

In the last days
the mountain of the LORD's temple will be established
  as chief among the mountains;
it will be raised above the hills,
  and peoples will stream to it.
MICAH 4:1

But he also believed he was called to expose the sins of his people:

But as for me, I am filled with power,
  with the Spirit of the LORD,
  and with justice and might,
to declare to Jacob his transgression,
  to Israel his sin.
MICAH 3:8

Isaiah condemned his own people, the southern kingdom of Judah, because 'justice is far from us':

Surely the arm of the LORD is not too short to save,
  nor his ear too dull to hear.
But your iniquities have separated
  you from your God;
your sins have hidden his face from you,
  so that he will not hear.
For your hands are stained with blood,
  your fingers with guilt.
Your lips have spoken lies,
  and your tongue mutters wicked things.
No one calls for justice;
  no one pleads his case with integrity.
They rely on empty arguments and speak lies;
  they conceive trouble and give birth to evil...
Their deeds are evil deeds,
  and acts of violence are in their hands.
Their feet rush into sin;
  they are swift to shed innocent blood.
Their thoughts are evil thoughts;
  ruin and destruction mark their ways.
The way of peace they do not know;

there is no justice in their paths.
They have turned them into crooked roads;
  no one who walks in them will know peace.

So justice is far from us,
  and righteousness does not reach us...
We look for justice, but find none;
  for deliverance, but it is far away.
ISAIAH 59:1–4, 6–9, 11

Those who appeal to the Old Testament to support Jewish claims to the land ought at the very least to be willing to take seriously what the prophets had to say about the practice of justice in the land. While biblical teaching about justice may be relevant to every party in the conflict, it is *specially* significant for Jews because their claim to the land is so intimately bound up with the Old Testament. While some Jews attach no authority to the Bible, many others have not only appealed to the Old Testament in general terms, but have been willing for Israel to be judged by a biblical understanding of justice.

Chaim Weizmann, for example, expressed his willingness for the whole Zionist programme to be judged in the light of the law and the prophets. Speaking to fellow Jews in the 1940s he said:

If you wish to secure your redemption through means... which do not accord with Jewish morality, with Jewish ethics or Jewish history, I say to you that you are worshipping false gods... Go and read Isaiah, Jeremiah and Ezekiel, and test that which we do and wish to do with the light of the teachings of our greatest prophets and wise men. They knew the nature and character of the Jewish people. Zion will be redeemed through righteousness, and not by any other means.[35]

Israel's Declaration of Independence makes no reference to the name of God, but recognizes the relevance of the Old Testament prophets to the life of the nation:

[The State] will promote the development of the country for the benefit of all its inhabitants; will be based on the principles of liberty, justice and peace as conceived by the Prophets of Israel; will uphold the full social and political equality of all its citizens, without distinction of religion, race, or sex; will guarantee freedom of religion, conscience, education and culture.[36]

Professor J.L. Talmon, an Israeli historian, in a conversation with **Saul Bellow** reflected on the 1973 war and the strange phenomenon of the whole world making strong moral judgments about the actions of Israel:

The 1973 war badly damaged their [i.e. Israel's] confidence. The Egyptians crossed the Suez Canal. Suddenly the abyss opened again. France and England abandoned Israel. The UN-bloc vote revived the feeling that she 'shall not be reckoned among the nations'. While Israel fought for life, debaters weighed her sins and especially the problem of the Palestinians. In this disorderly century refugees have fled from many countries. In India, in Africa, in Europe, millions of human beings have been put to flight, transported, enslaved, stampeded over borders, left to starve, but only the case of the Palestinians is held permanently open. Where Israel is concerned the world swells with moral consciousness. Moral judgment, a wraith in Europe, becomes a full-blooded giant where Israel and the Palestinians are mentioned. Is this because Israel has assumed the responsibilities of a liberal democracy? Is it for other reasons? What Switzerland is to winter holidays and the Dalmation coast to summer tourists, Israel and the Palestinians are to the West's need for justice – a sort of moral resort area.

The right of Israel to exist, Talmon says, has to be won by special exertions, 'by some special atonement through being better than others'. This is Israel's most persistent torment and paradox.[37]

Rabbi Elmer Berger, an American Jew speaking to a Christian audience in Holland after the end of the Second World War, said he believed that God must be allowed to stand in judgment, through his prophetic word, on *every* nation, including Israel. If critical voices from outside the Jewish community can be easily ignored, it should not be so easy to ignore such voices from *within* which challenge Zionism in the light of the Law and the Prophets:

Measured by any of the rigorous, covenanted criteria of the Prophetic tradition, the state of Israel is not 'the temple of the Lord'. Those who credit it with such sanctity, in my opinion, perform a disservice to the great, spiritual tradition we share. They do no lasting good, even in the world of realistic politics, to either the state of Israel itself or – more importantly – to the people who live there. And these two considerations, I think, are strong motivations in your country. For I believe I understand the particular poignancy with which the people of Holland recall those savage days of nearly three decades ago and I also understand, at least in part, the fundamental orientation of the religious commitment of perhaps a majority of the people of this country. Together with most of the people of the world, I share the tragic memory and I respect the religious commitment. But I earnestly suggest that the religious commitment can best help mankind avoid another Holocaust and more tragic memories, not by deifying the present state of Israel, but rather by insisting that the majestic vision of God in Zion must stand in the same rigorous, stern, moral judgment of this Zionist state as you demand this same God stand in judgment of this nation of yours, or as I demand – to the best of my powers – He stand in judgment of my own country.[38]

Do these *Jewish* voices help to explain why the rest of the world has every right to appeal to a biblical understanding of justice?

5.5 God's judgment in history

The writers of the Old Testament expressed their belief that God is in control of history by saying 'the Lord is king' (e.g. Psalm 97:1; 99:1, Zechariah 14:9). This meant for them that God is at work in the processes of history, not only in what happens to individuals but also to whole communities and nations. In reflecting on what was happening around them, they were trying to make connections, to see patterns and trace cause and effect. They believed that God is at work in all that happens, even in the apparent injustices of history. They were sustained by the conviction that because God is holy and righteous, he is concerned about rights and wrongs in the life of any nation, and irreconcilably opposed to all that is evil. This is what is meant by the concept of 'the wrath of God', an idea that is explained in this way by **Stephen Neill**:

The best way to understand the doctrine of the wrath of God is to consider the alternatives. The alternative is not love; since rightly considered, love and wrath are only the obverse and reverse of the same thing... The alternative to wrath is neutrality – neutrality in the conflict of the world... To live in such a world would be a nightmare. It is only the doctrine of the wrath of God, of his irreconcilable hostility to all evil, which makes human life tolerable in such a world as ours.[39]

Here are two examples of prophets who tried to understand how God might be at work not only in individuals but also of whole societies and nations.

'Woe to the Assyrian, the rod of my anger'

It cannot have been pleasant for the people of Judah to be told by the prophet **Isaiah** that God was about to use a foreign power, Assyria, as an instrument of judgment to punish them for their disobedience to the Law:

The LORD will bring on you and on your people and on the house of your father a time unlike any since Ephraim broke away from Judah – he will bring the king of Assyria...

In that day the Lord will use a razor hired from beyond the River – the king of Assyria – to shave your head and the hair of your legs, and to take off your beards also...
ISAIAH 7:17, 20

Before long, however, says Isaiah, the Assyrians themselves will be ready for judgment. For even while being used by God as an instrument of judgment on the people of Judah, they will provoke the judgment of God through their pride and arrogance, and through their excessive violence in war:

Woe to the Assyrian, the rod of my anger,
  in whose hand is the club of my wrath!
I send him against a godless nation,
  I dispatch him against a people who anger me,
to seize loot and snatch plunder,
  and to trample them down like mud in the streets.
But this is not what he intends,
  this is not what he has in mind;
his purpose is to destroy,
  to put an end to many nations.
'Are not my commanders all kings?' he says...
ISAIAH 10:5–8

When the Lord has finished all his work against Mount Zion and Jerusalem, he will say, 'I will punish the king of Assyria for the willful pride of his heart and the haughty look in his eyes. For he says:

"'By the strength of my hand I have done this,
  and by my wisdom, because I have understanding.
I removed the boundaries of nations,
  I plundered their treasures;
  like a mighty one I subdued their kings...'"
ISAIAH 10:12–13

O my people who live in Zion,
  do not be afraid of the Assyrians,
who beat you with a rod
  and lift up a club against you, as Egypt did.
Very soon my anger against you will end
  and my wrath will be directed to their destruction.
ISAIAH 10:24–25

Instead of trying to identify who 'the Assyrians' might stand for in the present scenario in the Middle East, we might notice that this passage provides one more example of the way that the prophets, when they spoke about future events, were not simply interested in the prediction of events. If all Isaiah had to do was to foretell the invasion of the Assyrians, he could no doubt have sat back with some complacency when he saw his predictions coming true. This is what God predicted – and look! It is happening before our eyes!

But the prophet had a much keener moral sense than this. He realized that being used by God as an instrument of judgment against the people of Judah did not mean that the Assyrians were exempt from God's judgment. If a listener had asked Isaiah 'is the Assyrian invasion "of God"?' he would certainly have answered that it *was* 'of God' – but that this did not mean that the Assyrians had *carte blanche* from God to act however they liked. Assyria had to pay the price at a later stage for overstepping the mark.

In the mind of the prophet, therefore, no individual and no nation is ever immune from judgment just because it is being used by God in a particular way at a particular stage of history. There can never be any exemption from responsibility and accountability before God.

Denys Baly suggests how the 'double judgment' described by Isaiah in this passage may have been working itself out in the twentieth century with the Jews and Arabs:

When we turn to consider what the events of the past forty years have meant to the people of the Middle East themselves, we see the double judgment of which Isaiah spoke. Only those whose enthusiasm for the Arab cause has blinded them to the facts should fail to take account of the tragic weakness of the Arabs. Their complacency, their certainty that they are the people and that wisdom will die with them, their rigidity, their high-sounding words, their inability to combine, the lack of courage of most of them save the Bedouin – these are the weaknesses which have put them at the mercy of Israel. Three things have been given to the Arab world at once: independence, the stimulus of new and exciting ideas and the possibility of quite overwhelming wealth, and with them at the same time has come the necessity of decision. The question is now what they will do with all these gifts. Will those in power use the new wealth for their own aggrandizement or for the benefit of the people? Will Egypt use her position of power for the benefit or the control of the other Arab nations? Will they struggle to overcome their past history in the face of the need for unity? Will the oil-countries consider their riches as something to be kept entirely within their own borders? Are the refugees always to remain a pawn in the game? These are the kind of questions of which the judgment is made, and the presence of Israel is the spur. Had there been no Israel, the questions would have come less sharply and the need for unity have been made less apparent. No one can deny the troubles of the Arabs. The West has not treated them fairly, not even with so much as common courtesy, but that is not now the question for them. Their crisis is now to know whether any of their own number will arise to tell them their own shortcomings, and, bluntly, whether they would rather listen to him or shoot him.

We must not, however, make the mistake of believing that the chastisement of Arab follies means that Israel is therefore justified. It is the tragedy of Israel that she has found no peace, and no peace is likely to be granted to her for a long time. She has gathered in those who were afraid, and they are afraid still. The security they longed for most earnestly is the thing which is still beyond their reach, the crock of gold at the rainbow's end.[40]

'Why do you make me look on injustice?'

When we read the sickening story of the violence which began with the first clashes between Jews and Arabs, we can understand the complaints which **Habakkuk** addressed to God:

How long, O LORD, must I call for help,
  but you do not listen?
Or cry out to you 'Violence!'
  but you do not save?
Why do you make me look at injustice?
  Why do you tolerate wrong?
Destruction and violence are before me;
  there is strife, and conflict abounds.
Therefore the law is paralysed,
  and justice never prevails.
The wicked hem in the righteous,
  so that justice is perverted.
HABAKKUK 1:2–4

O LORD, are you not from everlasting?
My God, my Holy One, we will not die.
O LORD, you have appointed them to execute judgment;
O Rock, you have ordained them to punish.
Your eyes are too pure to look on evil;
you cannot tolerate wrong.
Why then do you tolerate the treacherous?
Why are you silent while the wicked
swallow up those more righteous than themselves?
HABAKKUK 1:12–13

In his answer, God assures the prophet that he is not turning a blind eye to injustice, and that the Babylonians will be judged for all the crimes they are committing:

See, he is puffed up;
his desires are not upright –
but the righteous will live by his faith –
indeed, wine betrays him;
he is arrogant and never at rest.
Because he is as greedy as the grave
and like death is never satisfied,
he gathers to himself all the nations
and takes captive all the peoples.

Will not all of them taunt him with ridicule and scorn, saying,

'Woe to him who piles up stolen goods
and makes himself wealthy by extortion!
How long must this go on?'
Will not your debtors suddenly arise?
Will they not wake up and make you tremble?
Then you will become their victim.
Because you have plundered many nations,
the peoples who are left will plunder you.
For you have shed man's blood;
you have destroyed lands and cities and everyone in them.

'Woe to him who builds a city with bloodshed
and establishes a town by crime!
Has not the LORD Almighty determined
that the people's labor is only fuel for the fire,
that the nations exhaust themselves for nothing?
For the earth will be filled with the knowledge of the glory of
the LORD,
as the waters cover the sea.

Woe to him who gives drink to his neighbors,
  pouring it from the wineskin till they are drunk
  so that he can gaze on their naked bodies.
You will be filled with shame instead of glory.
  Now it is your turn! Drink and be exposed!
The cup from the LORD's right hand is coming around to you,
  and disgrace will cover your glory.
The violence you have done to Lebanon will overwhelm you,
  and your destruction of animals will terrify you.
For you have shed man's blood;
  you have destroyed lands and cities and everyone in them.'
HABAKKUK 2:4–8, 12–17

Are there any ways of relating the words of the prophet Habakkuk to the attitudes and actions of the different parties in the conflict over the land?

■ Would we not have to say that the Christian churches have 'humiliated and disgraced' (Habakkuk 2:15, TEV) their Jewish neighbours over many centuries?
■ When European governments exploited anti-Semitism in the nineteenth and twentieth centuries were they not like those in the prophet's time who 'plotted the ruin of many peoples' (2:10)?
■ Would we not have to admit that Western powers have been as 'greedy as the grave' (2:5) and have 'plundered many nations' (2:8)?
■ If Habakkuk were living today would he have to say that the *Irgun* and the *Haganah* 'shed man's blood' (2:8, 17) and 'built a city with bloodshed' (2:12)?
■ Would he in the same breath speak about the *fedayeen* and the Islamic suicide bombers as people who have 'shed man's blood' (2:8, 17) in their desperate attempt to resist Zionism and to win back their land?
■ Have some of the leaders of the Zionist movement over the years been trying to build 'a realm by unjust gain to set its nest on high, to escape the clutches of ruin' (2:9)?
■ Would the prophet want to say that the Arab countries which have been using their oil wealth as a political weapon have made themselves 'wealthy by extortion' (2:6)?
■ Is there a sense in which any imperial power of the past or present which desires to preserve its power and influence in the world, in the words of the prophet, 'gathers to himself all nations and takes captive all the peoples' (2:5)?

Is it too dangerous to make connections of this kind between the words of an Old Testament prophet and the attitudes and actions of individuals and nations in recent history? Does it depend too much on the subjective judgment of individuals who are bound to be influenced by their prejudices in relating the text of scripture to what has happened? Or is there a sense in which the words of the prophet give us at least a sense that since the God who is in control of history is a holy God, there *must* be some process of judgment (and also of mercy) that is being worked out before our eyes, even when we cannot discern it in detail?

5.6 Suffering injustice

The Jews look back to the Dispersion, the ghettos, the pogroms and the Holocaust. The Arabs look back to their oppression under the Turks, the broken promises of the Western powers, the establishment of the State of Israel in 1948 and the traumatic defeat of 1967. Both know the meaning of the words 'suffering' and 'injustice'.

The *Quaker Report* reminds us that the Middle East problem arises out of the sufferings of *both* the Jews *and* the Arabs, and out of their attempts to free themselves from oppression:

The Jews and the Arabs are ancient and long-suffering peoples, and their sufferings continue. Both have been cruelly dealt with by peoples of other cultures, and both are still subject to manipulation by forces beyond their control. Both are distrustful of other peoples and of each other, as they seek to establish their own identity, their right to respect, freedom and national self-development.

It is one of the great ironies of history that the roots of the present Arab-Jewish struggle should have grown, not in a poisoned soil of ancient mutual animosities, but in the mistreatment each has received at the hands of others. The Jews and the Arabs are Semitic cousins, share cultural traits and traditions, and through long centuries lived in relative peace with one another even during periods when Jews were subject to sustained persecution by the Christian West...

The intensified struggle of Jews and Arabs has come since the end of the First World War and most intensely since the end of the Second World War, as the two peoples, in their own ways, finally sought to put an end to persecution and to their common status as subject peoples – and ran head on into each other.

Zionism, the most dynamic force of nineteenth-century Jewish nationalism, burst upon the world scene just as Arab nationalism was beginning to rise from the dying Turkish empire. These simultaneously emerging nationalisms, unfortunately, were destined to fight for possession of the same territory in the Holy Land of Palestine.[41]

Anton La Guardia points out that *both* Jews *and* Arabs have been slow to recognize each other's suffering:

For the past half-century of the Israel-Arab dispute, each side has minimized, ignored or distorted the other side's pain to deny its right to exist as a people. In the struggle for Palestine, Israelis and Palestinians have not only fought over who has the oldest claim to the land, but have also argued over who has suffered the most...

The political architecture of peace, no matter how carefully the future borders are laid out, no matter how carefully the leaders finesse the questions of settlements and Jerusalem, no matter how much money the world pledges to support the 'peace process', cannot be complete without each side recognizing the other's agony, and abandoning the notion that it alone is the victim of history.[42]

Does the Bible have anything to say to people who suffer injustice? Does it encourage them to continue to fight, whatever the cost to themselves or others? Does it allow us to use evil ourselves in order to overcome evil? Or does it call for an acceptance of suffering?

Part of **Isaiah**'s answer to the awareness of injustice in his own nation and in other nations is the conviction that God will one day punish evildoers:

The LORD looked and was displeased
  that there was no justice.
He saw that there was no one,
  he was appalled that there
    was no one to intervene;
so his own arm worked salvation for him,
  and his own righteousness sustained him.
He put on righteousness as his breastplate,
  and the helmet of salvation on his head;
he put on the garments of vengeance
  and wrapped himself in zeal as in a cloak.
According to what they have done,
  so will he repay
wrath to his enemies
  and retribution to his foes;
  he will repay the islands their due…
ISAIAH 59:15–18

In his vision of the future reign of God, the figure described as 'the Servant of the Lord' plays a special role in bringing 'justice to the nations':

Here is my servant, whom I uphold,
  my chosen one in whom I delight;
I will put my Spirit on him
  and he will bring justice to the nations.
He will not shout or cry out,
  or raise his voice in the streets.
A bruised reed he will not break,
  and a smoldering wick he will not snuff out.
In faithfulness he will bring forth justice;
  he will not falter or be discouraged
till he establishes justice on earth.
  In his law the islands will put their hope.
ISAIAH 42:1–4

But when we ask *how* the Servant of the Lord is to establish justice on earth, the answer given is not the one we might have expected. Instead of dealing with injustice by force, and punishing evildoers, *the Servant himself suffers injustice*. Although he is totally innocent, and is not suffering for any wrong that he has done, he submits to all the injustice that is done to him:

He was oppressed and afflicted,
  yet he did not open his mouth;
he was led like a lamb to the slaughter,
  and as a sheep before her shearers is silent,
  so he did not open his mouth.
By oppression and judgment he was taken away.
  And who can speak of his descendants?
For he was cut off from the land of the living;
  for the transgression of my people he was stricken.
He was assigned a grave with the wicked,
  and with the rich in his death,
though he had done no violence,
  nor was any deceit in his mouth.
ISAIAH 53:7–9

By accepting injustice and bearing undeserved suffering, he is in some mysterious
way bearing the suffering and guilt of the whole people:

Surely he took up our infirmities
  and carried our sorrows,
yet we considered him stricken by God,
  smitten by him, and afflicted.
But he was pierced for our transgressions,
  he was crushed for our iniquities;
the punishment that brought us peace was upon him,
  and by his wounds we are healed.
We all, like sheep, have gone astray,
  each of us has turned to his own way;
and the LORD has laid on him
  the iniquity of us all.
ISAIAH 53:4–6

In Isaiah's picture of the Suffering Servant we find many of the same elements that
make up the conflict that we are studying – rejection, sorrow, suffering, wounds,
transgressions, oppression, violence and deceit. Could it therefore have anything to
say about situations where it seems that it is impossible for every party in a conflict
to see justice done?

Here in the Old Testament we find a principle that judgment and condemnation
are not the only answer to injustice. Evil cannot always be overcome by the punishment of evildoers. Sometimes the way to overcome injustice is to suffer it. The
divine answer to evil sometimes involves suffering. The Suffering Servant actually
overcomes evil by the way he responds to it. By enduring undeserved suffering, he
takes on himself the sins of others. He bears their sins, and instead of cursing those
who have wronged him, he prays for them.

In thinking about the conflict between Jews and Arabs **Denys Baly** points out the need to examine slogans like 'a just and durable peace', since it is *never* going to be possible for *everyone* to feel that justice has been done:

No peace can now be just. That is the lamentable fact, for whatever we do now will be unjust to somebody. If we confirm the Israeli immigrants in their homes, we shall be unjust to the Arab refugees, whose homes they once were, and who desperately long to return to them. If, however, we insist that justice shall be done to the Arabs, we shall be unjust to the Israeli immigrants, who cannot be held responsible for an exodus which took place before they set foot in the country... There are those on every side, it is true, who demand that justice be done to them and never mind about the others. But it is not this that 'justice' means.

The Middle East is admittedly not peculiar in this, for in any problem area of the world, in Kashmir, in South Africa, in Germany, in Indochina and in North Africa, the issues have become so complex, and so much unrighted wrong has been done, that justice is no longer feasible. To pretend that it is is to make any forward step impossible, because if we have proclaimed that justice is our purpose, then we shall unfailingly be condemned for the inevitable injustice, and we shall have added to the number of those who feel themselves to be betrayed.[43]

Many of those who experience injustice are determined never to give in and to fight with all their powers to the very end to overturn the injustice. For others, however, there may come a point when they cease to fight the injustice and begin to accept that the evil will never be overcome. They have not been overcome by the evil, but simply recognize that they cannot live for ever with anger, resentment and a desire for revenge. Does this amount to an acceptance of injustice, and is it a sign of weakness and surrender?

This may be the point at which we look again at the figure of the Suffering Servant in Isaiah, and notice how this picture is interpreted in the New Testament. At one level this can be seen simply as a poetic expression of the value of vicarious suffering. In the original context the figure of the Servants stands either for the whole people of Israel or for the prophet himself. But Christians believe that this picture finds its supreme fulfilment in the person of Jesus of Nazareth, who, instead of calling down the judgment of God on those who condemned him unjustly, was willing to suffer the injustice. He is the supreme example of the Servant who was 'despised and rejected by men, a man of sorrows, and familiar with suffering' (Isaiah 53:3).

Since Christians believe that this picture of the Suffering Servant finds its most perfect embodiment in the person of Jesus, the challenge to them is to see how they can follow in *his* footsteps when they face injustice and evil. They will of course seek redress (but not revenge); they will of course seek protection from the law in one way or another, and appeal to the consciences of others. But whether or not they succeed, they will refuse to give in to bitterness and despair, or take up the same weapons as their enemies, because they have the example of one who endured suffering that he did not deserve, committing his cause to God and praying for those who crucified him.

Naim Ateek sums up what is likely to be a fundamental attitude in the minds of Middle Eastern Christians:

The fundamental Christian attitude toward conflict and war familiar to the Christians in the Middle East is that of Jesus – the way of nonviolence... the only way of life that really makes sense to Eastern Christians is the way of Jesus.[44]

Similarly **Denys Baly** makes the point that reconciliation begins to be possible only when someone is willing to accept injustice. For Christians such an attitude can be inspired only by the spirit of Jesus:

In a situation where justice is no longer possible reconciliation can come only if some men accept injustice. There is no other way. But the very thought of it is abhorrent, for whatever else men are ready to forgo, justice, it would seem, is a permanent demand. This is, in fact, the root of nationalism. Only those in whom Christ lives can see the need to demand justice always for the other side and to accept injustice for themselves.[45]

5.7 Rethinking and repentance through disaster

It is generally agreed that during the period of Nazi power in Germany and Eastern Europe six million Jews were murdered in the Holocaust, the *Shoah*. Their only crime was that they happened to be Jews, and if Hitler had won the war, hardly a single Jew would have survived in Europe. **Rabbi Norman Solomon** describes the Hocaust as 'the most terrible event in history'.[46]

Palestinian Arabs look back to the events of 1948 and 1949 and the founding of the State of Israel as 'The Catastrophe' or 'The Disaster' (*nakbah*). 'One need not equate the two miseries,' says **Anton La Guardia**. 'The extermination of the *Shoah* belongs to a different universe of evil to the dispossession of Palestinians in the *nakbah*. For all the awful things that happened in the decades of conflict, the Jews did not gas the Palestinians. Yet the two tragedies are inextricably entwined. They are part of the same mosaic of conflict over Palestine. If the Jews were victims of the Nazis, the Palestinians are in many ways the victims of the victims.'[47]

How have Jews responded to the *Shoah*? How have Palestinians responded to the *nakbah* and all the disasters that have followed since then? And does the Bible shed any light on how a people responds to national disaster?

There is one book in the Bible, the book of **Lamentations**, which expresses the response of the people of Jerusalem to a national disaster, a response which involved profound rethinking and repentance. This short book, traditionally attributed to the prophet Jeremiah, was written some time after the Jews had witnessed the destruction of Jerusalem in 587 BC at the hands of the Babylonian army. According to tradition it was recited by the community in the remains of the temple in the following years. It has for many centuries held a special place in Jewish liturgical tradition, being read annually on the day commemorating the destruction of the temple (i.e. the Fast of the Ninth Ab).

What is specially significant about the way this prophet responds to the disaster? Firstly, instead of pouring out his anger on his enemies, the Babylonians, he is willing to ask the question: *why* has God allowed all this to happen? He points to particular leaders in the community who bear a large measure of responsibility for what has happened:

The visions of your prophets
  were false and worthless;
they did not expose your sin
  to ward off your captivity.
The oracles they gave you
  were false and misleading.
LAMENTATIONS 2:14

It happened because of the sins of her prophets
  and the iniquities of her priests,
who shed within her
  the blood of the righteous.
LAMENTATIONS 4:13

He also realizes that the people are reaping the consequences of the attitudes and actions of previous generations:

Our fathers sinned and are no more,
  and we bear their punishment.
LAMENTATIONS 5:7

He admits that God has only done what he warned he would do if they did not repent:

The LORD has done what he planned;
  he has fulfilled his word,
  which he decreed long ago.
LAMENTATIONS 2:17

He therefore encourages the people to examine themselves and turn to God in sincere repentance.

Secondly, the writer recognizes that there is a difference between suffering that is *deserved* (that is, suffering that comes as a judgment from God), and suffering that is *undeserved*. This means that if he and his people are willing to admit their share of responsibility and guilt for what has happened, they can then submit to God's heavy hand of judgment, knowing that he punishes only because he loves. When they have submitted to suffering that is deserved, they can begin to learn the secret of enduring suffering that is not deserved. In the midst of his suffering, therefore, he can overcome his feelings of despair, and face the future with hope and confidence.

These two themes are woven together in one key passage at the heart of the book:

I remember my affliction and my wandering,
  the bitterness and the gall.
I well remember them,
  and my soul is downcast within me.
Yet this I call to mind
  and therefore I have hope:

Because of the LORD's great love we are not consumed,
  for his compassions never fail.
They are new every morning;
  great is your faithfulness.
I say to myself, 'The LORD is my portion;
  therefore I will wait for him.'

The LORD is good to those whose hope is in him,
  to the one who seeks him;
it is good to wait quietly
  for the salvation of the LORD.
It is good for a man to bear the yoke
  while he is young.

Let him sit alone in silence,
  for the LORD has laid it on him.
Let him bury his face in the dust –
  there may yet be hope.
Let him offer his cheek to one who would strike him,
  and let him be filled with disgrace.

For men are not cast off
  by the Lord forever.
Though he brings grief, he will show compassion,
  so great is his unfailing love.
For he does not willingly bring affliction
  or grief to the children of men.

To crush underfoot
  all prisoners in the land,
to deny a man his rights
  before the Most High,
to deprive a man of justice –
  would not the Lord see such things?

Who can speak and have it happen
  if the Lord has not decreed it?
Is it not from the mouth of the Most High
  that both calamities and good things come?

Why should any living man complain
   when punished for his sins?

Let us examine our ways and test them,
   and let us return to the LORD.
Let us lift up our hearts and our hands
   to God in heaven, and say:
'We have sinned and rebelled
   and you have not forgiven.'
LAMENTATIONS 3:19–42

If this is the kind of rethinking that followed after the desctruction of Jerusalem in 536 BC, what kind of rethinking has there been among Jews following the Holocaust? In an address entitled *Jewish Responses to the Holocaust* **Rabbi Norman Solomon** acknowledges that for some 'after Auschwitz the metaphysical capacity is paralysed', but expresses his own conviction 'that some sort of talk is possible about the Holocaust'.[48] Some Jews lost their faith in God, while others continued to trust in God in spite of what they witnessed and suffered. As someone scrawled on a wall in Auschwitz before perishing, 'I believe in the sun even when it is not shining. I believe in God even when he is silent.'

   Summarizing the main types of what is called 'Jewish Holocaust Theology', Solomon describes traditional responses based on the teaching of traditional Jewish law and theology. One rabbi in a ghetto in Kovno in Lithuania, for example, wrote that 'despite our physical capacity, we were more obligated than ever to recite the blessing (of the sake of God) to show our enemies that as a people we were spiritually free.' The response of many ordinary believers is summed up by Solomon in this way:

'It is clear beyond all doubt that the blessed Holy One is the ruler of the universe, and we must accept the judgment with love.' These words of the Hungarian Rabbi Shmuel David Ungar exactly express the simple faith of those who entered the gas chambers with Ani Ma'min *('I believe') or* Shema Israel *('Hear, O Israel') on their lips. What was happening defied their understanding, but their faith triumphed over evil and they were ready, in the traditional phrase, to 'sanctify the name of God' –* kiddush Hashem. *Hence it is normal among Jews to refer to those who perished under the Nazis as* kedoshim, *'holy ones, saints'.*[49]

Some theologians tried to explain their suffering as 'God's punishment for Jewish sin', while most have found traditional answers of this kind to the problem of evil to be inadequate to explain the appalling suffering of the Holocaust. Others were able to 'rationalize the destruction of part of the people of Israel as part of God's redemptive process, leading ultimately to Israel's restoration, whether or not in terms of the land'.[50] One response was to see the suffering in the context of God's love ('suffering is… received as a token of God's special concern for Israel'), while another was to interpret both the *Shoah* and the strife surrounding the emergence of the State of Israel as 'birth pangs of the Messiah'.

It was not only Jews, however, who had to rethink their beliefs. The seriousness of the theological questions raised by the Holocaust both for Jews *and* Christians is summed up in these words of **Rabbi Irwing Greenberg**:

The Holocaust poses the most radical counter-testimony to both Judaism and Christianity... The cruelty and the killing raise the question whether even those who believe after such an event dare to talk about God who loves and cares without making a mockery of those who suffered.[51]

Solomon's final example of a Holocaust theology is that of **Emil Fackenheim** who started from 'the actual resistance of *Shoah* victims to whom no realistic hope remained', and pointed to the State of Israel as 'the central affirmation of Jewish survival':

A philosophical Tikkun *(Hebrew for 'mending' or 'restoration') is possible after the Holocaust because a philosophical* Tikkun *already took place, however fragmentarily, during the Holocaust itself. Before writing his main work Fackenheim had achieved note for his statement that there should be a 614th commandment – to survive as Jews, to remember, never to despair of God, lest we hand Hitler a posthumous victory. What one discerns in his evolving position is, at least, an affirmation of life and of God, and a challenge to Christian, Jew and all mankind to 'mend the world'. For Fackenheim, Israel (the Jewish State) is the central affirmation of Jewish survival, central in the process of* Tikkun; *hence, he has now made his home there.*[52]

A major section of Solomon's address summarizes the challenge *to Christians* which arises out of the Holocaust:

Jews tend to view the Shoah *as the culmination of their degradation and persecution at the hand of Christians. They see Christians by and large as persecutors, with a relatively small number as victims and an even smaller number showing the least concern for Jewish victims. Since the Holocaust, Jews have ceased to take the moral credibility of the Church seriously.*

The voice of the Shoah *was the voice of the pagan Hitler, but the hands that implemented it were the hands of ordinary Christians...*

Ninety per cent of Germans before the war, and in all probability an even larger proportion of Poles, attended Church weekly. Did the sermons they heard outspokenly condemn the demonic anti-Christ Hitler? By no means. First of all, in his early writings and speeches Hitler, seeking the support of the masses, spoke overtly Christian language. 'Hence I believe that I am acting in accordance with the will of the Almighty Creator: by defending myself against the Jew, I am fighting for the word of the Lord.' His attacks on Jews and Judaism were consciously expressed in the language of traditional Christian anti-Semitism, and the infamous laws of Nuremberg consciously modelled on the legislation of the mediaeval Church. It was the Church that had instigated trade restrictions against the Jews... It was the Church that sewed into the fabric of Western culture the images and stereotypes of the Jew that allowed so many of its faith-

ful sons to accept without demur the alienation and vilification of the Jew preached by
Hitler. For it was the Church whose gospel concerning the Jews was, as Jules Isaac
called it, l'enseignment du mépris, *the teaching of contempt. Hitler's* Judenhass *was*
not significantly greater than that of Luther – and it has taken all the courage of the
post-Holocaust Lutheran Church to repudiate that aspect of the 'Great Reformer's'
teaching.[53]

Naim Ateek as a Palestinian Christian priest recognizes that acknowledging the
Holocaust is a major part of the change in attitudes that is called for among Palestinians:

The Palestinians need to become conscious of and sensitive to the horror of the
Holocaust, Nazi Germany's attempt to exterminate the Jews. Granted, the Holocaust
was not a Middle Eastern phenomenon, and the Palestinians had nothing to do with
it; nevertheless, we need to understand the extent of the trauma for the Jews…
Admittedly, we as Palestiniaans have refused to accept, much less to internalize, the
horrible tragedy of the Holocaust. We have resisted even acknowledging it, believing
that we have been subjected to our own holocaust at the hands of the Jews. Many
Palestinians have doubted that the Holocaust even occurred; they could not believe
that those who suffered so much could turn around and inflict so much suffering
on the Palestinians. We have also refused to admit or acknowledge its uniqueness,
pointing to the attempt to destroy the Assyrian and Armenian Christians in this
century.
    Be that as it may, a new attitude is expected of us vis-à-vis the Holocaust. We
must understand the importance and significance of the Holocaust to the Jews,
while insisting that the Jews understand the importance and significance of the
tragedy of Palestine for the Palestinians. The new attitude would make us
Palestinians face Israel quite candidly and state that the only justification that
the Palestinians will accept for the creation of a Jewish state in Palestine is the
Holocaust. It was the Holocaust and only the Holocaust that necessitated the cre-
ation of a home for the Jews. Some Western countries did not open their doors to
the Jews, and the Zionist leadership at the time was glad about this because it
really wanted all the Jews to go to Palestine! The Palestinians, as hosts, have to
come to accept giving the Jews the best part of Palestine (western Palestine), not
because they had any right to it, not because of the Balfour Declaration, and not
even because of anti-Semitism, but because of the Holocaust.[54]

Ateek also, however, describes the kind of change of attitude that he believes the
Jews in Israel should be willing to articulate to Palestinians:

We are sorry that we came to you with arrogance and a feeling of superiority. We
came with good and not so good reasons. But we are now here in the land. Forgive
us for the wrong and the injustice that we have caused you. We took part of your
country. We ignored you. We pretended that you did not exist or, even worse, that
you did not matter. We stereotyped you, convincing others that you are all terror-
ists. We have refused to recognize that you have any rights, while we insisted that
you should recognize and legitimate our right to your land. We have insisted, and

convinced the United States and others to insist, that you recognize our claim to your land. And, amazingly, many governments in the world have agreed with us. We have refused to negotiate with your representatives, rejecting them as terrorists... We have done this and much more. We have wronged you. Now, we recognize that the healthiest solution to any conflict is the use of negotiation and compromise, as opposed to power, repression and control... We want to stay a part of the Middle East. We want to live among you, Muslims and Christians. Your own country of Palestine today used to be our country 2,000 years ago. We still have many cherished historic memories that keep pulling us to it. It is our 'holy land', too, our 'promised land'. There is room for both of us here.[55]

If the writer of Lamentations was able to go through such a painful process of rethinking and repentance after the disaster that befell his people and his city, can his words help others at the present time in reflecting on the disasters they have experienced?

5.8 Jew and Gentile in the Old Testament

What does it mean to be Jewish? Is Jewishness related to race or religion, or with *both* race *and* religion? Why is the world divided into two kinds of people: Jews and Gentiles? If Jews are different from other people, have they made themselves different, or have other people made them different?

And what does it mean for the State of Israel to define itself as a 'Jewish state', 'the creation of the entire Jewish people', 'the state of the Jewish people'? How can Jewishness be the defining factor in the creation of a modern state?

A strong sense of Jewish identity has developed over the centuries. These ideas, however, need to be traced back ultimately to the Old Testament, where the descendants of Abraham, the children of Israel, are told: 'You are a people holy to the LORD your God. The LORD your God has chosen you out of all the peoples . . . to be . . . his treasured possession' (Deuteronomy 7:6).

How then is the theme of election, the choice of Abraham and his descendants as a 'chosen people' developed in the Old Testament? We can trace at least six important strands in the development of these ideas in the Old Testament.

■ The call and election of Abraham and his descendants are understood in the context of God's concern for the whole human race. The first chapters of Genesis speak of the creation of the universe and of the human race (Genesis 1–2). After attempting to explain that things went wrong in God's creation (Genesis 3–11), the book goes on to speak about God's plan to put right what has gone wrong (Genesis 12 to the end). If ideas of exclusiveness come later, they are developed in the context of an inclusiveness which embraces the whole human race.

■ Election involves a special responsibility to follow God's ways in obedience. So, for example, at an early stage in the nation's life, Moses attempted to make the children of Israel aware of their identity. Being set apart from other nations, and entering into a special relationship with God meant that they were in some sense to be *like* the God who had called them: 'You shall be holy for I am holy' (Leviticus 11:45 NASB).

This special calling from God demanded rigid separation from surrounding nations, as Moses tells the people when they are about to enter the land:

When the LORD your God brings you into the land you are entering to possess and drives out before you many nations... and when the LORD your God has delivered them over to you and you have defeated them, then you must destroy them totally. Make no treaty with them, and show them no mercy. Do not intermarry with them. Do not give your daughters to their sons or take their daughters for your sons, for they will turn your sons away from following me to serve other gods, and the LORD's anger will burn against you and will quickly destroy you.
DEUTERONOMY 7:1–4

■ Because the idea of election is so easily misunderstood, it is constantly being challenged and clarified. The prophet **Amos**, for example, has to explain that election involves special responsibility and is not a calling to any status of privilege. In one very important verse which comes at the end of a detailed denunciation of the sins of Israel's neighbours, he tells his people that their punishment will be *more* severe than that of their neighbours, simply because they have been chosen for this special relationship and responsibility:

You only have I chosen
  of all the families of the earth;
therefore I will punish you
  for all your sins.
AMOS 3:2

Later he has to explain that God is at work in other nations just as much as he is in Israel. Election does not mean that God is not interested in other people:

Did I not bring Israel up from Egypt,
  the Philistines from Caphtor
  and the Arameans from Kir?
AMOS 9:7

Micah and other prophets have to tell their people that their election is no guarantee of safety and protection. Speaking of a situation in which the leaders of Israel 'despise justice and distort what is right' and seek to 'build Zion with bloodshed', he challenges their complacency. A false sense of confidence has been based on the idea that the temple is a sign of God's presence among his people and therefore a guarantee that whatever happens, he will always protect them:

Yet they lean upon the LORD and say,
  'Is not the LORD among us?
  No disaster will come upon us.'
MICAH 3:11

■ From time to time a number of non-Jews are included within the people:
– When Moses escaped for his life to the Sinai region, he married Zipporah, who was the daughter of 'a priest of Midian' (Exodus 2:15–22).
– In the events leading up to the conquest of the land under Joshua, the spies sent to explore the city of Jericho were protected by Rahab the prostitute. When the city was captured and destroyed, she and her family were spared, and the writer says that 'she lives among the Israelites to this day' (Joshua 2:1 – 6:25).
– In the time of the Judges, Ruth the Moabitess left her own people on the east bank of the Jordan and followed Naomi her mother-in-law with the well-known words 'your people will be my people and your God my God' (Ruth 1:16). In this way a foreigner, a Gentile, became an ancestor of King David. The book of Ruth was therefore a constant reminder that foreigners could be integrated into the life of the nation and not be rigidly excluded.

■ There were times when more exclusivist views prevailed. After their return from exile in Babylon around the middle of the sixth century BC, Ezra and Nehemiah felt compelled to enforce Moses' prohibition of foreign wives, even to the point of making men put away their foreign wives. Ezra writes:

After these things had been done, the leaders came to me and said, 'The people of Israel, including the priests and the Levites, have not kept themselves separate from the neighboring peoples with their detestable practices... They have taken some of their daughters as wives for themselves and their sons, and have mingled the holy race with the peoples around them. And the leaders and officials have led the way in this unfaithfulness.'
EZRA 9:1, 2

This is how Ezra wanted them to rectify the situation:

You have been unfaithful; you have married foreign women, adding to Israel's guilt. Now make confession to the LORD, the God of your fathers, and do his will. Separate yourselves from the peoples around you and from your foreign wives.
EZRA 10:10–11

■ The prophets sometimes look forward to a time when the strict separation between Jew and Gentile will be broken down.

'A blessing in the midst of the earth'
A whole chapter of **Isaiah** consists of 'an oracle concerning Egypt'. It speaks of God judging the nation of Egypt, and later restoring it – even to the extent of bringing the nation to acknowledge the God of Israel.

It must have sounded incredible, if not shocking, for Isaiah's listeners to hear that the people of Egypt, who centuries before had been their oppressors, would one day be converted and turn to worship Yahweh their God. It would have sounded as inconceivable for them as for an American Christian audience during the Cold War to be told that one day the Russian people as a whole would reject communism and embrace Christianity.

The oracle ends with the prophecy that Egypt, Israel and Assyria will one day be united together to become 'a blessing in the midst of the earth':

In that day there will be a highway from Egypt to Assyria. The Assyrians will go to Egypt and the Egyptians to Assyria. The Egyptians and Assyrians will worship together. In that day Israel will be the third, along with Egypt and Assyria, a blessing on the earth. The LORD Almighty will bless them, saying, 'Blessed be Egypt my people, Assyria my handiwork, and Israel my inheritance.'
ISAIAH 19:23–25

We must leave on one side the intriguing question of if and when this prophecy has been fulfilled: was it in the Camp David Agreements of 1979? Or was it fulfilled in the first few centuries AD when Egypt became in effect a Christian country, and enjoyed close links with the Syriac Church in the area of present-day Syria? The important point for us to notice is that Isaiah puts two *foreign* nations – pagan, godless nations at that – on the same level as Israel! The children of Israel had always thought of themselves as God's chosen people – but now God is calling *Egypt* 'my people!' What would happen to the concept of the chosen people if that ever happened? (See further Appendix 3.)

'My house shall be called a house of prayer for all nations'

The prophet **Isaiah**, writing in the eighth century BC, looked forward to the day when people of other nations would benefit from all that God had done for his people Israel. In the following passage he speaks of foreigners who 'join themselves' or 'bind themselves' to Jehovah, the Lord, and come to belong to his people:

This is what the LORD says:

*'Maintain justice and do what is right,
for my salvation is close at hand
    and my righteousness will soon be revealed...'*

*Let no foreigner who has joined himself to the LORD say,
    'The LORD will surely exclude me from his people.'
And let not any eunuch complain,
    'I am only a dry tree.'*

For this is what the LORD says:

*'To the eunuchs who keep my Sabbaths...
    and hold fast to my covenant –
to them I will give within my temple and its walls
    a memorial and a name
    better than sons and daughters;*

I will give them an everlasting name
  that will not be cut off.
And foreigners who bind themselves to the LORD
  to serve him,
to love the name of the LORD,
  and to worship him,
all who keep the Sabbath without desecrating it
  and who hold fast to my covenant –
these I will bring to my holy mountain
  and give them joy in my house of prayer.
Their burnt offerings and sacrifices
  will be accepted on my altar;
for my house will be called
  a house of prayer for all nations.'
The Sovereign LORD declares –
  he who gathers the exiles of Israel:
'I will gather still others to them
  besides those already gathered.'
ISAIAH 56:1–8

How does one begin to relate these themes in the Old Testament to the ways that Jews think of themselves today, and to the idea of Israel as a 'Jewish state' today? At this stage we are not asking how the idea of the Jews as the Chosen People is taken up and interpreted in the New Testament, and are simply trying to see the idea of the State of Israel in the light of the Old Testament.

Is the Zionist dream, therefore, closer to Ezra's idea of 'the holy race' or to Isaiah's vision of a people which welcomes 'foreigners who join themselves to the Lord'.

One can understand how Theodor Herzl could believe that the creation of a Jewish state would solve the problem of anti-Semitism in Europe. And one can have a strong sympathy for any Israeli who argues the need for Israel on the grounds of expediency – provided he is willing to consider the price that *others* have had to pay.

Although Herzl himself did not use the Old Testament at all in putting forward his idea of the Jewish state, other more devout, practising Jews were not slow to relate the Zionist vision to the Old Testament. But it is quite a different matter when we find Christians today who support this way of using the Old Testament.

But the *theological* question that needs to be asked is this: can the State of Israel be in any sense – for the Jew and for the Christian – the fulfilment of the promise that through Abraham and his descendants 'all peoples of the earth' would be blessed? How easy is it for anyone to say that '*this* (the Jewish state which we see today) is *that* which was spoken of by the prophets (like the visions of Isaiah and Zechariah)? Could it ever be seen even as one stage in the fulfilment of these visions?

When seen in the light of the idea of the chosen people as it developed in the Old Testament – from Moses to Ruth, Ezra and Nehemiah, to Isaiah and Zechariah – the modern Jewish state looks more like a step *backwards* than a step *forwards*.

Many Jews have commented on the problem that has been created within Judaism by the existence of the Jewish state.

Haim Cohen, a judge of the Supreme Court of Israel:

The bitter irony of fate has decreed that the same biological and racist arguments extended by the Nazis, and which inspired the inflammatory laws of Nuremberg, serve as the basis for the official definition of Jewishness in the bosom of the State of Israel.[56]

I.F. Stone, an American Jewish journalist, who was decorated by the *Irgun* in 1948, writing in 1967:

Israel is creating a kind of moral schizophrenia in World Jewry. In the outside world the welfare of Jewry depends on the maintenance of secular, non-racial pluralistic societies. In Israel, Jewry finds itself defending a society in which mixed marriages cannot be legalized, in which non-Jews have a lesser status than Jews and in which the ideal is racial and exclusionist. Jews must fight elsewhere for their very security and existence – against principles and practices they find themselves defending in Israel. Those from the outside world, even in their moments of greatest enthusiasm amid Israeli accomplishments, feel twinges of claustrophobia, not just geographical but spiritual. Those caught up in prophetic fervor soon begin to feel that the light they hoped to see out of Zion is only that of another narrow nationalism.

He comments on the tension between the universal vision of historic Judaism and the nationalism of the State of Israel:

It must also be recognized, despite Zionist ideology, that the periods of greatest Jewish accomplishment have been associated with pluralistic civilization in their time of expansion and tolerance: in the Hellenistic period, in the Arab civilization of North Africa and Spain, and in Western Europe and America. Universal values can only be the fruit of a universal vision; the greatness of the prophets lay in their overcoming of ethnocentricity. A lilliputian nationalism cannot distill truths for all mankind. Here lie the roots of a growing divergence between Jew and Israeli, the former with sense of mission as a witness in the human wilderness, the latter concerned only with his own tribes' welfare.[57]

5.9 Jew and Gentile after Jesus the Messiah

After the first century AD, as Judaism developed in radically new directions, the perception among Jews that they were different became even more pronounced. The differences between Jews and Gentiles became even more distinct.

This feeling is expressed, for example, in the prayer said by men each day: 'thank you that you have not made me a Gentile'.[58] It was expressed in an extreme form by **Rabbi Yitzhak Ginsburg**, the head of an ultra-orthodox Yeshiva (college) in Nablus, when he spoke at the trial following a rampage in which a Palestinian girl was shot dead in 1985: 'The people of Israel must rise and declare in public that a Jew and a goy (gentile) are not, God forbid, the same. Any trial that assumes that Jews and goyim are equal is a travesty of justice.'[59]

In contrast to the thinking of Judaism, the writers of the New Testament insisted that when Gentiles put their trust in Jesus and become his disciples, the distinction between Jew and Gentile is broken down.

Peter, for example, takes ideas and titles which, in their original context in the Old Testament, were reserved exclusively for the Children of Israel, and applies them to a group of Jewish and Gentile Christians:

You are a chosen people, a royal priesthood, a holy nation, a people belonging to God, that you may declare the praises of him who called you out of darkness into his wonderful light.
1 PETER 2:9

As a Jew, **Paul** was acutely conscious of the feelings of the Jewish people towards Gentiles in his own day. He believed, however, that God's intention was to create 'one new man', instead of two kinds of people – Jew and Gentile – and that God had begun to bring this about through the death of Jesus on the cross. This is the kind of relationship which God wanted to exist between Jews and Gentiles:

He himself is our peace, who has made the two [Jew and Gentile] one and has destroyed the barrier, the dividing wall of hostility, by abolishing in his flesh the law with its commandments and regulations. His purpose was to create in himself one new man out of the two, thus making peace, and in this one body to reconcile both of them to God through the cross, by which he put to death their hostility. He came and preached peace to you who were far away and peace to those who were near. For through him we both have access to the Father by one Spirit.

Consequently, you are no longer foreigners and aliens, but fellow citizens with God's people and members of God's household, built on the foundation of the apostles and prophets, with Christ Jesus himself as the chief cornerstone...

Through the gospel the Gentiles are heirs together with Israel, members together of one body, and sharers together in the promise in Christ Jesus.
EPHESIANS 2:14–20; 3:6

You are all sons of God through faith in Christ Jesus, for all of you who were baptized into Christ have clothed yourselves with Christ. There is neither Jew nor Greek, slave nor free, male nor female, for you are all one in Christ Jesus. If you belong to Christ, then you are Abraham's seed, and heirs according to the promise.
GALATIANS 3:26–29

This cannot mean that the difference between Jews and Gentiles is totally dissolved and becomes non-existent, any more than differences between males and females are done away with in Christ. It must mean, however, that differences between Jews and Gentiles can be transcended within the body of those who acknowledge Jesus as

Messiah. 'Through the Messiah' says **N.T. Wright**, 'and the preaching which heralds him, Israel is transformed from being an ethnic people into a worldwide family.'[60]

The origin of this new way of thinking in Peter and Paul is probably to be found in the teaching of Jesus himself. The vital link between the Old Testament and the radically new ideas in the New Testament is the claims that Jesus made about himself, and these can be illustrated in the following way:

How then do the writers of the New Testament understand the relationship between Israel in the Old Testament and Jesus? These are some of the ways in which these ideas are worked out in different parts of the New Testament, and especially in the letters of Paul:

Jesus represents Israel; Jesus is Israel

As we have already seen (4.3 Jesus and Jerusalem) 'the resurrection of Christ *is* the resurrection of Israel of which the prophets spoke' (C.H. Dodd).[61] Jesus was claiming in some sense to represent Israel in himself... he regarded himself as the one who summed up Israel's vocation and destiny in himself (N.T. Wright).[62]

As one who represents Israel, Jesus went through similar experiences to Israel. Thus, just as the Children of Israel spent time as exiles in Egypt, so Jesus was a refugee in Egypt during his earliest years (Matthew 2:13–15). Just as the Children of Israel wandered for forty years in the wilderness, so Jesus spent forty days being tempted by the Devil in the wilderness (Matthew 4:1–6). But whereas Israel failed and was disobedient, Jesus was fully obedient to the will of God (Hebrews 4:1–13; Romans 5:12–21).

'Loved on account of the patriarchs'

The Jews are still in a special relationship with God; they are 'loved on account of the patriarchs' (Romans 11:28–29). Jews who reject Jesus as Messiah forfeit the blessings of the covenant because of unbelief; they are 'broken off because of unbelief' (11:20). But the blessings of the covenant are still open to them (Romans 9:1–5).

This means that God has not finished with the Jewish people. 'Did God reject his people?' asks Paul; and his answer is 'By no means!' (Romans 11:1). 'God's gifts and his call are irrevocable' (Romans 11:29). There is something better to look forward to for them: 'and so all Israel will be saved' (11:26). But the only source of salvation for them, as for every other human being, is in Christ. When Jews believe in Jesus as Messiah, in Paul's picture of the olive tree, they are 'grafted back into their own olive tree' (Romans 11:23–24. See 5.10 The condemnation of anti-Semitism for a fuller discussion of Romans 9–11).

'Make disciples of all the nations'

Jesus sent his disciples out to 'make disciples of all nations' (i.e. of all the Gentiles – Matthew 28:19–20; compare John 12:32–33). Gentile Christians are therefore grafted into the people of God and inherit all the blessings of the covenant (Romans 11:13–24). Christians of any and every race therefore have all the privileges of the people of God, and titles applied to Israel in the Old Testament are applied to the church, as when Peter writes, 'you are a chosen people, a royal priesthood, a holy nation, a people belonging to God' (1 Peter 2:9–10).

It is important to note that although Christians often speak loosely of the church as 'the new Israel', this title is *not* found in the New Testament. **John Goldingay** explains where the title and the idea came from and why they should be avoided:

There is, actually, no point in the New Testament where 'Israel' denotes the Church. Although the New Testament uses terms to describe the Church which the Hebrew Bible uses to describe Israel, it does not describe the Church as 'Israel' or the 'New Israel' or the 'true Israel'. The transference of such terms from Israel to the Church begins with Justin Martyr, when the tension over Israel's position which is maintained in the New Testament is lost and the Church is distancing itself over against Judaism. In the New Testament, 'Israel' means 'Israel'. The Jewish-Gentile Church comes to share in Israel's privileges and so is described by means of the images that the Old Testament uses to describe Israel, but this does not mean in itself that the Church has replaced Israel.[63]

N.T. Wright similarly explains this understanding of the church, not as 'the new Israel', but rather as the renewed and restored Israel as follows:

From the earliest evidence, the Christians regarded themselves as a new family, directly descended from the family of Israel, but now transformed...
   Those who now belonged to Jesus' people were not identical with ethnic Israel, since Israel's history had reached its intended fulfilment; they claimed to be the continuation of Israel in a new situation, *able to draw freely on Israel-images to express their self-identity, able to read Israel's scriptures (through the lens of Messiah and spirit) and apply them to their own life. They were thrust out by that claim, and that reading, to fulfil Israel's vocation on behalf of the world.*[64]

If this is how the New Testament understands the relationship between the Jewish people and the Church, it is never appropriate for Christians to think that Christianity has 'taken the place of Israel'. This idea, which is sometimes described as 'supersessionism' and sometimes as 'Replacement Theology', find no support in the New Testament. While one can speak of Jesus 'replacing' the temple, there is no justification for saying that the church 'replaces' Israel.

In the minds of the Jewish disciples of Jesus, therefore, the destiny of the Jewish people had been fulfilled in their Messiah, Jesus of Nazareth. The dividing wall between Jews and Gentiles had been broken down, so that in Christ they become 'one new man' (Ephesians 2:15). There is no suggestion that they believed it was important for Jews to express their distinctive identity through having a Jewish state in the land. There is no hint that any of the New Testament writers continued to look forward to the establishment of an independent Jewish state.

Dow Marmur's *Beyond Survival: Reflections on the Future of Judaism* provides a valuable example of a Jewish rabbi wrestling with questions about Jewish identity and self-understanding in the world today. In a review of the book **Kenneth Cragg** summarizes its argument in the following way:

'The mystical bond... and the neurotic tangle' is a phrase that perhaps best sums up this frank, sensitive and, at times, exasperating, book. Its author is Rabbi of the North Western Reform Synagogue in London. He wants to take Judaism and Jews 'beyond' what he sees as their inordinate preoccupation with survival. This preoccupation he finds characteristic of the three main manifestations of Jewry. Traditional Orthodoxy finds survival through a rigorous loyalty to the past. Reform Judaism tends to emphasize present and future, but in his view, accommodates the world and its threat of assimilation too confidently. Zionism achieves a present, and – it hopes – a future security but only at the actual, or potential sacrifice of primary Jewish values.

The book pleads for a coming together of these three, each 'educating' the other in a unifying discipline so that they operate to alert each to dimensions which the others need but which also need them.

Cragg's further comments represent a serious attempt by a Christian theologian to engage with Marmur's thesis. This is how Cragg comments on Marmur's interpretation of the story of Jacob wrestling with the angel:

He sets his whole presentation in the context of Jacob wrestling with the angel at the brook, Jabbok. 'The elimination of the struggle deprives of the blessing.' Only in encounter with the future resolutely can the promise be reached, even if 'wrestling' Jacob is crippled in the process. The 'angel', for Dow Marmur, is 'the guardian angel of Esau', and perhaps, in a wider context, the spirit of the Gentile world. He does not mention the possibility that the struggle was about penitent honesty over Jacob's dubious past and the consequent 'new name' then bestowed. (Perhaps that is Gentile, Christian exegesis. But Jacob's apprehension about meeting Esau surely has to do not only with danger to his present gains but truth about his crooked past? Or does the duplicity at his old father's deathbed matter not?)

At all events, Jacob/Israel is called to perennial conflict. As at Peniel, his 'blessing' can only be had in being disadvantaged. His whole self-awareness is an awareness of actual or impending enmity. He has for ever to calculate in a crisis of survival.

He is a constant hostage to circumstance and can only triumph by struggling with real, feared, or imagined, adversity. This, mirrored in 'wrestling' Jacob, is the Jewish dilemma and gives to everything Jewish, whether Orthodoxy, Reform, Zionism, an incessant focus on self-ensuring response to hostility, actual or potential.

Cragg then goes on to express his response as a Christian to the argument of the book:

It is just this stance of Jewishness which Rabbi Marmur wants to exorcise (insofar as it makes 'survival' the be-all-and-end-all). Yet it is a stance to which he himself falls constantly victim. And this is where the book might be called exasperating. If only, somehow, Jewry could belong with mankind! But, somehow, tragically it never can. There is, as he sees it, the eternal problem of Anti-Semitism, a problem wholly at the door of the 'Gentile' world. There is persecution. There is the scapegoat 'syndrome' 'necessitating' Jews. There is assimilation, or the threat of it. Since, for example,

Old Testament	New Testament
Israel is the flock, with Yahweh their shepherd (Psalm 23:1; Ezekiel 34:1–31, especially 31)	Jesus speaks of himself as 'the good shepherd' (John 10:1–21, especially 11, 14, 16)
Israel is spoken of as the 'son' of God (Exodus 4:22–23; Psalm 80:15; Hosea 11:1)	Jesus speaks of himself as 'the son' who reveals 'the Father' (Matthew 11:27; John 14:5–14)
Israel is described as 'the vineyard' or 'the vine' (Psalm 80:8–16; Isaiah 5:1–7)	Jesus speaks of himself as 'the true vine' (John 15:1–17)
Israel in Daniel's vision is described as 'the son of man', a corporate figure which includes 'the saints of the Most High' (Daniel 7:13–28)	Jesus speaks of himself as 'the son of man' (Mark 2:10; 8:31; 14:62)
Israel is described by Isaiah as 'the servant of the Lord' (Isaiah 42:1–7; 49:1–7; 50:4–9; 52:13 – 53:12)	Jesus speaks of himself as the servant (Mark 10:45)

Oxford, with its culture and openness to Jewry, constitutes a danger of assimilation, 'both, Auschwitz and Oxford, have the same effect on the future of Judaism' (page 36). What an utterly desolating stance this is! Surely one of the sharpest needs of Jewish thought is a theology of 'the Gentiles', so that somehow what Marmur himself calls 'this neurotic tangle between Jews and their enemies' can be unravelled, and so ended...

There is much else that is perceptive and venturesome in this book. Yet it leaves a mere 'Gentile' reader who cares deeply about Jewry, the synagogue and Israel, and wants to understand 'the mystical bond', still aware that he, too, has only 'wrestled' (at this reconstruction of Peniel) with another occasion of the age-long problem that is 'the neurotic tangle'. When shall we all, Jew and Gentile alike, see 'the face of God' and know our life assured in that vision alone?[65]

Cragg speaks out of his conviction that in Jesus the Messiah the dividing wall between Jew and Gentile has been broken down. While he understands Jewish feelings about the relationship between Jew and Gentile, he finds it hard to believe that this was ever intended in the purposes of God to be a permanent relationship: 'If only, somehow, Jewry could belong with mankind!... When shall we all, Jew and Gentile alike, see "the face of God" and know that our life is assured in that vision alone?'

Jews and others have presented convincing *historical, political and psychological* arguments to justify the creation of a Jewish state in the land in the twentieth century. But on the basis of the New Testament understanding of the relationship between Jews and Gentiles outlined here, it is hard to see how *Christians* can pro-

duce convincing *theological* arguments based on the Bible for the appropriateness
and necessity of a Jewish state in the land.

5.10 The condemnation of anti-Semitism

'There is no shadow of doubt,' says **Rabbi Norman Solomon**, 'that in the historic
past the expression of Christianity has normally been anti-Semitic, sometimes vigor-
ously so'.[66] Does this mean that Christianity is inherently anti-Semitic? Can the source
of these attitudes towards Jews be traced back ultimately to the New Testament?

One of the best places to look for an answer is Romans chapters 9 to 11, which is
the most systematic discussion of the relationship between Jews and Gentiles in Paul's
letters. Much of the discussion about this passage has revolved around the sentence
'and so all Israel will be saved' (11:26), which has often been interpreted as a prediction
of a large-scale conversion of Jews – perhaps even of every Jew. This conversion is
sometimes linked with other ideas about the end of the world: the belief, for example,
that the return of Jews to the land and the recovery of Jerusalem have been highly significant events which will eventually lead to the conversion of many (if not all) Jews
and then to the second coming of Christ.

In response to this interpretation of the words 'and so all Israel will be saved'
three initial observations can be made:

■ 'Israel' in this verse probably does mean 'the Jewish people' and not 'the Church'.
In all the other thirteen instances in these chapters where he uses 'Israel', he clearly
means 'the Jewish people' (9:4, 6, 27, 31; 10:1, 16, 19, 21; 11:1, 2, 7, 11, 25). If Paul
here understands 'Israel' as 'the Church', he is using the word in two consecutive
sentences with two very different meanings: 'Israel [i.e. the Jewish people] has experienced a hardening' (11:25). 'And so all Israel [i.e. the church, the people of God,
including both Jews and Gentiles] will be saved' (11:26).

■ Paul has earlier argued that physical descent from Abraham is no guarantee of a
right relationship with God:

Not all who are descended from Israel are Israel. Nor because they are his descen-
dants are they all Abraham's children...
ROMANS 9:6–7

Circumcision has value if you observe the law, but if you break the law, you have
become as though you had not been circumcised... A man is not a Jew if he is only one
outwardly, nor is circumcision merely outward and physical. No, a man is a Jew if he
is one inwardly; and circumcision is circumcision of the heart, by the Spirit, not by the
written code. Such a man's praise is not from men, but from God.
ROMANS 2:25, 28–29

It would, therefore, be strange if Paul were to say that at some stage in the future
every Jew 'will be saved'.

■ This is the *only* sentence in *all* of Paul's letters which could possibly suggest the
idea of a large-scale conversion of Jews.

If Paul therefore has some idea about Jewish people 'being saved', what does he mean? How does he understand the relationship between Jews and Gentiles? The main points in Paul's argument in these chapters can be summarized as follows:

God has not rejected the people of Israel
The Jews are *still* heirs to all the promises made to their forefathers. Simply by virtue of being the physical descendants of Abraham, the privileges and blessings of the covenant are still theirs:

I ask then: Did God reject his people? By no means!... God did not reject his people, whom he foreknew.
ROMANS 11:1–2

... the people of Israel. Theirs is the adoption as sons; theirs the divine glory, the covenants, the receiving of the law, the temple worship and the promises. Theirs are the patriarchs, and from them is traced the human ancestry of Christ, who is God over all, forever praised! Amen.
ROMANS 9:4–5

As far as election is concerned, they are loved on account of the patriarchs, for God's gifts and his call are irrevocable.
ROMANS 11:28–29

The cost of unbelief
Although they are still the people of the covenant, Jews forfeit the blessings of the covenant through their unbelief. Since the majority of the Jewish people of his own time had rejected Jesus as their promised Messiah, they had forfeited the privileges of the covenant through their unbelief. Paul uses several vivid expressions to describe the unbelief of the Jews and its results:

Israel has experienced a hardening in part...
ROMANS 11:25 (COMPARE 11:7)

Their transgression... their loss...
ROMANS 11:12

They were broken off because of unbelief... God did not spare the natural branches...
ROMANS 11:20–21

'And so all Israel will be saved'
There is every reason to believe that Jews will continue to come to believe in Jesus and be 'grafted back' into the olive root. This is the confident expectation in the mind of Paul that is summed up in the sentence 'and so all Israel will be saved' (11:26). When Paul speaks of all Israel being saved, he seems to be saying that in contrast to the 'hardening *in part*' which Israel has experienced (11:25), what we

can now look forward to is the salvation of '*the full number*' of the Jews. This might mean a larger proportion than those who had already believed in Jesus, but it would still not mean every individual Jew.

The 'hardening in part' which has already taken place will eventually lead to 'the full number of the Gentiles' coming in; and this in turn will lead to the full number of the Jews (i.e. 'all Israel') being saved. The expression 'all Israel' would therefore have the same meaning as 'their fullness' ('their coming to full strength', 11:12, NEB).

Paul is not speculating about the *number* of Jews who would be saved, but rather insisting that they will continue to come to faith in Jesus as Messiah. The two quotations from the Old Testament (Isaiah 59:20–21; 27:9; Jeremiah 31:33–34) develop the idea of the salvation that God has been promising for his people. Since Paul is so insistent elsewhere that Jesus the Messiah *has already come* as deliverer and made a covenant to deal with the sins of his people, there is no suggestion that Jesus *has to come once again* to complete the special salvation of the Jews.

Correcting wrong attitudes

This hope should be a corrective to wrong attitudes of Christians towards the Jewish people. Paul does not unfold any detailed plan of how the full number of the Jews will one day come to believe. He is not presenting a grand blue-print for the future of the Jewish people. He says nothing about the land; and says nothing about political or national issues. His main concern is to correct wrong attitudes towards the Jewish people which he knew were there in the minds of many Gentile Christians. They had concluded that since the majority of the Jews had failed to accept Jesus as their Messiah, God had totally rejected them as a people, and they no longer had any role to play in the plan of God for the world.

These ideas, however, are totally unacceptable for Christians. Paul realizes that from now on the church is likely to be a largely *Gentile* church, but believes passionately that, in the words of **N.T. Wright**, there is to be 'total equality of Jew and Gentile within the church'.[67] He uses every argument he can find to correct any attitudes of pride and superiority towards the Jews:

I am talking to you Gentiles... If some of the branches have been broken off, and you, though a wild olive shoot, have been grafted in among the others and now share in the nourishing sap from the olive root, do not boast *over those branches. If you do, consider this: You do not support the root, but the root supports you. You will say then, 'Branches were broken off so that I could be grafted in.' Granted. But they were broken off because of unbelief, and you stand by faith.* Do not be arrogant, *but be afraid.*
ROMANS 11:13, 17–20

I do not want you to be ignorant of this mystery, brothers, so that you may not be conceited.
ROMANS 11:25

Paul ends the discussion by expressing the hope that Jews will turn to God and receive mercy through seeing evidence of God's mercy in the Gentiles:

Just as you who were at one time disobedient to God [i.e. you Gentiles] have now
received mercy as a result of their disobedience [i.e. of the Jews], so they too [the
Jews] have now become disobedient in order that they too may now receive mercy
as a result of God's mercy to you [Gentiles]. For God has bound all men over to dis-
obedience so that he may have mercy on them all.
ROMANS 11:30–32

His message to the largely Gentile church in Rome can therefore be paraphrased as
follows: 'Do not assume that since the majority of the Jewish people have now
rejected their Messiah, this will always be the case. The refusal of the Jews to recognize Jesus has meant that the gospel has spread all over the Gentile world. So
think what kind of a future we can look forward to when the full number of Jewish
believers are brought into the kingdom! Do not forget your own Jewish roots! And
do not write off the Jews!'

This understanding of the relationship between 'Israel' and 'the church' could never
be described as being 'supersessionism' or 'Replacement Theology'. 'Paul is writing,
with all the eleven chapters of theology behind him,' says **N.T. Wright**, 'in order to say
that "Gentile Christians" have not "replaced" Jews as the true people of God.'[68]

If we ask how the Christian Church could have generally developed a more critical and negative attitude towards Jews and Judaism, part of the answer is to be
found in what happened in AD 135 and the following years. **Peter Schneider**
explains the origin of these ideas as follows:

The fall of Jerusalem in AD 70 and the collapse of Bar Cochba's national Jewish
revolt in AD 135 and Hadrian's subsequent establishing and renaming of Jerusalem
as Aelia Capitolina *was almost as great a watershed for the Church as it was for the*
Jewish people. The Apostolic Fathers of the second century reflecting on this Jewish
tragedy had no difficulty in deciding to interpret it as a further piece of evidence
that Jewry had not only been displaced and dispersed physically but precisely
because of this forfeited her place spiritually as the true Israel to which the Church
then thought itself to be the rightful heir.

Justin Martyr, a convert from Pagan philosophy and worthy representative of the
second-century Apostolic Fathers, is the author of the so-called Dialogue with
Trypho *the Jew shortly after the collapse of Bar Cochba's national Jewish revolt in*
AD 135 and Hadrian's explusion of Jews from Jerusalem renamed as Aelia
Capitolina. *Because of this Justin had no hesitation in claiming that the Church is*
not the 'true Israel', *an expression that in its absoluteness is not found in the New*
Testament. So he boldly says, 'We are the true and spiritual Israelitish nation, and
the race of Judah and of Jacob and Isaac and Abraham' (Dialogue *11:5).*[69]

Far from allowing or encouraging anti-Semitism, therefore, Paul's argument in
Romans 9–11 contains a strong condemnation of anti-Semitic attitudes. Paul was
very aware of a tendency among Gentile Christians to think that God had finished
with the Jews, and that they no longer had any special significance in the purposes
of God.

His response is to say that while Jews forfeit the full blessings of the covenant because of their unbelief, 'God did not reject his people whom he foreknew'. Instead of thinking that they have stepped into the place of the Jewish people, Gentile Christians are to recognize that they have somehow been 'grafted into' the Jewish people. There is therefore no place for Gentile Christians to boast, to be arrogant or conceited in their attitude towards the Jews. The present unbelief of the majority is not the end of the story, since there is something better for them that has still to unfold.

Paul's understanding of the relationship between 'Israel' and the church should have provided the Christian church with a permanent antidote to the attitudes which later developed into anti-Semitism. Properly understood, his argument could have provided the Church with 'the best antidote it could have had for identifying and combating some of the worst evils of the Third Reich' (**N.T. Wright**).[70]

A confession of Christian shame over its contribution towards anti-Semitism might therefore be expressed like this:

If only Christians in the past had listened to Paul's warning and challenged and corrected every attitude of arrogance and superiority towards the Jews whenever it raised its ugly head!

If only John Chrysostom, Augustine, Aquinas and Luther had soaked themselves in these chapters, and not written the Jewish people off as being beyond the pale!

If only they had seen that these chapters were not intended as a theological treatise about predestination and freewill, but as a challenge to think in a truly Christian way about the people who are 'loved on account of the patriarchs' (Romans 11:28)!

If only they had got Paul's point and tried to look forward to the time – even if it was not to be in their day – when the full number of the Jews 'would be grafted into their own olive' (Romans 11:24)!

If only Christians today would use Paul's words for the purpose of correcting wrong attitudes towards the Jews, and not for speculating about how and when the Jews are going to join the church in large numbers!

5.11 The possibility of reconciliation

The present state of conflict between Jews and Arabs in the land makes it hard even to think in terms of *coexistence* between the two peoples – let alone of *reconciliation*. Given the realities of all that has happened in recent years, the idea that the Jews and Palestinians might actually make peace and be reconciled with each other may seem so unrealistic that it is not even worth considering as a possibility.

But there *are* examples of reconciliation – even if only on a small scale. And if the alternative is mutual destruction, it is never too late to go back to basics and to ask what would be required if everyone – both participants and spectators – were determined to go on seeking for peace and reconciliation.

Before turning to the Bible we ought to recognize that most cultures have their own approaches to peacemaking and reconciliation. If we put together these ideas from different traditions, these would appear to be some of the basic preconditions of reconciliation:

■ We have to admit the existence of the other, and attempt to understand something of their experience.

■ While seeking justice for ourselves, we need to put aside the thirst for revenge.

■ There must be a *desire* for reconciliation.

■ At some stage there has to be face-to-face meeting.

■ We need to be willing to admit our faults. Even if we cannot bring ourselves to admit these too publicly to the other side, we must be willing to admit them at least to ourselves and to our own community.

■ There needs to be at least a willingness to forgive the other party.

■ We need to be able to look beyond our own interests and to allow the other person to claim the things that we have claimed for ourselves. If *we*, therefore, need a sense of identity, and claim security and independence for ourselves, we should be willing to allow *the other party* to claim these same things for themselves.

■ Sometimes reconciliation is only possible when there is a mediator. In many situations there needs to be a third party which is not identified with one side or the other and can deal fairly and evenly with both sides.

Many of these ideas come together in 'Resist with Peace', an article written in March 2001 by **Eyad El-Sarraj**, a Palestinian psychiatrist, who lives and works in the Gaza Strip:

I was brought up to hate Jews. Jews, I was told, had robbed me of my home in Beir-Sheva and forced my people out of Palestine. Jews were monstrous killers. I lived dreading the day when I would meet my first Jew.

In 1956, during the Suez War, when Israel occupied Gaza, I met him. I was 12; he was a soldier pointing a gun at my back as he ordered me to lead him into our underground dark shelter. I was terrified of the gun but amused that the soldier was apparently frightened too. I asked myself then if they have the same feelings as we do.

The second Jew was shocking. It was in 1971, when I finished my medical degree in Alexandria and was driven by a Red Cross bus across the Suez Canal to serve in Gaza. The Israelis had then occupied Gaza again, along with the West Bank, Sinai desert and Golan Heights following their victory in the Six-Day War.

I was sitting in the front seat of the bus facing an Israeli soldier and his gun. I was angry and frightened. It must have shown on my face because suddenly the young Israeli soldier looked at me with a reassuring smile and said. 'Have you been away from your family for long?'

'Yes,' I said, shocked. He then said, 'I hope you will find them all safe and in good health.' I will never forget his face. I think that I decided then that Jews are humans as we are and that I would never be able to kill.

Living and working in Gaza under Israeli military occupation for the past 30 years has been a rich but painful experience. I was interrogated many times. I was asked to 'cooperate'. I was treated with arrogance, and I was fired from my job twice, and listened to hundreds of stories of pain and tears. But I met many wonderful Israelis and some became my friends. I learned much from them.

One of my best friends is Tamar, a clinical psychologist from Tel Aviv. She called me on the eve of Ariel Sharon's victory. She was depressed. While we were talking, I realized how Israel has turned inward, radicalized in fear and united behind Sharon. I wondered if Palestinian rocks have shaken Israeli democracy and were decisive in his victory. I always believed, but now increasingly so, that both peoples are trapped.

Israelis who appear as the masters are in fact victims of a history of pain, suffering persecution and ghettos. They are surrounded by an ocean of hatred as Arabs could not accept defeat, and their rhetoric was fierce.

Palestinians are hurt. They felt betrayed by the Arab regimes and unjustly treated by the Western world. Their anger turned into cycles of defiance and rage. Now they fire bullets of despair on a suicidal path.

For any peace process to succeed, people need to be liberated. Palestinians and Israelis have yet to realize that they are interdependent.

Liberation of the Palestinians from the Israeli occupation of their land, from the humiliation and suffering, will happen when Israelis are liberated from their fear and insecurity. Palestinian bullets only strengthen Israelis' sense of victimization and paranoia.

I believe that Palestinians should take the initiative along the road of nonviolent resistance. Such an idea will not be easy to accept or implement. Some would argue that our culture is bent on Jihad, but Jihad does not exclude nonviolence. In fact, the most challenging Jihad is that within one's self.

The road of nonviolence will empower the masses and the individual while they learn how weakness can be turned into strength. It will make Israelis peer from behind their shield to see the Palestinian man and woman in their true size, in their true form. Imagine if we take a bus, loaded with Palestinians to Tel Aviv, not to explode but to meet Israelis.

They will then be secure enough to feel, share the pain and empathize. And many Israelis, Jews and friends of peace and justice will join the struggle for Palestinian liberation. Palestinians will then begin to see the Israelis in a human form and relate to them as equals. Both will be 'free at last' and partners in peace.[71]

Is there beyond this anything distinctive about a Christian approach to the idea of reconciliation? If Christians make so much of the idea of our reconciliation with God, one would expect to find teaching in the Bible about what is involved in reconciliation between human beings. The following are just some of these ideas as they are found in the Bible, and especially in the teaching of Jesus:

■ Jesus said that his disciples should never hate their enemies: 'You have heard that it was said, "Love your neighbor and hate your enemy." But I tell you: Love your enemies and pray for those who persecute you, that you may be sons of your Father in heaven' (Matthew 5:43–45). The command 'love your neighbor as yourself' (Matthew 22:39) must mean that we must want for our neighbor what we want for ourselves.

■ Jesus taught that there is a close connection between our relationship with God and our relationships with fellow human beings. If we are aware that there is something wrong in any relationship, we need to take the initiative to attempt to put things right: 'if you are offering your gift at the altar and there remember that your brother has something against you, leave your gift there in front of the altar. First go and be reconciled to your brother; then come and offer your gift' (Matthew 5:23–24).

■ At some stage in the process of reconciliation there has to be face-to-face meeting. When Jacob had cheated his brother Esau out of his birthright, they remained estranged from each other for many years. It was only when they met face to face that the relationship could be restored. When they finally met and Jacob offered gifts to Esau, he expressed his enormous sense of relief in seeing his brother face to face: 'If I have found favor in your eyes, accept this gift from me. For to see your face is like seeing the face of God, now that you have received me favorably' (Genesis 33:10).

■ There needs to be at least a willingness to forgive the other party. Jesus linked our receiving forgiveness from God with our willingness to forgive others who have wronged us. The parable of the unforgiving servant, for example, shows how we cannot expect God to forgive us if we are unwilling to forgive other people. In the same spirit Paul writes, 'Be kind and compassionate to one another, forgiving each other, just as in Christ God forgave you' (Ephesians 4:32). 'Forgiveness is to be the hallmark of all social relationships,' says **N.T. Wright**, and goes on to add: 'One only has to live for a short time in a society where forgiveness is not even valued in theory – where, for instance, "losing face" is regarded as one of the greatest misfortunes – to realize how revolutionary this challenge really is.'[72]

We end, therefore, with two examples of writers whose thinking about reconciliation springs out of a Christian understanding of the way God's love and forgiveness have been demonstrated in Christ.

Naim Ateek, the Palestinian priest who was evicted from his home in 1948 and now lives in Jerusalem, urges his fellow Palestinian Christians to adopt genuinely Christian attitudes in the conflict:

The challenge to the Palestinian Christians, and indeed of all Christians faced with situations of bitterness and hate, is to keep up the struggle and never to succumb to despair and hate. I am speaking out of my own experience with Israel since 1948. I have learned much from my father, who had to come to terms with the hate and resentment in his life after he lost everything to the Israelis in Beisan. His struggle was real but he did not succumb to hate. For when people hate, its power engulfs them and they are totally consumed by their hatred. So I consider the challenge to my fellow Palestinians to be threefold:

Keep struggling against hate and resentment. Always confess that the struggle goes on and the battle is not over. At times you will have the upper hand, at times you will feel beaten down. Although it is extremely difficult, never let hatred completely overtake you. By the power of God the struggle will go on until the day comes when you begin to count more victories than defeats.

Never stop trying to live the commandment of love and forgiveness. Do not dilute the strength of Jesus' message: do not shun it, do not dismiss it as unreal and impractical. Do not cut it to your size, trying to make it more applicable to real life in the world. Do not change it so that it will suit you. Keep it as it is; aspire to it, desire it, and work with God for its achievement.

Remember that so often it is those who have suffered most at the hands of others who are capable of offering forgiveness and love.[73]

Kenneth Bailey's story of the two sons and their father's land explores what can happen when a person begins to seek justice *for the other person* and not simply *for himself or herself.* The story is part of a longer poem, 'Ode on a Burning Tank: The Holy Lands, October 1973', and was written immediately after the October War in 1973. It is based on similar stories found in both Jewish and Arab sources and adapts them in such a way as to draw out what may be distinctive in Christian thinking about reconciliation.

A certain man had two sons.
One was rich and the other was poor.
  The rich son had no children
  while the poor son was blessed with many sons and many
    daughters.

In time the father fell ill.
  He was sure he would not live through the week
  so on Saturday he called his sons to his side
  and gave each of them half of the land of their inheritance.
  Then he died.

Before sundown the sons buried their father with respect
  as custom required.

That night the rich son could not sleep.
  He said to himself,
  'What my father did was not just.
  I am rich, my brother is poor.
  I have bread enough and to spare,
    while my brother's children eat one day
      and trust God for the next.
I must move the landmark which our father has set in the
    middle of the land
so that my brother will have the greater share.
  Ah – but he must not see me.
  If he sees me he will be shamed.
  I must arise early in the morning before it is dawn and
    move the landmark!'

With this he fell asleep
  and his sleep was secure and peaceful.

Meanwhile, the poor brother could not sleep.
  As he lay restless on his bed he said to himself,
  'What my father did was not just.
  Here I am surrounded by the joy of my many sons and
    many daughters,
  while my brother daily faces the shame
  of having no sons to carry on his name
  and no daughters to comfort him in his old age.
  He should have the land of our fathers.
  Perhaps this will in part compensate him
  for his indescribable poverty.
  Ah – but if I give it to him he will be shamed.
  I must awake early in the morning before it is dawn
  and move the landmark which our father has set!'
  With this he went to sleep
  and his sleep was secure and peaceful.

On the first day of the week –
  very early in the morning,
  a long time before it was day,
the two brothers met at the ancient landmarker.
  They fell with tears into each other's arms
  And on that spot was built the city of Jerusalem.[74]

The first three lines of the last stanza are an unmistakable echo of the account of the resurrection of Jesus in the Gospels of Luke and John (Luke 24:1 and John 20:1). The idea therefore is that belief in the resurrection of Jesus the Messiah makes this kind of reconciliation possible at the deepest level.

If the struggle between Jews and Arabs in Israel/Palestine is about the land, perhaps the cross and the empty tomb might ultimately have something to do with establishing peace with justice in the land.

5.12 Conclusions

A passion for truth

All who are concerned about the conflict over the land should demonstrate their concern by doing all they can to find out the truth about what has actually happened in the past and what is happening at the present. If Christians know little or nothing about the history of the conflict, or if they have been fed a very one-sided version of what happened, there is a real danger in turning first to the Bible to find clear interpretations of what has been happening. We need 'the most complete truth' that we can understand (5.1 A passion for truth).

The problem of prejudice

It is often prejudice that makes it difficult for people to acknowledge the truth about any situation. Those who are not themselves involved in the conflict need to beware of total identification with one side or the other, and try to be as even-handed as possible. When outsiders take their stand openly with one side or the other in any conflict they tend to become so prejudiced and partisan in their approach that they lose the right and the opportunity to say anything positive to either side. Some believe that in this conflict it is possible to be 'both pro-Jewish and pro-Arab' at the same time (5.2 The problem of prejudice).

The demands of the law

If Jews appeal to the Abrahamic promise as the title deed which gives them the right to the land for all times, they automatically put themselves under the authority of the law of Moses. The more they seek to interpret what has happened in the land in the light of the divine promise, the more they should be willing for their actions to be judged in the light of the divine law. The more they want to see recent history as the fulfilment of prophecy, the more they should be prepared to submit themselves to the demands of the law. If Jews are to be judged in the light of their own law, it is not out of place to ask questions about *how* they have acquired land and *how* they have treated the Arabs (5.3 The demands of the law).

The prophetic concern for justice

Interpreting the Old Testament prophets today should mean very much more than trying to find how their predictions have been fulfilled in history. If, in addition to predicting future events, the prophets sought to interpret what was going on around them, our study of the prophets today should encourage and enable us to make moral judgments about all that has happened in the land in recent history. If God judges individuals for breaking his law, he also judges nations for the ways in which they break his law in their relationships with each other. If the prophets were concerned about justice for all who were oppressed, those who accept these scriptures ought to have the same concern for every individual and community in the Middle East which feels that it is oppressed and denied the justice for which it longs (5.4 The prophetic concern for justice).

God's judgment in history

If God is holy and if he is in control of history, there must be a process of judgment that is at work in the rise and fall of nations. If it is true in the life of *individuals* that they reap what they sow, it must also be true for *nations*. One of the most distinctive marks of a Christian response to the conflict over the land should be repentance (5.5 God's judgment in history).

Suffering injustice

Alongside every call for *justice* to be done, there needs to be an awareness that justice *cannot* always be done, and that many people have to live with *injustice*. The figure of Isaiah's Suffering Servant suggests that there should be something distinctive about the way in which the people of God respond to injustice. In some situations the way to overcome evil is to suffer it (5.6 Suffering injustice).

Rethinking and repentance through disaster
If disaster forces some to despair and unbelief, others find ways of responding which lead to a deep rethinking and repentance: 'Let us examine our ways and test them, and let us return to the LORD' (Lamentations 3:40).While fully aware of the enormity of what they have suffered, they are able to hold onto their faith in the love of God (5.7 Rethinking and repentance through disaster).

Jew and Gentile in the Old Testament
Jews today believe that Zionism is one valid expression of Judaism in the modern world. It is hard to see, however, how the concept of a Jewish state in Palestine can be related to the universalist vision presented by several of the prophets. If these prophetic visions were more than pious hopes for the future, they challenge the whole idea of a modern state in which citizenship is based primarily on being Jewish (5.8 Jew and Gentile in the Old Testament).

Jew and Gentile after Jesus the Messiah
The New Testament writers believed that in Jesus the Messiah the dividing wall between Jews and Gentiles had been broken down. In Jesus 'there is neither Jew nor Greek... for you are all one in Christ Jesus' (Galatians 3:28). 'For he himself, is our peace, who has made the two one... to create in himself one new man...' (Ephesians 2:14–15) (5.9 Jew and Gentile after Jesus the Messiah).

The condemnation of anti-Semitism
Gentile Christians should never think that the church has superseded the Jewish people or taken their place. Paul's image of the olive tree suggests that instead of thinking that a largely Gentile church has taken the place of the Jewish people in the plan of God, it is nearer the truth to see Gentile Christians as shoots from a wild olive that are grafted back into the original stock. There is no place for Christian arrogance in relation to the Jewish people (5.10 The condemnation of anti-Semitism).

The possibility of reconciliation
While every culture and every society has its own approach to reconciliation, what is distinctive in the Christian approach arises out of the example of Christ. If 'God was in Christ reconciling the world to Himself' (2 Corinthians 5:19 NASB), the attitude of Jesus points to the possibility of real and lasting reconciliation between people (5.11 The possibility of reconciliation).

If these are some of the ideas in the Bible that are relevant to the conflict over the land, how can they be worked out in the real world of today?

PART 3

Appreciating
the Issues Today

Part 3 explores questions about the outworking of the conflict at the present time. Does the present crisis raise concerns about the original vision of Zionism? What are the realties of international power politics today, and how are they likely to affect any possible resolution? If Zionism is open to question, is Christian Zionism also open to question? And what are the reasons for the opposition to Zionism that are inspired not only by nationalism but also by the religion of Islam? What are the options for Israel and for the Palestinians at the present time?

Chapter 6

Realities Today

Is There Any Hope of Resolving the Conflict?

*I am certain that the world will judge the
Jewish state by how it will treat the Arabs.*[1]
CHAIM WEIZMANN, IN 1944

*We would not like to dominate another people
against their will... It is a moral issue. It is a political
issue. Throughout our history as Jewish people, we have
never dominated other people, and whoever dominated us disappeared from
history. We do not want to copy that.*[2]
SHIMON PERES

*If 1948 was a just war, then Israel's subsequent actions,
however unpleasant, were in defence of a just cause. If
Israel was born morally tainted, however, then it remains
for ever besmirched and nothing it does, especially in its
conflict with the Palestinians, is morally defensible.*[3]
ANTON LA GUARDIA

*The first Intifada was to force the Israelis to the negotiating
table. This Intifada is to get rid of the occupation... The Intifada
is a milestone – a place from which to consider the tumultuous
road to Palestinian statehood, the experiment in Palestinian autonomy, and the
forces that destroyed this attempt at 'peace'.*[4]
ANTON LA GUARDIA

*Rabin knew that if they [Jewish fundamentalist settlers]
were to succeed, if the conflict were to be theologized,
there never would be peace. For, to theological conflict,
there are no compromises, and therefore no solutions.*[5]
MARTIN GILBERT

To get peace, we must return to the pre-1967
borders. Peace is more important than real estate.[6]
DAVID BEN-GURION, IN 1967

6.1 A crisis for Zionism

Is land more important than peace? Or, as Ben-Gurion seemed to think in 1967, six
years before his death, is making peace more important than holding on to land?
Israel's continuing occupation of the West Bank and Gaza since 1967 – against the
wishes of the Palestinians and in defiance of UN Resolutions – has brought it to a
moment of truth: Is Zionism inevitably committed to the vision of a 'Greater Israel'
which includes the maximum amount of Palestine?

The questions raised by the present stage of the conflict are far from new, since
they have been there from the beginning. It could be argued that the present crisis
simply draws attention to weaknesses that have existed in the Zionist vision from
the beginning. If the present difficulties lead people to question the Zionist vision,
these questions and doubts echo voices that have been raised – either by Zionists
themselves, by Jews outside the movement, by Palestinian Arabs or by observers –
in one form or another at every stage of the conflict.

Zionists have generally been unable to come to terms with the Palestinians

The land was already inhabited and largely Arab – and the Zionists knew it. So how
did they proceed?

Inevitably there was a large element of deception. Herzl and Weizmann gave
assurances to the Arabs, but their real intentions were evident to the Arabs and are
now there for everyone to read in their diaries. The denial of the conflict by David
Ben-Gurion for a period of twenty years was, in **Norman Finkelstein**'s view, 'a
calculated tactic, born of pragmatism rather than profoundly of conviction. The idea
that Jews and Arabs could reconcile their differences... was a delaying tactic. Once
the Yishuv had gained strength, Ben-Gurion abandoned it. This belief in a compromise solution... was also a tactic, designed to win continued British support for
Zionism.'[7] They could hardly have survived if they had openly declared their ultimate goal from the beginning.

Alongside this deception there was a profound unwillingness to understand the
Arabs and to allow that they might have the same aspirations as the Zionists had
themselves. This is how **David Vital** in his book *The Origins of Zionism* sums up
the attitudes of the visionaries of the 'Lovers of Zion' in the nineteenth century:

*The question of the future relations between the Jews of Eretz-Israel on the one
hand and the Arabs and members of other ethnic and religious communities in
the country on the other did not register in their minds... All in all, it is difficult
not to conclude that they assumed that the manifest legitimacy of their ideas and
the sheer force of their personal example would suffice to ensure their moral
supremacy in the evolving society around them and the acceptance of their leadership and guidance by all concerned.*[8]

Similarly **Simha Flapan**, an Israeli Jewish historian, in *Zionism and the Palestinians* writes of the inability of the Jews – right up to the present day – to come to terms with the Palestinians:

When the former Israeli Prime Minister Golda Meir was criticized for her widely publicized pronouncement that 'there is no such thing as a Palestinian people', it escaped the notice of her critics that the view she expressed was the cornerstone of Zionist policy, initiated by Weizmann and faithfully carried out by Ben-Gurion and his successors. This policy has been pursued despite abundant proof of the tenacity with which the Palestinians have clung to their national identity in the most adverse circumstances.

Non-recognition of the Palestinians remains until the present the basic tenet of Israel's policy-makers who, like the Zionist leadership before 1948, nurture the illusion that the Palestinian national problem disappeared with the creation of the state of Jordan, leaving only the residual humanitarian problem of the refugees to be solved.[9]

David Ben-Gurion was very frank about the realities of the conflict and the clash of the two nationalisms:

Everybody sees a difficulty in the question of relations between Arabs and Jews. But not everybody sees that there is no solution to the question. No solution! There is a gulf and nothing can fill this gulf. It is possible to resolve the conflict between Jewish and Arab interests (only) by sophistry. I do not know what Arab will agree that Palestine should belong to the Jews... We, as a nation, want this country to be ours; the Arabs, as a nation, want this country to be theirs.[10]

Part of the tragedy that we see unfolding at the present time, therefore, is that the majority of Jews in the land who have been so intent on establishing their own national identity have generally found it impossible to allow Palestinian Arabs to do the same. In affirming their own right to be a people and a nation, they have consistently denied that right to the people who happened to be living in the land before they arrived. If they have thought about the possibility of coexistence with the Palestinian presence alongside them, it has generally been only on their own terms.

Violence was implicit in the original vision of Zionism

Even as early as 1841 it was possible for **David Millard**, an American Christian preacher, to reach this conclusion after a visit to the Holy Land:

Should the time ever take place when the Jews shall again possess the land of their fathers, a very important overturn must first take place with the nations and tribes that surround it. The land is at present inhabited by native Arabs, who till the soil and mainly people the towns and villages. The question arises, how are these inhabitants to be dispossessed of the land? Is a purchase contemplated? Who, or what power is to enforce such a purchase, and where would the present inhabitants emigrate to? Or is it contemplated that they are to be driven out by the sword? This, I am convinced is the only means by which the land can be cleared of its present population. But in this case, the native inhabitants would, of course, be driven back upon Arabia, which bends like a crescent round the south and east of the Holy Land. The present inhabitants would not thus be driven out without obstinacy and bloodshed, carrying with them at the same time, the most malignant inveteracy. From Arabia, aided by other tribes, they would sally from time to time, to ravage and lay waste the whole land. In that case, the Jews could not protect themselves, and must fall a prey to the tribes of Ishmael. Nor could a standing army, kept by the powers of Europe, protect them.[11]

Being 'driven out by the sword' and 'bloodshed' seemed to Millard to be 'the only means by which the land could be cleared'. This was not someone writing with the benefit of hindsight, but someone simply visiting the land as a pilgrim/tourist forty years *before* Jewish immigration began to increase. He could understand facts on the ground well enough to predict accurately what would be involved in a widespread return of Jews to the land.

David Hirst is convinced that for Theodor Herzl 'violence… was implicit in Zionism from the outset' and that Palestinian violence was to a large extent a response to the violence that was done to them:

The prophet of Zionism foresaw that coercion and physical force were inevitable; they were not unfortunate necessities thrust, unforeseen, on his followers. To his diaries, not published until twenty-six years after his death in 1904, Herzl confided the beliefs which, in his public utterances, he had been careful to omit: that military power was an essential component of his strategy and that, ideally, the Zionists should acquire the land of their choice by armed conquest…

'Qui veut la fin, veut les moyens' ('he who desires the end desires the means') is a saying which Herzl cited with approval. But in proposing such an end – a Jewish State in Palestine – and such means he was proposing a great deception, and laying open his whole movement to the subsequent charge that in any true historical perspective the Zionists were the original aggressors in the Middle East, the real pioneers of violence, and that Arab violence, however cruel and fanatical it might eventually become, was an inevitable reaction to theirs.[12]

Norman Finkelstein comes to the same conclusion:

Mainstream Zionism adapted its tactics to accommodate new contingencies. But force was a constant throughout. Zionism did not come to use force despite itself. The recourse to force was not circumstantial. It was 'inherent' in the aim of transforming Palestine, with its overwhelmingly Arab population, into a Jewish state…

None of the Zionist movement's standard rationales – divine right, historical right, compelling need – could justify its aim to transform Palestine into a Jewish state. A violent conflict with the indigenous Arab population was thus inevitable. As the dissident Zionist intellectual Judah Magnes succinctly put it, 'The slogan

Jewish state... is equivalent, in effect, to a declaration of war by the Jews on the Arabs.[13]

Arthur Ruppin, head of land purchasing for the Jewish National Fund, writing in 1930, was fully aware of the implications of the Zionist drive to acquire land:

On every side where we purchase land and where we settle people the present cultivators will inevitably be dispossessed. There is no alternative, but that lives should be lost. It is our destiny to be in a state of continual warfare with the Arabs.[14]

Even before the conflict began, therefore, and at many stages along the way it was obvious that the Zionist dream could never be fulfilled without violence. It was almost inevitable that the people who set the pace and pushed the Zionist movement forward at crucial stages were not the moderates who wanted peaceful coexistence with the Arabs, but the leaders with more aggressive and hardline approaches. A more gentle and pacific approach would never have brought the state to where it is today. The violence involved in the present confrontation in the West Bank and Gaza has been implicit from the beginning.

A Jewish state requires a majority that has political power
At the beginning of the process of immigration the Jews were outnumbered by twenty to one. A basic conviction of the early Zionists, according to **Norman Finkelstein**, was that 'the creation of a Jewish majority... was the fundamental aim of Zionism... the term "Jewish state"... means a Jewish majority... Palestine will become a Jewish country at the moment when it has a Jewish majority.'[15] If Jews had returned to the land simply to find a homeland, a haven from persecution, and had determined to find a political formula which recognized both the demographic facts as well as the aspirations of the Palestinian Arabs, there might never have been any conflict. But as long as the Zionists believed that *the Jewish homeland* meant *the Jewish state*, they had to work for the time when Jews would eventually outnumber the Arabs and take over power. The Zionist refusal to consider any kind of power-sharing with the Palestinians, and their insistence on creating a Jewish state in which they themselves were in control would inevitably put the Palestinians in the position of being a minority of second-class citizens.

Martin Buber, the Jewish philosopher who died in Jerusalem in 1965, repeatedly addressed the question of numbers and the balance of power between the Jews and Arabs. He argued repeatedly for a binational state in which there was proportionate power-sharing between the two communities. **Paul Mendes-Flohr** has described Buber's challenge to the Zionists in this way:

From as far back as the time of the Balfour Declaration on through to the end of his life, Martin Buber was earnestly reminding his fellow Zionists of the moral dimensions of Zionism – specifically in terms of the Arab problem... Buber essentially saw the entire Zionist enterprise as a test of Jewish humanism and morality... He was an enthusiastic supporter of the return of the Jews to their land. But he

*never forgot that... two peoples exist in that land. For this reason, he maintained
some positions that were extremely unpopular with his fellow Zionists.*

*Some of those positions – like not insisting on a Jewish majority in Palestine –
stagger the imagination today. But... such an idea was grounded in what Buber
insisted was the utter realism dictating his moral stance.*

*The prevailing Zionist view had long been to settle as many Jews as possible in
the Land of Israel. Only by creating facts on the ground, and by eventually establishing a Jewish majority, would the Jews be able to assert sovereignty here and
neutralize Arab claims.*

*Buber, however, violently disagreed with this approach. Instead of aiming to set-
tle as many Jews as possible, he argued for settling only as many Jews as necessary.
That's because he believed that with two peoples in the land, sovereignty had to be
shared on a parity basis. So he wanted as many Jews here as would be necessary to
allow Jewish national life to flourish – but not so many that a majority rule would
be artificially imposed at the expense of others.*

*Buber argued further that this was the only morally realistic approach to the
problem of two national groups residing in one territory. Mass immigration would
only alert the Arabs to the threat of being displaced, which would then lead to
resistance, bloodshed and suffering on both sides.*

*It didn't matter if the Arabs had been in Palestine for hundreds of years or for just
a few generations. They were there, they were human facts, and they had to be
accommodated. In fact, Buber reasoned, the Jews were the interlopers, the newcom-
ers, and as such it was incumbent on them to establish and earn the trust of the
Arabs.*

*In other words, Buber saw the Zionist problem as one of pursuing national goals
while avoiding the dangers of nationalism... If such things as theft and killing and
domination are hateful to us in our personal morality, how can we sanction them
on a national level? People in fact do accept these things on a national level, in the
name of the so-called greater good.*

*Buber insisted that Zionism not be guilty of such hypocrisy. This was precisely
the message that our prophets were forever levelling at our kings, and to ignore
their moral message, Buber said, was to ignore the essence of Jewish civilization...*

*He was rejecting the tragic principle of realpolitik, which says that morality is
irrelevant... He was concerned about the problems arising out of what he saw as
the reality of the situation. So he acknowledged that the assertion of Jewish national
rights would have to entail encroaching on Arab rights. But what he insisted on
was keeping that encroachment to a minimum.*

The way he expressed it was we must not sin more than is necessary. *I think that's
an awfully good way of putting it. It's something that as a nation we're wrestling with
right now – or at least perhaps ought to be...*[16]

A Jewish state inevitably contains an element of racial and/or religious discrimination

When the United Nations General Assembly passed the resolution which included
the notorious sentence that 'Zionism is a form of racism', the President of the
Assembly, **Gaston Thorn** from Luxembourg, was critical of the decision: 'The spirit

of the United Nations has been jeopardized by the adoption of a resolution that was stupidly and needlessly pressed to the vote by extremists who did not know when they had gone too far. I fear the evil consequences of this vote will appear only too quickly.'[17] When attempts were made at the UN Conference Against Racism in Durban, South Africa, in September 2001, to revive the charge that Zionism is racism, the Israeli and American delegations felt compelled to walk out, saying that the conference had become 'a cesspool of racism'.

Even if it is acknowledged that a resolution equating Zionism with racism was unwise and unnecessarily provocative, the original resolution expressed a widespread feeling about the anomaly of having a state 'whose main purpose', in the words of **Edward Said**, 'is to establish and enshrine Jewishness alone as its *raison d'être*... Israel is the only state in the world which is not the state of its actual citizens, but of the whole Jewish people, who consequently have rights that non-Jews do not.'[18] **Norman Finkelstein** is expressing the same unease when he says that 'The realization of the Zionist project in Palestine thus, in effect, implied the transformation of the indigenous Arab population into a gratuitous presence living on the sufferance of the Jewish majority.'[19] Similarly for **Morris Cohen**, 'A national Jewish Palestine must necessarily mean a state founded on a peculiar race, a tribal religion, and a mystic belief in a peculiar soil.'[20]

If non-Jews can understand the instincts of Jews that have made them feel that the only place in the world where they can feel safe is in a Jewish state, is it possible for Jews to understand why many non-Jews (as well as many Jews) feel obliged to draw attention to the inevitable exclusivity at the heart of this vision? If we agree to put aside the simplistic charge that 'Zionism is racism', can we not at least be willing to address the issue that lies at the heart of this incredibly sensitive issue?

A Jewish state has not solved the problem of anti-Semitism

One of the ironies – or the tragedies – in what has happened is that having escaped from anti-Semitism in Europe (which developed out of a pernicious convergence of theological, social, political and economic factors), Jews have imposed themselves on people who have a *different* set of reasons for antipathy towards them. We have already seen that the political stance of an Islamic fundamentalist group like *Hamas* is grounded in a particular understanding of the Qur'an's teaching about the Jews (see 2.10 The different voices of the Palestinians).

When every allowance is made for the fact that groups of this kind are regarded by many Arabs and fellow Muslims as extremist, it is hard to ignore the hard feelings towards the Jews which seem to go back to Muhammad's time in Mecca and the difficulties he faced with Jewish tribes. While there have been many periods in history when Jews and Muslims have lived peacefully together, the creation of the Jewish state in the heartlands of Islam has inevitably brought ancient feelings of distrust and antipathy to the surface once again. For, in the words of **Andrew Kirk**:

The existence and policies of Israel have also in other parts of the world increased anti-Jewish sentiments. In many Arab countries the state of Israel has caused the very anti-Semitism it was designed in part to alleviate... the presence again of Jews after 1,800 years in Palestine appears to many outside observers as a classical case

of cultural misfit. It is like a transplanted organ which the rest of the body rejects...
It would well be argued, simply from observation, that pro-Zionism often fans the
flames of anti-Semitism.[21]

Zionists can dismiss this kind of critique of Zionist ideology when it comes from
outside the Jewish community and when it seems like being wise after the event.
When they respond by saying that such criticisms are nothing more nor less than
anti-Semitism, it seems as if they have played the trump card and brought the discussion to an end. But what if these same concerns have been expressed not just
within the Jewish community, but within the Zionist movement itself, and they have
been expressed at many stages in the past? We have already noted the passionate
protest made by people like Ahad Ha'Am (2.3 Jewish settlement in the land and 2.4
Arab reactions to Jewish settlement). And the ideas of **Martin Buber**, as summed
up by **Paul Mendes-Flohr** in 1988, represent a similar critique and have a very contemporary ring:

His advocacy of binationalism was to point us in a direction, to alert us to the very
real practical necessity of coming to terms with the Arabs. For the same reason...
Buber did not favour the Partition Plan of 1947. Pushing Arabs and Jews apart, he
reasoned, would only exacerbate the conflict and lead to endless wars as each side
tried to regain what partition has taken away.

Rather, he said, the two peoples had to learn to live together. And he reasoned
that mutual interests would overlap to the point where cooperation would be possi-
ble... he advocated cooperation as opposed to one side attempting to dominate the
other. In short, he tried to be realistic while remaining within the boundaries estab-
lished by his moral concerns, rather than vice-versa...

There is no question he would be enraged by the national hubris, particularly as
manifested by Gush Emunim... And since Buber found fault with every Israeli
leader of his time, there's every reason to assume he would do so today... Look at
our leaders, look at the policies they're pursuing. Do you see anything that suggests
dialogue? Anything that suggests concern for the dignity and well-being of Arabs?
There's little doubt as to what Martin Buber would say.[22]

6.2 The power equation in the world today

If everything is ultimately a question of power, where does it lie in the conflict over
the land? If Jews and Arabs cannot simply sit round a table and sort out their problems between themselves, and if there is no single power that can use its muscle to
impose a solution, how does the power equation work in the world today?

What follows is simply an attempt to recognize the main powers and the main
factors which have determined the development of the conflict in recent years and
are likely to influence it in the immediate future.

Israeli power

Israel has won every war it has fought – in 1948–49, 1956, 1967, 1973 and 1982 –
and was therefore able to enter all the negotiations from Madrid onwards from a
position of confidence and strength. With American support, it has quietly ignored

international law relating to territories occupied in war and every UN resolution following the 1967 war. When occasionally restrained by the US because of its policies on the West Bank, it has only been a matter of months before moral, political and financial support has been resumed. Successive Israeli governments have been creating facts on the ground in the West Bank and Gaza by building settlements, creating networks of roads, controlling water supplies and encircling Jerusalem with a ring of Jewish settlements. Their declared aim has been to guarantee their own security and to provide land for new immigrants from Russia. But a further aim has evidently been to prevent any Palestinian state from coming into existence, or if it ever were to be created, to ensure that it would be little more than a Bantustan – in the words of one Israeli, nothing more than a 'trussed chicken'.

Palestinian weakness

Since the Arabs had been defeated in war at every stage, the Palestinians, represented by the Palestine Liberation Organization (PLO), entered the peace process at Madrid and Oslo from a position of extreme weakness. Ever since they surrendered their last card by accepting the existence and legitimacy of the Jewish state, Israel has held all the cards. Since Oslo the Palestinian Authority has been placed in the impossible position of policing its own angry and embittered communities (with weapons supplied by the Israelis), so that every act of violence has strengthened Israel's hand and increased its unwillingness to concede independence and sovereignty to the Palestinians.

Most Israelis are able to justify the actions of their government on the grounds of security, while the Palestinians are portrayed as the terrorists who have no desire for peace. Concessions made by Arafat and his Palestinian negotiators in an attempt to reach an agreement are condemned by the more hardline elements in their own community, because they appear to amount to a kind of surrender. The more moderate elements among the Palestinians say, 'If our backs are against the wall, what else can we do but latch on to every concession that seems to offer a gleam of hope? What room do we have for manoeuvre? What do we do if it is a choice between humiliation and/or extinction on the one hand and these meagre crumbs that are offered by Israel and the US on the other?'

American mediation

One of the most elementary rules of peacemaking is that a mediator needs to be as neutral as possible. Too much sympathy for one side or the other makes it impossible to play a genuinely mediating role. When the Norwegians were able to bring Israelis and Palestinians together in the secret process which led to the Oslo Accord in 1993, it was partly because they could not be accused of self-interest or bias. Recent American administrations have certainly tried on occasions to respond to Palestinian and Arab agendas. Bill Clinton was genuinely committed to finding a lasting political solution, and at Camp David in June 2000 enabled the Jews and the Palestinians to come closer than ever before to a final agreement. And immediately after the events of 11 September 2001, the US government gave the impression that it wanted to address the grievances of the Arabs. Until now, however, America's sympathy for Israel has appeared to override every other consideration. The horrific results of Palestinian suicide bombings have no doubt strengthened this support. Some believe that being themselves largely a nation of settlers who have driven back its original inhabitants and taken over a whole continent, it is only natural that many of them identify with the Jews who have done basically the same thing in Palestine. Most of the rest of the world has felt that this bias disqualifies the USA from being an honest broker. It remains to be seen whether the war against terrorism creates a new dynamic which forces the USA to a position of greater neutrality in relation to Israel, or whether the Israeli connection is so strong that it allows Israel to influence, if not to control, American foreign policy.

Zionist political organizations and representation in the USA

Six million Jews in the USA have an influence that is out of all proportion to their numbers in the total population of 281 million. Through wealth, education, skill and single-mindedness over many years they have gained positions of power in government, business and the media. It is widely recognized, for example, that no one could ever win the presidential race without the votes and the financial support of substantial sections of the Jewish community. This is how **Edward Said** perceives the extent of Zionist influence in recent years:

The role of organized Zionist groups and activities in the United States has not been sufficiently addressed during the period of the 'peace process', a neglect that I find absolutely astonishing, given that Palestinian policy has been essentially to throw our fate as a people in the lap of the United States without any strategic awareness of how US policy is in effect dominated, if not completely controlled, by a small minority of people whose views about Middle East peace are in some way more extreme than even those of the Israeli Likud...

The official discourse is totally dominated by Zionism and, except for a few individual exceptions, no alternatives to it exist. Therefore all peace arrangements undertaken on the basis of an alliance with the US are alliances that confirm rather than confront Zionist power... The irony is that there exists inside the US a vast body of opinion ready to be critical of both Israel and of US foreign policy. The tragedy is that the Arabs are too weak, too divided, too disorganized and ignorant to take advantage of it.[23]

Arab paralysis

One result of the Al-Aqsa Intifada is that it has created a certain kind of unity in the Arab world in its opposition to Israel. But while Arab Summits have produced impressive statements of resolution, Arab governments do not seem to be able to work together in ways which have a significant effect on the situation. Although they provide important moral and financial support for the Palestinians, they are widely perceived to be powerless in substantially altering the balance of power in the Middle East.

Patrick Seale's biography of Hafiz al-Asad explains one basic motive which determined much of his foreign policy: his determination to keep the major Arab states working together against what al-Asad saw as the schemes of Israel.[24] The success of Israel's diplomacy over the years, however, with the active cooperation of the USA, has meant that first Egypt and then Jordan were detached from the Arab

fold and made peace separately with Israel. Arab rhetoric and the use of certain television images, combined with Islamic appeals to *Jihad* against the Zionist state,
keep the Palestinian cause very much alive in the Arab world. Hizbollah took a
major share of the credit for the Israeli withdrawal from South Lebanon in May 2000,
and has commended its example of armed resistance to the Palestinians within Israel
and Palestine. In spite of this, however, the Arabs give the impression of being both
divided and paralysed, and therefore unable to work together to produce any significant change to the prevailing balance of power.

The politics of oil
Alongside its fundamental support for Israel, the USA has carefully nurtured its relationship with Saudi Arabia ever since the first discovery of oil there in the 1920s. It
therefore has to perform a delicate balancing act between its loyalty to Israel and
its economic interests in the Arab world. In the build-up to the Gulf War in 1992 it
looked as if *one* reason why the West reacted so strongly to the Iraqi invasion of
Kuwait was that it felt its oil supplies were being threatened, and that further Iraqi
control of Middle Eastern oil would only strengthen Iraq's position in its confrontation with Israel and the West. One does not have to be a Marxist to recognize the
importance of economic factors in the Middle East.

The vagaries of democracy
If democratic processes give a country the leaders it chooses, the policies they adopt
are generally determined less by high principles than the need to obtain power and
then remain in power. Ehud Barak was no doubt elected in 1999 because he convinced enough people that he could deliver some kind of peace with the Palestinians.
His inability to reach a settlement and his dependence on the votes of Orthodox religious groups, however, weakened his position and made him call for early elections.
Ariel Sharon was elected in 2001 as the strong man who would put the Palestinians in
their place. The widespread and vocal opposition to recent government policies that
has been expressed by many Jewish individuals and organizations within Israel in
recent years does not seem to be able to translate itself into sufficient votes to win an
election.

In the US the power of the Jewish lobby ensures that, whoever is president and
whichever party has the majority on Capitol Hill, American Middle Eastern policies
are likely to be more in the interest of Israel than of the Arabs. So, for example, having proclaimed her earlier support for a Palestinian state and her opposition to moving the US embassy from Tel Aviv to Jerusalem, Hillary Clinton changed her tune
on both these issues during her campaign for election in New York. In both Israel
and the USA, therefore, the message seems to be that to get yourself elected you
have to choose the policies which are acceptable to the majority and/or to the most
powerful.

Fundamentalisms – Jewish, Christian and Islamic
One of the most disturbing aspects of the conflict in the last thirty years has been
the growing power of fundamentalisms within the Jewish, Christian and Muslim
communities.

■ Yitzhak Rabin is said to have regretted to his dying day that he had given in to *Gush Emunim* over an incident near Eilon Moreh, beside Nablus on the West Bank, because he saw them as 'a threat to Israel's democracy'.[25] Many years before this, Weizmann in his diaries expressed his fears about the role that religious parties would one day play in the Jewish state: 'We must clearly differentiate between legitimate aspirations and the State's obligation to defend them, and the excess of power sometimes revealed by supposedly religious groups… We must be firm if we lust for life.'[26]

■ Around forty million fundamentalist Christians exercise considerable influence in the USA because their interpretation of the Bible leads them to support the Zionist vision in general and the policies of Israel in particular. Prime Ministers of Israel in recent years have made no secret of their appreciation for this lobby which adds significant weight to the Zionist lobby within the community of six million American Jews. They have frequently received an enthusiastic welcome from Christians who come to Jerusalem to celebrate the Feast of Tabernacles as a token of solidarity with the Jewish people and the State of Israel. Grace Halsell some years ago documented the influence of certain kinds of millennial thinking on the US government and especially on President Reagan.[27] Christian magazines from time to time report that the stones for a new temple in Jerusalem have already been cut and are ready somewhere in the USA to be shipped out to Jerusalem. When the instinctive gut-level sympathy for Israel among so many Western Christians coincides with the perceived political interests of Israel and the USA, it is bound to make a significant impact on the general thinking of the nation (see further 6.3 Christian Zionism and Dispensationalism). Thus, according to the influential evangelical journal, *Christianity Today*, 'the close connection between evangelicals and Israel… has shaped popular opinion in America and, to some extent, US foreign policy'.[28]

■ The increasing focus on Osama Bin Laden and the al-Qa'ida network since 11 September 2001 has made the whole world aware of the ideology of certain groups which loudly proclaim their opposition to Israel and the USA in terms of *Jihad*. Groups like *Hamas* and *Islamic Jihad* make no secret of the fact that their political beliefs are based on the Qur'an. The vast majority of Muslim leaders and scholars in the world dissociate themselves from these Islamic groups, saying that Islam does not allow the terrorism that we have seen recently. But many ordinary Muslims all over the world have considerable sympathy with the political stance of these Islamic groups, even if they do not approve of their terrorism. And since 11 September no one can afford to underestimate the power of Islamic fundamentalism or 'Islamism', as it is increasingly being called (see further 6.4 Zionism and Islam).

Psychological factors

Since international politics are never simply about power, in this conflict perhaps more than any other it is wise to reckon that we are dealing with two suffering peoples whose deep wounds profoundly affect their worldview and their reactions. These are just three of the factors which are at work beneath the surface:

■ *The appeal to the Holocaust.* The dream of a Jewish homeland had been drawing thousands of Jews to Palestine for fifty years before the Nazis began to carry out their 'Final Solution'. The Holocaust simply increased the numbers of those who needed to find a homeland, and accelerated the process of sending refugees to settle in Palestine. Historians are still at work documenting every detail of the whole appalling story, and human rights workers have tried to bring individuals to justice. Yad Vashem in Jerusalem, the Holocaust Museum in Washington and films like *Schindler's List* ensure that memories of the Holocaust are kept alive in the minds of both Jews and Gentiles. When Jews in Israel are concerned about their security, it is because of their awareness that it could all happen again, since some of their neighbours really would like to see them driven into the sea.

When Jewish fears are fed in this way by the Holocaust, the Arabs want to point out that the Holocaust is being used as a kind of psychological weapon to support the Zionist cause. 'You people in the West,' they say, 'have salved your guilty conscience over your treatment of the Jews in Europe by supporting Israel. You're glad that so many Jews have left your countries to settle in Israel. But it was you Europeans who slaughtered the Jews – not us Arabs. But *we* have had to pay and are still paying the price for *your* clear conscience. *You've* dealt with *your* problem by supporting the Jews in what they have wanted to do – and *we* are the ones who have suffered in the process.'

■ *The psychology of fear.* Jews have good reason to be afraid when they hear certain kinds of Arab and Islamic rhetoric, and see the violence inflicted on innocent Israeli civilians. Fear creates the siege mentality which has developed over 2000 years of persecution in various settings, and convinces them that only by superior force and constant vigilance can they ensure their own survival.

Palestinians also have good reason to be afraid because of all that they have suffered at the hands of the Jews, and because of the superior power in the hands of the Jews. In the words of **Hanan Ashrawi**, they see themselves as 'subject to the dual injustice of dispossession, dispersion and exile on the one hand, and of occupation and oppression on the other.'

What makes the conflict so difficult to resolve is that *both* parties are dominated so much by fear that they are unable to see the others as human beings. Perhaps it is only when individuals from both sides can meet each other face to face and get to know and respect each other as people that fear can be overcome (see 5.11 The possibility of reconciliation).

■ *The psychology of abuse.* It is widely recognized that a considerable proportion of adults who abuse others emotionally, physically or sexually, have themselves suffered from abuse in childhood. Does this help us to understand why the Palestinian Authority has used torture against fellow Palestinians in prison? Does it help to explain why Jewish settlers on the West Bank are so abusive towards Palestinians, and why Israeli soldiers in uniform have sometimes been so brutal and violent? This is no simple rule of thumb that explains everything. But if the psychologists tell us that the abused can easily become the abusers, something needs to be done to help both Jews and Arabs to find the resources to help them to resist the inevitable temptation to punish others in the way that they themselves have been punished.

If such a brief analysis of the power equation leads some to despair over the complexity of the issues and the possibility of ever seeing an end to the conflict, it may help others to give names to the various forces at work in the region and the wider world, and to see what can and must be done at every level by individuals and communities who want to be genuine peacemakers.

6.3 Christian Zionism and Dispensationalism

Christian Zionism can be defined simply as 'Christian support for Zionism that is based on theological reasons'. Christian Zionists believe that the establishment of the Jewish state is a very significant part of God's plans both for the Jewish people and for the world, and that for this reason they should support the State of Israel. 'Christian Zionists', says **Stephen Sizer**, 'see themselves as defenders of and apologists for the Jewish people and, in particular, the State of Israel. Their support involves opposing those deemed to be critical of, or hostile toward Israel.'[29]

This definition of Christian Zionism would exclude the view of those Christians who might call themselves 'Zionists' in the sense that they support the idea that there should be a Jewish state in at least part of the land. They believe that Jews have a right to some of the land and that, because of the animosities between the two communities, the only viable solution is to have a Jewish state and a Palestinian state. Although Christians who hold this view might call themselves 'Zionists', they would not be included in the above definition of 'Christian Zionism' because their support of Zionism is not based on theological considerations.

If Christian Zionism gained in strength in the twentieth century, the biblical and theological basis for this outlook was laid in the nineteenth century by Dispensationalism. This system gets it name from the belief that history has to be divided into a number of different periods of time or 'dispensations'. In each of these periods 'God reveals a particular purpose to be accomplished in that period, to which men respond in faith or unbelief.'[30] These ideas were first developed from the 1820s onwards by an Irishman, John Nelson Darby, and popularized by men like William E. Blackstone in the USA and by the *Schofield Reference Bible* (1909), and more recently by writers like Hal Lindsey, whose first book, *Late Great Planet Earth* was first published in 1970.

Since 1998, a Dispensationalist worldview has been communicated very skillfully through the books of the *Left Behind* series. Presented as a kind of science fiction which is especially popular among children and young people, the story assumes that at any time in the future, history will begin to unfold according to the scheme agreed on by Dispensationalists. The basic message of the series is described on the cover of the first book, *The Vanishings*, in these dramatic terms:

In one shocking moment millions around the globe disappear. Those left behind face an uncertain future – especially four kids who now find themselves alone. As the kids search for help and for answers, they are told the truth behind the disappearances. But are they ready to believe it?

In this new series based on the bestselling book Left Behind, Jerry B. Jenkins and Tim LaHaye present the Rapture and Tribulation through the eyes of four young friends – Judd, Vicki, Lionel and Ryan. As the world falls in around them, they band together to find faith and fight the evil forces that threaten their lives.

According to this way of understanding history, we are at present living in the dispensation of 'grace', and this will be followed by 'the millennium' (see 4.7 The land and the millennium). What is specially significant for us about this view of history is that, in the words of **Timothy Weber**, 'the key to this entire prophetic plan is the refounding of Israel as a nation state in Palestine. Without Israel the whole plan falls apart.'[31]

According to **Stephen Sizer**,

Dispensationalism is one of the most influential theological systems within the universal church today. Largely unrecognized and subliminal, it has increasingly shaped the presuppositions of fundamentalist, evangelical, Pentecostal and charismatic thinking concerning Israel and Palestine over the past 150 years... dispensationalism is now "a theological system that in all probability is the majority report among current American evangelicals" (Gerstner).[32]

Sizer summarizes the main features of the Dispensationalist view of how the history of the world will come to its climax as follows:

Crucial to the dispensationalist reading of biblical prophecy is the conviction that the period of tribulation is imminent, along with the secret rapture of the church and the rebuilding of the Jewish temple in place of, or alongside, the Dome of the Rock. This will signal the return of the Lord to restore the kingdom to Israel centred on Jerusalem. This pivotal event is also seen as the trigger for the start of the war of Armageddon, in which most of the world's population, together with large numbers of Jews, will suffer and die (Hal Lindsey).[33]

He also points out that Jimmy Carter and Ronald Reagan were dispensationalists, and that virtually all the 'televangelists' such as Jerry Falwell, Pat Robertson, Jimmy Swaggart and Billy Graham belong to the same school. The influence of this system has been so pervasive that many people have absorbed this way of thinking without knowing it, from simple Bible teaching and from maps and charts on the wall at Sunday school. Dispensationalists therefore 'think the Promised Land belongs to them as much as it does to Israelis' (Timothy P. Weber). They may not even know the word 'dispensationalism', but all the essential ideas of the system have come to be taken for granted by them as essential Christian beliefs.

Christian Zionists and Dispensationalists frequently differ among themselves over the details of how history will unfold in the future. All of them, however, would probably accept four basic assumptions, which can be summarized as follows and illustrated from statements by different Christians who have held these views over the last 120 years.

A divine right to the land
The Jews have a divine right to the land for all times. The land belongs to Jews because of God's promise to Abraham.

*According to God's distribution of nations, the land of Israel has been given to the
Jewish people by God as an everlasting possession by an eternal covenant. The
Jewish people have the absolute right to possess and dwell in the land, including
Judea, Samaria, Gaza and Golan (Third International Christian Zionist Congress,
1996).[34]*

*The promise of the Land of Israel is for ever, and the plain sense of this is that the
Jewish people will possess the Land (at least in trusteeship...) and live there. To say that
the New Covenant transforms this plain sense into an assertion that those who believe
in Yeshua come into some vague spiritual 'possession' of a spiritual 'territory' is intellectual sleight-of-hand aimed at denying, canceling and reducing to nought a real
promise given to real people in the real world! This is an intellectually unacceptable
way of dealing with a text or with ideas (David Stern).[35]*

The fulfilment of God's promises

The return of Jews to the land in the last 100 years and the establishment of the
State of Israel should be (or can be) interpreted as a fulfilment of Old Testament
promises and prophecies concerning the land, or at the very least as signs of God's
continuing mercy and faithfulness to the Jewish people.

*Zionism is a new power in the world and has come to stay. Its object is the arrange-
ment of the national future of the Jews. Consciously or unconsciously, the Zionists
are working out God's purposes for His ancient people, namely, their return to the
land of their forefathers (London Jews Society, 1897).[36]*

*Surely 1948 has been one of the most momentous years in the history of the world,
perhaps the most momentous since that amazing time when God Himself appeared
upon the earth in the form of a man... in this amazing year of 1948, another God-
planned and prophet-foretold wonder has taken place – the rebirth of the unchang-
ing, undying, unassimilated Jewish state...*

*Years ago some of us were taught and brought up to believe that Ezekiel chapters
36, 37 and 38 were an outline of the history of what might be called 'modern
Zionism' and were led to believe that the Jewish people would be brought back in
their thousands to Palestine, where they would acquire not only land but a resemblance of power also... Whether this interpretation is correct or not, there is no
denying the fact that many of the features portrayed in Ezekiel 38 bear a striking
resemblance to conditions in Palestine today (Revd Maxwell, writing in 1929).[37]*

*For many Christians today the greatest visible sign of God's faithfulness is the sur-
vival of the Jewish people. God has preserved them, cared for them, directed them,
against all the odds. And so, in a sense, the greatest sign of all is the State of Israel,
and Jewish sovereignty over Eretz Israel; such is a classic Christian Zionist position
(Walter Riggans, 1988).[38]*

The significance of the State of Israel

The establishment of the State of Israel in 1948 has special theological significance because of what it means for the Jews. It will eventually lead to the conversion of the Jewish people to their Messiah and finally to the second coming of Christ.

We regard the incorporation of the Balfour Declaration of 1917 in the Peace Treaty with Turkey... as one of the most wonderful instances on record of the working out of God's promises to that nation that He loves with an everlasting love... students of Holy Writ know... that a time is coming when 'all Israel shall be saved', and when the Jews will rejoice in the Messiah, and that previous to the turning of the nation to Christ must first come the re-establishment of the Chosen Race in their own land (London Jews Society, 1920).[39]

[Concerning the establishment of Israel in 1948] I consider it the greatest event, from a prophetic standpoint, that has taken place within the last 100 years, perhaps even since AD 70, when Jerusalem was destroyed (Louis Talbot, 1949).[40]

[Concerning the event of 1967]: that for the first time in more than 2,000 years Jerusalem is now completely in the hands of the Jews gives a student of the Bible a thrill and a renewed faith in the accuracy and validity of the Bible (Nelson Bell, 1967).[41]

I see everywhere in the Bible prophecies of the restoration of a theocracy in Israel. We may ask, how could it happen in modern Israel, since it is a secular state? But God will resolve the problem. Is it possible that God might have to expel the Jews from the Land again because of their unrighteousness? No, it won't happen again. What will happen in the future is the spiritual return and restoration, and it is on its way. We Christian Zionists announce the Kingdom of Israel. One day everybody will see a spiritual Israel again (David Pawson, 1985).[42]

Christian support for the Jewish state

Christians should not only support the idea of a Jewish state, but (at least in general terms) support what it stands for and defend it against attack.

The Lord in His zealous love for Israel and the Jewish people blesses and curses peoples and judges nations based upon their treatment of his Chosen People of Israel (Third International Christian Zionist Congress, 1996).[43]

In the most modest of ways I would suggest that Christians as Christians must give support in principle to the State of Israel as a sign of God's mercy and faithfulness, and as a biblical mark that God is very much at work in the world (Walter Riggans, 1998).[44]

The biblical and theological basis of Dispensationalism

Dispensationalism rests on two basic assumptions: the first about the necessity of a literal interpretation of the Bible, and the second about the relationship between

'Israel' (as understood in the Bible) and the Christian church. Both of these assumptions need to be challenged, since it is difficult to support them from the evidence of the New Testament.

ALL PROPHECY IN THE BIBLE MUST BE INTERPRETED LITERALLY

Not one instance exists of a 'spiritual' or figurative fulfilment of prophecy...
Jerusalem is always Jerusalem, Israel is always Israel, Zion is always Zion...
Prophecies may never be spiritualized, but are always literal (Cyrus I. Schofield).[45]

Dispensationalists hold that the promises made to Abraham, and through him to the Jews, although postponed during this present church age, are nevertheless eternal and unconditional and therefore await future realization, since they have never yet been literally fulfilled. For example, it is an article of normative dispensational belief that the boundaries of the land promised to Abraham and his descendants from the Nile to the Euphrates will be literally instituted and that Jesus Christ will return to a literal and theocratic Jewish kingdom centred on a rebuilt temple in Jerusalem. (Stephen Sizer).[46]

The basic hermeneutical principle is literal interpretation, which does not rule out symbols, figures of speech and typology, but does insist that throughout 'the reality of the literal meaning of the terms involved' is determinative. Consequently, the promises of an earthly kingdom given to Israel as a nation must be fulfilled literally in a future, millennial kingdom (on the analogy of the literal fulfilment of the messianic promises relating to Jesus (New Dictonary of Theology).[47]

The basic weakness of this approach is that the New Testament writers do not seem to be bound to this kind of literal interpretation of the Old Testament. The whole of chapters 3, 4 and 5 have developed a different approach to the Bible which is based on the assumption that there is one fundamental question which Christians need to ask: how did Jesus and his disciples interpret the Old Testament? The following are examples of the very *non-literal* way in which ideas from the Old Testament are handled in the New Testament.

■ When David first became king, God made a promise to him concerning his descendants: 'Your house and your kingdom will endure forever before me; your throne will be established forever' (2 Samuel 7:16). Taken at its face value, this would seem to be a promise that God would ensure that the royal line of David would continue throughout history; there would always be a descendant of David sitting on a royal throne in Jerusalem.

This inevitably creates a problem for the literalists, since the royal line of David came to an end at the time of the Exile in Babylon in 586 BC. Those who ruled as kings in Jerusalem after this time, like Herod, were not descendants from the line of David. Because dispensationalists insist on a *literal* interpretation of these verses, they have to postpone their fulfilment until after the second coming of Christ, when he will reign *literally* over the world from his throne in the city of Jerusalem for 1,000 years (i.e. the millennium).

The New Testament, however, points to a different way of understanding the fulfilment of the promise made to David. In Luke's account of the birth of Jesus, Mary is told by an angel that she is to be the mother of a child who will have a very special role in the purposes of God: 'Do not be afraid, Mary, you have found favor with God. You will be with child and give birth to a son, and you are to give him the name Jesus. He will be great and will be called the Son of the Most High. The Lord God will give him the throne of his father David, and he will reign over the house of Jacob forever; his kingdom will never end' (Luke 1:30–33).

The most natural interpretation of these words is that Luke believed that the coming of Jesus was the fulfilment of the original promise made to David about his descendants. Luke later traces the line of Jesus from his legal father, Joseph, back to King David (Luke 3:23–38). And the words of the angel who announces his coming birth express the idea that *Jesus himself* (not his physical descendants) will reign for ever, and that his kingdom, his kingly rule, will never end. The rest of the gospel of Luke and the book of Acts make it clear that Jesus, in his life, death, resurrection and ascension, was thought by Christians to have fulfilled all the main promises and prophecies of the Old Testament (see further 4.1–4.4).

■ We have already seen (in 4.6 John's vision of the final fulfilment of the covenant) that three Old Testament prophets describe in slightly different ways the same vision of a time when water will flow down from the temple in Jerusalem down across the wilderness to the Dead Sea. If we ask whether there is any way of knowing how Jesus or any writer of the New Testament might have understood the vision, we find a saying recorded in John's gospel which suggests that Jesus claimed that *he himself* was in some way the fulfilment of this vision: 'If anyone is thirsty, let him come to me and drink. Whoever believes in me, as the Scripture has said, streams of living water will flow from within him.' John goes on to give this explanation: 'By this he meant the Spirit, whom those who believed in him were later to receive' (John 7:37–39). The phrase 'as the Scripture says' makes a deliberate link with the Old Testament, and there are no other passages in the Old Testament which could remotely be linked to the idea in the words of Jesus.

A *literal* interpretation of the vision about the water from the temple would be that these three prophets are predicting a time when a spring will appear under the remains of the temple in Jerusalem and when fresh water from this spring will flow (through pipes or over the ground?) down to the salty waters of the Dead Sea. The *figurative* interpretation is that Jesus was claiming that he himself in his own person summed up all that the temple was supposed to be, and that all who believe in him will find that their deepest thirst and longings satisfied through trust in him.

■ If literalists are prepared to accept figurative interpretation of this kind, they continue to insist on literal fulfilment of everything related to the land. The whole of Part 4 has explored the way in which the theme of the land is interpreted in the New Testament. It was noted there, for example, that whereas the land was a fundamental theme of first century Judaism, there is only *one* clear reference to the land in the teaching of Jesus: 'Blessed are the meek, for they will inherit the earth'

(Matthew 5:5, which is actually a straight quotation from Psalm 37:11). Jesus proclaimed his message in terms of the coming of the kingly rule of God: 'The time has come' (i.e. the time to which the whole of the Old Testament looks forward), 'the kingdom of God is near' (Mark 1:15).

All the major themes of the covenant and Old Testament prophecy (including the land and the kingdom of God) are therefore interpreted *within the context of the kingdom of God* which has begun through Jesus. When Jesus speaks about the future, he speaks of the judgment that is to fall on the city of Jerusalem, but says nothing at all about the future establishment of a Jewish kingdom in the land. His prediction of the conquest of Jerusalem by Gentiles ('Jerusalem will be trampled on by the Gentiles until the times of the Gentiles are fulfilled', Luke 21:24) far from looking forward to Jewish sovereignty being re-established in the land, probably means that Jerusalem will be under God's judgment until the time comes for the judgment to fall on the Gentiles who have destroyed the city (see 4.3 Jesus and Jerusalem).

After his resurrection Jesus tried to explain to his disciples that *he had already* achieved 'the redemption of Jerusalem' – although not in the way that his disciples expected (Luke 24:13–35; Acts 1:1–8). It would seem that after these meetings with the risen Jesus between the time of the resurrection and the ascension, the disciples finally got the point about the nature of the kingdom that had come through Jesus. There is absolutely nothing in the rest of the New Testament to suggest that the disciples continued to look foward to the kingdom of God as something that was for Jews only and centred in Jerusalem. This cannot be dismissed simply as an argument from silence, because there is much to suggest that the Apostles continued to use *language* associated with the land, but that they now interpreted it in a new way – that is, in the light of the kingdom that had come through Jesus (e.g. Acts 20:32; Hebrews 4:1–13; 1 Peter 1:3–5).

This method of interpreting the Old Testament is frequently dismissed by literalists with the accusation that it represents a 'spiritualizing' of the Old Testament. The assumption is that there is a straightforward choice to be made between 'literal interpretation' and 'spiritualizing interpretation', and that most of the Old Testament (including what it says about the land) can *only* be interpreted literally. The approach that has been developed in this book suggests that this is a thoroughly unhelpful distinction which can never do justice to the way the New Testament interprets the Old Testament.

In the teaching of Jesus, the coming of the kingdom of God is *the real, the substantial, the essential fulfilment* of the promises given to Abraham about the land and the visions of the prophets about the land. In the teaching of the Apostles, the life, death, resurrection of Jesus are *the real, the substantial, the essential fulfilment* of what God promised in the Old Testament. So when Ezekiel described his vision of a restored temple in Jerusalem he was using the only images and the only language that were at his disposal to describe something that would be much more wonderful than the literal re-building of the temple, namely what Christians today understand as the incarnation of the eternal Son of God. When John wrote, 'The Word became flesh and made his dwelling among us. We have seen his glory', he believed that he had seen the glory of God resting not on Ezekiel's restored temple in Jerusalem but on the person of Jesus (John 1:14). Are John and the writer of the letter to the Hebrews to be accused of 'spiritualizing' what should have been interpreted literally? They would probably have rejected totally the distinction between the 'literal' and the 'spiritual', since as far as they and the other writers of the New Testament were concerned, Jesus was *the real, the perfect fulfilment* of all the hopes and longings of the Jewish people.

Examples of this kind could be multiplied to demonstrate the impossibility of insisting on a literal interpretation of everything in the Old Testament. If Western Christians from the nineteenth century onwards have wanted to interpret the Old Testament in such a literal way, this is not the way that Jesus seems to have interpreted it, nor the way that his disciples interpreted it in the light of what they had seen and experienced in Jesus.

ISRAEL IS DIFFERENT FROM THE CHURCH
'Israel' (i.e. the Jewish people) is distinct from the Church; 'Israel' is the people of God on earth, while the church is the people of God in heaven.

Dispensationalists believe that God has two separate but parallel means of working: one through the church, the other through Israel, the former being a parenthesis to the latter. Thus there is, and always will remain, a distinction 'between Israel, the Gentiles and the Church' (Ryrie).[48]

The dispensationalist believes that throughout the ages God is pursuing two distinct purposes; one related to the earth with earthly people and earthly objectives involved, which is Judaism; while the other is related to heaven with heavenly people and heavenly objectives involved, which is Christianity... Israel is an eternal nation, heir to an eternal land, with an eternal kingdom, on which David rules from an eternal throne... (Lewis Sperry Chafer).[49]

The biblical material already surveyed (especially in 4.3 Jesus and Jerusalem and 4.5 The land in the teaching of the apostles.) suggests that the writers of the New Testament did not understand the relationship between the Jewish people and the church in terms of such total discontinuity. Some of these ideas can be summarized as follows:

■ The way that Jesus spoke about his ministry suggests that he believed that *he himself* represented Israel. Jesus 'saw himself as in some way the heir of Israel's hopes' (R.T. France). 'The resurrection of Christ *is* the resurrection of which the prophets spoke' (C.H. Dodd). 'Jesus was claiming in some sense to represent Israel in himself... he regarded himself as the one who summed up Israel's vocation and destiny in himself' (N.T. Wright).
■ In the thinking of the apostles, Jesus and his disciples from all nations together form a renewed Israel. Paul uses the picture of a wild olive being grafted into a cultivated olive to convey the idea that Gentiles who believe in Jesus are grafted into the Jewish people (Romans 11:13–24). In Jesus the Messiah all the barriers

separating Jews from Gentiles have been broken down, with the result that Jewish and Gentile believers together become 'one new man' (Ephesians 2:15). While God's promises to the Jewish people still stand because he has not cancelled the original covenant he made with them, they fail to enjoy the blessings of the covenant because they have not recognized Jesus as Messiah. Because Jesus represents Israel, however, and because his church includes both Jews and Gentiles, all the privileges and titles that are related to the Jewish people in the Old Testament (like 'a chosen people, a royal priesthood, a holy nation, a people belonging to God') can now be applied to people of all nationalities who believe in Jesus
(1 Peter 2:9).

This is a much more natural way of reading the New Testament than the dispensationalist interpretation that makes a radical and permanent distinction between the Jewish people and the church. In the words of **N.T. Wright**,

Through the Messiah and the preaching which heralds him, Israel is transformed from being an ethnic people into a worldwide family... The Christians regarded themselves as a new family, directly descended from the family of Israel, but now transformed... they claimed to be the continuation of Israel in a new situation. (See 5.9 Jew and Gentile after Jesus the Messiah.)

Further implications of Christian Zionism and Dispensationalism

A LACK OF UNDERSTANDING OF THE NATURE OF THE CONFLICT
Christian Zionism and Dispensationalism make no attempt to understand the conflict between Zionism and the Palestinians in its own terms. Christian Zionists tend to think about the present Middle East situation primarily and largely in biblical or theological categories. If God has said in the Bible that the land belongs to the Jews for ever and that they would return to the land, the only problem for Christian Zionists is to know how to help the Jews to establish and defend themselves in the land. Any questions related to politics, human rights or religion are seen to be secondary and have to be answered in Zionist terms. The problem of Israel's relations with the Palestinians is treated almost as a footnote, a mere detail to be considered when the main argument has been established and accepted on the basis of a particular way of interpreting history.

So, for example, if we ask Christian Zionists what kind of state there should be in the land, it goes without saying that it has to be a Jewish state. If there is a question about human rights, the Palestinians are told that they must simply accept their minority status and their lack of a homeland. If we wonder about our responses as Christians to the aspirations of Jews and Muslims, we are told that Judaism is witnessing the redemption of the land, and that Islam is a sinister and perhaps even Satanic force which seeks to annihilate God's Chosen People.

Everything tends to be seen through the lens of this particular understanding of how God is working in history. Or, to change the metaphor, Christian Zionists have forced themselves into a strait-jacket which makes it impossible for them to understand the human and political problems in any terms other than their own particu-

lar set of biblical categories. None of the many popular Christian books about Israel
make any serious attempt to understand the history of the Jews and Arabs over the
last 2,000 years, or to unravel the different stages of the conflict in the past 120
years. By starting with a schema that is imposed on the Bible and does not arise
naturally out of the text itself, Christian Zionists find it hard to recognize the human
realities of what is actually happening on the ground.

A ONE-SIDED POLITICAL STANCE
Christian Zionism and Dispensationalism lead to a one-sided political stance. It is
interesting to note that in certain Christian circles in the USA in the nineteenth century support for the restoration of Jews to Palestine was stronger than it was among
Jews in Europe or North America. Christian Zionists were among the most enthusiastic supporters of Herzl and Weizmann. Christians of this kind 'seemed more eager
for Jews to move back to Palestine than did Jews themselves' (Timothy P. Weber).[50]

Grace Halsell, a Christian journalist, analyzed the phenomenon of Christian
Zionism in the USA with particular reference to its political implications in a book
called *Prophecy and Politics: Militant Evangelists on the Road to Nuclear War.*[51]
Among other things she explained why forty million evangelicals in the USA, many
of whom would call themselves Fundamentalists, are totally and almost blindly committed to the support of Israel, why the Israeli government has been delighted for
many years to have the support of a lobby which is at least five times larger than
the Jewish community, why the Israeli government provided Jerry Falwell with his
own jet and a pilot to fly it, and how even some of Ronald Reagan's utterances
revealed the Armageddon mentality of Christian Zionism.

Although Christian Zionists in other countries would not necessarily identify
themselves with all of these positions, they still end up with a political stance that is
very one-sided. Their message to the Palestinians seems to be: 'It is hard luck on
you! You may have suffered some injustices, but it is largely your own fault for
resisting the Jews. Since it was God's plan to bring the Jews back to their land, your
only hope lies in accepting Jewish rule and seeing how God wants to bless you and
the whole world through the Jews.'

A LACK OF CONCERN FOR PEOPLE OF OTHER FAITHS
Christian Zionism and Dispensationalism have no real message or concern for the
Jews and Muslims, and little desire to share their Christian faith with them. Some of
the prophetic schemes of Dispensationalism paint a horrifying picture of the future
in store for the Jews. In the words of **DeMar and Leithart**, they describe 'a holocaust indescribably more savage and widespread than any vision of carnage that
could have been generated in Adolf Hitler's criminal mind'.[52] Jews are no doubt disgusted if they know all the details of the scenarios that await the Jews in these
prophetic schemes; or if they are aware of them, may simply ignore them because
of the political advantages of gaining support from Christians like these. As
Netanyahu used to say, American evangelicals are the best friends that Israel has.

The International Christian Embassy in Jerusalem believes that Christians are
called to 'comfort Zion', and not to bear witness to Jesus as Messiah. The proclamation at the end of the Second Christian Zionist Congress held in Jerusalem in

April 1988 called for strong support for Israel and defended its policies in the Occupied Territories since the start of the Intifada, but had nothing at all to say about Christian witness to Jews. Some Christian Zionists dissociated themselves from this aspect of the Embassy's teaching. But many hold a 'two covenant' theory which says that God has his own way of dealing with the Jewish people and bringing them salvation which is completely different from the way provided for Gentiles.

The message for the Muslim world, on the other hand, seems to be: 'Take your hands off God's Chosen People, the Jews! You Muslims are descendants of Ishmael, and your religion is of the devil. God's plan is to bless the world through the Jews and through what he is doing in the Jewish state. If you are enemies of Israel, you are enemies of God; and God will judge you, as he will judge the whole world, by your attitude to Israel.' If Christian Zionists were to live anywhere in the Muslim world for even for a short time, or share what they believe with thoughtful Muslims, they might realize what an impossible stumbling block they are placing in their way. When the Muslim world sees how many millions of so-called 'Bible-believing Christians' in the West support the policies of Israel, they reject the Christian message out of hand and are unwilling to listen to any Christians who want to speak about the love of God in Jesus.

This kind of message coming from Dispensationalism does not seem to spring out of any kind of love or concern for Jews or Muslims. The only people who can draw any message of comfort from it are confident Western Christians who are made to feel even more secure than they already are: 'We Western Christians have nothing to worry about, because in the final battle of human history that is about to unfold before our eyes, God is in control, and we are on the winning side! Faithful Christians will be taken up to heaven in "the Rapture" before the worst of the calamities begin. But we will be safe, and our future is secure.'

Part of the tragedy here is that Christian Zionists seem to be so concerned about how God is going to bless the world *in the future* they have no prophetic word and no message of comfort for people living *here and now*. They believe that 'human history is following a predetermined divine script, and they and Israel are simply playing their assigned roles' (Timothy P. Weber).[53] It is so much easier, of course, to watch what amounts to a kind of 'video of the future', and to accept the pre-packaged predictions of what is to happen *in the future* than to attempt to analyse the complexities of history and politics *in the past and present*, or to relate to real people, most of whom belong to faiths other than Christianity, in the actual situations in which they live and suffer *today*.

CHRISTIAN ZIONISM IS UNREPRESENTATIVE

Christian Zionism does not represent the views of the vast majority of the Christians in the Middle East. 'It is not surprising,' says **Stephen Sizer**, 'that, among the indigenous Christians of the Holy Land especially, dispensationalism is regarded as a dangerous heresy, an unwelcome and alien intrusion, advocating an exclusive Jewish political agenda and undermining the genuine ministry of justice, peace and reconciliation in the Middle East'.[54] Similarly the **Middle East Council of Churches**, which represents almost all the Catholic, Orthodox, Oriental and Protestant Christians in the Middle East, has repeatedly made strong statements like this against

Christian Zionism:

*[They] force the Zionist model of theocratic and ethnocentric nationalism on the
Middle East [rejecting] the movement of Christian unity and inter-religious understanding which is promised by the churches in the region. The Christian Zionist
programme, with its elevation of modern political Zionism, provides the Christian
with a worldview where the gospel is identified with the ideology of success and mil-
itarism. It places its emphasis on events leading up to the end of history rather than
living Christ's love and justice today.*[55]

WHAT HAPPENS IF THE FUTURE DOES NOT FOLLOW THE PREDICTED SCENARIO?

Some Dispensationalists in the past have made confident assertions concerning
events in the future which have not taken place. In the 1930s, for example, some
predicted an important role for Mussolini, and had to change their story in the light
of what actually happened. During the Cold War it may not have seemed totally
impossible that Russia might one day join forces with the Arabs to invade Israel and
fight a pitched battle in the Jezreel valley in Israel at the site of Armageddon. But at
the beginning of 2002, because of all the new alliances that are being formed, such
a scenario seems much less likely than it did in the 1970s. Hal Lindsey has on more
than one occasion predicted the end of the world, only to find that it has not happened. It is strange that instead of being discredited, some Dispensationalist teachers seem to be able simply to rewrite the script of the future and carry on as before.

Until now Israel has had its way, and it has been possible for Christian Zionists
to interpret (almost) everything that has happened as a kind of success story, a miracle of divine intervention in history. But can we be sure that it will always remain
like this? Britain was the first country to work actively for the creation of the Zionist
homeland, and when the potato became too hot for Britain to handle, it was handed
over to the United Nations, and America became the main protector of Israel. But
what would happen if the potato were ever to become too hot even for America to
handle? What if public opinion there were to change as drastically as it did over
Vietnam? What would happen if America were to turn off the life-support machine
which keeps Israel alive? What if the whole Arab and Muslim world were to unite to
reject what it sees as a foreign body, a transplant, or even a cancerous growth so
near to its heart?

No one would dare to *predict* that any of these things will happen, and no one
should be *wishing* that they will happen. But if the whole scenario as conceived by
Christian Zionists and Dispensationalists turns out to be seriously wrong – either in
major details or in its grand design – what will this do to the faith of ordinary
Christians? Will their teachers be able to go on revising the plot indefinitely? Or will
there come a time when the flaws in the system become so obvious that they are
clear for everyone to see? In this case we would be faced with a whole generation of
Christians who would feel that they have been badly let down by their 'prophets'.

The apostle Peter had to prepare some churches in his day for the damage that
would be caused by disillusionment over the fulfilment of prophecy. 'You must
understand that in the last days scoffers will come... They will say, "Where is this

'coming' he promised?'" (2 Peter 3:3–4). It is not impossible that Christian Zionism and Dispensationalism will produce more and more 'scoffers' within the churches in the years to come.

If, therefore, the crisis that has been coming to a head in recent years in Jerusalem, the West Bank and Gaza has brought *Zionists* to a moment of truth, perhaps it should also be bringing *Christian Zionists* and *Dispensationalists* to a moment of truth. Do they realize the practical implications of their theology? Are they aware of how their biblical interpretation works out in practice on the ground? Do they know that their beliefs are being used, whether they like or not, to support not only Israeli government policies and actions in Jerusalem and the West Bank, but those of Jewish extremists and fundamentalists on the West Bank and Gaza? This interpretation of the Bible and these beliefs about God's plan for the world inevitably lead to a very one-sided political stance, which in turn leads to acute suffering for Palestinians (both Muslim and Christian).

Christians of various traditions have for many years dissociated themselves very strongly from the teaching of Christian Zionism and Dispensationalism. The vast majority of Christians in the Middle East feel that the time has come for this dissociation and disavowal to be made even stronger and clearer. Perhaps the time has come when more and more *evangelical* Christians will have to reject Christian Zionism and Dispensationalism with greater vigour and dissociate themselves more clearly from these views. If Dispensationalism is recognized to be deeply flawed, and if Christian Zionism is seen to be lending support more and more openly to policies that are profoundly unjust and inhuman, has the time not come for more *evangelical* Christians all over the world to reject Christian Zionism and Dispensationalism with greater vigour and dissociate themselves more clearly from these views?

If this interpretation of the Bible and these beliefs about God's plan for the world are recognized to be deeply flawed, and if they are seen to be lending support more and more openly to political policies that are profoundly unjust and inhuman, will there not be a need for drawing some clearer lines?

6.4 Zionism and Islam

The history of the conflict no doubt provides adequate explanations for Palestinian resistance to the whole Zionist movement. But are there any specifically *Islamic* reasons for Palestinian opposition to Zionism? If more than ninety-five per cent of Palestinians happen to be Muslims, does their faith influence their thinking in any way? Are they likely to think differently from Christian Palestinians, for example?

There are three reasons in particular why this question needs to be asked. Firstly, if we have tried to understand how *Jews* and *Christians* think about the land and the conflict over it, we can hardly avoid considering how *Muslims* think about these same issues. Secondly, Islamic claims to the land are not widely known or recognized by non-Muslims, and when they are known they are sometimes scornfully dismissed. Thirdly, appreciating Islamic viewpoints on these issues should help to explain the significant differences between the *secular* standpoint of the PLO and the unashamedly *Islamic* approach of organizations like *Hamas* and *Islamic Jihad*, which have consistently opposed the peace process since Madrid and Oslo and actively sought to undermine it.

How then has it come about that Palestine as a whole has a special place in Islam, and that Jerusalem is regarded as the third most holy site in Islam? The reasons for these convictions can be summarized as follows:

The land in the Qur'an

There are at least three clear references to the land in the Qur'an. The first is in a passage which speaks about Moses encouraging the Children of Israel to enter the land: 'O my people! Go into the holy land (*al ard al-muqaddasa*) which Allah hath ordained for you' (Qur'an 5:21, Pickthall). This conveys the idea that this land has been set apart and destined by God for the Children of Israel, who are, as it were, Semitic cousins of the Arabs, and related to the Arabs through their ancestor, Ishmael. The second is a verse which speaks about Abraham and Lot in the land, where God says, 'We delivered him (Abraham) and Lot, and brought them to the land which We had blessed for all mankind' (Qur'an 21:71, Dawood). The third is a verse which refers to Muhammad's Night Journey from Mecca to Jerusalem: 'Glory be to him who made His servant go by night from the Sacred Temple [of Mecca] to the Farther Temple [of Jerusalem] whose surroundings We have blessed (*alladhi barakna hawlahu*), that We might show him some of our signs' (Qur'an 17:1, Dawood). Muslims have speculated whether this special blessing refers to the area immediately surrounding the mosque, the whole of Jerusalem or the whole of the land.

These verses about the land, together with the role that the land played in subsequent Islamic history, make Muslims feel that the whole land is sacred. It is interesting to note that the phrase 'the holy land' is found only once in the Old Testament, in Zechariah 2:12. Jerusalem is referred to in the psalms as 'your holy hill' and 'your holy mountain'. But 'holy land' is not found in the New Testament at all. There are good Qur'anic reasons, therefore, for Muslims to feel that the land is 'the holy land' not only for the Jews but also for Muslims, and that there is a special blessing from God upon this land.

Muhammad and the land

According to Islamic tradition, earlier in his life before his call to be a Prophet, Muhammad visited Gaza and Palestine, perhaps including Jerusalem. When he first received his revelations, he and the first Muslims said their prayers facing in the direction of Jerusalem for 13 years, until he received a further revelation instructing them to change the direction to face Mecca. During the first stage of Muhammad's ministry in Mecca, soon after the death of his first wife, Khadijah, and his uncle Abu-Talib, he experienced what is known as the Night Journey (the *isra'*), in which either literally (as some believe) or in a mystical experience, he was transported during the night from Mecca to Jerusalem, and from there taken up into heaven (*mi'raj*), where he met with Abraham, Moses and Jesus. The magic steed which transported Muhammad from Mecca to Medina, known as Buraq, was tied up at the Wailing Wall, which is therefore known to Muslims as the Buraq Wall. This whole event plays an important part in Muslim thinking about the life of Muhammad.[56]

Jerusalem in Islamic tradition

In the course of time a rich body of traditions (*hadith*) developed about what Muhammad had said and done. These, for example, are some of his reported sayings which illustrate the special sanctity that Jerusalem came to have for Muslims:

- 'Journeys should not be made except to three mosques: this my mosque (in Medina), the sacred mosque (in Mecca), and Al-Aqsa.'
- 'God, the Supreme Being, has blessed what lies between Al-Arish (in Egyptian Sinai) and the Euphrates, with a special sanctification of Palestine.'
- [Concerning the Jerusalem sanctuary] 'Go to it and worship in it, for one act of worship there is like a thousand acts of worship elsewhere.'
- 'Whoever dies in the Jerusalem sanctuary is as if he has died in heaven.'
- 'Whoever goes on pilgrimage to the Jerusalem sanctuary and worships there in one and the same year will be cleared of his sins.'[57]

Jerusalem also came to play an important role in Muslim stories about the Day of Judgment. One widely accepted idea that developed was that when Jesus comes again to the earth, he will kill the Antichrist and return to Jerusalem, where he will pray in the mosque, kill all the pigs, break all the crosses, and destroy the synagogues and churches, thus vindicating Islam as the one true religion. He will reign in Jerusalem for fifty years, then die and be buried in Medina beside the Prophet Muhammad.[58]

The following account of what will happen on the Day of Judgment also shows the important place of Jerusalem in Muslim imagination:

When Christ is sitting on the wall between the Golden Gate and Al-Aqsa Mosque, and the Prophet on the mountain opposite, a single hair will be stretched from a column there across the valley, over which the multitudes assembled on the Haram (the area where Al-Aqsa and the Dome of the Rock stand) and will have to pass. The hills will recede and the valley deepen, and the righteous will walk fearlessly across, well knowing that, if they falter, their guardian angels are ready to hold them up by their forelocks, and save them from tumbling headlong into hell, which is gaping beneath. Thus will they cross until only a handful are left, who seem ill at ease, and reluctant to set foot on so narrow a bridge. Muhammad inquires why they linger, and is informed that they are the wicked Muslims who, having been smitten with a sense of their misdoings, and realizing that their virtue will not suffice to help them over the abyss, are awaiting the Prophet's pleasure on this side in fear and misgiving. Muhammad looks stern, and rebukes them for their neglect of his rules and ordinances; and then he smiles a little to himself, and in a moment is across the bridge and among them. Then they repent, and so they cross the bridge without mishap.[59]

Jerusalem in Islamic history

Muslims point out repeatedly that the land was in Muslim hands for around 1,300 years, that is ever since the first Islamic conquest in AD 638, until the end of the Ottoman empire in 1918 (except for the years of Crusader rule), and under Arab rule for around 900 of those years. When the caliph Umar reached Jerusalem with his army in AD 638, Sophronius, the leader of the Christian community, came out of the city wearing his patriarchal robes to surrender to Umar who was wearing his battle clothes. Umar gave orders that a place of worship should be built on the site of Muhammad's 'ascension' into heaven, which was also the place where Abraham was going to offer his son as a sacrifice and the site of the previous Jewish temples of Solomon and Herod.

It was here that the Umayyad caliph Abd al-Malik built the Dome of the Rock (*qubbat al-sakhra*) in AD 691. This shrine was designed not as an ordinary mosque, but as a pilgrim ambulatory, providing Muslims with a place of pilgrimage similar to the Christian Church of the Holy Sepulchre a few hundred yards to the west. The Al-Aqsa mosque was built a few hundred yards to the south of the Dome of the Rock in around AD 810, to replace the original mosque that had been built there by Umar. Many other important names in Islamic history are associated with Jerusalem, including the Umayyad caliph Mu'awiya, Bilal, the first muezzin who called the Muslims to prayer, Rabi'a the mystic, the legal scholar al-Shafi'i, and the theologian al-Ghazali. Many hospices were built for pilgrims and travellers.

Jerusalem and the Crusades
It was the Crusaders who, according to **Zaki Badawi**, 'transformed Jerusalem into a potent symbol of Islam once again'.[60] Many Muslims draw attention to the contrast between the behaviour of the Crusaders who, when they entered Jerusalem killed every person in sight (Jews, Christians and Muslims) and Saladin, who killed no one and later even allowed Jews to return to Jerusalem.

There is one particular incident during the Crusades which gives a special insight into the thinking of Muslims concerning Jerusalem. At the time when the Crusaders had temporarily lost Jerusalem to Saladin in 1191 and were trying to re-establish their control over the whole country, Richard the Lion-Hearted wrote to Saladin making the bold suggestion that Richard's sister, Joanna, should marry Saladin's brother, Malik al-Adil; they should reign together as king and queen of Jerusalem, and all Palestine should come under Christian rule. **Saladin**, in his reply, explained how unthinkable it was for him as a Muslim to surrender the land to Christian rule:

Jerusalem belongs to us just as much as to you, and is more precious in our eyes than in yours, for it was the place of our Prophet's Journey and the place where the angels gathered. Therefore, do not imagine that we will give the city up to you, or that we shall suffer ourselves to be persuaded in this matter. As regards the land, it belonged originally to us, and you came to attack us; if you succeeded in getting possession of it, it was only because you came unexpectedly, and on account of the weakness of the Muslims who then held it; as long as the war lasts, God will not suffer you to raise one stone upon another in this country.[61]

For reasons such as these, **H.S. Karmi**, a Muslim writer, sums up the significance of the Crusades in these striking words, comparing them to events in the nineteenth and twentieth centuries:

The Crusades... gave Jerusalem a new significance in the eyes of the Muslims. The Crusaders were not regarded as Christians, impelled only by religious zeal, but were found to be Europeans who were desirous of expansion and conquest – an adumbration of European colonialism later on. This blend of Christianity and imperialism was counteracted by a blend of Arabism and Islamism. It sharpened the Arab-Muslim interest in Jerusalem, and the proof of it is the lavish care bestowed upon Jerusalem by the Ayyubid and the Mamluk Sultans... The position of Palestine as a holy country for Muslims derives very strongly from the Crusades... The Crusaders did not conquer Jerusalem alone, but they conquered the whole of Palestine...

It is little wonder that Arabs and Muslims regard Palestine as holy, as a reaction to such aggressive designs... The same historical pattern was repeated after nearly 800 years. The Jewish immigration into Palestine under the Mandate (1920–48), and the establishment of Israel in 1948, have had the electrifying effect of making Palestine holy in a wider Islamic frame and in a narrower Arab one. Now the question of Palestine, especially after the Israeli Occupation of Jerusalem, June 1967... is no longer a local one, concerning only the Arabs of Palestine or the Arab world, but it has also become the concern of the Islamic world...[62]

Similarly a British Muslim, **Abdul-Majid Davies**, describes Zionism and all that flowed from it as 'the most momentous event of our century (i.e the twentieth century)'. In seeking to give a religious reflection from an Islamic standpoint on why God could have permitted it to happen, he seeks to explain it all as 'a foretold precursor of Antichrist, and as a punishment and reproach to an Arab world emasculated and made venal by the exclusion of the religious ethic from politics.[63]

The land in popular tradition
In addition to Jerusalem there are other places that are important for Muslims, including Hebron, the burial place of Abraham, Sarah, Isaac, Jacob and Joseph, and Gaza, situated at the meeting point of major trade routes and at one time the largest city in Palestine, and the place where Muhammad's grandfather was buried. The land also plays an important role in popular tradition, with Muslims regularly visiting the shrines of prophets, saints and sheikhs in different places. Annual festivals have always drawn large numbers of people together at places like Nabi Musa, located in a valley between Jericho and Jerusalem, and reputed to be the place where Moses was buried.

These six factors taken together explain why the land has come to play such an important role in Islam. The following summary of Islamic beliefs about the land is written by **Father John Sansour**, a Roman Catholic priest originally from Bethlehem, and links many of these factors together. Although written by a Christian, it reflects accurately the ideas and feelings of many Muslims.

The theology of the Land, launched by Jews to justify their presence by force in the Holy Land, created a new Muslim theology of the Land. It is, in general, identical to the Jewish one... Those who hold this (Islamic) view maintain that God cannot fulfill his promises concerning the Land with such people (i.e. the Jews). He has fulfilled and is still fulfilling all his promises with Ishmael and his sons (i.e. the Muslims)... The Holy Land is entirely a Muslim waqf (possession) belonging to God. The rights of Palestinian Christians are preserved by orders of Caliph Omar. Palestinian Christians with the Muslims of the whole world must unite and fight against the Jews. There will be no peace and Jihad, holy war, is declared until victory.

If the Jews are back in Palestine it is God's will that they are there. Their presence is a punishment for the Muslims who have left the way of Islam. Muslims must convert, increase and prepare themselves to execute God's will, which is to again control the Holy Land... It is the duty of all Arabs to punish these aggressors until they establish justice with the Palestinians. This group of Muslims expects Israel to reach a solution satisfactory to the Palestinians and then for them to live together peacefully.[64]

Having outlined the place of the land in Islamic thinking, there are two other subjects that need to be noted before we move on to note the relevance of this history to the conflict over the land: Muhammad's relations with the Jews of Medina, and the status of Jews living under Islamic rule.

Muhammad was invited to come from Mecca to Medina in AD 622 because a group of Medinans who had already accepted the faith of Islam believed that he could act as an arbitrator between some of the different tribes in and around Medina. Among these there was a considerable number of Jews, and three Jewish tribes in particular caused problems for Muhammad. The reason for their opposition was partly that they could not accept the new faith of Islam, and partly that they found it difficult to recognize his growing power in the community.

During the series of battles that took place between the Muslims and the Meccans, the Muslims felt that although the Jews in Medina were bound by a covenant to support the new Islamic community, they were in fact working against them and conspiring with the Meccans. As a result, one Jewish tribe, the Banu Nadir, were expelled from Medina and sought refuge in a Jewish community at Khaybar to the north. Between 600 and 900 men from another tribe, the Banu Qurayza, were beheaded and thrown into a ditch and their wives and children sold into slavery, while a third tribe, Qaynuqa, were expelled from Medina and went eventually to Syria. The source of the conflict between Muhammad and the Jews is explained by **William Montgomery Watt** as follows:

The intellectual or ideational conflict between Muhammad and the Jews became as bitter as it did because it threatened the core of the religious ideas of each. If prophets could arise among the Gentiles, the Jews were not God's chosen people, and that was tantamount to having no religion left. If Muhammad was not God's prophet and messenger, then in his own eyes he could only be a self-deceived impostor. This was at the root of the quarrel.[65]

During the following centuries during which the Islamic empire spread from Morocco in the West to the borders of China in the East, Jewish communities were allowed to practise their religion because they were regarded (along with Christians) as 'people of the Book' and as protected communities (*dhimmis*). Since small Jewish communities presented no threat to the Muslim authorities, relationships were reasonably good most of the time. This is why **Zaki Badawi** is able to say, 'We have always had a good relationship in history with the Jews but it is this which has been put at risk by the fifty years of conflict with Israel.'[66]

Christians and Jews would argue that they were treated as second-class citizens, and that there were often pressures, sometimes subtle but sometimes overt, to convert to the religion of the conquerors. Muslims would argue that persecution was the exception rather than the general rule, and that Islam worked out its own kind of tolerance and pluralism long before the West developed its own pluralist societies. If this is true for most of the 1,400 years of Islamic history, what seems to have happened is that the conflict with the Zionist Jews from the end of the nineteenth century revived memories of the difficult relationship that Muhammad had had with Jews. It looked as if Jews in the modern period were simply repeating in modern history the behaviour of fellow Jews many years before towards the Prophet of Islam.

Against this background the position of radical Islamic groups like *Hamas* and *Islamic Jihad* is more understandable. Here are committed Muslims who see Muhammad as the model for every Muslim individual and community today, and see the Qur'an as the very words of God, to be obeyed faithfully. Many of them therefore believe that they need to take serious note of what the Qur'an says about the Jews and how the Prophet dealt with them. Thus Article 8 of the Covenant of *Hamas* states: 'Allah is the target, the Prophet is its model, the Qur'an its constitution; *Jihad* is its path and death for the sake of Allah is the loftiest of its wishes'. *Hamas* is therefore, in the words of **Peter Riddell**, 'an organization which has founded its ideology on scripture and revelation'.[67]

He goes on to say that for this reason 'it was inevitable that the detailed policies of *Hamas* with regard to the organization's attitude towards Jews and Judaism would reflect Islamic scriptural teaching on the issue. The Qur'an reflects the controversy between Muhammad and Jews, and this controversy served to cement the basis of future Jewish-Muslim relations.'[68] He quotes the following statements made to the media by Palestinians expressing strong opposition to the Oslo Accords of September 1993:

I don't believe in peace. People who believe in peace did not read in the Koran what Jews did to Jesus. The Jews killed Jesus and the prophet Zechariah and wanted to kill Moses.

The people are very angry and very mad... We have known the Jews 2,000 years and Mohammad said that they cannot be trusted.[69]

Riddell draws attention to the difference between the approaches of these Islamic groups and those of the PLO:

While the PLO has engaged to a certain degree in a review of its National Covenant, supporters of Hamas will always refer to the Qur'an as their primary and ultimate point of reference in determining their political approach… This fact precludes the type of compromise formulae which have been explored by both nationalist Palestinians and Israelis in recent years.

Quite simply, because of Qur'anic imperatives, land which has once been part of the Islamic domain, and especially holy sites such as Jerusalem, can never be allowed to pass under non-Muslim, in this case Jewish, authority. Such is the approach of Hamas, an approach which is well articulated by M.A. Rauf in relation to Jerusalem as follows: 'Any property belonging to a Muslim has sanctity. When that property is the "house of God", it becomes a permanent, inalienable property, with sanctity that is incalculable, and the violation of such sanctity is a severe offence to Muslim sensibility.'[70]

He quotes the words of three other Muslims to illustrate the same basic way of thinking:

Israel will exist and will continue to exist until Islam will obliterate it, just as it obliterated others before it (Hasan al-Banna, founder of the Muslim Brotherhood, writing in the 1940s).

Whether during, before, or after Moses these Israelis display a consistency of misbehaviour, disobedience, defiance, and malfeasance… the Qur'an is speaking to these Israelis about an affair of their own deviation… it was Allah who succored and supported them and made it possible for them to move into the appointed land… But, as usual, the children of Israel flouted and frustrated the divine design… they misquoted what was in effect a divine address to all the children of Israel and not only to those who took it upon themselves to misdirect the words or the meaning of the divine communique. 'And We sent down on them a calamity from the sky because of their iniquity' (Mohammed al-Asi).

The first quarter of the next century will witness the elimination of the Zionist entity and the establishment of the Palestinian state over the whole of Palestine (Ahmad Yassin, leader of Hamas, 1988).[71]

At this point one cannot help noting a strange series of ironies in the twists of history. Jews lived in the land for centuries until they were mostly turned out by the Romans in the first and second centuries. Then from the fourth and fifth centuries until well after the coming of Islam in the seventh century, the area became mostly Christian. So when Islam first burst out of Arabia and conquered Palestine and Syria, these areas were largely Christian and only gradually converted to Islam over the following centuries. Then it was the *Christian* intrusion of the Crusades which made Muslims more aware of the significance of Jerusalem and Palestine within the faith and history of Islam. Now in recent years it has been *Jewish/Zionist* intrusion into the land that has stimulated Islamic thinking about the land once again and encouraged it to develop a theology of the land which has strong similarities to Jewish theologies about the land.

Reflections of this kind, however, seem largely academic in comparison with the questions that now face the Palestinians, the Israelis and the rest of the world, in which for many people the faith of Islam is now thoroughly mixed up with the politics of Israel and Palestine:

■ Is the Palestinian movement now in danger of being split apart? If, as **Peter Riddell** says, the Palestine Authority represents 'an essentially secular, nationalist perspective' and *Hamas* in contrast draws its guidance 'from its interpretation of scriptural imperatives', and if the Islamist position results in 'an absolute rejection of any possibility of seeking a compromise solution for the Israel-Arab dispute',[72] is it ever going to be possible for them to work together?

■ What is going to happen in the confrontation over Jerusalem between Jewish and Arab/Muslim nationalism, and between Jewish and Muslim fundamentalisms? Since the peace process began in 1991, Israel has been able to postpone discussion of the question of Jerusalem, while making it clear that it will never even open up the subject for discussion. But can the discussion be postponed for ever? What happens when two fundamentalist claims to Jerusalem are totally incompatible and non-negotiable?

■ If and when a Palestinian state is created, will it be a secular state or an Islamic state? If it becomes an Islamic state, what kind of Islamic state will it be, and to what extent will it be influenced by Islamic beliefs? And how would such an Islamic state be perceived by the rest of the world?

■ Have politicians and military commanders in the Middle East and the rest of the world taken into account the power of religion to motivate people?

■ Has Zionism, especially as expressed by extremist Jewish individuals and groups that have been so active on the West Bank since 1967, unleashed forces that are rapidly becoming uncontrollable? If Israel had made its peace with the Palestinians in 1967, is it possible that *Hamas* and *Islamic Jihad* might never have been formed? Is it now too late for anyone to make a genuine peace? Do Zionist extremists and fundamentalists recognize the role they have played in stimulating Islamic extremists and fundamentalists? Does the outside world understand the dynamic that has created these expressions of Islamism? Where are they likely to end?

6.5 Conclusions: The options for Israel and questions for the Palestinians

Having reflected on the crises facing both Zionism and Christian Zionism and tried to understand the realities of power in the world today, including the renewed power of Islam, we end this part of the book by simply spelling out the options from which Israel needs to choose and the dilemmas that face the Palestinians as they contemplate the future.

Options for Israel

All the possible options for Israel can be reduced to variations of these five options:

THE ONE-STATE SOLUTION

This is for Israel to remain as a Jewish state and to annex the West Bank, Gaza (and the Golan Heights, if there is no peace with Syria), making them part of Israel. This of course is unthinkable for most Israelis, and was the bad dream that used to torment Golda Meir. For if Israel is to remain a democracy, all the Arabs of the West Bank and Gaza would become citizens of the Jewish state and be given a vote. But since there is a higher birth rate among the Arabs than among the Jews, before long the Arabs would outnumber the Jews and defeat them in elections. As a Palestinian once said, 'If they beat us in the battle at the borders, we will beat them in the battle in our beds!'

THE CREATION OF A SINGLE SECULAR STATE
This would include the whole of Israel, the West Bank and Gaza and would require a new kind of state altogether: a state in which race and religion would be irrelevant and Jews and Arabs would be on a level of complete equality. This solution challenges the very concept of Israel as 'a Jewish state' and is therefore as unthinkable to most Israeli Jews as the first solution. A single secular state would also arouse a great deal of opposition from some Palestinians, especially from Islamists.

THE CRUSHING OF THE PALESTINIANS
The frequent Israeli blockades of the West Bank and Gaza since October 2000 have ruined the economy of the West Bank and Gaza. If the present Israeli government continues to suppress the Intifada with even greater force than has been used until now, it will simply increase and intensify the anger and bitterness of the Palestinians. If journalists and TV cameras are able to convey accurately to the rest of the world what is taking place, Israel and the US are likely to face even fiercer criticism than they have already received. If Jewish extremists were to lay their hands on the Islamic sites on the Temple Mount, they would bring upon themselves the wrath of the whole Islamic world. Palestinians are very serious in their willingness to die for their cause. 'Are you really going to try to kill us *all*?' they say to the Israelis, 'in order to take over our land?' Sometimes this is what they feel in their desperation. It feels to them as if the Israelis have long ago coolly and calmly worked out a whole range of strategies in order to crush the spirit of the Palestinians or to reduce their numbers by forcing them to leave.

THE DESTRUCTION OF THE STATE OF ISRAEL BY THE PALESTINIANS AND ARABS
Arabs frequently draw comparisons between the establishment of Israel and the establishment of the Crusader kingdoms in Palestine between 1099 and 1291. They tell themselves that if they are willing to take a long-term view, Israel will ultimately share the same fate as the Crusader kingdoms. There are of course very significant differences between the State of Israel and the Crusader kingdoms, and the present balance of power in the world makes such a scenario seem impossible. The bloodbath that it would entail should make everyone shrink from even contemplating an outcome of this kind.

THE TWO-STATE SOLUTION
This was the original proposal of the United Nations in 1947, but it was rejected out of hand by the Palestinians and all the Arabs, partly because it was felt to be

imposed without consultation, and partly because the division of the land was felt to be unfair. It was not until 1988 that the Palestinian National Congress in Algiers was willing to revise its earlier goals, accept the existence of the State of Israel and adopt the two-state solution.

The creation of a Palestinian state on the West Bank and Gaza would give them sovereignty over twenty-two per cent of the land. Many (or most?) of the Israeli settlements would need to be dismantled, since it makes a mockery of any recognition of Palestinian sovereignty to have so many Jewish settlements on the West Bank and forty per cent of the Gaza Strip occupied by Jews. The Palestinians are not likely to give up their insistence on retaining East Jerusalem as their capital and establishing the right of return for at least some of their refugees. There would need to be firm guarantees for any peace agreement, perhaps based on the concept of 'mutually assured security'.

The only way that Israel can guarantee its own security is to make peace with the Arabs. And the only conceivable way to do this at the present time is for Israelis to concede to the Palestinians the right that the Jews fought for from the beginning, namely the right to establish their own sovereign, independent state.

If the two-state solution sounds totally idealistic and unworkable, and if it seems to demand far too many concessions on the part of Israel, it only proves the point that Israel has been allowed by the rest of the world to do far too much on the West Bank and in Gaza with impunity since 1967. Now that the only real alternative to this solution – a brutal suppression of the Intifada – is becoming a real possibility, the international community needs to find the will and the means to convince both sides that only within the framework of two separate states can some kind of peaceful coexistence become a possibility.

Questions for the Palestinians

VIOLENCE OR NEGOTIATION?
Are Palestinians going to continue to use violence as a weapon to draw attention to their cause?

If many already want to renounce violence, will others like *Hamas* and *Islamic Jihad* ever be willing to lay down their weapons? Or do the Islamists really intend to fight on till death to achieve their goals?

If one can understand the distrust and despair which have driven them to violence, will they ever reach the point at which they recognize that violence becomes counter-productive and only leads to further violence?

Is there ever going to be a time when they say 'enough is enough' and when they renounce violence in order to trust the process of face to face negotiation? Having been let down so badly and so often in the past, will they ever have enough confidence in the process of international mediation?

DO THEY REALLY ACCEPT THE EXISTENCE OF ISRAEL?
If it is recognized that Zionists have at many stages practised deception to further their cause, are Palestinians willing to face up to the deception there may have been in Palestinian nationalism?

After years of armed struggle, many Palestinian leaders have been forced to make public statements in which they publicly recognize the right of Israel to exist. But do they really mean it?

Are there many Palestinians who never will reach the point of accepting the State of Israel? How do the rest of the Palestinians respond to this situation?

TO WHAT EXTENT ARE THEY WILLING TO ACCEPT COMPROMISE?

Is there a willingness to compromise, to be flexible, to meet half way, to accept less than they actually want, in order to gain at least *some* of their goals and to ensure some kind of peaceful coexistence? Having missed the opportunity (for understandable reasons) to establish a Palestinian state in 1948, are they willing to settle now for something that is less than the best?

Or will they continue to stand firm on what they see as the justice of their cause and adopt an 'everything or nothing' approach, being prepared, if necessary, to be totally destroyed in the process?

DO THEY HAVE THE LEADERSHIP THEY NEED?

Do the Palestinians have leaders of integrity and vision who are able to unite their people, who know when to stand firm and when to make compromises, and who can argue the Palestinian case before the world?

How do the official leaders of the Palestinians, whether in the PLO or the Palestine Authority, respond to the criticisms that have been leveled against them – of dictatorial leadership, suppression of dissent, torture of opponents, corruption and lack of financial accountability? Do they recognize that some of the fiercest criticism of Palestinian leadership comes from Palestinians themselves and from journalists and observers who have strong sympathy for the Palestinian cause?

If Palestinians feel that the justice of their cause enables them to occupy the moral high ground, do they recognize the extent to which they sometimes lose that high ground because of the way their leaders are perceived to function and because of the suicide attacks on civilian Jewish targets?

ISLAMIC IDEOLOGY AND/OR THE LANGUAGE OF HUMAN RIGHTS?

How important are Islam and Islamic beliefs for Palestinians in articulating their opposition to Zionism and arguing their case before the world?

While it may be hard for many Muslims to separate religion from politics, and while Islamic ideology is fully understood by fellow-Muslims, how necessary and helpful is it for Muslims to appeal to Islamic ideology when speaking to the non-Muslim world?

Is it sufficient to use the language of human rights and international law in appealing to people in the world who do not share their Islamic beliefs? Is there a danger of losing support from some who fully accept the justice of their cause through excessive use of Islamic ideas?

A SECULAR OR ISLAMIC STATE?

If and when a democratic Palestinian state comes into existence, will it be a secular state or an Islamic state? If Islamic, how Islamic will it be?

If it is the religious groups which win more support among the people and are more successful in pursuing the struggle against Jewish occupation, will Palestinian Muslims (who make up well over ninety-five per cent of the Palestinian population) insist that it is an Islamic state rather than a secular state?

If they choose an *Islamic* state, how would this reflect on their basic rejection of the idea of a *Jewish* state? Would the creation of a Palestinian Islamic state legitimize the idea of a Jewish state, just as the creation of a Christian state in parts of Lebanon (which many Israeli leaders wanted to do in the early 1980s) would have legitimized the idea of the Jewish state? Is it consistent to challenge the idea of a Zionist state because it is based on race and/or religion, and then create another state which is identified with a particular religion?

How comfortable would Christian Palestinians feel in an Islamic state? Christian minorities have not always found it easy to live within majority Islamic communities. Christian Palestinians, for example, sometimes speak privately about intimidation that they have suffered at the hands of Muslim Palestinians, but are hesitant to speak publicly about it for fear of seeming disloyal to the Palestinian community. Can ordinary Muslim Palestinians as well as their leaders reassure Christian Palestinians that they are genuinely appreciated in the community and not regarded as second-class citizens?

Conclusion
Whose Land?

Any conclusion to a book of this kind will inevitably be a very personal view. It will need to attempt to draw together some of the different themes of this book, which include the Christian understanding of the land in the Bible and the history and politics of the conflict over the land in the last 120 years. It will inevitably be coloured by the fact that it is being written in the months immediately following the events of 11 September 2001.

Immediate questions

The second Intifada which began in October 2000 has forced the rest of the world to face up to what has been happening on the West Bank and Gaza since 1967. Israel has somehow been able to defy the United Nations resolutions calling for its withdrawal from the Occupied Territories.

It may be that the attacks of 11 September have changed almost everything in international relations. While Sharon has tried to paint Arafat as Israel's own Bin Laden, many Western leaders have expressed considerable frustration over Arafat's leadership. At the same time they seem to have heard the message about the anger and cynicism that have built up over the years because of Western support for Israel and its policies. It remains to be seen whether international pressure will be strong enough to bring moderates on both sides together and to silence, or at least restrain, the extremists on both sides who have no interest in making peace.

Will Israel finally be forced to do what the UN required it to do in 1967 and withdraw from the territories it has occupied against the will of the Palestinians, against international law, and against the wishes of the UN? Will Israel be willing to allow the creation of a viable Palestinian state? Or has Israel been creating so many facts on the ground in and around Jerusalem, the West Bank and Gaza as a way of forcing its will on the Palestinians and the international community, and making it impossible for any meaningful Palestinian entity to be created? Has the Israeli occupation of the West Bank and Gaza proved to be 'a conquest too far'?

Long-term questions

Has the conflict escalated so much in recent years that it is in danger of setting the whole region ablaze?

Will it ever be possible for the different Arab states to make peace with Israel, to coexist alongside Israel and even to trade with it? Or is the antipathy towards Israel and the Jews so strong in the Arab world and the Muslim world that, even if there were to be peace in the near future, it will only be a matter of time before they re-group, muster their forces and attempt to destroy the Jewish state?

Is Christianity going to survive in the Middle East? In view of all the pressures felt by Christians – economic, political and religious – how many Christians will be left in Israel, Palestine and the rest of the Middle East in fifty years' time? What kind of coexistence is possible between Jews, Christians and Muslims? And how do the difficult relationships in the Middle East affect relationships in other parts of the world?

The seeds of conflict

The newer histories that are being written are making it even clearer that the poten-tial for conflict between the Zionists and the Palestinian Arabs was there from the beginning. The land to which the Jews returned from the 1880s onwards was not empty, and they knew it. But with the typical arrogance of Western colonialists they believed that they had a right to settle where they wished and that they would bring the benefits of Western civilization to a backward region. If they ever tried, they failed at almost every stage to come to terms with the people who were already there, people who like the Jews in the biblical period, had been rooted in the land for centuries and whose identity was bound up in this particular piece of land.

The coming of the Zionists stimulated Palestinian nationalism. It also provoked Palestinian Muslims to articulate the religious reasons why they believed they had a claim to the land. If we want to say that both sides have been guilty of violence, we should at least stop to enquire what were the first actions which triggered off the whole conflict.

Politics and religion

It is hard to think of another situation anywhere in the world where politics have come to be so closely bound up with religion, and where scriptures have such a pro-found effect on political action. But however much religion is tied up with politics in this conflict, political problems require political solutions, and if people of religion in the three faiths cannot learn how to talk to each other and make compromises in the real world for the sake of survival, peace and coexistence, they should be asked to retreat to their ghettos and talk only to those within their closed circle.

All religious Jews base their claim to the land on scripture, and all Muslims have strong Islamic reasons (which are both theological and historical) for claiming the land, and especially Jerusalem, for Palestinians. The problem is that fundamentalists of all kinds, Jewish, Christian and Muslim, put themselves beyond the reach of rea-son. The clash of fundamentalisms (especially Jewish and Islamic) is particularly acute over the question of Jerusalem, and it is virtually impossible to carry on any meaningful dialogue with a real fundamentalist.

It is not much comfort for anyone to be told by certain kinds of Christians that 'the situation is so bad and the problems so complex that things will only be resolved when Jesus comes again'. It *ought* to be possible at least for *some* people of faith to work out what the problem is all about and, instead of opting out and hoping for the best in a future millennium or in heaven, to get involved in the hard work of peacemaking here and now.

Jews and the land

While communities of religious Jews continued to live in the land from the second century, most of the first Zionists were very secular Jews who had little interest in religion. They came back to the land as a way of affirming their identity and to escape from the evil of anti-Semitism. It was only later that orthodox Jews began to be associated with the Zionist movement, and consciously related their vision to their Hebrew Bible. But if they were drawn back to the land because of their Jewish faith and their association with it in the past and because they needed a safe haven, they had to reckon with the land as it actually was, not as they had imagined it, and that land was occupied by others.

For many Israeli Jews today the Hebrew Bible is simply part of their history and culture, and it might never occur to them to think that it gives them a right to live in the land today. For a number of religious Jews, however, it is still treated as the scripture which gives them a divine right to the land for all time. Those who read the sacred texts in this way need to ask themselves whether the settlers on the West Bank and in Gaza and their governments have ever seen the need to listen to the command in the *Torah* about not oppressing the alien or the stranger. And is there any sense in which they can see the State of Israel as a fulfilment of the dreams of the prophets who saw the restored nation as a blessing to the whole human race? If Jewish claims to the land are based on the Hebrew Bible, are Jews willing for the State of Israel to be judged in the light of everything contained in these scriptures?

Christians and the land

Christians see the gift of the land to Abraham and his descendants as the preparation of the context in which God was going to reveal himself gradually to a particular group of people, but with a view to revealing himself eventually to the whole human race. The gift of the land was not an end in itself, but a means to the end of enabling the revelation of God's love to reach to the ends of the earth.

The climax of that process of revelation through the history of the Children of Israel came in the person of Jesus of Nazareth. He claimed that through him God was breaking into history in a new way, revealing God's love not only to the Jews, but also to every nation and tribe. While God's original covenant with the Jews still stands, therefore, enjoyment of the blessings of that covenant now has little or nothing to do with the land. All the major themes of the Old Testament, the land, the *Torah*, the Chosen People and the temple all point beyond themselves to a new reality – a person of flesh and blood through whom God was revealing himself and 'reconciling the world to himself'.

If this is how many Christians articulate their faith today, however, they have to think long and hard about the role of the Christian church over the centuries in allowing anti-Semitism to grow within it and then watering the soil in which Nazism could carry out its murderous designs. When Christians are inclined to pontificate on any of these issues, they need a special dose of humility to recognize and own up to these darker sides of their history which have contributed to the conflict.

Christian Zionism

From the standpoint developed in this book, Christian Zionism appears to be a well-meant but misguided attempt to interpret the recent history of the Middle East and to show sympathy for the Jewish people in their painful dilemmas in the modern world. Basing itself on a profoundly flawed method of interpreting the Bible, it seems to read the New Testament through the eyes of the Old Testament, rather than reading the Old Testament through the eyes of the New Testament. It fails to grasp how the coming of the Messiah was meant to transform first-century Jewish ideas about the *Torah*, the land, the temple, the Chosen People and how new wineskins were needed to contain the new wine of the gospel of Jesus. It represents a regression to the mentality of the Jewish disciples of Jesus *before* they finally got the point and began to understand the significance of who Jesus was and what he had accomplished.

In so far as Christian Zionism supports the basic vision of Zionism and the actions of Zionists from the beginning to the present day, they are supporting something that has led to some disastrous consequences. While one cannot hold *all* Christian Zionists responsible for *all* the actions of Zionists, it is hard to see how Christian Zionists can be enthusiastic about the basic vision of Zionism and at the same time be critical of the direction in which the movement has developed in recent years. If conflict and violence were implicit in the original vision from the very beginning, how can Christians support Zionism as a solution to the problem of anti-Semitism and believe that the Zionist movement can be seen even as a part of God's plan for the Jewish people as understood in the Bible?

The land and Islam

If secular Westerners have thought until now that we are dealing simply with two ethnic groups, Jews and Palestinian Arabs, they have been forced to reckon with the new forces that have emerged through the resurgence of Islam in the modern world. They now have to recognize that the land played an important part not only in the life of the Prophet, but also in subsequent Islamic history. The history of Islam has been intertwined with Christianity and Judaism from the beginning through Muhammad's relationships with Jews and Christians and through his followers who lived alongside Jews and Christians in the region for many centuries.

Muslims are proud of their history. For 1,300 years they ruled the land, from the first conquest in AD 638 until the end of the Ottoman empire in 1918, with the sole exception of around 90 years when it was under Crusader rule. Even if the Christian and Jewish perception of this history is not as positive as the Muslim perception was, Muslims can with some justification argue that Islam has generally been more tolerant towards Jews and Christians than Christian Europe was tolerant towards Jews and Muslims. Islam certainly developed its own kind of tolerance and pluralism.

But Palestinians and Muslims now face difficult questions over the place of Islamic ideology in arguing and fighting for the Palestinian cause. If Zionism can be defined as 'religious reasons for exclusive political control of the land', are Muslims in danger of adopting a kind of 'Islamic Zionism', especially in the way they sometimes argue for exclusive control over East Jerusalem? The challenge to Muslims and

Palestinians is to find the most convincing language to commend their cause in a world which understands the language of human rights better than it understands the language of Islam.

The world has a role

This is no local conflict between two tribes which they can sort out between themselves. Western nations have been active (or rather interfering) in the Middle East for centuries. Their interests in the region in the nineteenth and twentieth centuries have been tied up with their own regional rivalries and conflicts, with the need to protect their empires in India and the East, with their need for markets and for oil, with academic scholarship and with tourism, with Christian mission, with their desire to limit the number of Jews coming into the West, and with their guilty conscience over the Holocaust.

Having broken their promises to the Arabs made during the first World War, Britain took responsibility for Palestine during the period of deepening conflict between 1920 and 1948, and then handed the problem over to the United Nations. The State of Israel therefore owes its existence first to Britain and then to the United Nations. It has also been the subject of numerous resolutions from the UN General Assembly and the Security Council, but has somehow found a way of ignoring most of them and carrying on with its plans.

If the peace process which began in 1991 seems to have stalled or failed until now, it is largely because it has not attempted to deal with the root of the problem and the fundamental injustices at the heart of all that has happened, and because most of the self-appointed mediators have either been too closely identified with one side in the conflict or been cowed by the strength and skill with which that side has pursued its policies.

If the two Intifadas have been the Palestinian way of saying 'Enough is enough!', the events of 11 September 2001 may have made some Western leaders wake up to the reality of what has been happening and to say 'Enough is enough! For the sake of the peace of the region and the world, we cannot allow this conflict to go on for ever!' Surely the time has come for the international community – through whatever means it chooses – to sit down with the main parties to work out a way of living together which the majority of both sides are willing to accept.

Tragedy and suffering

'The conflict over the Holy Land – or Israel, or Palestine', says **Anton La Guardia**, 'is a vast story of tragedy and redemption.' Within the worldview of the ancient Greeks, the tragedy might be seen in terms of noble but flawed characters and communities being sucked into a series of events leading to disaster, through the interplay of superhuman forces that are beyond their control. A more rational approach to the problem attempts patiently to understand not only what happened but why it happened. While it is careful not to oversimplify the issues, it says that it ought to be possible to understand the major factors which have led us to where we are. It does not need, therefore, to resort too quickly to purely supernatural explanations of historical events in terms of the miraculous.

But however well or badly we understand the ingredients of the tragedy, it is important that we recognize that we are dealing with *two* peoples who have suffered injustice, and not just with one. The title of Benny Morris's outstanding history of the Zionist-Palestinian conflict, *Righteous Victims*, recognizes that it is not just Jews who see themselves as the victims of injustices done to them by others, but Palestinian Arabs as well. And if Jews are to recognize the suffering they have caused for the Palestinians, the Palestinians and other Arabs for their part need to admit the enormity of the Holocaust and not try to argue that it never happened or that it has been grossly exaggerated, as some still try to do.

It is easier, however, to see what La Guardia means by 'tragedy' than to see any signs of 'redemption'. The depth of the tragedy and the suffering should be forcing Jews, Christians and Muslims to look again to the roots of their faith to see what resources they have for dealing with suffering and evil. Do their teaching and their spirituality satisfy the mind and the heart, and do they give ordinary people the resources to 'overcome evil with good'? Are they willing to look outside their own tradition to learn from each other?

Wanted – peacemakers!

The peacemakers required in this particular conflict need to be of a very special kind. While being able to understand the history, to appreciate the aspirations of both sides and to empathize with them, they need to be genuinely impartial and not committed ideologically or emotionally to one side or the other. They need to be prepared to speak the truth to both sides and to different groups within the two sides. They need to understand the realities of geopolitics and be willing and able when necessary to speak the truth to the most powerful nations in the world.

They need to be tough enough to say to the fundamentalists of all kinds, 'Look, if you want to belong to the human race, if you want to live in the global village, you will have to learn the language of human rights which has been accepted by the vast majority of the nations. You cannot go on imposing your worldview, your scriptures, your understanding of your rights on the rest of the world at the expense of your neighbours who live beside you. If you want to live in the real world and if you accept the need for coexistence, there are some things that you simply cannot do, and you'll have to be willing to sit down and negotiate with others.'

Time may be running out

Sober predictions of the future should add an element of even greater urgency, warning us that soon there could be nothing left for anyone. By the year 2020 the population density in Israel will be similar to that of Holland, the most densely populated country in Europe. The expected increase in the population for the year 2050 among both Jews and Arabs, both through natural increase and immigration, point to projected figures of twelve million in Israel/Palestine. The country already faces acute problems over water, and these are only likely to increase.

Have the events of 11 September 2001 made the Western world, and especially the USA, aware of the depth of the anger felt by most Muslims, most Arabs and all Palestinians over the way they have been treated by the West? One particular focus for this anger has been the way the West has created and then supported what they see as the Zionist transplant at the heart of the Muslim world. One can only hope that this time the West will begin to hear what so many have been saying for so long. It will be a further tragedy if, instead of trying to address the root causes of the anger, the Western world goes on proclaiming its innocence, trying simply to treat the symptom of terrorism without seeking to deal with at least *one* of its root causes.

The land belongs to God

So who does the Promised Land belong to after all? Whenever Jews, Christians or Muslims use their scriptures to claim the land for themselves, they need to hear again this simple sentence buried away in the book of Leviticus where God insists that ultimately *the land belongs to him*: 'the land is mine and you are but aliens and tenants' (Leviticus 25:23). If God gave it to one group of people for a particular period of time, they were to see it as a *gift*, and not as something that they owned *by right*. The gift was a means to a greater end, not an end in itself.

When the promise of the land to Abraham and his descendants is read *only in the context of the Old Testament*, it is understandable that Jews (and some Christians) will interpret it as a divine gift for all time to Jews as the Chosen People. But within the context of the Old Testament there is also plenty of teaching about the ethical standards required of the people who live in this land. There is no suggestion that anything like the conquest under Joshua would ever have to be repeated again. And there are plenty of visions about a future that will bring blessing not only to this people living in the land but also to the rest of the world.

When seen *in the context of the whole Bible*, however, *both Old and New Testaments*, the promise of the land to Abraham and his descendants does not give *anyone* a divine right to possess or to live in the land for all time, because the coming of the kingdom of God through Jesus the Messiah has transformed and reinterpreted all the promises and prophecies in the Old Testament. God has acted *in the land* not only to demonstrate his love but also to deal with the root causes of injustice and evil. Jesus the Messiah, who lived, died and was raised from death *in the land*, has opened the kingdom of God to people of all races, making all who follow him into 'one new humanity' (Ephesians 2:15, NRSV).

'Like everything,' therefore, says **W.D. Davies**, 'the land also in the New Testament drives us to ponder the mystery of Jesus, the Christ, who by his cross and resurrection broke not only the bonds of death for early Christians but also the bonds of the land.' This same Jesus has also pointed out ways of being peacemakers among those who live and suffer *in the land* today.

It ought to be possible for the rest of the world to support Jews and Palestinian Arabs in finding ways to recognize each other's existence and aspirations, and to make their home *in the land* as they live there side by side.

Appendix I
Principles of Christian Interpretation of Old Testament Prophecy

If we are to establish any agreed principles of interpreting prophecy, and in particular prophecies about the return to the land and the future of the nation, these are some of the questions we will need to ask:

Q What kind of language is the prophet using?

Sometimes the prophet is making *a simple prediction of an event* which does not need any interpretation. For example:

This is what the Sovereign LORD says... 'I will take you out of the nations; I will gather you from all the countries and bring you back into your own land.'
EZEKIEL 36:22, 24

At other times he describes *a future event in poetic language*. For example:

The desert and the parched land will be glad;
* the wilderness will rejoice and blossom...*
and the ransomed of the LORD will return...
ISAIAH 35:1, 10

In many cases the prophet is describing *a vision*. Thus, for example, the book of Ezekiel begins with an explanation of where and when the prophet saw his 'visions of God':

In the thirtieth year, in the fourth month on the fifth day, while I was among the exiles by the Kebar River, the heavens were opened and I saw visions of God.
EZEKIEL 1:1

The prophet sometimes describes what he sees, and is then given an interpretation of what he sees. For example:

Vision
I saw a great many bones on the floor of the valley, bones that were very dry.
EZEKIEL 37:2

Interpretation
These bones are the whole house of Israel.
EZEKIEL 37:11

Vision
The bones came together, bone to bone... and breath entered them; they came to life and stood up on their feet – a vast army.
EZEKIEL 37:7, 10

Interpretation
I am going to open your graves and bring you up from them; I will bring you back to the land of Israel.
EZEKIEL 37:12

In other cases we are not given any interpretation of the details of the visions. For example, Ezekiel's vision of the new Jerusalem contains details like these:

The remaining area, 5,000 cubits wide and 25,000 cubits long, will be for the common use of the city, for houses and for pastureland. The city will be in the center of it and will have these measurements: the north side 4,500 cubits, the south side 4,500 cubits, the east side 4,500 cubits, and the west side 4,500 cubits....
EZEKIEL 48:15–16

Does the prophet really intend to give us an architect's blueprint of the new Jerusalem? If so, we must interpret the visions very literally and see them as a kind of visual preview of history. The alternative is to try to interpret the language of the vision and translate it into a message which was relevant to the original hearers and is relevant to anyone who wants to listen today.

Q When were these prophecies delivered, and can we see any fulfilment of them during or soon after the time of the prophet?

The writer of 2 Chronicles and Ezra wants us to understand that the return to the land in 537 BC was the fulfilment of the prophecies of Jeremiah. This does not present any problems.

It is more complicated when we come to Zechariah's prophecy of a return of exiles *both* from the southern kingdom of Judah, *and* from the northern kingdom of Israel (Zechariah 10:6–10). If he was writing around 520 BC, the first wave of exiles of the people of Judah had already returned from Babylon seventeen years before; and more exiles were to return many years later with Ezra and Nehemiah. It is therefore easy to see how this part of the prophecy was fulfilled soon after his lifetime.

But what of the prophecy of a return of exiles from the northern kingdom of Israel, which implies the eventual union of the two kingdoms of Israel and Judah (Zechariah 10:6–10; compare Ezekiel 37:15–23)? There is nothing in the history of the centuries immediately following Zechariah's time which could by any stretch of the imagination be described as the fulfilment of these prophecies.

When we are faced with this kind of dilemma, we have to make a choice: *either* we insist that we must continue to look for a literal fulfilment in history – in which case we may see the return of Jews to the land in the twentieth century and the establishment of the State of Israel as the intended fulfilment, *or* we look for other ways in which these prophecies could have been fulfilled already in the past or could yet be fulfilled in the future.

Q Do the prophecies themselves contain any clues which help us to interpret them?

One important clue is that in many of the prophecies there are echoes of the four promises which made up the original covenant with Abraham. For example:

■ *The land*: 'you will live in the land I gave your forefathers' (Ezekiel 36:28).
■ *The nation*: 'I will make their people as numerous as sheep' (Ezekiel 36:37).
■ 'I will redeem them; they will be as numerous as before' (Zechariah 10:8).
■ *The covenant relationship*: 'you will be my people, and I will be your God' (Ezekiel 36:28).
■ 'They will be my people, and I will be their God' (Jeremiah 24:7).
■ 'They will be my people, and I will be faithful and righteous to them as their God' (Zechariah 8:8).
■ *Blessing for all people*: 'then the nations… will know' (Ezekiel 36:36).

This suggests that the fulfilment of the promises about the land must be seen in the context of the fulfilment of the whole covenant with Abraham.

Q How are these prophecies related to other divine promises in the Old Testament?

Several of these prophecies contain the phrase 'for ever', which is associated in other parts of the Old Testament with the continuation of the line of David and the line of Aaron, and the presence of God in the temple:

■ *The promise of a king in the line of David*: 'Your house and your kingdom will endure *forever* before me; your throne will be established *forever*' (2 Samuel 7:16; compare Psalm 89:3–4).
■ *The commissioning of Aaron and his descendants*: 'Aaron was set apart, he and his descendants *forever*, to consecrate the most holy things, to offer sacrifices before the LORD, to minister before him and to pronounce blessings in his name *forever*' (1 Chronicles 23:13).
■ *The promise concerning the temple built by Solomon*: 'I have heard the prayer and plea you have made before me; I have consecrated this temple, which you

have built, by putting my Name there *forever*. My eyes and my heart will always be there' (1 Kings 9:3).

In Ezekiel 37 the phrase 'for ever' is linked to four out of the fifteen themes:

■ 'They and their children's children will live there *forever*' (37:25).
■ 'David my servant will be their prince *forever*' (37:25).
■ 'It will be an everlasting covenant' or 'this covenant shall be theirs *for ever*' (37:26 NEB).
■ 'I will put my sanctuary among them *forever*' (37:26).

If God promised that the descendants of Abraham would live in the land for ever, he also promised that the royal line of David would continue for ever, that the priestly line of Aaron would continue for ever, and that the temple in Jerusalem would bear the name of God for ever. Do we therefore have any right to separate these promises and interpret one of them very literally (the one about the land), but interpret all the others in a totally different way?

If we insist on a *literal* interpretation of everything that the Old Testament says about the land, we ought to be consistent and give a literal interpretation to *all* the other promises in the Old Testament. A strictly literal interpretation would require a descendant of David being installed as king in Jerusalem, the temple being rebuilt and the whole sacrificial system reinstituted… Since it has not happened yet, is it still to happen in the future?

If, however, we interpret everything about the land in a *literal* and *spiritual* way at the same time, once again we have to be consistent and interpret *all* the promises in the same way. But the Davidic monarchy did *not* continue in Jerusalem after 587 BC; and although sacrifices were offered in the temple after the exile, the temple was destroyed in AD 70 and completely obliterated in AD 135. So how can we combine a spiritual and literal interpretation of these promises if the literal interpretation makes nonsense of history? There is no reason why we should be content with a *spiritual* interpretation of the Davidic monarchy, the temple and its sacrifices, but at the same time insist that the teaching about the land has both a *spiritual* and a *literal* meaning.

The only solution to this problem is to link all these Old Testament promises and prophecies together and see them in the same light. When we do this, it begins to look as if their fulfilment may also somehow be bound up together.

Q How did Jesus and the biblical writers interpret these prophecies?

This question is hardly relevant for the Jew. But for Christians it is crucial, because they feel bound to try to read the Old Testament through the eyes of Jesus and the apostles.

There are basically three different ways in which the writers of the Old and New Testaments understood the fulfilment of prophecy. These can be indicated by the symbols F1, F2 and F3:

F1 Fulfilment in the original context in which the prophet spoke
In other words, fulfilment in historical events at, or soon after, the time of the prophet.

For example, the return of the exiles from Babylon in 539 BC is described in 2 Chronicles 36:22 and Ezra 1:1 as the fulfilment of the prophecies of Jeremiah.

F2 Fulfilment in the first coming of Jesus Christ
In other words, fulfilment in the birth, life, death, resurrection and ascension of Jesus Christ, and therefore also in the new age which has been inaugurated through his coming.

For example, the angel announcing the birth of Jesus told Mary that Jesus would be the fulfilment of the promise that a descendant of David would sit on his throne 'forever' (Luke 1:30–33).

F3 Fulfilment in the second coming of Jesus Christ
In other words, fulfilment in events in the future associated with the second coming of Jesus Christ and the end of the world.

For example, the apostle John saw the final fulfilment of Ezekiel's vision of the new Jerusalem and the new temple in 'a new heaven and a new earth' (Revelation 21:1 – 22:6).

These three ways of understanding the fulfilment of prophecy are not mutually exclusive. We are not forced in every case to choose between these different kinds of fulfilment. Some prophecies can be interpreted as referring to *all three periods* of time, while others can be related to *two different periods* – for example, the immediate future (F1) and the first coming of Jesus (F2), or the first coming of Jesus (F2) and the second coming (F3).

The following words, for example, are found in a passage in the prophet Zechariah which speaks about the whole people of Judah and Jerusalem returning to God in a spirit of deep repentance:

And I will pour out on the house of David and the inhabitants of Jerusalem a spirit of grace and supplication. They will look on me, the one they have pierced, *and* they will mourn for him *as one mourns for an only child, and grieve bitterly for him as one grieves for a firstborn son.*
ZECHARIAH 12:10

There is a clear echo of these words in Matthew's version of the saying about the coming of the Son of man. If the coming of the Son of man refers primarily to the vindication of Jesus in the years immediately following his death (see section 3:8), the mourning of all the nations of the earth must also refer primarily to this period:

At that time the sign of the Son of Man will appear in the sky, and all the nations of the earth will mourn. They will see *the Son of Man coming on the clouds of the sky, with power and great glory.*
MATTHEW 24:30

The words are also quoted in John's Gospel, in his description of the crucifixion, and related to the piercing of the side of Jesus' body with a spear:

When they came to Jesus and found that he was already dead, they did not break his legs. Instead, one of the soldiers pierced Jesus' side with a spear, bringing a sudden flow of blood and water... These things happened so that the scripture would be fulfilled: 'Not one of his bones will be broken,' and, as another scripture says, 'They will look on the one they have pierced.'
JOHN 19:33–37

In the book of Revelation John relates the same prophecy to something in the future – to the time when Jesus comes with the clouds and is seen by all those who crucified him:

Look, he is coming with the clouds,
    and every eye will see him,
even those who pierced him;
    and all the peoples of the earth will mourn because of him.
So shall it be! Amen.
REVELATION 1:7

Q What was God trying to teach his people through these prophecies at the time they were given?

When the prophets spoke the message that they believed God had given them for the people of their day, they must have expected that it would mean something to their hearers at the time and in the context in which they were living. It is hard to think that a prophet would be given a message to his people in the eighth century BC which related to events that would not take place until the twentieth or twenty-first centuries.

When we read the prophecies we need to ask what God might be trying to teach *us* in our context today. Understanding the message of the prophet in his original context should help us in working out the message for ourselves today. Two well-known Christian writers make this point as follows:

James I. Packer:

The heart of the hermeneutical problem does not lie in the determining of the historical meaning of each passage... it lies, rather, in seeing how it applies to you, me and us at the point in history and personal life where we are now.[1]

John Goldingay:

As the word of God, those prophecies have things to say to us about contemporary world events and contemporary church life. They reveal God's will to us by revealing God's will embodied in particular contexts. But when Ezekiel declared that such and such a return to the land or such and such a battle was to take place, he was not announcing events scheduled for two and a half millennia after his day. He was addressing and bringing God's word to people in his own day, warning them of calamities and promising them blessings that could come about in their day. He was not revealing a timetable or fixture list of events that had to unfold over thousands of years; he was bringing a specific message to a particular context. A fulfilment in 1948 of a prophecy given by Ezekiel to people who lived in the 580s BC is thus nonsense: it is not a fulfilment of promises and warnings that were part of God's relationship with those people. Prophets did sometimes speak about the End of all things, but there are relatively few of these prophecies. The ones applied to the recent history of the Jews are prophecies that relate to the circumstances of the Jews in particular contexts.

When we seek to understand the significance of Old Testament prophecy, then we must treat this, too, as an act of communication between God and his people in the contexts in which they lived. We have to work out its implications for us from that, not by treating it as a coded preview of things to take place in the far future which were not in any direct sense God's good news to the people to whom they were announced.[2]

Appendix 2
Examples of Christian Interpretation of Old Testament Prophecy

Because of the flexibility in the New Testament's interpretation of Old Testament prophecy, we need to take account of the fact that in many cases there may be more than one way of interpreting a particular passage of prophecy. We now approach five passages from Old Testament prophets with three questions in mind:

■ Were these words fulfilled in any way during the time of the prophet or soon after (F1)?
■ Were these words fulfilled in any way in the first coming of Jesus Christ? Is there any indication that Jesus regarded himself, or that his disciples regarded him, as the fulfilment of this prophecy (F2)?
■ Are these words to be fulfilled in the future at the second coming of Jesus Christ? Is there any indication that either Jesus himself or the disciples related these prophecies to the end of the world (F3)?

When we have attempted to answer these questions, we will not have exhausted the meaning of these prophecies. They may have much to teach us about Christian history between the first and second comings of Jesus Christ. But we shall see how difficult it is, if not impossible, to relate the prophecy to specific events in the twentieth century in the way that many are suggesting today. We dare not try to reduce the whole of biblical prophecy to a neat and tidy system. But we do need to make sure that we have understood how the New Testament writers handled Old Testament prophecy *before* we start using it to interpret contemporary events in detail.

In each passage all the words, phrases or sentences which are quoted or echoed in other parts of the Old Testament or the New Testament are in roman type, and the references to the relevant passages are in the column on the right.

The planting of Israel in the land (Amos 9:8–15)
'Surely the eyes of the Sovereign LORD
  are on the sinful kingdom.
I will destroy it
  from the face of the earth –
yet I will not totally destroy

the house of Jacob,' declares the LORD.
'For I will give the command,
 and I will shake the house of Israel among all the nations
as grain is shaken in a sieve,
 and not a pebble will reach the ground.
All the sinners among my people
 will die by the sword,
all those who say,
 "Disaster will not overtake or meet us."

ACTS 15:16–17

In that day I will restore
   David's fallen tent.
I will repair its broken places,
   restore its ruins,
   and build it as it used to be,
so that they may possess the remnant *of Edom*
   and all the nations that bear my name,'
   declares the LORD, *who will do these things.*

'The days are coming,' declares the LORD,
 'when the reaper will be overtaken by the ploughman
 and the planter by the one treading grapes.
New wine will drip from the mountains
 and flow from all the hills.
I will bring back my exiled people Israel;
 they will rebuild the ruined cities and live in them.
They will plant vineyards and drink their wine;
 they will make gardens and eat their fruit.
I will plant Israel in their own land,
 never again to be uprooted
from the land I have given them,'
 says the LORD *your God.*

F1 The prophet Amos came from the *southern* kingdom of
Judah, but was called to exercise his prophetic ministry in the
northern kingdom of Israel. After preaching in the capital of
Samaria from approximately 760 to 750 BC, he was ordered to
return home to Judah. He warned the people of the northern
kingdom of a severe judgment to come (Amos 9:8), and this
was fulfilled in 721 BC when Samaria was captured and the
people taken into exile in Assyria.

Most commentators find it difficult to point to any clear fulfilment of this prophecy of a return from the exile in Assyria. It
would seem that the exiles were scattered all over the Assyrian
empire, and that the vast majority were assimilated with the
local population. Even if a few individuals were able to return

to their land, there was nothing resembling the return of the exiles from Babylon to Judah in the mid-sixth century BC.

F2 At the Council of Jerusalem described in Acts 15, Peter and Paul argue that the way in which the Gentiles had received the gospel message and the way in which God had given his Spirit and worked signs and wonders among them proved beyond doubt that he intended them to be accepted as full members of the church. James, apparently acting as a kind of chairman to the Council, accepted their argument, and went on to quote from Amos 9:11–12 to support his position.

The two verses quoted cannot be isolated from the rest of the passage. So, for example, verse 11 ('I will... restore its ruins, and build it as it used to be') is echoed in verse 14 ('they will rebuild the ruined cities and live in them'). The original passage in Amos speaks about the restoration of the *people* of Israel to the land, the rebuilding of the ruined cities, and the permanent replanting of the people in the land. When James quotes the passage, he is trying to show that the inclusion of the Gentiles in the church is *a* fulfilment – or should we not rather say *the* fulfilment? – of the prophecies of Amos.

The restoration of Israel is not understood as something still in the future, but as something that has already taken place. And the inclusion of the Gentiles in the church is described as a result of the restoration of Israel ('... *that* the remnant of men may seek the Lord, and all the Gentiles who bear my name' Acts 15:17).

Hopes for the restored nation (Ezekiel 37:15–28)

The word of the LORD came to me: 'Son of man, take a stick of wood and write on it, "Belonging to Judah and the Israelites associated with him." Then take another stick of wood, and write on it, "Ephraim's stick, belonging to Joseph and all the house of Israel associated with him." Join them together into one stick so that they will become one in your hand.

'When your countrymen ask you, "Won't you tell us what you mean by this?" say to them, "This is what the Sovereign LORD says: I am going to take the stick of Joseph – which is in Ephraim's hand – and of the Israelite tribes associated with him, and join it to Judah's stick, making them a single stick of wood, and they will become one in my hand." Hold before their eyes the sticks you have written on and say to them,
"This is what the Sovereign LORD says: I will take the Israelites   JOHN 10:16
out of the nations where they have gone. I will gather them   11:51–52
from all around and bring them back into their own land. I
will make them one nation *in the land, on the mountains of*

Israel. There will be one king *over all of them and they will
never again be two nations or be divided into two kingdoms.
They will no longer defile themselves with their idols and vile
images or with any of their offenses, for I will* save them from
all *their sinful backsliding, and I will* cleanse them. *They will
be my people, and I will be their God.*

   *"My servant David will be king over them, and they will
all have one shepherd. They will* follow my laws and be careful to keep my decrees. *They will live in the land I gave to my
servant Jacob, the land where your fathers lived. They and
their children and their children's children will live there forever, and* David my servant will be their prince forever. *I will
make a* covenant *of peace with them; it will be* an everlasting
covenant. *I will establish them and increase their numbers,
and I will put* my sanctuary *among them forever...* My
dwelling place will be with them; I will be *their God, and
they will be my people. Then the nations will know that I the
Lord make* Israel holy, *when* my sanctuary is among them
forever. *"'*

HEBREWS 9:14
1 JOHN 1:7
1 PETER 2:9–10
LUKE 1:31–33
JOHN 10:11
HEBREWS 8:7–13

LUKE 22:20
HEBREWS 13:20

JOHN 2:18–22
JOHN 1:14
REVELATION 21:3
1 PETER 2:9

F1 Some of these words found their immediate fulfilment in
the return of the Jewish exiles from Babylon to Jerusalem
beginning in 537 BC.

F2 The reference to the 'one shepherd' (Ezekiel 37:24) and the
'one nation' (37:22) are echoed in Jesus' claim that he is 'the good
shepherd' who brings together 'one flock' (John 10:11, 14, 16).
John believed that Jesus had died not only for the Jewish nation,
'but also for the scattered children of God, to bring them together
and make them one' (John 11:51–52).

   The promise about the Davidic king who will rule over his
people for ever (37:22, 24, 25), is fulfilled in the person of
Jesus and his kingly rule (Luke 1:31–33). Since the rule of the
Davidic king is inevitably associated with the land (37:22, 25),
we must assume that the promise about his people living in
the land 'forever' (37:25) must also be related to Jesus Christ
and his church.

   Jesus spoke of his death as the inauguration of a new
covenant (Luke 22:20), and the writer to the Hebrews relates
the 'everlasting covenant' (Ezekiel 37:26) to this same covenant
(Hebrews 13:20).

   John sees Jesus as the new temple in which the glory of
God has been revealed (John 1:14; 2:26).

   Peter describes all Christian believers as being 'a holy
nation' (1 Peter 3:9), and thus fulfilling the promise that God
would make Israel 'holy' (Ezekiel 37:28).

It demands an impossible kind of surgery to cut out and iso-late references to the land in this passage (Ezekiel 37:22, 25) and expect them to be fulfilled in a literal way (and not only in the sixth century BC but also in the twentieth century AD), while accepting that every other aspect of the prophecies has been ful-filled in Jesus Christ and his people.

Jerusalem under attack (Zechariah 12:1–10)

This is the word of the LORD concerning Israel. The LORD, who stretches out the heavens, who lays the foundation of the earth, and who forms the spirit of man within him, declares: 'I am going to make Jerusalem a cup that sends all the sur-rounding peoples reeling. Judah will be besieged as well as Jerusalem. On that day, when all the nations of the earth are gathered against her, *I will make Jerusalem an immovable* rock *for all the nations. All who try to move it will* injure themselves. *On that day I will strike every horse with panic and its rider with madness,' declares the LORD. 'I will keep a watchful eye over the house of Judah, but I will blind all the horses of the nations. Then the leaders of Judah will say in their hearts, "The people of Jerusalem are strong, because the LORD Almighty is their God."*

REVELATION 20:7–9
MATTHEW 21:44

'On that day I will make the leaders of Judah like a firepot in a woodpile, like a flaming torch among sheaves. They will consume right and left all the surrounding peoples, but Jerusalem will remain intact in her place.

'The LORD will save the dwellings of Judah first, so that the honor of the house of David and of Jerusalem's inhabitants may not be greater than that of Judah. On that day the LORD will shield those who live in Jerusalem, so that the feeblest among them will be like David, and the house of David will be like God, like the Angel of the LORD going before them. On that day I will set out to destroy all the nations that attack Jerusalem.

MATTHEW 16:18
REVELATION 20:7–10

JOHN 19:37
REVELATION 1:7
MATTHEW 24:30

'And I will pour out on the house of David and the inhabi-tants of Jerusalem a spirit of grace and supplication. They will look on me, the one they have pierced, *and* they will mourn *for him as one mourns for an only child, and grieve bitterly for him as one grieves for a firstborn son.'*

F1 Some of Zechariah's earlier prophecies could be regarded as having been fulfilled in the Maccabean struggle for inde-pendence from Seleucid rule in 165 BC. But he is not writing here about the immediate future, but about a more distant time, which he speaks of as 'that day'.

F2 Jesus relates the picture of the rock (Zechariah 12:3) to himself in Matthew 21:44.

In Matthew 24:30 there is an echo of Zechariah 12:10, when he says that all nations of the earth will 'mourn' at the coming of the Son of man, in other words, in the period immediately after his death (see 3:8 Conclusions).

John connects verse 10 with the crucifixion of Jesus (John 19:37).

F3 John also relates the vision of all nations of the earth mourning to the second coming of Jesus Christ (Revelation 1:7).

When he later takes up the picture of all nations attacking Jerusalem, he describes it as 'the camp of God's people, the city he loves' (Revelation 20:9). This could hardly refer to the Jewish people or the city of Jerusalem, and must therefore refer to the church.

If Jesus and the apostles relate these verses so clearly to the first and second comings of Jesus, it is difficult to believe that they could *also* be applied to the modern city of Jerusalem as the capital of Israel withstanding attacks from all nations of the world. If we insist on this kind of literal interpretation, we must lengthen the list to include *every other occasion* on which Jerusalem has withstood attacks – for example, during the Muslim conquest in the seventh century, the Crusades in the eleventh and twelfth centuries, the Byzantine wars, and the First World War.

'The day of the Lord' (Zechariah 14:1–9, 21)

A day of the LORD is coming when your plunder will be divided among you.   REVELATION 20:7–9

I will gather all the nations to Jerusalem to fight against it; *the city will be captured, the houses ransacked, and the women raped. Half of the city will go into exile, but the rest of the people will not be taken from the city.*

Then the LORD will go out and fight against those nations,   REVELATION 20:7–9 *as he fights in the day of battle. On that day his feet will stand on the Mount of Olives, east of Jerusalem, and the Mount of Olives will be split in two from east to west, forming a great valley, with half of the mountain moving north and half moving south. You will flee by my mountain valley, for it will extend to Azel. You will flee as you fled from the earthquake in the days of Uzziah king of Judah. Then the LORD my God will come, and* all the holy ones with him.

On that day there will be no light, no cold or frost. It will be   MATTHEW 16:27; *a unique day,* without daytime or nighttime – *a day known to*   25:31 *the LORD. When evening comes, there will be light.*   REVELATION 22:5

On that day living water will flow out from Jerusalem, *half to the eastern sea and half to the western sea, in summer and in winter.*

The LORD will be king over the whole earth. *On that day there will be one LORD, and his name* the only name.

And on that day there will no longer be a Canaanite [or merchant] in the house of the LORD Almighty.

JOEL 3:18
JOHN 7:37–39
REVELATION 22:1–2
REVELATION 11:15–17
ACTS 4:12
MARK 11:15–17
JOHN 2:13–19

F1 The capture of Jerusalem described in Zechariah 14:2 could perhaps be related to the capture of Jerusalem in AD 70 by the Romans.

F2 Mark summarizes the message preached by Jesus in the words: 'The time has come... The kingdom of God is near' (Mark 1:15). All his teaching about the coming of the kingdom (compare Mark 9:1) must be related to Zechariah's prophecy 'The LORD will be king over the whole earth' (Zechariah 14:9).

The cleansing of the temple by Jesus is a clear fulfilment of the words 'there will no longer be a Canaanite [or merchant] in the house of the LORD Almighty' (Zechariah 14:21; compare Mark 11:15–17 and John 2:13–19).

The picture of living water flowing from Jerusalem (Zechariah 14:8) is found in two other prophets (Ezekiel 47:1–12 and Joel 3:18). It must be to this that Jesus was referring when he said, 'Whoever believes in me, as the Scripture has said, streams of living water will flow from within him' (John 7:38). There is no other passage in the Old Testament which could account for his using the phrase 'as the Scripture has said'. Jesus therefore takes the original vision of living water flowing from the temple in Jerusalem down to the Dead Sea and interprets it as a picture of the life-giving influence of the believer who is filled with the Holy Spirit, or of himself as the one through whom the Spirit is given.

The words 'On that day there will be one LORD, and his name the only name' (Zechariah 14:9) are echoed by Peter's claim about Jesus: 'Salvation is found in no one else, for there is no other name under heaven given to men by which we must be saved' (Acts 4:12).

F3 There is an echo of Zechariah 14:5 in Jesus' words about the coming of the Son of man (Matthew 16:27 and 25:31), since 'the holy ones' are probably to be understood as 'angels'.

Several of the themes that are mentioned here are taken up by John in his vision of 'a new heaven and a new earth'

(Revelation 21:1ff) – for example, the defeat of the nations attacking Jerusalem (Zechariah 14:2–3; compare Revelation 20:7–9), and the unique day in which there is no day or night (Zechariah 14:7; compare Revelation 22:5). The picture of living water flowing from the temple is here given a completely different interpretation: it now becomes 'the river of the water of life, as clear as crystal, flowing from the throne of God and of the Lamb' (Revelation 22:1).

However closely, therefore, some of Zechariah's words seem to correspond to events in and around Jerusalem since 1948, we must resist the temptation to draw the connection *until and unless* we have answered these two basic questions:

■ How do the New Testament writers understand the fulfilment of the prophecies of Zechariah?
■ Do the New Testament writers encourage us in any way to relate Zechariah's words to historical events in Jerusalem between the first and second comings of Jesus Christ?

Since they relate Zechariah's prophecies at so many points to the first and second comings of Jesus, and since they give us no encouragement whatsoever to relate them to events in the city of Jerusalem between the two comings, is there any good reason why we in the twentieth century should want to do so? When the New Testament writers have opened our eyes to see how Jesus fulfilled some of Zechariah's prophecies in his first coming, and when they have given us a vision of how others will be fulfilled at his second coming, the attempt to relate them, for example, to Arab attacks on the State of Israel seems to be a step backward rather than forward. It is rather like lighting a candle when the sun is already shining.

The conversion of Egypt (Isaiah 19:18–25)

In that day five cities in Egypt will speak the language of Canaan and swear allegiance to the LORD Almighty. One of them will be called the City of Destruction.   JOSHUA 10

In that day there will be an altar to the LORD in the heart of Egypt, and a monument to the LORD at its border. It will be a sign and witness to the LORD Almighty in the land of Egypt.   GENESIS 28:18
When they cry out to the LORD because of their oppressors, he will send them a savior and defender, and he will rescue them.   EXODUS 2:23 – 3:10
So the LORD will make himself known to the Egyptians; and in   EXODUS 6:1–8
that day they will acknowledge the LORD. They will worship with sacrifices and grain offerings; they will make vows to the LORD and keep them. The LORD will strike Egypt with a plague;

he will strike them and heal them. They will turn to the LORD, and he will respond to their pleas and heal them.

1 PETER 2:9–10
EPHESIANS 2:10

In that day there will be a highway from Egypt to Assyria. The Assyrians will go to Egypt and the Egyptians to Assyria. The Egyptians and Assyrians will worship together. In that day Israel will be the third, along with Egypt and Assyria, a blessing on the earth. The LORD Almighty will bless them, saying, 'Blessed be Egypt my people, Assyria my handiwork, and Israel my inheritance.'

F1 This prophecy was probably written in the period between 720 and 711 BC, when the small kingdom of Judah felt it was at the mercy of the two great powers of the day – Egypt and Assyria. In the first part of the chapter (19:1–17) the prophet has described God's judgment on Egypt: civil war leads to a violent struggle, which in turn leads to a cruel and tyrannical government. All Egypt's national resources – spiritual, moral, economic and material – fail one after the other and are unable to arrest the rapid decline.

This passage, the second half of the chapter (18–25), describes the restoration and renewal of Egypt in terms that would have sounded very surprising to Israel's first listeners. The basic idea seems to be that at some day in the future Yahweh is going to 'make himself known to the Egyptians'. First of all there will be a nucleus of people in Egypt who worship the true God, and through this small community God will reveal himself to the whole of the Egyptian people. So these people who had in the past been the idolatrous oppressors of the Children of Israel will one day come to worship Yahweh! Similarly, Assyria, the powerful, expansionist kingdom to the north will one day come to worship the one true God!

Although the 'five cities' cannot be identified with any certainty, we know that from the time of the Exile in 586 BC there were Jewish colonies in several places in Egypt. Jeremiah speaks of Israelites living in the cities of 'Migdol, Tahpanhes and Memphis – and in Upper Egypt' (Jeremiah 44:1). It may well be that Isaiah is speaking figuratively and using ideas taken from the conquest of the land of Canaan. His idea would then be that just as the book of Joshua describes the conquest of the five Amorite cities in Canaan which led to the conquest of the whole land (Joshua 10), so now he speaks of the conversion of the five Egyptian cities as the beginning of the spiritual conquest of the whole land of Egypt. We know from archaeology that a garrison of Jewish mercenaries established themselves at Elephantine beside Aswan in Upper Egypt in 528

BC. And Philo the Jewish historian from Alexandria tells us that by his time (i.e. the time of Christ) there were a million Jews living in Egypt.

The 'altar to the Lord in the heart of Egypt' could be an echo of the altar which Jacob erected at Bethel (Genesis 28:18). In this case Isaiah is saying that 'Egypt is going to have its own Jacob-like figures who will meet with God as Jacob did at Bethel'. This is then followed by the prediction that Egypt will also experience its own exodus and deliverance from oppression (compare Exodus 2:23 – 3:10; 6:1–8). Thus the Egyptians will come to enjoy the same blessings as the Children of Israel had done in the past.

F2 Luke includes both Egypt and the area formerly known as Assyria in his list of places from which Jews came to Jerusalem for the day of Pentecost (Acts 2:9–10). Thus on the day when the church came into being we see people from Egypt and Assyria coming together to worship God in the name of Jesus. And it was not long before there were thriving, indigenous churches in both these areas. Thus there was a sense in which the Egyptians did 'know the Lord' during the first centuries of the Christian era. There was a strong monastic movement both in Egypt and the Fertile Crescent, and a great deal of coming and going between the monasteries in these two regions. During the medieval period also, continuous exchange between monasteries in Syria and Egypt meant that there was a well-worn 'highway' between these two areas.

The most striking echo of these ideas in the New Testament, however, is the way in which titles that are given by Isaiah to Egypt and Assyria are given to *all* believers in Christ. Thus Peter, writing to a mixture of Jewish and Gentile Christians says, in effect, 'You Gentiles are not foreigners or strangers any longer; you are now fellow citizens with God's people and members of God's family' (1 Peter 2:9–10). Similarly, Paul speaks of the church as God's 'workmanship' (Ephesians 2:10, RSV), echoing the description of Assyria as 'my handiwork'.

Some students of prophecy became very excited in 1958 when Egypt and Assyria joined together to form the United Arab Republic (UAR). Here, it was thought, was a very obvious and literal fulfilment in modern times of Isaiah's prophecy. The fact that this union came to an end a few years later in 1961, however, simply illustrates the difficulty in trying to relate Old Testament prophecy to events in contemporary history. What sense does it make to think that Isaiah, in the eighth century BC, was making a detailed prediction about an alliance between two countries in the Middle East in the twentieth century AD which would last for only three years?

In its original context Isaiah's prophecy would have sounded very shocking, because it was looking forward to the time when Egyptians and Assyrians, people who had been enemies of Israel in the past, would one day know Yahweh, the God of Israel. The main thrust of Isaiah's message, therefore, was that God was going to reveal himself to the most unlikely people!

Appendix 3
The Covenant of Hamas, the Islamic Resistance Movement[1]

Article	Issue addressed	Qur'an/Hadith ref.
1	Hamas is based on Islam.	
2	Hamas = Palestinian branch of Muslim Brotherhood.	
3	Hamas is for Muslims who favour Jihad.	Q21:18
4	Hamas welcomes every Muslim.	
5	Allah is target, Prophet is example, Qu'ran is constitution.	Q14:24–25
6	Hamas aims for every inch of Palestine.	
7	Hamas is a universal movement, for Muslims throughout the world. Struggle is indefinite.	Q5:48; Hadith
8	As per Article 5, plus Jihad is path, and death for the sake of Allah is the loftiest of its wishes.	
9	Hamas emerged from a State of decay of Islamic values; its objective is the establishment of the State of Islam.	Q2:251
10	Hamas supports the oppressed; fights injustice.	
11	Palestine is Islamic 'waqf' till Judgment Day. No part of it should be given up.	Q56:95
12	Fighting the enemy is the duty of every Muslim, male and female.	Q2:256
13	Hamas is opposed to initiatives, peaceful solutions and international conferences. Jihad is the only solution.	Q2:120
14	Palestine is sacred land.	Q17:1 and Q59:13
15	Islamic consciousness is to be instilled through the education system.	Hadith (x2)
16	Importance of Islamic curriculum, and the detailed study of the enemy.	Q31:16–18
17	Role of Muslim woman; avoid Western concepts.	
18	Woman's role: family, children and housekeeping.	Q33:25
19	Role of Islamic art in the battle for liberation.	
20	Society should unite – mutual responsibility.	
21	Support for those in need.	
22	Enemy (i.e. Jews) responsible for the French Revolution, the Communist Revolution, etc.	
	Allies of enemy: Freemasons, Rotary, Capitalist West, Communist East.	Q5:64;
	Enemy caused the First and Second World Wars, etc.	Q3:118
23	Hamas respects and appreciates other Islamic movements.	Q3:102
24	Hamas is against slander.	Q4:147–48
25	Hamas respects Palestinian nationalist movements.	Q44:6
26	Hamas will discuss new options with nationalists.	
27	PLO is kinsman with Hamas. But Hamas is against secularism. PLO should adopt Islam as its banner.	Q2:130
28	Arab and Islamic countries should assist the anti-Zionist struggle.	

29	Support from international Islamic community sought.	*Q58:21*
30	Beware of Zionist control of international finances and media. Jihad can be fought with various weapons.	*Hadith*
31	All can coexist under Islamic sovereignty.	*Q59:14 and Q60:8*
32	No concessions. Camp David was treachery. Zionists want to expand from the Nile to the Euphrates.	*Q5:114*
33	Appeal for funds to Allah-fearing Muslim nations.	*Q22:40*
34	As the Crusaders were defeated, so will the Zionists be.	*Hadith; Q3:12; Q37:171–72*
35	As the Crusaders and Tartars were defeated, so will the Zionists be.	
36	Hamas represents committed Muslims.	*Q7:89*

Notes

Introduction

1. David Ben-Gurion, quoted in Martin Gilbert, *Israel: A History*, London: Doubleday, 1998, p. 146.

2. Anton La Guardia, *Holy Land, Unholy War: Israelis and Palestinians*, London: John Murray, 2001, p. 43.

3. Bill Clinton's pastor, quoted in La Guardia, *Holy Land, Unholy War*, p. 327.

4. La Guardia, *Holy Land, Unholy War*, p. 9.

5. Edward Said, *The End of the Peace Process: Oslo and After*, Granta Books, 2000, p. 319.

6. David Ben-Gurion, quoted in Jonathan Quigley, *Palestine and Israel: A Challenge to Justice*, Duke University Press, 1990, p. 25.

7. Moshe Dayan, 14 May 1967, quoted in Gilbert, *Israel: A History*, p. 422.

8. Benny Morris, *Righteous Victims: A History of the Zionist-Arab Conflict, 1881–1999*, London: John Murray, 1999, p. 669.

9. La Guardia, *Holy Land, Unholy War*, p. 337.

10. David Grossman, 'Where Death is a Way of Life', *Guardian Weekly*, 17–23 June 2001.

Chapter 1: The Land in History: Basic Facts and Their Interpretation

1. John H. Davis, *The Evasive Peace: A Study of the Zionist-Arab Problem*, London: John Murray, 1968.

2. Norman G. Finkelstein, *Image and Reality of the Israel–Palestine Conflict*, London: Verso, 1995, p. 4.

3. David Ben-Gurion in 1938, quoted in Simha Flapan, *Zionism and the Palestinians*, Croom Helm, 1979, p. 141.

4. Morris, *Righteous Victims*, p. 652.

5. La Guardia, *Holy Land, Unholy War*, p. xi.

1.15 Conflicts since 1948

6. Morris, *Righteous Victims*, p. 596.

1.17 Jerusalem and the West Bank since 1967

7. Quigley, *Palestine and Israel*, p. 177.

Chapter 2: The Seeds of Conflict: Call the Next Witness

1. Najib Azuri, *Le réveil de la nation Arabe*, Paris: Libraire Plon, 1905.

2. Yitzhak Epstein, 'A Hidden Question', lecture at the Seventh Zionist Congress, Basle, 1905, reprinted in *New Outlook*, December 1985, p. 27.

3. Asher Ginsberg (Ahad Ha'Am), quoted in Moshe Menuhin, *The Decadence of Judaism in Our Time*, Beirut: Institute of Palestinian Studies, 1969.

4. David Ben-Gurion, quoted in Said, *The End of the Peace Process*, pp. 313–14.

5. Moshe Dayan, *Ha'olam Hazeh*, 8 July 1968.

6. Maxime Rodinson, *Israel and the Arabs*, London: Penguin, 1970, 1982.

2.1 Anti-Semitism

7. Theodor Herzl, quoted in John Bagot Glubb, *Peace in the Holy Land: An Historical Analysis of the Palestine Problem*, London: Hodder and Stoughton, 1971, p. 258.

8. Theodor Herzl, quoted in La Guardia, *Holy Land, Unholy War*, p. 168.

9. Max Nordau, quoted in David Vital, *The Origins of Zionism*, Oxford: Oxford University Press, 1975, pp. 362–66.

10. Max Nordau, quoted in Vital, *The Origins of Zionism*, pp. 362–66.

11. Dagobert D. Runes, *The Jew and the Cross*, New York: Philosophical Library, 1965, pp. 12, 14–15, 25, 40, 41, 61, 62, 87.

12. James Parkes, *The Emergence of the Jewish Problem (1878–1939)*, Oxford: Oxford University Press, 1946, pp. 195–98.

2.2 Zionism

13. Denys Baly, *Multitudes in the Valley: Church and Crisis in the Middle East*, New York: Seabury Press, 1957, pp. 22ff.

14. Vital, *The Origins of Zionism*, pp. 118–19.

15. Vital, *The Origins of Zionism*, pp. 128–31.

16. Noah Lucas, *A Modern History of Israel*, London: Weidenfeld and Nicolson, 1974, pp. 24–25, 27.

17. Theodor Herzl, *The Jewish State* (fifth edition), Henry Pordes, 1967.

18. Ahad Ha'Am, quoted in Vital, *The Origins of Zionism*, p. 373.

19. Vital, *The Origins of Zionism*, pp. 371–73.

20. Chaim Weizmann, 'States must be built up…', quoted in ESCO Zionist Institute, *Palestine: A Study of Jewish, Arab and British Policies*, vol. 1, New Haven: Yale University Press, pp. 98–99; 'The Balfour Declaration…' and 'I trust to God…', quoted in *Chaim Weizmann: Excerpts from His Historic Statements, Writings and Addresses*, New York: The Jewish Agency for Palestine, 1952, pp. 48, 302; 'All fears…', 'I need hardly say…' and 'The Zionists are not demanding…', quoted in Glubb, *Peace in the Holy Land*, pp. 266, 267, 277; 'Palestine must be built up…' and 'It is not our objective…', quoted in David Hirst, *The Gun and the Olive Branch: The Roots of Violence in the Middle East*, London: Futura, 1978, p. 39.

21. Sir Charles Webster, 'The Art and Practice of Diplomacy', *The Listener*, 28 February 1952.

2.3 Jewish settlement in the land

22. Hirst, *The Gun and the Olive Branch*, pp. 29, 78–79, 79–80.

23. David Ben-Gurion, *The History of the Haganah*, World Zionist Organization, 1954.

24. Joseph Weitz, *My Diary and Letters to the Children*, vol. 2, Tel Aviv: Massada, 1965, pp. 181–82.

25. Moshe Dayan, *Jerusalem Post*, 10 August 1967.

2.4 Arab reactions to Jewish settlement

26. Azuri, *Le réveil de la nation Arabe*, pp. 6ff.

27. Asher Ginsberg, 'Palestine is not an uninhabited country…' and 'As to the war…', quoted in Menuhin, *The Decadence of Judaism in Our Time*, 'We abroad…', quoted in H. Kohn, *Nationalism and Imperialism in the Hither East*, London, 1923, p. 126 (footnote).

28. The Emir Faisal and Chaim Weizmann, quoted in Davis, *The Evasive Peace*, pp. 14–15, 46.

29. Moshe Sharett, quoted in Davis, *The Evasive Peace*, p. 149.

30. David Ben-Gurion, quoted in Davis, *The Evasive Peace*, pp. 141–42.

31. Commander Hogarth, quoted in Davis, *The Evasive Peace*, p. 58.

32. Herbert Samuel, quoted in Davis, *The Evasive Peace*, p. 61.

33. Gilbert Clayton, quoted in Davis, *The Evasive Peace*, pp. 28–29.

34. Eric Mills, quoted in Naomi Shepherd, *Ploughing Sand: British Rule in Palestine*, London: John Murray, 1999, p. 97.

2.5 The role of Britain

35. Arthur Balfour, quoted in Oskar K. Rabinowicz, *Winston Churchill on Jewish Problems*, New York: Thomas Yoseloff, 1960, p. 167.

36. Arthur Koestler, *Promise and Fulfilment*, London: Macmillan, 1949, p. 4.

37. Sir Henry McMahon, quoted in George Antonius, *The Arab Awakening*, Beirut: Libraire du Liban, 1969, pp. 435–36.

38. Sir Edward Grey, quoted in Walid Khalidi (ed.), *From Haven to Conquest: Readings in Zionism and the Palestine Problem Until 1948*, Beirut: Institute for Palestine Studies, 1971, pp. 219–20.

39. Lord Balfour, quoted in Doreen Ingrams, *Palestine Papers 1917–1922*, London: John Murray, 1972, p. 73.

40. Erskine Childers, in *Jubilee Volume of the Netherlands–Arabia Association 1955–1966*, Leiden: E.J. Brill, 1966.

2.6 The role of the United Nations

41. Hirst, *The Gun and the Olive Branch*, pp. 131–32.

42. President Truman, 'I am sorry…', quoted in William Eddy, *FDR Meets Ibn Saud*, New York: American Friends of the Middle East, 1954, p. 36; 'The facts were…', in *Memoirs*, vol. 2, London: Doubleday, 1958, pp. 158ff.

43. Hirst, *The Gun and the Olive Branch*, p. 132.

44. Maxime Rodinson, 'Israel, fait colonial?', *Les Temps Modernes*, no. 253, 1967.

45. *Towards Understanding the Arab-Israeli Conflict*, London: British Council of Churches Report, 1982.

46. Edward Said, *The Question of Palestine*, New York: Vintage Books, 1980.

47. The Quaker Report, *The Search for Peace in the Middle East*, London: Friends Peace and International Relations Committee, 1970.

48. Erskine Childers, quoted in the *Jubilee Volume of the Netherlands–Arabia Association 1955–1966*.

2.7 Partition and war (1948–49)

49. Baly, *Multitudes in the Valley*, p. 85.

50. Morris, *Righteous Victims*, p. 206.

51. David Ben-Gurion, quoted in La Guardia, *Holy Land, Unholy War*, p. 188.

52. David Ben-Gurion, quoted in Gilbert, *Israel: A History*, p. 166.

53. David Ben-Gurion, *Rebirth and Destiny of Israel*, New York: Philosophical Library, 1954, pp. 530–31.

54. Joseph Weitz, quoted in Quigley, *Palestine and Israel*, p. 25.

55. Menachem Begin, quoted in Glubb, *Peace in the Holy Land*, p. 299.

56. Said, *The End of the Peace Process*, pp. 157–58.

57. Morris, *Righteous Victims*, p. 179.

58. Morris, *Righteous Victims*, pp. 207–208.

59. Morris, *Righteous Victims*, p. 209.

60. Edgar O'Ballance, *The Arab-Israeli War of 1948*, London: Faber and Faber, 1956, p. 64.

61. I.F. Stone, quoted in Department of Information and Interpretation of the Middle East Council of Churches, *Zionism: A Preliminary Memo*, Geneva: Commission of the Churches on International Affairs of the World Council of Churches, 1976, pp. 30–31.

62. Benny Morris, quoted in Finkelstein, *Image and Reality of the Israel–Palestine Conflict*, p. 52.

63. Finkelstein, *Image and Reality of the Israel–Palestine Conflict*, p. 54.

64. Yitzhak Rabin, quoted in Gilbert, *Israel: A History*, p. 486.

65. Joseph Weitz, quoted in Gilbert, *Israel: A History*, p. 159.

66. Joseph Weitz, quoted in Gilbert, *Israel: A History*, p. 714.

67. Yigal Allon, *Ha Sepher La Palmach*, vol. 2, pp. 43, 286.

68. Chaim Weizmann, quoted in James McDonald, *My Mission to Israel*, New York: Simon and Schuster, 1952, p. 176.

69. Davis, *The Evasive Peace*, p. 121.

2.8 The voice of Israel

70. David Ben-Gurion, quoted in Davis, *The Evasive Peace*, p. 84.

71. Abba Eban, *An Autobiography*, London: Weidenfeld and Nicholson, 1978, p. 609.

72. Moshe Davis, *I Am a Jew*, London: Mowbray, 1978, p. 88.

73. Golda Meir, quoted in Hirst, *The Gun and the Olive Branch*.

74. Moshe Dayan, *Story of My Life*, London: Weidenfeld and Nicolson, 1976, pp. 58–59.

75. W. Laqueur, *A History of Zionism*, New York: Schocken Books, 1978, pp. 595–97.

76. Ecumenical Theological Research Fraternity in Israel, *An Appeal to the Churches Around the World*, Geneva: Commission of the Churches on International Affairs of the World Council of Churches, 1976.

77. Moshe Dayan, quoted in Gilbert, *Israel: A History*, pp. 311–12.

78. Yitzhak Rabin, quoted in Gilbert, *Israel: A History*, p. 567.

79. La Guardia, *Holy Land, Unholy War*, p. 9.

80. La Guardia, *Holy Land, Unholy War*, p. 136.

81. Gilbert, *Israel: A History*, pp. 406–407.

82. Rabbi Shlomo Avner, quoted in Gilbert, *Israel: A History*, p. 524.

83. *Gush Emunim*, quoted in Gilbert, *Israel: A History*, p. 469.

84. Morris, *Righteous Victims*, pp. 659–60.

2.9 Other Jewish/Israeli voices

85. Board of Deputies of British Jews and the Anglo-Jewish Association, *The Times*, May 1917.

86. Asher Ginsberg, quoted in Hans Kohn, 'Zion and the Jewish National Idea', *Menorah Journal*, Autumn–Winter 1958, pp. 39ff.

87. Albert Einstein, *Out of My Later Years*, New York: Philosophical Library, 1950, pp. 262ff.

88. Rabbi Benjamin, quoted in James and Marti Hefley, *Arabs, Christians and Jews*, Logos International, 1978, p. 149.

89. Marc Ellis, 'A Place for Palestinians in Passover Prayers', *Houston Chronicle*, 11 April 2001.

90. Abba Eban, quoted in Gilbert, *Israel: A History*, p. 514.

91. Arie Lova Eliav, quoted in Gilbert, *Israel: A History*, pp. 529–30.

92. Benny Barabash, quoted in Gilbert, Israel: A History, p. 401.

93. Quoted in Gilbert, *Israel: A History*, p. 401.

94. Ze'ev Schiff, quoted in Gilbert, *Israel: A History*, p. 512.

95. La Guardia, *Holy Land, Unholy War*, p. 134.

96. La Guardia, *Holy Land, Unholy War*, p. 270.

97. La Guardia, *Holy Land, Unholy War*, p. 125.

2.10 The different voices of the Palestinians

98. Everett Mendelsohn, in the Quaker Report, *A Compassionate Peace*, London: Penguin, 1982, p. 40.

99. Said, *The Question of Palestine*, pp. 51, 117–18.

100. La Guardia, *Holy Land, Unholy War*, p. 114.

101. Davis, *The Evasive Peace*.

102. Abdel-Shai, quoted in La Guardia, *Holy Land, Unholy War*, p. 157.

103. Fawaz Turki, *The Disinherited*, New York: Monthly Review Press, 1974, p. 168.

104. Said, *The Question of Palestine*, pp. 125–26.

105. La Guardia, *Holy Land, Unholy War*, p. 119.

106. Tawfiq Zayyad, *Baqun* ('We Shall Remain'), in *Enemy of the Sun: Poetry of Palestinian Resistance*, ed. Naseer Arari and Edmund Ghareeb, Washington: Drum and Spear Press, 1970, p. 66.

107. Kamal Nasr, *Jirah Tughanni*, Beirut, 1960.

108. Mahmoud Darwish, quoted in La Guardia, *Holy Land, Unholy War*, p. 3.

109. Mendelsohn, *A Compassionate Peace*, pp. 42–43, 44, 47–48.

110. Yehoshafat Harkabi, *Guardian Weekly*, 14 August 1988.

111. *Palestine National Charter*, quoted in Walter Laqueur and Barry Rubins (eds), *The Israel-Arab Reader: A Documentary History of the Middle East Conflict*, Gretna: Pelican, 1984, pp. 366–69.

112. Hirst, *The Gun and the Olive Branch*, p. 292.

113. Salah Ta'mari, quoted in La Guardia, *Holy Land, Unholy War*, p. 147.

114. Quoted in Hirst, *The Gun and the Olive Branch*, pp. 336–37.

115. Palestinian Declaration of Independence.

116. Peter Riddell, 'From Qur'an to Contemporary Politics: *Hamas* and the Role of Sacred Scripture', in Christopher Partridge (ed.), *Fundamentalisms*, Paternoster, to be published 2002.

117. Said, *The End of the Peace Process*, p. 190.

118. Said, *The End of the Peace Process*, p. 164.

119. Edward Said, *Guardian Weekly*, 8 May 1988.

120. Said, *The End of the Peace Process*, pp. 188–89.

121. Said, *The End of the Peace Process*, p. 126.

122. Said, *The End of the Peace Process*, p. 246.

123. Said, *The End of the Peace Process*, p. 152.

124. Said, *The End of the Peace Process*, p. 136.

125. Said, *The End of the Peace Process*, p. 232.

126. Said, *The End of the Peace Process*, p. 126.

127. Said, *The End of the Peace Process*, p. 192.

128. Said, *The End of the Peace Process*, p. 198.

129. Said, *The End of the Peace Process*, p. 166.

130. Said, *The End of the Peace Process*, p. 112.

131. Said, *The End of the Peace Process*, p. 315.

2.11 Conclusions

132. Morris, *Righteous Victims*, p. 661.

133. Morris, *Righteous Victims*, p. 652.

134. Morris, *Righteous Victims*, p. 654.

135. Morris, *Righteous Victims*, p. 654.

136. Morris, *Righteous Victims*, p. 656.

Chapter 3: The Land *Before* Christ: 'A Land Flowing with Milk and Honey'

1. Walter Brueggemann, *The Land: Place as Gift, Promise and Challenge in Biblical Faith*, London: SPCK, 1978, p. 3.

2. E.A. Martens, *God's Design: A Focus on Old Testament Theology*, Leicester: Apollos, 1994, p. 121.

3. Peter Walker, 'The Land in the New Testament: The Land in the Apostles' Writings', in Philip Johnston and Peter Walker (eds), *The Land of Promise: Biblical, Theological and Contemporary Perspectives*, Leicester: Apollos, 2000, p. 87.

3.2 The boundaries of the land

4. Paul R. Williamson, 'The Land in Israel's Story: Promise and Fulfilment of the Territorial Inheritance', in Johnston and Walker (eds), *The Land of Promise*, pp. 21–22.

3.3 The conquest of the land

5. Alan Millard, 'The Cities of Conquest', in *The Lion Handbook to the Bible*, Oxford: Lion Publishing, 1989, p. 213.

3.4 The land and the temple

6. N.T. Wright, *Jesus and the Victory of God*, London: SPCK, 1996, p. 205.

7. Peter Walker, 'The Land and Jesus Himself', in Johnston and Walker (eds), *The Land of Promise*, p. 101.

8. R. Kreider, 'The Covenant and the Land' (unpublished paper), in Johnston and Walker (eds), *The Land of Promise*, p. 101.

9. W.D. Davies, *The Gospel and the Land: Early Christianity and Jewish Territorial Doctrine*, Berkeley: University of California Press, 1974, p. 152.

3.6 The return to the land

10. Davies, *The Gospel and the Land*, p. 95.

11. Dagobert D. Runes, quoted in Davies, *The Gospel and the Land*, p. 122.

3.7 The land and the hopes of Israel

12. *The Lion Handbook to the Bible* (second revised edition), Oxford: Lion Publishing, 1983, p. 429.

Chapter 4: The Land *After* Christ: 'The Meek Shall Inherit the Earth'

1. Davies, *The Gospel and the Land*, p. 375.

2. O. Palmer Robertson, 'A New Covenant Perspective on the Land', in Johnston and Walker (eds), *The Land of Promise*, p. 139.

3. Davies, *The Gospel and the Land*, pp. 178, 179, 182, 213, 217.

4. D.E. Holwerda, *Jesus and Israel: One Covenant or Two?*, Leicester: Apollos, 1995, p. 104.

5. N.T. Wright, *The New Testament and the People of God*, London: SPCK, 1992, p. 366.

4.1 The birth of Jesus the Messiah

6. Wright, *The New Testament and the People of God*, p. 300.

7. Wright, *The New Testament and the People of God*, p. 459.

4.2 Jesus and the land

8. Davies, *The Gospel and the Land*, p. 68.

9. Wright, *The New Testament and the People of God*, p. 302.

10. Wright, *The New Testament and the People of God*, p. 476.

11. Kittel, *Theological Dictionary of the New Testament*, vol. VI, p. 36.

12. R.T. France, 'Old Testament Prophecy and the Future of Israel: A Study in the Teaching of Jesus', *Tyndale Bulletin*, no. 26, 1975, p. 58.

13. France, 'Old Testament Prophecy and the Future of Israel', *Tyndale Bulletin*, p. 73.

14. Wright, *Jesus and the Victory of God*, p. 446.

15. Wright, *Jesus and the Victory of God*, p. 471.

4.3 Jesus and Jerusalem

16. France, 'Old Testament Prophecy and the Future of Israel', *Tyndale Bulletin*, p. 68.

17. Wright, *Jesus and the Victory of God*, pp. 517, 537.

18. R.T. France, *Jesus and the Old Testament*, Tyndale Press, 1971, pp. 227–39.

19. Wright, *Jesus and the Victory of God*, p. 521.

20. John Nolland, *Word Biblical Commentary: Luke 18:35 – 24:53*, Dallas: Word Books, 1993, pp. 1002–1003.

4.4 The redemption of Israel

21. John Calvin, *Commentary on the Acts of the Apostles*, tr. W.J.D. McDonald, Grand Rapids: Eerdmans, 1989, p. 29.

22. Johnston and Walker (eds), *The Land of Promise*, p. 108.

23. Wright, *The New Testament and the People of God*, p. 476.

4.5 The land in the teaching of the apostles

24. Wright, *The New Testament and the People of God*, p. 367.

25. Kenneth E. Bailey, 'St Paul's Understanding of the Territorial Promise of God to Abraham: Romans 4:13 in its Historical/Theological Context', *Near East School of Theology Review*, 15.1, 1994, p. 63.

26. C.J.H. Wright, 'A Christian Approach to Old Testament Prophecy Concerning Israel', in Peter Walker (ed.), *Jerusalem Past and Present in the Purposes of God*, Carlisle: Paternoster, 1994, p. 18.

4.6 John's vision of the final fulfilment of the covenant

27. Wright, *Jesus and the Victory of God*, pp. 435, 526.

28. Wright, *The New Testament and the People of God*, p. 451.

4.7 The land and the millennium

29. Anthony A. Hoekema, 'Amillennialism', in Robert G. Clouse, *The Meaning of the Millennium: Four Views*, Downers Grove: InterVarsity Press, 1977, pp. 161–69.

Chapter 5: Other Biblical Themes: 'Is There Any Word from the Lord?'

1. Rabbi Elmer Berger, 'Prophecy, Zionism and the State of Israel', an address delivered at the University of Leiden, Holland, 20 March 1968, published by Arnold J. Toynbee, p. 17.

2. Baly, *Multitudes in the Valley*, p. 268.

3. Naim Stefan Ateek, *Justice and Only Justice: A Palestinian Theology of Liberation*, Orbis, 1989, p. 111.

5.1 A passion for truth

4. Walter Barker, *Third Way*, February 1981, p. 24.

5. Margaret Brearley, *A Christian Response to the Middle East and the Palestinian Question*, The Anglo-Israel Association, 1988, p. 3.

6. Edward Said, 'Propaganda and War', *Al-Ahram Weekly*, 30 August–5 September, 2001.

7. William Zuckermann, *Jewish Newsletter*, 7 December 1958.

8. General Carl von Horn, *Soldiering for Peace*, London: Cassell, 1966, p. 85.

9. The Quaker Report, *The Search for Peace in the Middle East*, pp. 5–7.

10. Von Horn, *Soldiering for Peace*, pp. 282ff.

11. Stephen Sizer, book review in *Al-Aqsa*, vol. 2, no. 22, Leicester: Friends of *Al-Aqsa*, April 2000.

12. Baly, *Multitudes in the Valley*, pp. 96, 268, 281–83.

13. Said, *The End of the Peace Process*, p. 123.

5.2 The problem of prejudice

14. Mark Twain, quoted in La Guardia, *Holy Land, Unholy War*, p. 11.

15. Wright, *Jesus and the Victory of God*, pp. 404–405.

16. The Quaker Report, *The Search for Peace in the Middle East*, p. 7.

17. Denys Baly, 'The Things that Belong unto Peace', The Sprigg Lectures, 1971, quoted in Johan Bouman, *Biblical Interpretation... and the Middle East*, Geneva: World Council of Churches, 1974, pp. 40–41.

5.3 The demands of the law

18. Chaim Weizmann, quoted in Gilbert, *Israel: A History*, p. 139.

19. Chaim Weizmann, 'In all humbleness...', in *Report of the UN Special Committee on Palestine*, Document A/364, 1947, p. 77.

20. W. Brunn, quoted in Department of Information and Interpretation of the Middle East Council of Churches, *Zionism: A Preliminary Memo*, p. 30.

21. Flapan, *Zionism and the Palestinians*, pp. 12, 78–79, 83.

22. David Ben-Gurion, quoted in I.F. Stone, 'For a New Approach to the Israeli-Arab Conflict', *The New York Review of Books*, 3 August 1967.

23. Golda Meir, *The Sunday Times*, 15 June 1969.

24. Samuel Katz, *The Jewish Presence in Palestine*, Israel Academic Committee on the Middle East, p. 35.

25. Menachem Begin, *The History of the Haganah*, World Zionist Organization, 1954.

26. Nahum Goldmann, quoted in Flapan, *Zionism and the Palestinians*, p. 126.

27. La Guardia, *Holy Land, Unholy War*, p. 204.

28. Chaim Weizmann, *Trial and Error*, 1949.

5.4 The prophetic concern for justice

29. Derek Prince, *The Destiny of Israel and the Church: Restoration and Redemption at the End of the Age*, Derek Prince Ministries, 1999, pp. 73–74.

30. Ateek, *Justice and Only Justice*, p. 87.

31. Max Nordau, quoted in Hirst, *The Gun and the Olive Branch*, p. 19.

32. Moshe Dayan, in *Haaretz*, 4 April 1969.

33. Nathan Chofshi, *The Jewish Newsletter*, 9 February 1959.

34. Martin Buber, quoted in Gilbert, *Israel: A History*, p. 256.

35. Chaim Weizmann, quoted in Lucas Grollenberg, *Palestine Comes First*, SCM Press, 1980, p. 6.

36. 'Declaration of Independence', in Laqueur and Rubins (eds), *The Israel–Arab Reader*, p. 127.

37. Professor J.L. Talmon, quoted in Saul Bellow, *To Jerusalem and Back*, London: Penguin, 1977, pp. 135–36.

38. Rabbi Elmer Berger, 'Prophecy, Zionism and the State of Israel', p. 17.

5.5 God's judgment in history

39. Stephen Neill, 'The Wrath of God and the Peace of God', in Max Warren, *Interpreting the Cross*, London: SCM Press, 1966, pp. 22–23.

40. Baly, *Multitudes in the Valley*, p. 258.

5.6 Suffering injustice

41. The Quaker Report, *The Search for Peace in the Middle East*, pp. 8–9.

42. La Guardia, *Holy Land, Unholy War*, pp. 156–57.

43. Baly, *Multitudes in the Valley*, pp. 277–78.

44. Ateek, *Justice and Only Justice*, p. 134.

45. Baly, *Multitudes in the Valley*, p. 300.

5.7 Rethinking and repentance through disaster

46. Norman Solomon, *Jewish Responses to the Holocaust*, Selly Oak Colleges, Birmingham: Centre for the Study of Judaism and Jewish/Christian Relations, 1988, p. 23.

47. La Guardia, *Holy Land, Unholy War*, p. 155.

48. Solomon, *Jewish Responses to the Holocaust*, p. 1.

49. Solomon, *Jewish Responses to the Holocaust*, p. 8.

50. Solomon, *Jewish Responses to the Holocaust* p. 7.

51. Rabbi Irwing Greenberg, quoted in Solomon, *Jewish Responses to the Holocaust*, p. 12.

52. Solomon, *Jewish Responses to the Holocaust*, p. 15.

53. Solomon, *Jewish Responses to the Holocaust*, pp. 15, 17.

54. Ateek, *Justice and Only Justice*, pp. 168–69.

55. Ateek, *Justice and Only Justice*, pp. 170–71.

5.8 Jew and Gentile in the Old Testament

56. Haim Cohen, quoted in Joseph Badi, *Fundamental Laws of the State of Israel*, New York: Twaine Publishers, 1960, p. 156.

57. I.F. Stone, quoted in *Zionism: A Preliminary Memo*, pp. 31–32.

5.9 Jew and Gentile after Jesus the Messiah

58. Quoted in La Guardia, *Holy Land, Unholy War*, p. 47.

59. Rabbi Yitzhak Ginsburg, quoted in Gilbert, *Israel: A History*, p. 539.

60. N.T. Wright, *The Climax of the Covenant: Christ and the Law in Pauline Theology*, London: T. & T. Clark, 1991, p. 240.

61. C.H. Dodd, quoted in France, 'Old Testament Prophecy and the Future of Israel', *Tyndale Bulletin*, No. 26, p. 68.

62. Wright, *Jesus and the Victory of God*, pp. 517, 537.

63. John Goldingay, 'The Jews, the Land and the Kingdom', *Anvil*, vol. 4, no. 1, 1987, p. 10.

64. Wright, *The New Testament and the People of God*, pp. 447, 457–58.

65. Kenneth Cragg, *Bible Lands*, Jerusalem and the Middle East Church Association, spring 1982, pp. 24–26.

5.10 The condemnation of anti-Semitism

66. Solomon, *Jewish Responses to the Holocaust*, p. 18.

67. Wright, *The Climax of the Covenant*, p. 234.

68. Wright, *The Climax of the Covenant*, p. 253.

69. Peter Schneider, *The Christian Debate on Israel*, Selly Oak Colleges, Birmingham: Centre for the Study of Judaism and Jewish/Christian Relations, 1985.

70. Wright, *The Climax of the Covenant*, pp. 282–83.

5.11 The possibility of reconciliation

71. Eyad El-Sarraj, email 31, 2001, the Washington Post Company.

72. Wright, *Jesus and the Victory of God*, p. 240.

73. Ateek, *Justice and Only Justice*, p. 184.

74. Kenneth Bailey, extract from 'Ode on a Burning Tank: The Holy Lands, October 1973', in *Through Peasant Eyes: More Lucan Parables*, Eerdmans, 1980, pp. 71–73.

Chapter 6: Realities Today: Is There Any Hope of Resolving the Conflict?

1. Weizmann, *Trial and Error*, 1949.

2. Shimon Peres, quoted in Gilbert, *Israel: A History*, p. 550.

3. La Guardia, *Holy Land, Unholy War*, p. 189.

4. La Guardia, *Holy Land, Unholy War*, pp. xi, 268.

5. Gilbert, *Israel: A History*, p. 566.

6. David Ben-Gurion, quoted in Anthony Lewis, 'At Home and Abroad: The Price of Occupation', *New York Times*, 2 June 2001.

6.1 A crisis for Zionism

7. Finkelstein, *Image and Reality of the Israel–Palestine Conflict*, p. 105.

8. Vital, *The Origins of Zionism*, p. 87.

9. Flapan, *Zionism and the Palestinians*, pp. 11–12.

10. David Ben-Gurion, quoted in Finkelstein, *Image and Reality of the Israel–Palestine Conflict*, p. 110.

11. David Millard, quoted in *Arabia: Islamic World Review*, 1985.

12. Hirst, *The Gun and the Olive Branch*, pp. 18–19.

13. Finkelstein, *Image and Reality of the Israel–Palestine Conflict*, pp. 104, 109.

14. Arthur Ruppin, quoted in Quigley, *Palestine and Israel*, p. 20.

15. Finkelstein, *Image and Reality of the Israel–Palestine Conflict*, p. 8.

16. Paul Mendes-Flohr, *Jerusalem Post Magazine*, 4 March 1988.

17. Gaston Thorn, quoted in Gilbert, *Israel: A History*, p. 468.

18. Said, *The End of the Peace Process*, pp. 203, 268.

19. Finkelstein, *Image and Reality of the Israel–Palestine Conflict*, p. 12.

20. Morris Cohen, quoted in Quigley, *Palestine and Israel*, p. 12.

21. Andrew Kirk, 'The Middle East Dilemma: A Personal Reflection', *Anvil*, vol. 3, 1986, pp. 238, 255.

22. Paul Mendes-Flohr, *Jerusalem Post Magazine*, 4 March 1988.

6.2 The power equation in the world today

This section is adapted from an article, 'Peace Under Siege', in *New Routes: Journal of the Life and Peace Institute*, vol. 6, no. 1, Uppsala, Sweden: Life and Peace Institute, 2001, pp. 12–19.

23. Edward Said, 'The Misunderstood and Misjudged Role of American Zionism in the Question of Palestine', *Al-Ahram*, 23 October 2000.

24. Patrick Seale, *Asad: The Struggle for the Middle East*, Berkeley: University of California Press, 1990.

25. Yitzhak Rabin, quoted in Gilbert, *Israel: A History*, p. 470.

26. Chaim Weizmann, quoted in Gilbert, *Israel: A History*, p. 150.

27. Grace Halsell, *Prophecy and Politics: Militant Evangelists on the Road to Nuclear War*, Lawrence Hill & Co., 1986.

28. Timothy P. Weber, 'How Evangelicals Became Israel's Best Friends', *Christianity Today*, 5 October 1998, p. 39.

6.3 Christian Zionism and Dispensationalism

29. Stephen Sizer, 'Christian Zionism and its Impact on Justice', *Al-Aqsa Journal*, October 2000, p. 9.

30. Sinclair B. Ferguson, David F. Wright and J.I. Packer (eds), *New Dictionary of Theology*, InterVarsity Press, 1988, p. 200, under 'Dispensational Theology'.

31. Weber, 'How Evangelicals Became Israel's Best Friends', *Christianity Today*, p. 41.

32. Stephen Sizer, 'Dispensational Approaches to the Land', in Johnston and Walker (eds), *The Land of Promise*, p. 142.

33. Sizer, 'Dispensational Approaches to the Land', in Johnston and Walker (eds), *The Land of Promise*, p. 146.

34. Third International Christian Zionist Congress in 1996, quoted in Sizer, 'Christian Zionism and its Impact on Justice', *Al-Aqsa Journal*, p. 11.

35. David Stern, *Making the Issues Clear: The Land from a Messianic Jewish Perspective*, Jerusalem: Musalaha, 2000, pp. 41–42.

36. London Jews Society, quoted in Kelvin Crombie, *For the Love of Zion: Christian Witness and the Restoration of Israel*, London: Hodder and Stoughton, 1991, p. 140.

37. Revd Mansell, quoted in Crombie, *For the Love of Zion*, p. 222.

38. Walter Riggans, *Israel and Zionism*, The Handsell Press, 1988, p. 19.

39. London Jews Society, quoted in Crombie, *For the Love of Zion*, p. 176.

40. Louis Talbot, quoted in Weber, 'How Evangelicals Became Israel's Best Friends', *Christianity Today*, p. 45.

41. Nelson Bell, quoted in Weber, 'How Evangelicals Became Israel's Best Friends', *Christianity Today*, p. 45.

42. David Pawson, address at the Christian Zionist Congress, Basle, August 1985.

43. Third International Christian Zionist Congress in 1996, quoted in Sizer, 'Christian Zionism and its Impact on Justice', *Al-Aqsa Journal*, p. 11.

44. Riggans, *Israel and Zionism*, p. 21.

45. Cyrus I. Schofield, quoted in Sizer, 'Dispensational Approaches to the Land' in Johnston and Walker (eds), *The Land of Promise*, p. 145.

46. Sizer, 'Dispensational Approaches to the Land', in Johnston and Walker (eds), *The Land of Promise*, p. 146.

47. Ferguson, Wright and Packer (eds), *New Dictionary of Theology*, p. 201, under 'Dispensational Theology'.

48. Ryrie, quoted in Sizer, 'Dispensational Approaches to the Land', in Johnston and Walker (eds), *The Land of Promise*, p. 144.

49. Lewis Sperry Chafer, quoted in Sizer, 'Dispensational Approaches to the Land', in Johnston and Walker (eds), *The Land of Promise*, pp. 144–45.

50. Weber, 'How Evangelicals Became Israel's Best Friends', *Christianity Today*, p. 41.

51. Halsell, *Prophecy and Politics*.

52. DeMar and Leithart, quoted in Sizer, 'Dispensational Approaches to the Land', in Johnston and Walker (eds), *The Land of Promise*, p. 147.

53. Weber, 'How Evangelicals Became Israel's Best Friends', *Christianity Today*, p. 39.

54. Sizer, 'Dispensational Approaches to the Land', in Johnston and Walker (eds), *The Land of Promise*, pp. 166–67.

55. Middle East Council of Churches, quoted in Sizer, 'Dispensational Approaches to the Land', in Johnston and Walker (eds), *The Land of Promise*, pp. 166–67.

6.4 Zionism and Islam

56. See, for example, Zaki Badawi, 'Jerusalem and Islam', in Ghada Karmi (ed.), *Jerusalem Today: What Future for the Peace Process?*, Ithaca, 1997, pp. 137–43, and H.S. Karmi, *How Holy is Palestine to Muslims?*, Islamic Cultural Press, pp. 1–28.

57. Quoted in Karmi, *How Holy is Palestine to Muslims?*, p. 5.

58. *Encyclopedia of Islam* (new edition), vol. IV, p. 84, under *Isa*.

59. Karmi, *How Holy is Palestine to Muslims?*, p. 6.

60. Badawi, 'Jerusalem and Islam', in Karmi (ed.), *Jerusalem Today*, p. 141.

61. Saladin, quoted in K.J. Asali (ed.), *Jerusalem in History*, London, 1989, p. 179.

62. Karmi, *How Holy is Palestine to Muslims?*, pp. 18–19, 25–26.

63. Abdul-Majid Davies, *Q-News*, January 1998, p. 34.

64. Father John Sansour, 'Hearing the Different Voices: Issues Amongst Jews, Christians and Muslims', in L. Loden, P. Walker and M. Wood (eds), *The Bible and the Land: An Encounter*, Jerusalem: Musalaha, 2000, pp. 141–43.

65. William Montgomery Watt, *Muhammad: Prophet and Statesman*, Oxford: Oxford University Press, 1975, p. 193.

66. Badawi, 'Jerusalem and Islam', in Karmi (ed.), *Jerusalem Today*, p. 142.

67. Peter Riddell, 'From Qur'an to Contemporary Politics: *Hamas* and the Role of Sacred Scripture', in Christopher Partridge (ed.), *Fundamentalisms*, Paternoster, to be published 2002.

68. Riddell, 'From Qur'an to Contemporary Politics', in Partridge (ed.), *Fundamentalisms*.

69. Riddell, 'From Qur'an to Contemporary Politics', in Partridge (ed.), *Fundamentalisms*.

70. Riddell, 'From Qur'an to Contemporary Politics', in Partridge (ed.), *Fundamentalisms*.

71. Riddell, 'From Qur'an to Contemporary Politics', in Partridge (ed.), *Fundamentalisms*.

72. Riddell, 'From Qur'an to Contemporary Politics', in Partridge (ed.), *Fundamentalisms*.

Appendix 1: Principles of Christian Interpretation of Old Testament Prophecy

1. James I. Packer, 'Infallible Scriptures and Hermeneutics', in Carson and Woodbridge (eds), *Scripture and Truth*, Grand Rapids: Zondervan, p. 346.

2. 'The Jews, the Land and the Kingdom', *Anvil*, vol. 4, no. 1, 1987, p. 17.

Appendix 3: The Covenant of Hamas, the Islamic Resistance Movement

1. Riddell, 'From Qur'an to Contemporary Politics', in Partridge (ed.), *Fundamentalisms*.

Index of Biblical Passages

Genesis

1–2   216
3–11   216
12:1–3   114, 216
12:5   117
12:6–20   115
15:4–6   116
15:7–8   134
15:13–14, 16   119, 122
15:18   114, 117
15:19–21   22, 117
16:1–16   116
17:1, 8   14, 114
17:7–11, 13   114
18:1–15   116
21:1–7   116
22   115
22:16–18   116
23:17–18   115
26:2–4   116
28:13–15 116, 158
28:18   302, 304
33:10   234
50:22–26   119

Exodus

2:14   187
2:15–22   218
2:23–3:10   302
3:8   113
4:22–23   226
6:1–8   302
19:6   163
20:13, 15, 17   190
21:12–14   190
22:21   191
23:9   191
23:31   117

25:8   126
29:44–46   126
40:34–35   126

Leviticus

11:45   216
18:24–27   122
18:28   123
25:23   122, 285
26:1–45   123

Deuteronomy

1:8   122
4:25–27   127
7:1–4   217
7:6   216
8:19   124
9:1, 4–6   124
11:24   118
13:1–18   123
18:9–15   123
18:30   123
19:2   123
19:14   190
20:18   123
27:15–26 123, 190
28:1–68   123
30:1–5130
34:1–3   118

Joshua

1:4   118
1:11   163
2:1–6:25   218
5:13–6:27   119
7   163
8:1–10:45   119
9:1–27   119

10   302
11   119
11:23   163
13:1–32   119
14:15   163
21:44   119
23:1   119

Judges

1:1–36   119

Ruth

1:16   218

2 Samuel

7:11–14, 16   43
12:1–7   195

1 Kings

4:24–25   118
8:12–13   126
8:27–30   126
8:60   126
9:3   290
9:6–7   127
17:1   195
21:2   195

2 Kings

17:5–8, 18   128
24:13–14, 20   129
25:8–12, 21   129

1 Chronicles

9:2   132
23:13   289

2 Chronicles
9:26   118
36:22–23   132, 291

Ezra
1:1–3   132, 291
2:1   132
9:1–2   218
10:10–11   218

Psalms
23:1   226
37   147, 260
78:52–55   162
80:8–16   226
89:3–4   289
106:6   188
107   149–50
137:1–4   129–30

Isaiah
5:1–7   226
6:5   188
7:17, 20   201
10   201–2
13   156
13:10   153
19   219, 302–3
27:9   229
27:13   155
33   158
35:1–10   134–35, 287
40:1–10   130–31
42:1–7   207, 226
43:5–7   149
47   158
49:1–7   226
50:4–9   226
52:13–53:12   226
53:3   209
53:4–9   208
56:1–8   219–20
59:1–11   198–99
59:12–15   182
59:15–18   207
59:20–21   229
61:1–2   148–49

Jeremiah
7:28–29   182
9:5–6   182

9:13–16   128
12:7–11   128
16:14–15   131
24:5–7   135
29:10–14   131
31:33–34   229
37:16–17   179
44:1   303
50–51   158

Lamentations
2:14   211
2:17   211
3:19–42   212–13
3:40   238
4:13   211
5:7   211

Ezekiel
1:1   287
11:14, 16–18   132
34:1–31   226
35:1, 10   287
36   135–36, 287, 289
37   135–36
38   136
38–39   136
40–48   136
40:1–2   136
43:1–9   136
47   136
47:13–23   136

Daniel
7:13–28   153–54, 226
9:26–27   158
11:31   152
12:11   152

Hosea
6:1–2   151
11:1   226

Joel
3:18, 20   170, 301

Amos
3:2   197, 217
5:10   182
5:21–24   197–98
9:7   217
9:8–15   295–96

Micah
3:8   198
3:11   217
4:1   198

Habakkuk
1:2–4   203
1:11–2:3   158
1:12–13   204
2   204–205

Haggai
2:6   167

Zechariah
2:6–7   155
2:12   267
10:6–10   137–38, 288–89
12:1–10   291, 299–300
14   170, 200, 301–302

Matthew
2:13–15   223
4:1–6   223
5:3–10   146
5:5   141, 260
5:23–24   234
5:43–45   233
7:5   188
8:10–12   149
11:27   226
16:18   299
16:27   300
21:24   300
21:44   299–300
22:39   233
24:30   300
24:31   155
25:31   300
28:19–20   223

Mark
1:15   146, 260, 301
2:10   226
8:31   151, 226
9:1   154, 301
10:45   226
11:15–17   301
13   152–56
14:62   226

Luke

1:30–33   142, 259, 291
1:46–55   143
1:68–75   143–44
1:76–79   144
2:25–26   144, 157
2:29–32   144
2:36–38   145
3:23–38   259
4:17–21   148
7:21–22   148
12:13–16   187
18:31–33   151
21:20–28   156–57, 260
22:20   298
24:1   157
24:13–35   260

John

1:14   169, 261, 298
2:13–19   301
2:18–22   169, 298
2:26   298
7:37–39   171, 259, 301
8:1–11   187–88
10   226
11:51–52   150, 298
12:32–33   223
14:5–14   226
15:1–17   226
19:33–37   292
20:1   236

Acts

1:1–8   163, 260
2:9–10   304
2:30–31   161

2:36   161
2:47   163
4:12   301
5:1–11   163
6:7   163
9:31   163
12:24   163
13:49   163
15   295–96
19:20   163
20:32   163, 260

Romans

2:25, 28–29   227
4:13   164
5:12–21   223
9 – 11   164, 223, 227–28, 230

2 Corinthians

1:21   164
5:19   238

Galatians

3:26–29   165, 222, 238
4:24–26   165
6:14–16   166

Ephesians

2:10   303–304
2:14–20, **3:6**   222, 238
4:32   234

1 Thessalonians

2:14–16   165

Hebrews

1:1–2   124

3:12–4:11   167
4   167
6:13–20   167
8:1   167
8:7–13   298
9:14   298
10:11–21   166–67
11:9–16   167
12   167
13:10–14   167
13:20   298

James

3:17–18   10

1 Peter

1:3–5   162, 260
2:9–10   162–63, 222–24, 262,
    298, 303–304
3:9   298

2 Peter

3:3–4   265

1 John

1:7   298

Revelation

1:5–7   292, 300
7:4–9   172
11:15–17   301
20:1   172–73, 175, 299–300,
    302
21   169, 172, 298, 302
21:1–22:6   291

General Index

Abbasids   26

Abdel-Shai   94

Abraham 13–14, 16, 21–22, 111, 113–17, 119, 122, 124, 129, 138, 142–49, 164–65

Ahad Ha'Am   43, 52–53, 55–56, 61, 87, 191–92, 248, 309–10

Al-Aqsa Intifada   9, 36, 180, 250, 268–69, 313

Allon, Yigal   78

amillennialism   174

anti-Semitism   44–49, 53–54, 73, 84, 106–107, 188, 205, 214–15, 220, 223, 225, 227, 230–31, 238, 247–48, 281–82

Aquinas, Thomas   46, 231

Arabs 13, 15–16, 19, 21, 26–31, 34, 37, 39–41, 43–44, 56–64, 66–80, 82–84, 86–87, 90, 93, 95, 98, 102, 106–108, 111, 180–81, 183–85, 188, 191–94, 196–97, 202–203, 206, 209–210, 231, 233, 236–37, 241–43, 245–51, 253, 263, 265, 267, 270–71, 275–76, 280, 282–85

Arafat, Yasser   34–36, 41, 96–100, 104, 249, 279

Argentina   54

Ashrawi, Hanan   253

Assyria   127, 130, 138–39, 155, 201–202, 215, 219, 296, 303–305

Ateek, Naim Stefan   196, 210, 215, 234

Augustine   231

Auschwitz   213

Avner, Rabbi Shlomo   86

Azuri, Najib   43, 61

Babylon, Babylonians   24–25, 49, 128–132, 135, 139, 148–49, 153, 155–56, 168, 174, 204, 210, 218, 258, 288, 291, 297–98

Badawi, Zaki   269, 272

Bailey, Kenneth   164, 235

Balfour Declaration   27–28, 56–57, 62, 65–68, 70, 86, 107, 215, 245, 257

Baly, Denys   49, 73, 179, 185, 202, 209–210

Barak, Ehud   36, 251

Barker, Walter   180

Basle Congress   44, 56

Begin, Menachem   37, 74, 76, 193

Beirut   9, 11, 33, 96

Ben-Gurion, David   13, 15, 21, 43, 60, 63, 74, 80–82, 91, 191, 197, 242–43

Benjamin, Rabbi   88

Berger, Rabbi Elmer   179, 200

Bible: New Testament   9, 111, 120, 124–25, 136, 139, 141–236

Bible: Old Testament   16–17, 113–38, 179–236, 287–93

Brearley, Margaret   180

British Council of Churches   71–72

Brueggeman, Walter   111, 113

Brunn, W.   191

Buber, Martin   197, 245–46, 248

Bush, George   35

Byzantium, Byzantines   25–26, 300

Calvin, John   161

Camp David   33, 36, 219, 249

Canaan, Canaanites 22–23, 114, 117–20, 123, 125, 301–303
Carter, Jimmy 255
Childers, Erskine 38, 73
Chofshi, Nathan 197
Christian Zionism 239, 252, 254, 262–66, 274, 282
Chrysostom, John 46, 231
Clayton, Gilbert 64
Clinton, Bill 14, 35, 249
Cohen, Haim 221
Cohen, Morris 247
Constantine, Constantinople 25
covenant 114–17, 119, 123, 127, 129–30, 134–46, 164–65, 167–69, 172, 176
Cragg, Kenneth 224–26
Crusades, Crusaders 27, 45, 50, 73, 121, 269–70, 273, 299, 308

Darby, John Nelson 254
Darwish, Mahmoud 96
David, King 23, 39, 47, 124, 129, 134, 136, 142–43, 161, 195, 218, 258–59, 261, 289–91, 296, 298–99, 308
Davies, Abdul-Majid 270
Davies, W.D. 127, 133, 141, 145, 285
Davis, John H. 21, 79, 94
Davis, Moshe 81
Dayan, Moshe 61, 82, 84, 91, 102, 196–97
Dead Sea 23, 25, 49, 136, 171, 259, 301
Deir Yassin 30, 75–77
Dispensationalism 9, 174, 252, 254–55, 257, 262–66
Dispersion of Jews 49–50
Dodd, C.H. 152, 223, 261
Dreyfus, Alfred 53

Eban, Abba 80, 89
Egypt, Egyptians 22, 26, 30–33, 35, 45, 60, 66, 76, 88, 95, 108, 113–19, 126, 128, 138, 155, 187, 190–91, 199, 202–3, 217–19, 223, 250, 268, 302–5
Einstein, Albert 87
Eliav, Arie Lova 89–90
Ellis, Marc 88
El-Sarraj, Eyad 232
Epstein, Yitzhak 43
ethnic cleansing 41, 120–21, 124
Europe 14–15, 26, 28, 39–41, 44–47, 50–53, 55–56, 58, 71–73, 82–83, 92, 106–107, 120, 191, 200, 210, 220, 244, 253, 263, 282, 284
exile, Babylonian 24, 127–30, 139, 168–69
exodus 22, 33, 76

Fackenheim, Emil 214
Faisal, Emir 62–63
fedayeen 97–98, 205
Finkelstein, Norman 21, 78, 242, 244–45, 247
First World War 27, 40, 65–66, 68, 93, 107, 206, 283, 300
Flapan, Simha 191, 243
France 28, 32, 35, 53, 66–67, 69, 94, 199
France, R.T. 149–51, 153, 261
fundamentalism 15, 41, 85, 102, 106, 251–52, 274, 280

Gaza 32–37, 40–41, 84–86, 89–92, 95, 99–100, 103, 109, 118, 180, 232, 242, 245, 249, 256, 266–67, 270, 274–76, 279, 281
George, Lloyd 58, 68–69
Geneva Convention 37
Gentiles 51, 144, 151, 156–58, 164–65, 176, 216, 221–24, 226–30, 238, 253, 260–62, 264, 271, 297
Germany 40, 48, 65, 68, 209–210, 215
Gilbert, Martin 9, 85
Ginsberg, Asher *see* Ahad Ha'Am
Ginsburg, Rabbi Yitzhak 222
Golan Heights 32–33, 61, 86, 232, 274
Goldingay, John 224, 292
Goldman, Nahum 193

Graham, Billy   255
Great Britain   57, 63, 66–67
Greece, Greeks   24–25, 163, 283
Greenberg, Rabbi Irwing   214
Grey, Edward   67–68
Grollenberg, Lucas   180
Grossman, David   16
Guardia, Anton La   9, 14, 21, 85, 91,
   93, 95, 193, 206, 210, 241, 283–84
Gulf War (1991)   9, 34–35, 251
Gush Emunim   37, 41, 86, 248, 252

Hadassah Hospital   30
hadith   268, 307–308
Haganah   60, 73–79, 205
Halsell, Grace   252, 263
Hamas   35–36, 41, 101–102, 109, 247,
   252, 266, 272–76, 307–308
Harkabi, Yehoshafat   97
Herzl, Theodor   15, 44, 53, 55–56,
   107, 193, 196, 220, 242, 263
Hirst, David   58, 69–70, 98–99, 244
Hitler, Adolf   73, 83, 210, 214–15, 263
Hizbollah   251
Hoekema, Anthony A.   175
Hogarth, Commander   64
Holocaust   28, 71–72, 82–83, 85, 108,
   179, 181, 194–95, 200, 206, 210,
   213–15, 253, 283–84
Holwerda, D.E.   142
Horn, General Carl von   181, 183
Hussein, King   36
Hussein, Saddam   34–35

International Commission of Jurists
   39
Intifada, first   19, 34, 102, 241
Intifada, second   *see* Al-Aqsa Intifada
Iraq   30, 34–35, 61, 63, 66, 92, 108,
   113, 251
Irgun   30, 74–75, 77, 193, 205, 221
Islam, Muslims   9, 13, 15, 26–27, 39,
   45, 64, 92, 102, 106, 186, 216,
   239, 247, 252–53, 262–64, 266–78,
   280, 282, 283, 307, 308

Islamic Jihad   35, 41, 109, 252, 266,
   272, 274, 276
Israel
   in the New Testament   141–75,
      221–36
   in the Old Testament   21–24,
      113–38, 216–26
   State of   37, 40–41, 61, 70, 72–73,
      80–81, 84, 92, 98, 108, 172,
      179–80, 183, 194–96, 200, 206,
      210, 213–16, 220–21, 247, 252,
      254, 256–57, 275–77, 281, 283,
      289, 302
IZL (Irgun Z'vai Leumi)   *see* Irgun

Jerusalem   10, 13, 23–27, 30–33,
   35–37, 39, 42, 49–50, 52, 61, 73,
   75–77, 86, 89, 95, 97, 99, 101,
   108, 125, 127, 129–39, 143–45,
   151–61, 163, 165–72, 176, 182–84,
   202, 206, 210, 213, 223, 227, 230,
   234, 236, 245, 249, 251–53, 255,
   257–61, 263, 266–70, 273–74, 276,
   279–80, 283, 288, 290–91,
   297–304
Jesus   45–46, 111, 124–25, 139,
   141–76, 186–88, 209–10, 221–24,
   226, 228–30, 233–36, 338, 258–64,
   267–68, 272, 280–82, 285, 290–92,
   295, 298–302, 304
Jews   10, 13–16, 24–32, 39–41, 43–67,
   70–73, 75–93, 98–99, 102,
   106–111, 119–20, 130, 132–34,
   145–46, 168–71, 174–76, 189–99,
   213–18, 220–33, 242–50, 252–60,
   269–73, 304
Johnston, Philip   9
Jordan   23, 30–31, 36, 61, 66, 76,
   92–93, 108, 119
Joshua   22, 119, 121–25, 133–34, 138,
   163, 167, 218, 285
Judah   23–24, 118, 128–29, 131–39,
   143, 148, 150, 158, 170, 183,
   197–98, 201–202, 230, 234, 288,
   289, 291, 296–97, 299–300, 303

Judea   15, 37, 45, 60, 152, 156,
    160–61, 163, 171, 256
June Six-Day War (1967)   31–32, 85,
    89, 232
justice   10, 187–210

Karmi, H.S.   69–70
Katz, Samuel   193
kingdom of God   125, 145–46,
    150–51, 154, 156, 160–62, 166,
    175, 260, 285, 301
Kirk, Andrew   247–48
Koestler, Arthur   66
Kreider, R.   127
Kuwait   34, 251

land
    and Abraham   14, 111, 113–16
    and Jesus   16–17, 141–75
    and the apostles   159–75
    and the temple   125
    boundaries   22, 33, 36, 61, 69, 88,
        117–19, 136, 138, 258
    conquest   22–23, 119–25, 138, 163,
        218, 303
    exile from   82, 127–30, 139, 168–69
    in history   21–40
    in the Bible   122–75
    in the Prophets   125–38
    Jewish claims   14, 39–41
    Jewish immigration   14, 28, 63
    Palestinian claims   14, 39–41
    promise to Abraham   14, 122, 189
    restoration of   138–39
    return to   10, 49–50, 119, 130–34,
        139, 146, 148, 150, 176, 287–88
    sale of Palestinian land   59–60
    under the Arabs   26
    under the Babylonians   24–25
    under the British   27–28
    under the Byzantines   25–26
    under the Crusaders   26–27
    under the Greeks   24–25
    undr the Mamluks   26–27
    under the Persians   24–25
    under the Romans   25
    under the Turks   27

Laqueur, Walter   82–83
law   189–94
League of Nations   29, 40, 100
Lebanon   9, 30, 33, 66, 69, 90–92, 95,
    97–98, 108–109, 118, 138, 183,
    205, 251, 278
Lilienblum, Moshe Leib   50–51
Lindsey, Hal   254–56
Lucas, Noah   52
Luther, Martin   46, 215, 231

Maccabeus, Judas   25
McMahon, Henry   66
McMahon–Hussein Agreement   40
Madrid Peace Conference (1991),   94
Mamluks   26–27
Mandate   27–30, 40, 49, 69–71, 73,
    108, 270
Marmur, Dow   224–26
Martens, E.A.   113
Mary   142–45, 259, 291
Meir, Golda   81, 192, 243, 275
Mendelsohn, Everett   92, 96
Mendes-Flohr, Paul   245, 248
Messiah   90, 142, 149, 152, 158–59,
    161–62, 165–66, 168, 175–76, 213,
    221, 223–24, 226, 228–30, 236,
    238, 257, 261–63, 282, 285
Middle East Council of Churches   264
Millard, Alan   120
Millard, David   243–44
millennium   168, 172–76, 255, 259,
    281
Mills, Eric   64
Montefiore, Moses   50
Morris, Benny   9, 15, 21, 34, 73–78,
    86, 107–108, 185, 284
Moses   22, 89, 119, 123–27, 159, 167,
    187, 189, 195, 216–18, 221, 237,
    267, 270, 272–73
Muhammad   26, 247, 267–72, 282

Nasr, Kamal   96
Nasser, President   31–32, 97
Nazis, Nazism   40, 72, 82–83, 120,
    210, 213, 215, 221, 253, 281
Neill, Stephen   201

Netanyahu, Benjamin   36, 263
Nolland, John   158
Nordau, Max   44, 196
Norway   35, 249

O'Ballance, Edgar   77
Occupied Territories   31, 33–34, 37,
    96, 91, 102–103, 133, 264, 279
October War (1973)   33, 235
Oslo Peace Accords   35–36, 103–104
Ottomans   27–28, 58, 65, 92, 100, 268,
    282

Palestine, Palestinians   9, 145–15, 21,
    24–31, 33–37, 39–41, 49–50,
    52–74, 78–80, 82–83, 86–87,
    92–109, 115, 118, 125, 145, 147,
    150, 160–61, 172, 174–76, 180–81,
    186, 191–94, 196–97, 206, 210,
    215–16, 232, 236, 238, 243–51,
    253, 255–56, 263, 267–75, 277,
    280, 283–84, 307
Palestine Authority   35–37, 92, 274,
    277
Palestine Liberation Organization
    (PLO), 33, 35, 41, 96–104, 109,
    249, 266, 272–73, 277, 307
Palestine National Charter   97–98
Palestinian National Council   34, 99,
    101
Parkes, James   46–47
partition   69–70
Paul   141, 163–66, 222–23, 227–31,
    234, 238, 261, 297, 304
Pawson, David   257
peace, peacemaking   10, 15, 23,
    32–36, 40–41, 84–88, 90, 94, 96,
    100, 102–106, 108–109, 118, 136,
    144, 163, 183, 185, 187, 189, 193,
    198–99, 222, 231–33, 242, 249,
    250–51, 264, 266, 271–72, 274,
    276, 281
Peres, Shimon   241
Persia, Persians   24–26, 45, 132
Philistines   23
Philo   133

Pinsker, Leon   51
postmillennialism   173–74
prejudice   186–89, 237
premillennialism   173–74
Prince, Derek   194–95
prophets   84, 87, 111, 130–43, 150–53,
    158–59, 169–70, 173–75, 181, 195,
    199, 201–202, 217–18, 220–23,
    237–38, 259–61, 265, 270–71, 281,
    292, 295, 301

Quaker Report   72, 92, 183, 188, 206
Qur'an   102, 247, 252, 267, 272–73

Rabin, Yitzhak   35, 78, 84–85, 91, 241,
    252
racism   83, 246–47
Rauf, M.A.   273
Reagan, President Ronald   252, 255,
    263
reconciliation   10, 84, 105–106, 189,
    210, 232–38, 253
refugees   35, 65, 77, 79–80, 88, 92, 94,
    96, 106, 109, 181, 185, 192, 196,
    199, 203, 209, 243, 253, 276
Riddell, Peter   11, 102, 272, 274
Riggans, Walter   256–57
Robertson, O. Palmer   141
Rodinson, Maxime   44, 71
Rome, Romans   45, 121, 125, 133, 142,
    163–64, 273, 301
Runes, Dagobert D.   45
Ruppin, Arthur   245
Russia   41, 50, 52, 65, 249, 265

Sadat, President   33
Said, Edward   15, 72, 75, 92, 95, 102,
    180, 186, 247, 250
Saladin   27, 58, 269
Samuel, Herbert   64
Sansour, Father John   270
Saudi Arabia   35
Schiff, Ze'ev   90–91
Schneider, Peter   230
Schofield, Cyrus. I.   254, 258
Seale, Patrick   250

second coming   153–56, 173, 175, 291
Second World War   28, 71, 184, 200,
    206
settlements   32, 35–42
Shamir, Yitzhak   37
Sharon, Ariel   36, 89, 218, 233, 251,
    279
Sharett, Moshe   63
Sinai   22, 32–33, 61, 69, 86, 165, 167,
    190, 218, 232, 268
Sizer, Stephen   79, 185, 254–55, 258,
    264
Solomon   23, 118, 125–27, 129, 134,
    143, 269, 289
Solomon, Rabbi Norman   213–14, 227
Stern, David   256
Stone, I.F.   77, 221
Suez War (1956)   31–33, 232
Syria   21, 24–26, 28, 20, 32, 35, 61,
    66–69, 108, 219, 271, 273–74, 304

Talmon, J.L.   199–200
Ta'mari, Salah   99
temple   24–25, 125–27, 129, 132–33,
    136, 138–39, 141–46, 152, 154,
    156, 158, 164, 166–73, 210, 217,
    224, 252, 255, 258–61, 269,
    281–82, 289–91, 298, 301–302
terrorism   10, 36–37, 63, 77, 97,
    100–101, 190, 252, 285
Thorn, Gaston   246–47
Truman, President   69–71
Turkey, Turks   24, 26–27, 43, 55, 62,
    65–66, 68, 206, 257
Turki, Fawaz   94–95
Twain, Mark   186

Umayyads   226, 269
UN Partition Plan (1947)   13, 29–30,
    40, 69, 71–73, 78
UN Resolutions   35, 41, 242
UN Security Council   32, 35, 37, 100,
    283

United Nations (UN)   10, 29–35,
    40–41, 69, 71–73, 78, 82, 99–101,
    108, 183–84, 190, 199
USA   10, 14, 16, 28, 30, 33–34, 39,
    70–72, 99, 250–554, 263, 284

Versailles Peace Conference   27, 69,
    108
Vital, David   50–51, 55, 242

Walker, Peter   9, 127, 161
war of 1948–49   30, 77–78, 192
war of 1982   9, 33, 90, 109
Watt, William Montgomery   271
Weber, Timothy P.   255, 263
Webster, Charles   58
Weitz, Joseph   60, 74, 78
Weizmann, Chaim   30, 56, 58, 62, 64,
    79, 87, 107, 190–94, 199, 242–43,
    252, 263
West Bank   10, 15, 31–41, 85–86,
    89–92, 95, 98–100, 103–104, 109,
    119, 180, 232, 242, 245, 249,
    252–53, 266, 274–76, 279, 281
Williamson, Paul   118
Wright, C.J.H.   167
Wright, N.T.   9, 125–26, 142, 151–52,
    154, 161, 163–64, 169, 171, 187,
    223–24, 229–31, 234, 261–62

Yom Kippur War   see October War

Zayyad, Tawfiq   95
Zionism, Zionist   9, 14–15, 21, 27, 37,
    41, 44, 49–50, 52–53, 55–61,
    63–65, 67–70, 72–73, 80, 82–93,
    98–99, 102, 107–109, 174, 179–81,
    185, 190–93, 196–97, 199–200,
    205–206, 215, 220–21, 225,
    238–39, 242–48, 250, 252, 254,
    256, 262–66, 270, 274, 277,
    282–83
Zuckermann, William   181

Text Acknowledgments

Extracts from Naim Stefan Ateek, *Justice and Only Justice: A Palestinian Theology of Liberation*, published by Orbis Books, 1989, and reproduced by permission.

Kenneth Bailey, extract from 'Ode on a Burning Tank: The Holy Lands, October 1973', in *Through Peasant Eyes: More Lucan Parables*, published by Eerdmans, 1980. Permission sought from Eerdmans Publishing.

Extracts from Denys Baly, *Multitudes in the Valley: Church and Crisis in the Middle East*, published by Seabury Press, New York, 1957. Reproduced courtesy of the Archives of the Episcopal Church, USA.

Extracts from John H. Davis, *The Evasive Peace: A Study of the Zionist-Arab Problem*, published by John Murray, 1968, and reproduced by permission.

Extracts from David Hirst, *The Gun and the Olive Branch: The Roots of Violence in the Middle East*, published by Futura, 1978, and reproduced by permission of Little, Brown and Company.

Extracts from Anton La Guardia, *Holy Land, Unholy War: Israelis and Palestinians*, published by John Murray, 2001, and reproduced by permission.

Extracts from Benny Morris, *Righteous Victims: A History of the Zionist-Arab Conflict, 1881–1999*, published in the UK by John Murray, 1999, and reproduced by permission. Permission sought from Knopf Publishing Group, a Division of Random House, Inc., for the USA and Canada.

Extracts from *The Search for Peace in the Middle East*, published by the American Friends Service Committee, 1970. Permission sought from the American Friends Service Committee.

Extracts from Edward Said, *The End of the Peace Process: Oslo and After*, published in the UK by Granta Publications, 2000, and reproduced by permission. Permission sought from Pantheon Books, an imprint of Knopf Publishing Group, for the USA.

Extracts from Norman Solomon, *Jewish Responses to the Holocaust*, published by the Centre for the Study of Judaism and Jewish/Christian Relations, Selly Oak Colleges, Birmingham, 1988.

Extracts from David Vital, *The Origins of Zionism*, published by Oxford University Press, 1975, and reproduced by permission.

Extracts from N.T. Wright, *The New Testament and the People of God*, published by SPCK, 1992. Pemission sought from SPCK.

Tawfiq Zayyad, *Baqun* ('We Shall Remain'), in *Enemy of the Sun: Poetry of Palestinian Resistance*, ed. Naseer Arari and Edmund Ghareeb, published by Drum and Spear Press, Washington, 1970.

Extracts from the Palestinian Declaration of Independence.

Adaptation from an article, 'Peace Under Siege', in *New Routes: Journal of the Life and Peace Institute*, vol. 6, no. 1, published by the Life and Peace Institute, Uppsala, Sweden, 2001, and used by permission.

Picture Acknowledgments

All maps by Derek West.

1.11a adapted from Walid Khalidi, *From Haven to Conquest: Readings in Zionism and the Palestine Problem Until 1948* (edited with introduction), Beirut: Institute for Palestine Studies, 1971, p. 94.

1.11b, 1.12, 1.13, 1.17a and 1.17b adapted from Martin Gilbert, *Israel: A History*, Doubleday, 1998, pp. 622, 623, 629, 657, 648, copyright © 1998 Martin Gilbert.

Colin Chapman has been, since 1999, Lecturer in Islamic Studies at the Near East School of Theology, Beirut, Lebanon. He is the author of several books, including *Christianity on Trial* and *The Case for Christianity* (both Lion), *Cross and Crescent: Responding to the Challenge of Islam* (InterVarsity Press) and *Islam and the West: Conflict, Coexistence or Conversion?* (Paternoster).